W9-AXA-482

SOUTH CAROLINA

JIM MOREKIS

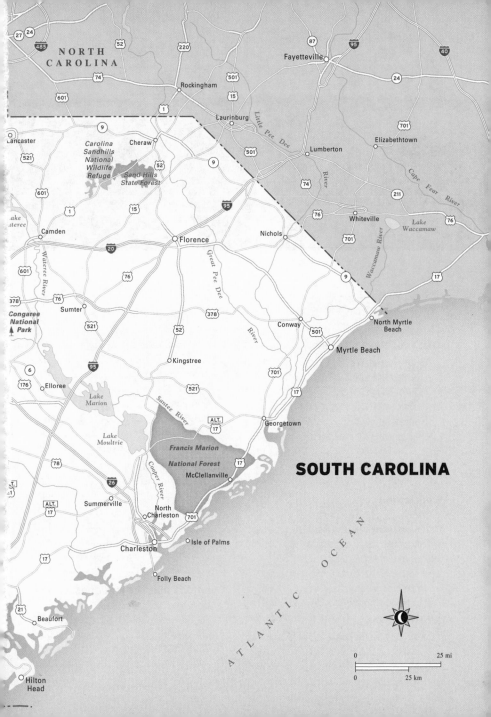

Contents

Even by Southern standards, South Carolina is bathed in a certain mystique. The Spanish moss hangs low, people catch their own seafood for dinner, and the creeks are like highways in the marsh.

Few states provide such a wealth of experience in such a small package. You can traverse its entire width in half a day, going from a beautiful white-sand beach to a stunning mountain overlook. Along the way you'll experience a sampler of Southern culture encompassing the genteel remnants of the Lowcountry plantations, echoes of the old shag scene on the Grand Strand, and the very edge of Appalachia in the fast-growing Upstate region.

The common thread linking these disparate strands together is the people. Once here, you'll immediately tune in to a particularly South Carolinian vibe that's easygoing yet flamboyant, laid-back yet cocksure. This unique twist on proverbial Southern hospitality—a sort of assertive niceness—is a product of the extraordinary resilience of South Carolinians, who have proudly maintained their identity despite centuries of war, strife, and natural disaster.

Clockwise from top left: St. Philip's Episcopal Church in Charleston; an ornate gate at Brookgreen Gardens in the Lower Grand Strand; golfing in Myrtle Beach; Caesars Head State Park; the Pineapple Fountain in Charleston; Charleston's skyline at dusk.

While history buffs flock to the region for its seemingly endless supply of colonial and Civil War sites, easily its most underrated attribute is the beauty of its environment and the scope of its outdoor recreation. You'll find the oldest cypress stands in the world, a wealth of mountain waterfalls, and some of the best fishing, kayaking, and white-water rafting in the country.

As for its essence, South Carolina has long been something of a paradox. Notorious as the cradle of secession during the Civil War, the state is today home to some of the nation's most patriotic citizens. Often caricatured as hopelessly retro, South Carolina's larger cities have quietly become magnets for high-tech jobs and foreign investment.

While the rest of the world tries to figure out what makes them tick, South Carolinians do what they've always done: make their way in the world, often too stubbornly, practicing their take on Southern hospitality and having as much fun as they can along the way.

Clockwise from top left: the Angel Oak on Johns Island; Myrtle Beach; azaleas and an oak tree in Charleston; the lobby of the South Carolina State House in Columbia.

5 TOP EXPERIENCES

1 **Historic Charleston:** Enjoy this historic city's well-preserved sights with a walking tour of its charming, winding streets (page 29).

2 **Myrtle Beach:** This family-friendly getaway is designed for maximum convenience and enjoyment, with enough kitsch factor to keep things interesting. Oh, and the beaches are the best (page 100)!

3 **Golf Galore:** Tee up a links-centric vacation at top-ranked, public courses, especially around Charleston, Myrtle Beach, and Hilton Head Island (page 16).

4 **Southern BBQ:** No trip to South Carolina is complete without partaking of the pork goodness (page 20)!

5 **African American Heritage:** This region has shaped the history of African Americans since before the nation's inception (page 18).

<<<

The Best of South Carolina

Lowcountry Romance

Spanish moss, balmy beaches, good food—the Palmetto State is a great place for a romantic getaway. This trip centers on **Charleston** and the **Lowcountry.**

DAY 1

Spend your first morning walking or biking around peaceful **downtown Beaufort.** In the afternoon, take a short drive to **Hunting Island State Park** and walk on the windswept beach. Then enjoy a tasty dinner at **Saltus River Grill** on the scenic waterfront. Spend the night at one of Beaufort's many classic B&Bs, such as the **Beaufort Inn** or the **Rhett House Inn.**

DAY 2

Drive to **Old Town Bluffton,** walk down to the beautiful May River, and browse the many local **art galleries** around Calhoun Street. Visit the relaxing **Pinckney Island National Wildlife Refuge** before going into Hilton Head proper. Walk on the beach and enjoy live music and a great meal at **The Jazz Corner.** Head up to Charleston and check into a romantic room at **The Vendue** or the **Andrew Pinckney Inn.**

DAY 3

Start your day in Charleston in its bustling heart, **Marion Square.** Maybe do a little shopping on **King Street** and at **Old City Market** afterward. Take a sunset stroll around **the Battery**

Fresh Catch

South Carolina—especially the coastal region—is a paradise for **seafood lovers.** The state offers a wide range of epicurean pleasures, from the self-conscious high cuisine of Charleston's hot young chefs to rustic roadside seafood shacks. Here are some highlights you shouldn't miss.

SHRIMP AND GRITS

The most iconic South Carolina seafood dish combines surf (delectable shrimp) with turf (stoneground hominy) in a stunning yet deeply comforting taste combination. Enjoy this classic entrée in its most mouthwatering form at **Poogan's Porch** (page 78) and **Slightly North of Broad** (page 78) in Charleston.

LOWCOUNTRY BOIL

Also called Frogmore stew after the township on St. Helena Island where it originated, this deceptively simple dish, commonly found in family-style neighborhood restaurants, offers all the basic nutrients you need boiled together in one big pot: shrimp, sausage, potatoes, and corn on the cob, all

with a spicy kick. Try it at **Marshside Mama's** (page 180) on Daufuskie Island.

FRIED CATFISH

The lowly cat is a renowned freshwater fish in South Carolina, and fried up right it's a treat. This is what to order when you're inland and need a fresh-seafood fix. Try it at **Yesterday's** (page 196) in Columbia.

MAY RIVER OYSTERS

While most of the great South Carolina stocks are long gone, the well-preserved May River at Bluffton still provides some of the best-quality oysters in the world. Buy them fresh at the **Bluffton Oyster Company** (page 176), which brings them in right off the boat during the season (Sept.-Apr.).

HAUTE CUISINE

Not everything is rustic in South Carolina. Fine dining spots, such as **McCrady's** (page 77) in Charleston or **Charlie's L'Etoile Verte** (page 173) in Hilton Head, serve seafood prepared with panache in a spirit of diverse experimentation.

Charleston's Old City Market

and admire **Rainbow Row** before diving right into a great meal at one of the city's fine restaurants—maybe the **Peninsula Grill.**

DAY 4

Today you put your historian's hat on and visit one of Charleston's great house museums, such as the **Aiken-Rhett House** or the **Edmondston-Alston House.** Have a hearty Southern-style lunch, then take an afternoon trip to **Fort Sumter.** After another fantastic Charleston dinner at **Husk,** take a stroll or carriage ride through the French Quarter to close the evening.

DAY 5

Have a cozy brunch at **Poogan's Porch** downtown. Then make the 20-minute drive over the Ashley River to gorgeous **Middleton Place,** where you'll tour the gardens. Then stop at adjacent **Drayton Hall** and see one of the oldest and best-preserved plantation homes in the nation. Return to downtown Charleston for a late afternoon **carriage ride** through the French Quarter before dining at romantic **McCrady's.**

Family Fun on the Grand Strand

This long weekend gives you a taste of life in **Myrtle Beach** and the rest of the **Grand Strand.** The area is small enough to stay in one place for both nights, but so popular that travel along the 60-mile-long Strand can be slow. Be sure to leave enough time to get from place to place.

DAY 1

Begin the day at historic **Hampton Plantation** before taking a guided **kayak tour** around Winyah Bay or Hobcaw Barony. Have an early dinner on the waterfront in nearby **Georgetown,** then drive up to Myrtle Beach for the night. If you want to stay away from the resorts, camp at **Huntington Beach State Park.**

DAY 2

In the morning explore **Brookgreen Gardens,** one of the most unique sights in the Grand Strand. Spend the afternoon in Myrtle Beach: Shop at **Broadway at the Beach.** After dinner go for a fun, cheesy round of **miniature golf** under the stars. Or perhaps take in a show at the

Golf Galore

With great weather, beautiful land, and an abundance of retirees, South Carolina offers some of the best golf courses in the world. While a handful of courses are more exclusive, many of the best are public and even have reasonable prices.

MYRTLE BEACH AND VICINITY

- **Barefoot Resort and Golf Club, Fazio Course** (page 115): Strangely not as popular as the affiliated Love course, but many say it's way better.

- **Caledonia Golf and Fish Club and True Blue Golf Club** (page 128): These sister courses compete for the fierce affections of serious golfers; it's sublime.

- **Myrtle Beach National** (page 115): With its South Carolina-shaped sand trap at hole 3, the National is one of the state's legendary courses, not to mention a heck of a deal.

- **Waccamaw Golf Trail** (page 128): Down the road from Myrtle Beach and near Pawleys Island, this area features some of the best courses in the state, including that of the famous Litchfield Resort.

HILTON HEAD ISLAND AND THE LOWCOUNTRY

- **Harbour Town Golf Links** (page 171): The host course of the RBC Heritage features a final three holes that are among the most challenging in the sport.

- **Palmetto Dunes, Arthur Hills Course** (page 172): Put away the drivers at this finesse course artfully situated in a residential area.

Kiawah Island Golf Resort

- **Legends at Parris Island** (page 160): Always considered one of the best military courses, a recent redesign of the 1957 original has been getting rave reviews.

CHARLESTON AND VICINITY

- **Kiawah Island Golf Resort, Ocean Course** (page 58): This Pete Dye design is considered the most wind-affected course outside the British Isles and possibly the most difficult resort course in the United States.

- **Wild Dunes Links Course** (page 75): This windy, winding beauty is the Holy City's most challenging course.

Carolina Opry, or learn to dance the shag at old **Ocean Drive Beach.**

DAY 3
Spend the morning **on the beach.** After lunch visit one of the **Ripley's** attractions or take in

a concert at the **House of Blues** in **Barefoot Landing.**

Southern Living in the Midlands

Sandwiched between the coast and the mountains, the **Midlands** are easily overlooked, but not for lack of attractions. This central section of the state is large and spread out. To fully experience the breadth of the area, bunk one night in **Columbia** and the next in **Camden.**

DAY 1

Devote a full day to touring South Carolina's capital, **Columbia.** Downtown sights include the **South Carolina State Museum,** the **South Carolina State House,** and the **University of South Carolina.** In addition, don't miss the **Riverbanks Zoo and Garden.** Have dinner in the trendy **Vista** area and finish with a nightcap in boisterous **Five Points.** Spend the night at the venerable **Inn at USC.**

DAY 2

Get up bright and early and drive out of town to **Congaree National Park** to walk along its primordial cypress swamp and old-growth forest. If you have time, go down to Orangeburg to see the **Edisto Memorial Gardens.** Head east and end the day in **Camden.** Explore the picturesque historic district with its many antiques shops.

DAY 3

Drive up U.S. 1 to **Cheraw** to see its charming historic district and visit the nearby **Dizzy Gillespie** home site and park. Scoot over to Darlington and check out **Darlington Raceway,** the grandfather of all stock car tracks. Spend the rest of the afternoon near Florence at **Woods Bay State Natural Area,** enjoying the well-preserved Carolina Bay.

High Times in Horse Country

You don't have to own a horse to enjoy a weekend in **Aiken.** If you're here in spring, you can aim to see a polo match on Sunday.

DAY 1

Explore Aiken's historic **Winter Colony** district and **racetracks.** After lunch, check out the **Carolina Bay Nature Preserve.** Stay in Aiken at the classy **Willcox** or the old **Hotel Aiken.**

DAY 2

Get up bright and early to explore Aiken's **Hitchcock Woods** on a long, relaxing hike. If you're here in the fall and it's a Saturday, you might even catch a **fox hunt.** Or, if you're here in the spring and it's a Sunday, grab lunch after your hike and aim to catch a **polo match** at Whitney Field.

In the Shadow of the Blue Ridge

This weekend trip highlights the best of the Upstate, from the beautiful natural setting to city life and early American history. Spend one night in the shadow of the **Blue Ridge Mountains** and another in cosmopolitan **Greenville.**

DAY 1

Begin at the **South Carolina Botanical Garden** in Clemson before heading over to little **Pendleton** and enjoying lunch on the **Village Green.** Head up to Walhalla in the afternoon and check out the unique **Stumphouse Tunnel and Issaqueena Falls.** Stay in a B&B or camp at **Oconee State Park.**

DAY 2

Spend the day in **Greenville:** enjoy **Falls Park on the Reedy;** do some shopping on restored **Main Street;** and maybe check out artworks by the great masters at the **Bob Jones University** Museum and Gallery. In the evening, take in a **minor-league baseball** game at Fluor Field. Splurge for the night at the classy **Westin Poinsett** downtown.

DAY 3

Drive to **Cowpens National Battlefield** outside Spartanburg to learn about this pivotal Revolutionary War battle. After a classic greasy-spoon lunch at Spartanburg's **Beacon Drive-In,** head over to York County to check out **Historic Brattonsville** and its excellently restored upcountry homestead site, complete with living-history demonstrations.

Back to Nature

South Carolina packs a lot of habitat into a small area. Here's where to focus your environmental attention for maximum benefit.

Lowcountry

- Kayak the inlet at **Hunting Island State Park,** where portions of *Forrest Gump* were filmed, then enjoy the **scenic beach,** concluding with a view from the top of the **lighthouse.**

- Canoe in the **ACE Basin,** touring the Edisto River—the longest **blackwater river** in the world—on a guided trip. Head to Charleston and visit the **South Carolina Aquarium** to learn more about the entire state's vibrant water-oriented ecosystem.

- North of Charleston, find the Sewee Visitor Center at the **Cape Romain National Wildlife Refuge** and see their family of rare **red wolves.** Then stop by **Hobcaw Barony** and take a guided kayak tour of the excellently preserved marsh.

Midlands

- Visit the well-preserved Carolina Bay at the **Woods Bay State Natural Area** near Florence, right off I-95. Just outside the state's capital, Columbia, is the stunning **Congaree National Park** and its old-growth cypress swamp.

- Enjoy some **white-water rafting** on the Broad and Saluda Rivers, which run through Columbia. Spend an afternoon at Columbia's nationally renowned **Riverbanks Zoo and Garden.**

Upstate

- Head to the Upstate and choose between camping or a cabin at **Devil's Fork State Park,** which provides the only public access to beautiful **Lake Jocassee** at the base of the Blue Ridge Mountains.

- **Hike** at **Table Rock State Park** in the Mountain Bridge Natural Wilderness Area or on the **Foothills Trail** along the Blue Ridge Escarpment.

- Take the **Cherokee Foothills Scenic Highway** over to the wild and scenic **Chattooga River** for an equally wild and scenic day of **white-water rafting.**

African American Heritage

There's no way to truly and completely understand South Carolina without a close look at its African American background, so integral to the state's history. Of particular interest is the story of **the Gullah people,** descendants of slaves whose culture survived in relative isolation on South Carolina's Sea Islands after the Civil War. This one-week journey takes you to all the key stops.

Day 1

From your base in Beaufort, explore the Gullah community of **St. Helena Island,** including the Penn Center, where **Dr. Martin Luther King Jr.** once organized civil rights activists. In the afternoon, pay your respects to African American **Civil War hero** Robert Smalls at his memorial at the **Tabernacle Baptist Church,** and see his former home on Prince Street. View the Berners Barnwell Sams House, where **Harriet Tubman** once worked as a nurse.

Day 2

Get up bright and early for a drive to **Hilton Head Island** to explore the remnants of African American history here, including the old Fort Mitchel and Mitchelville site where the **first freedmen's community**

Civil War Sites

While most Civil War battles took place elsewhere, South Carolina was the cradle of secession and has many sites of great historical importance in the War Between the States, as it's sometimes called here.

BATTLE REENACTMENTS

- Experience the reenactment of the **Battle of Secessionville** each November at Boone Hall Plantation in Charleston. While you're here, visit the restored brick slave cabins, a reminder of what the war left behind.

WAR HOSPITALS AND CEMETERIES

- See **St. Helena's Episcopal Church** in Beaufort, used as a hospital by Union troops. Nearby is **Beaufort National Cemetery,** one of the few in the country where both Union and Confederate troops are interred.

REMNANTS OF THE WAR

- Take the ferry out to **Fort Sumter,** target of Confederate batteries on the eve of war (ironically, none of the shots came from Charleston's Battery itself, as it was too far away).

- See the newly raised **CSS Hunley** submarine on the old Navy base in North Charleston, and marvel at the bravery of the men on this suicide mission.

- Visit historic **Drayton Hall** on the Ashley River, saved from torching by Union troops by

Beaufort National Cemetery

a quick-thinking local who erected smallpox warning flags.

MONUMENTS AND MUSEUMS

- In Columbia, tour the **South Carolina State House** and its numerous monuments to Civil War figures. Note the Yankee cannonball damage on the walls.

- Visit the **Confederate Museum** on the 2nd floor of Charleston's City Market to see its collection of military memorabilia.

---

in the country once stood. Take the ferry to **Daufuskie Island** and spend the balance of the day relaxing and getting in touch with the substantial Gullah culture, including the **Mary Field School,** where author **Pat Conroy** once taught.

Day 3

Drive inland a little way to **Walterboro,** where

you can pay your respects at the **Tuskegee Airmen Memorial** and browse the folk art at the **South Carolina Artisans Center.** Then head to Charleston to begin a two-day stay. On the way into town, stop at Drayton Hall along the Ashley River, a meticulously conserved **plantation home.** There's a program exploring African American life at the plantation as well as a **slave cemetery.**

The importance of barbecue in the South cannot be overstated. It's a noun down here, something you eat rather than a verb that you do. To the Southerner, barbecue is both delicacy and staple: one of life's greatest luxuries, but one without which a person cannot be said to be truly living.

South Carolina holds a rare distinction. It's the only state in the union that represents all known variants of barbecue sauce: vinegar and pepper, light tomato, heavy tomato, and the Palmetto State's own contribution, a hot, sweet mustard-based sauce. A culinary legacy of the German settlers who numbered heavily in that interior region, this indigenous mustard sauce is found mostly in the central Midlands portion of the state from Newberry almost to Charleston. The extreme Upstate leans toward the heavier tomato-based sauce, while a sweeter, ketchupy sauce is the trend along the Savannah River. The vinegar-and-pepper concoction—an eastern North Carolina transplant—holds sway everywhere else, especially east of the Wateree River in the Pee Dee region.

As for the meat itself, in all regions there's no question about what kind you mean when you say barbecue. It's always pork, period. And connoisseurs agree that if it isn't cooked whole over an open wood fire, it isn't authentic barbecue, merely a pale—if still tasty—imitation. Sides are important in South Carolina, especially the item known as hash, made from pork byproducts served over rice. In any genuine barbecue place you'll also encounter cracklin's (fried pork skin), whole loaves of white bread, and, of course, sweet iced tea (called simply "sweet tea").

Aficionados further insist that a real barbecue place is open only on Friday and Saturday (some generously extend the definition to include Thursday), chops its own wood, and proffers its pig not à la carte but in a distinctive "all you care to eat" buffet style, which generally means one huge pass at the buffet line.

Key purveyors of the culinary art form include:

- **Fiery Ron's Home Team BBQ,** Charleston (page 83)

- **Henry's Smokehouse,** Greenville (page 222)

- **McCabe's Bar-B-Que,** Manning (page 205)

- **Po Pigs Bo-B-Q,** Edisto Island (page 162)

- **Sweatman's Bar-b-que,** outside of Holly Hill (page 205)

- **Duke's Barbecue,** Walterboro (page 182)

Charles Pinckney National Historic Site

Day 4

Spend the day exploring the well-preserved African American history at the **Aiken-Rhett House** and visit the **Old Slave Mart** museum downtown. For a more intensive educational experience, pay a visit to the **Avery Research Center** for African American History and Culture at the College of Charleston. **Randolph Hall** and the historic **"Cistern"** on the campus hosted **Barack Obama** during a campaign rally in January 2008.

Day 5

Your last day in Charleston will be spent in and around the suburb of **Mount Pleasant,** visiting several key sites. With a stop along U.S. 17 to buy a **sweetgrass basket** from a roadside vendor, head to **Boone Hall Plantation,** which has 10 of the best-restored **antebellum slave quarters** in the country, with excellent interpretive programming. Just down the road is the **Charles Pinckney National Historic Site,** commemorating the life of the early abolitionist and coauthor of the U.S. Constitution. End your day with a visit to relaxing **Sullivan's Island** and Fort Moultrie. Nearby, you'll find the **"bench by the road,"** a monument to the million or so slaves who first arrived in America at Sullivan's Island, which was inspired by a line from a book by **Toni Morrison.**

Day 6

Drive up U.S. 17 to **Georgetown,** once the main seaport for South Carolina's rice economy. Visit the **Rice Museum** to learn about the history and daily life of area plantations.

Day 7

This optional day takes you on a drive inland to the town of **Cheraw,** birthplace of the jazz great **Dizzy Gillespie.** Visit his home site, now a delightful park, and view his statue downtown.

Planning Your Trip

Where to Go

Charleston

One of America's oldest cities and an early national center of **arts and culture,** Charleston's legendary taste for the high life is matched by its forward-thinking outlook. The birthplace of the **Civil War** is not just a city of museums resting on its historic laurels; the "Holy City" is now a **vibrant, creative hub** of the New South.

Myrtle Beach and the Grand Strand

The 60-mile Grand Strand focuses on the **resort activity** of Myrtle Beach and the adjacent, faster-growing **North Myrtle Beach.** Down the strand are the more peaceful areas of **Pawleys Island** and **Murrells Inlet,** with **historic Georgetown**

and its scenic plantations anchoring the bottom portion of the long, skinny peninsula.

Hilton Head and the Lowcountry

The Lowcountry's **mossy, laid-back pace** belies its former status as the heart of American plantation culture and the original cradle of secession. Today it is a mix of **history** (Beaufort and Bluffton), **natural beauty** (the ACE Basin), **resort development** (Hilton Head), **military bases** (Parris Island), and **relaxed beaches** (Edisto and Hunting Islands).

Columbia and the Midlands

The state capital and home of South Carolina's largest university, Columbia is still a very

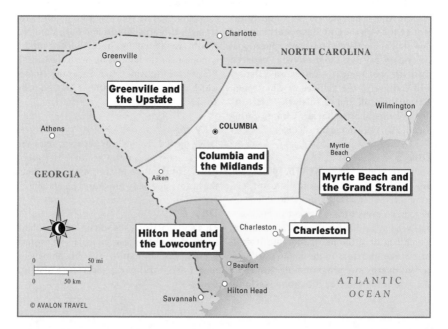

manageable, fun place. Visit the nationally known **Riverbanks Zoo and Garden** and the very good **South Carolina State Museum,** and enjoy the restaurants and nightlife of the **Vista** and **Five Points** neighborhoods. The surrounding area, the "real" South Carolina, offers a look at a **small-town way of life** usually seen in Norman Rockwell paintings. A resurgent polo scene is bringing affluent but accessible Aiken back to its full **equestrian glory.**

Greenville and the Upstate

Fast-growing Greenville can teach many other cities a lesson in tasteful, efficient renovation. **Shopping** is great, and **Bob Jones University** offers an excellent collection of religious art by old masters. A short drive away are the treats and treasures of South Carolina's **Blue Ridge** region—a more user-friendly, less expensive version of the trendy **mountain towns** over the border in North Carolina.

When to Go

Springtime is when most love affairs with South Carolina begin. Unless you have severe pollen allergies, you should experience this area at its peak of natural beauty during the magical period of **mid-March** to **mid-May.** Not surprisingly, lodging is typically at a premium at that time.

My **favorite time of year** in South Carolina, though, is the middle of **November,** when the tourist crush subsides. The days are delightful, the nights are crisp but not frigid, and you can also get a room at a good price.

For those interested in South Carolina's excellent **state park** system, be aware that there are minimum stays, usually one week, for cabin rentals during March-October. In the off-season, this doesn't apply.

June-October is **hurricane season** on the coast, with September in particular the time of highest risk.

By Region

The hardest time to get a room in **Charleston** is during Spoleto, Memorial Day to mid-June. **Hilton Head**'s busiest time is during the RBC Heritage Classic Golf Tournament in mid-April.

Unlike in the rest of the state, in **Myrtle Beach** the absolute hottest months of summer are the big season—the better to enjoy the water. Prices are higher and availability is lower

during this time. **Golfers,** however, will see bigger crowds on the links as the weather cools—though Myrtle Beach's oversupply of courses means there are usually tee times available and some good deals. About the middle of November, you can find some good prices on lodging in the entire Myrtle Beach area.

Under its touristy veneer, **Columbia** is still a college town. **Fall** means **football,** and that means the most competition for lodging, especially when the Gamecocks are playing at home. Summer can get *really* slow in Columbia—and hot. I advise avoiding it during summer.

Aiken has two big **equestrian seasons.** Most of **March** is taken up by the Triple Crown equestrian events, and October is big for tournament polo and steeplechase. Indirectly, **April** is also very competitive lodging-wise, largely because nearby Augusta, Georgia, hosts the insanely popular Masters golf tournament, with much spillover into Aiken.

The **Upstate** is great most any time of year. Spring is best weather-wise, and while summers can get quite hot, there's some real relief at night. Fall foliage can be surprisingly glorious well into December. During Tiger football home games at **Clemson University,** lodging is more difficult to find in a wide radius around Clemson.

Charleston

Everyone who spends time in Charleston comes away with a story about the locals' courtesy and hospitality.

Mine came while walking through the French Quarter and admiring a handsome old single house on Church Street, one of the few that survived the fire of 1775. To my surprise, the woman chatting with a friend nearby turned out to be the homeowner. Noticing my interest, she invited me, a total stranger, inside to check out the progress of her renovation. This is a city that takes civic harmony seriously—it even boasts the country's only "Livability Court," a legally binding board that meets regularly to enforce local quality-of-life ordinances.

In 2015, however, Charleston gained national prominence when a white gunman murdered nine worshippers in the historically black Emanuel AME Church on Calhoun Street downtown. The nation was transfixed not only by the horror of the incident, but also by Charleston's community response, which was wholly in keeping with its character: hopeful, forgiving, resilient, and compassionate. Charleston's nickname, the "Holy City," derives from the skyline's abundance of church steeples rather than any excess of piety among its citizens, but its response to the Mother Emanuel tragedy seemed to lend a new meaning.

While many visitors come to see the historical south of Charleston—finding it and then some, of course—they leave impressed by the diversity of Charlestonian life. It's a surprisingly cosmopolitan mix of students, professionals, and longtime inhabitants—who discuss the finer points of Civil War history as if it were last year, party on Saturday night like there's no tomorrow, and go to church on Sunday morning dressed in their finest.

This city, so known for its history, is also quietly booming as one of the nation's key centers of tech and digital development. Highly educated and motivated millennials from all over the country are flocking to Charleston for its blend of start-up friendliness, great nightlife, eco-friendly sensibilities, and vibrant arts and cultural scene.

HISTORY

Unlike the many English colonies in America that were based on freedom from religious persecution, Carolina was strictly a commercial venture from the beginning. The tenure

Previous: the view down Broad Street from the Old Exchange; Charles Towne Landing. **Above:** the veranda at Husk.

Look for ★ to find recommended sights, activities, dining, and lodging.

Highlights

© AVALON TRAVEL

★ **The Battery:** Tranquil surroundings combine with beautiful views of Charleston Harbor, historical points key to the Civil War, and amazing mansions (page 31).

★ **Rainbow Row:** Painted in warm pastels, these old merchant homes near the cobblestoned waterfront take you on a journey to Charleston's antebellum heyday (page 33).

★ **South Carolina Aquarium:** Experience the state's surprising breadth of habitat (page 37).

★ **Fort Sumter:** Take the ferry to this historic place where the Civil War began, with gorgeous views along the way (page 37).

★ **St. Philip's Episcopal Church:** A sublimely beautiful sanctuary and two historic graveyards await you in the heart of the evocative French Quarter (page 39).

★ **Aiken-Rhett House:** There are certainly more ostentatious house museums in Charleston, but none that provide such a virtually intact glimpse into real antebellum life (page 46).

★ **Drayton Hall:** Don't miss Charleston's oldest surviving plantation home and one of the country's best examples of professional historic preservation (page 48).

★ **Middleton Place:** Wander around one of the world's most beautifully landscaped gardens—and the first in North America (page 49).

★ **CSS Hunley:** The first submarine to sink a ship in battle is a moving example of bravery and sacrifice (page 51).

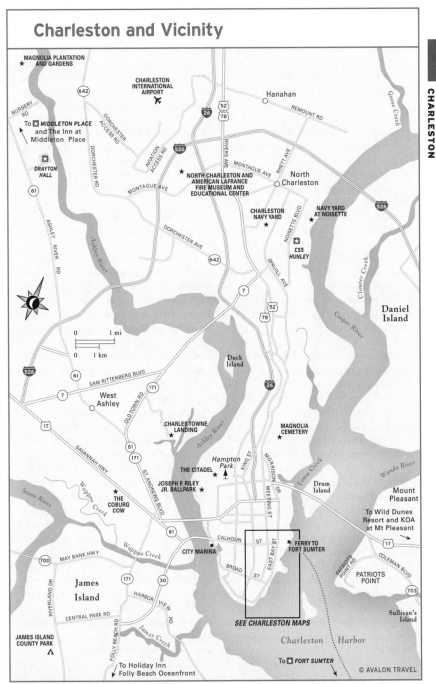

of the Lords Proprietors—the eight English aristocrats who literally owned the colony—began in 1670 when the *Carolina* finished its journey from Barbados at Albemarle Creek on the west bank of the Ashley River.

Those first colonists set up a small fortification called Charles Towne, named for Charles II, the first monarch of the Restoration. A year later they were joined by settlers from the prosperous but overcrowded British colony of Barbados, who brought a Caribbean sensibility that exists in Charleston to this day.

Finding the first Charles Towne not very fertile and vulnerable to attack from Native Americans and the Spanish, they moved to the peninsula and down to "Oyster Point," what Charlestonians now call White Point Gardens. Just above Oyster Point they set up a walled town, bounded by modern-day Water Street to the south (then a marshy creek, as the name indicates), Meeting Street to the west, Cumberland Street to the north, and the Cooper River on the east.

Charles Towne came into its own after two nearly concurrent events in the early 1700s: the decisive victory of a combined force of Carolinians and Native American allies against the fierce Yamasee people, and the final eradication of the pirate threat with the deaths of Blackbeard and Stede Bonnet.

Flush with a new spirit of independence, Charles Towne threw off the control of the anemic, disengaged Lords Proprietors, tore down the old defensive walls, and was reborn as an outward-looking, expansive, and increasingly cosmopolitan city that came to be called Charleston. With safety from hostile incursions came the time of the great rice and indigo plantations. Springing up all along the Ashley River soon after the introduction of the crops, they turned the labor and expertise of imported Africans into enormous profit for their owners. However, the planters preferred the pleasures and sea breezes of Charleston, and gradually summer homes became year-round residences.

As the storm clouds of civil war gathered in the early 1800s, the majority of Charleston's population was of African descent, and the city had long been America's main importation point for the transatlantic slave trade. The worst fears of white Charlestonians seemed confirmed during the alleged plot by slave leader Denmark Vesey in the early 1820s to start a rebellion. The Lowcountry's reliance on slave labor put it front and center in the coming national confrontation over abolition, which came to a head with the bombardment of Fort Sumter in Charleston Harbor in April 1861.

By war's end, not only did the city lay in ruins—mostly from a disastrous fire in 1861, as well as from a 545-day Union siege—so did its way of life.

World War II brought the same economic boom that came to much of the South, most notably through an expansion of the Navy Yard and the addition of a military air base. By the 1950s, the automobile suburb and a thirst for "progress" had claimed so many historic buildings that the inevitable backlash inspired the formation of the Historic Charleston Foundation, which continues to lead the fight to keep intact the Holy City's architectural legacy.

Civil rights came to Charleston in earnest with a landmark suit to integrate the Charleston Municipal Golf Course in 1960. The biggest battle, however, would be the 100-day strike in 1969 against the Medical University of South Carolina—then, as now, a large employer of African Americans.

Charleston's next great renaissance—still ongoing today—came with the redevelopment of its downtown and the fostering of the tourism industry under the nearly 40-year tenure of Mayor Joe Riley, during which so much of the current visitor-friendly infrastructure became part of daily life here. Today, Charleston is completing the transition away from a military and manufacturing base, and by some measures is the nation's leader in tech startups, even ahead of Silicon Valley.

PLANNING YOUR TIME

Even if you're just going to confine yourself to the peninsula, plan on spending at least **two nights** in Charleston. You'll want half a day for shopping on King Street and a full day for seeing various attractions and museums. Keep in mind that one of Charleston's key sights, Fort Sumter, takes almost half a day to see once you factor in ticketing and boarding time for the ferry out to the fort and back; plan accordingly.

If you have a car, there are several great places to visit off the peninsula, especially the three plantations along the Ashley—Drayton Hall, Magnolia Plantation, and Middleton Place—and Charles Towne Landing. They are all no more than 30 minutes from downtown, and because they're roughly adjacent, you can visit all of them in a single day if you get an early start. The sites and excellent down-home restaurants on Johns Island are about 45 minutes out of downtown.

ORIENTATION

Charleston occupies a peninsula bordered by the Ashley River to the west and the Cooper River to the east, which "come together to form the Atlantic Ocean," according to the haughty phrase once taught to generations of Charleston schoolchildren. Although the lower tip of the peninsula actually points closer to southeast, that direction is regarded locally as due south, and anything toward the top of the peninsula is considered due north.

The peninsula is ringed by islands, many of which have become heavily populated suburbs. Clockwise from the top of the peninsula, they are: Daniel Island, Mount Pleasant, Isle of Palms, Sullivan's Island, Morris Island, Folly Island, and James Island. The resort island of Kiawah and the less-developed Edisto Island are farther south down the coast.

Charleston is made up of many small neighborhoods, many of them quite old. The boundaries are confusing, so your best bet is to simply look at the street signs (signage in general is excellent in Charleston). If you're in a historic neighborhood, such as the French Quarter or Ansonborough, a smaller sign above the street name will indicate that.

Other key terms you'll hear are "the Crosstown," the portion of U.S. 17 that goes across the peninsula; "Savannah Highway," the portion of U.S. 17 that traverses "West Ashley," which is the suburb across the Ashley River; "East Cooper," the area across the Cooper River that includes Mount Pleasant, Isle of Palms, and Daniel and Sullivan's Islands; and "the Neck," up where the peninsula narrows. These are the terms that locals use, and hence what you'll see in this guide.

Sights

TOURS

Because of the city's small, fairly centralized layout, the best way to experience Charleston is on foot—either yours or via hooves of an equine nature. For more tour information in Charleston, visit the **Charleston Visitor Reception and Transportation Center** (375 Meeting St., 800/774-0006, www.charlestoncvb.com, Mon.-Fri. 8:30am-5pm), where they have entire walls of brochures for all the latest tours and an on-site staff of local tourism experts.

Walking Tours

Since 1996, **Ed Grimball's Walking Tours** (Waterfront Park, Concord St., 843/813-4447, www.edgrimballtours.com, $22 adults, $8 children) has run twice-weekly historical tours that take you through the heart of Charleston, courtesy of the knowledgeable and sprightly Ed himself, a native Charlestonian. All of Ed's walks start from the big Pineapple Fountain in Waterfront Park, and reservations are a must.

Original Charleston Walks (Market St. and State St., 843/408-0010, www.charlestonwalks.com, times and prices vary) has received much national TV exposure. Its two-hour tours leave from the corner of Market and State Streets and cover a full slate, including a popular adults-only pub crawl.

Charleston Strolls (Mills House Hotel, 115 Meeting St., 843/722-8687, www.charlestonstrolls.com, daily 10am and 2pm, $25 adults, $10 children) is another popular tour good for a historical overview and tidbits. The two-hour tours leave twice daily from the Mills House Hotel.

Art lovers should check out the offerings from **Charleston Art Tours** (53 Broad St., 843/860-3327, www.charlestonarttours.com, $48-55). Sandra and Teri provide a selection of visual art-themed packages, including a French Quarter Tour and a Charleston Renaissance Tour.

Ghost tours are very popular in Charleston. **Bulldog Tours** (18 Anson St., 843/722-8687, www.bulldogtours.com, $22 adults, $10 children) has exclusive access to the Old City Jail, which features prominently in most of its tours. The most popular tour, the Haunted Jail Tour, leaves daily at 7pm, 8pm, 9pm, and 10pm; meet at the jail at 21 Magazine Street. The Ghosts and Dungeons Tour runs March-November Tuesday-Saturday at 7pm and 9pm and leaves from 18 Anson Street.

Carriage Tours

There's not a lot of difference in service or price among the carriage companies, and that's chiefly by design. The city divides the tours into three routes, or "zones." Which zone your driver explores is determined by lottery at the embarkation point—you don't get to decide the zone and neither does your driver. Typically, rides take 1-1.5 hours and hover around $25 per adult, about half that per child.

Tours sometimes book up early, so call ahead. The oldest and in my opinion best service in town is **Palmetto Carriage Works** (40 N. Market St., 843/723-8145, www.palmettocarriage.com), which offers free parking at its "red barn" base near City Market. Another popular tour is **Old South Carriage Company** (14 Anson St., 843/723-9712, www.oldsouthcarriage.com) with its Confederate-clad drivers. **Carolina Polo & Carriage Company** (16 Hayne St., 843/577-6767, www.cpcc.com) leaves from several spots, including the Doubletree Hotel and the company's Hayne Street stables.

Motorized Tours

Adventure Sightseeing (Charleston Visitor Reception and Transportation Center, 375 Meeting St., 843/762-0088, www.adventuresightseeing.com, daily various times, $20 adults, $11 children) offers several comfortable 1.5- to 2-hour rides, including the only motorized tour to the Citadel area, leaving the visitors center at various times throughout the day.

You can make a day of it with **Charleston's Finest Historic Tours** (Charleston Visitor Reception and Transportation Center, 375 Meeting St., 843/577-3311, www.historictoursofcharleston.com, daily 10:30am, $21 adults, $10.50 children), which has a basic two-hour city tour each day at 10:30am and offers some much longer tours to outlying plantations. The company offers free downtown pickup from most lodgings.

The old faithful **Gray Line of Charleston** (Charleston Visitor Reception and Transportation Center, 375 Meeting St., 843/722-4444, www.graylineofcharleston.com, Mar.-Nov. daily 9:30am-3pm, Dec.-Feb daily 9:30am-2pm, $21-34 adults, $12-19 children) offers a 90-minute Historic Charleston Tour. Tours depart from the visitors center every 30 minutes. Hotel pickup is available by reservation. The last tour leaves at 2pm during the off-season.

African American History Tours

Al Miller's **Sites & Insights Tours**

(Charleston Visitor Reception and Transportation Center, 375 Meeting St., 843/552-9995, www.sitesandinsightstours. com, tour times vary, $13-18) has several packages, including a Black History and Porgy & Bess Tour as well as a good combo city and island tour, all departing from the visitors center.

Alphonso Brown's **Gullah Tours** (African American Art Gallery, 43 John St., 843/763-7551, www.gullahtours.com, Mon.-Fri. 11am and 1pm, Sat. 11am, 1pm, and 3pm, $18) features stories told in the Gullah dialect. Tours run Monday-Saturday and leave from the African American Art Gallery, near the visitors center.

SOUTH OF BROAD

Wander among these narrow streets and marvel at the lovingly restored old homes, but keep in mind that almost everything down here is in private hands. Don't wander into a garden or take photos inside a window unless you're invited to do so.

The Battery

★ The Battery

For many, **The Battery** (S. Battery St. and Murray Blvd., 843/724-7321, daily 24 hours, free) is the single most iconic Charleston spot, drenched in history and boasting dramatic views. South is the Cooper River, with views of Fort Sumter, Castle Pinckney, and Sullivan's Island; north is the old carrier *Yorktown* moored at Mount Pleasant; and landward is the adjoining, peaceful **White Point Gardens,** the sumptuous mansions of the Battery.

Once the bustling (and sometimes seedy) heart of Charleston's maritime activity, the Battery was where "the gentleman pirate" Stede Bonnet and 21 of his men were hanged in 1718. The area got its name for hosting cannons during the War of 1812, with the current distinctive seawall structure built in the 1850s.

Contrary to popular belief, no guns fired from here on Fort Sumter, as they would have been out of range. However, many inoperable cannons, mortars, and piles of shot still reside here, much to the delight of kids. This is where Charlestonians gathered in a giddy, party-like atmosphere to watch the shelling of Fort Sumter in 1861, blissfully ignorant of the horrors to come.

Edmondston-Alston House

The most noteworthy attraction on the Battery is the 1825 **Edmondston-Alston House** (21 E. Battery St., 843/722-7171, www. middletonplace.org, Sun.-Mon. 1pm-4:30pm, Tues.-Sat. 10am-4:30pm, $12 adults, $8 students), the only Battery home open to the public for tours. This is one of the most unique and well-preserved historic homes in the United States, thanks to the ongoing efforts of the Alston family, who acquired the house from shipping merchant Charles Edmondston after the Panic of 1837 and still lives on the 3rd floor (tours only visit the first two stories).

Over 90 percent of the home's furnishings are original items from the Alston era. Originally built in the Federal style, second owner Charles Alston added several Greek

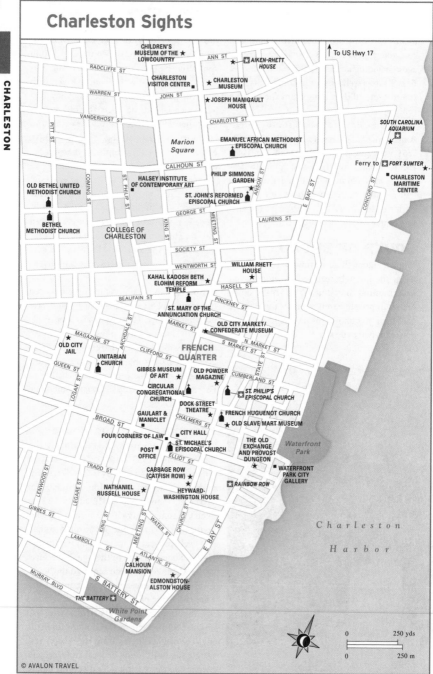

Charleston Sights

Revival elements, notably the parapet, balcony, and piazza, from which General P. G. T. Beauregard watched the attack on Fort Sumter. Today, the house is owned and administered by the Middleton Place Foundation, best known for its stewardship of Middleton Place along the Ashley River.

★ Rainbow Row

At 79-107 East Bay Street, between Tradd and Elliot Streets, is one of the most photographed sights in the United States: colorful **Rainbow Row,** nine pastel-colored mansions facing the Cooper River. The bright, historically accurate colors are one of the vestiges of Charleston's Caribbean heritage, a legacy of the English settlers from the colony of Barbados who were among the city's first citizens.

The homes are unusually old for this fire-, hurricane-, and earthquake-ravaged city, with most dating from 1730 to 1750. These houses were originally right on the Cooper River, their lower stories serving as storefronts on the wharf. The street was created later on top of landfill, or "made land" as it's called locally.

Besides its grace and beauty, Rainbow Row is of vital importance to American historic preservation. These were the first Charleston homes to be renovated and brought back from early 20th-century seediness. The restoration projects on Rainbow Row directly inspired the creation of the Preservation Society of Charleston, the first such group in the United States.

Nathaniel Russell House

Considered one of Charleston's grandest homes despite being built by an outsider from Rhode Island, the **Nathaniel Russell House** (51 Meeting St., 843/724-8481, www. historiccharleston.org, Mon.-Sat. 10am-5pm, Sun. 2pm-5pm, last tour begins 4:30pm, $12 adults, $5 children) is now a National Historic Landmark and one of the country's best examples of neoclassicism. Built in 1808 by Nathaniel Russell, aka "King of the Yankees," the home is furnished as accurately as possible to represent not only the lifestyle of the Russell family, but also the 18 African American servants who shared the premises.

When you visit, keep in mind that you're in the epicenter of not only Charleston's historic preservation movement but perhaps the nation's as well. In 1955 the Nathaniel Russell House was the first major project of the Historic Charleston Foundation, which raised $65,000 to purchase it. For an extra $6, you can gain admission to the Aiken-Rhett

Rainbow Row

Know Your Charleston Houses

Charleston's homes boast not only a long pedigree, but an interesting and unique one as well. Here are the basics of local architecture.

- **Single House:** Thus named for its single-room width. With full-length piazzas, or long verandas, on the south side to take advantage of breezes, the single house is perhaps the nation's first sustainable house design. The house is lengthwise on the lot, with the entrance on the side. This means the "backyard" is actually the side yard. Church Street has great examples, including 90, 92, and 94 Church Street, and the oldest single house in town, the 1730 Robert Brewton House (71 Church St.).

- **Double House:** This layout is two rooms wide with a central hallway and a porched facade facing the street. Double houses often had separate carriage houses. The Aiken-Rhett and Heyward-Washington Houses are good examples.

- **Charleston Green:** This uniquely Charlestonian color—extremely dark green that looks pitch black in low light—has its roots in the aftermath of the Civil War. The government distributed surplus black paint to contribute to the reconstruction of the ravaged peninsula, but Charlestonians were too proud to use it as-is. So they added a tiny bit of yellow, producing Charleston green.

- **Earthquake Bolt:** Due to structural damage after the 1886 earthquake, many buildings were retrofitted with one or more wall-to-wall iron rods to keep them stable. The rod was capped at both ends by a "gib plate," often disguised with a decorative element such as a lion's head, an S or X shape, or some other design. Notable examples are at 235 Meeting Street, 198 East Bay Street, 407 King Street, and 51 East Battery (a rare star design); 190 East Bay Street is unusual for having both an X and an S plate on the same building.

- **Joggling Board:** This long (10-15 ft.) flexible plank of cypress, palm, or pine with a handle at each end served various recreational purposes. Babies were bounced to sleep, small children used it as a trampoline, and it was also a method of courtship. A couple would start out at opposite ends and bounce until they met in the middle.

- **Carolopolis Award:** The Preservation Society of Charleston hands out these badges, to be mounted near the doorway, to local homeowners who have renovated historic properties downtown. On the award is "Carolopolis," the Latinized name of the city; "Condita AD 1670," the Latin word for "founding" with the date of Charleston's inception; and the date the award was given.

- **Ironwork:** Wrought iron was a widely used ornament before the mid-1800s. Charleston's best-known blacksmith, Philip Simmons, worked in wrought iron. His masterpieces are visible most notably at the Philip Simmons Garden (91 Anson St.), a gate for the visitors center (375 Meeting St.), and the Philip Simmons Children's Garden at Josiah Smith Tennent House (Blake St. and E. Bay St.). Chevaux-de-frise are iron bars on top of a wall that project menacing spikes. They became popular after the Denmark Vesey slave revolt conspiracy of 1822. The best example is at the Miles Brewton House (27 King St.).

House farther uptown, also administered by the Historic Charleston Foundation.

Calhoun Mansion

The single largest of Charleston's surviving grand homes, the 1876 **Calhoun Mansion** (16 Meeting St., 843/722-8205, www.calhounmansion.net, tours daily 11am-5pm, $16) boasts 35 opulent rooms (with 23 fireplaces!) in a striking Italianate design taking up a whopping 24,000 square feet. The grounds feature some charming garden spaces. A 90-minute "grand tour" is available for $75 per person; call for an appointment. Though the interiors at this privately run house are packed with antiques and furnishings, not all of them are accurate for the period.

Heyward-Washington House

The **Heyward-Washington House** (87 Church St., 843/722-0354, www.charleston-museum.org, Mon.-Sat. 10am-5pm, Sun. noon-5pm, $12 adults, $5 children, combo tickets to Charleston Museum and Manigault House available) takes the regional practice of naming a historic home for the two most significant names in its pedigree to its logical extreme. Built in 1772 by the father of Declaration of Independence signer Thomas Heyward Jr., the house also hosted George Washington during the president's visit to Charleston in 1791. It's now owned and operated by the Charleston Museum. The main attraction at the Heyward-Washington House is its masterful woodwork, exemplified by the cabinetry of legendary Charleston carpenter Thomas Elfe.

Cabbage Row

You'll recognize the addresses that make up **Cabbage Row** (89-91 Church St.) as "Catfish Row" from Gershwin's opera *Porgy and Bess* (based on the book *Porgy* by the Charleston author DuBose Heyward, who lived at 76 Church St.). Today this complex—which once housed 10 families—is certainly upgraded from years past, but the row still has the humble appeal of the tenement housing it once was, primarily for freed African American slaves after the Civil War. The house nearby at 94 Church Street was where John C. Calhoun and others drew up the infamous Nullification Acts that eventually led to the South's secession.

St. Michael's Episcopal Church

The oldest church in South Carolina, **St. Michael's Episcopal Church** (71 Broad St., 843/723-0603, services Sun. 8am and 10:30am) is actually the second sanctuary built on this spot, the first being St. Philip's, which was rebuilt on Church Street. As a response to the overflowing congregation at the new St. Philip's, St. Michael's was built from 1752 to 1761, in the style of Christopher Wren. Other than a small addition on the southeast corner in 1883, the St. Michael's you see today is unchanged, including the massive pulpit, outsized in the style of the time.

Services here over the years hosted such luminaries as the Marquis de Lafayette, George Washington, and Robert E. Lee, the latter two of whom are known to have sat in the "governor's pew." Two signers of the U.S. Constitution, John Rutledge and Charles Cotesworth Pinckney, are buried in the sanctuary.

St. Michael's offers informal, free guided **tours** after Sunday services; contact the greeter for more information.

Four Corners of Law

The famous intersection of Broad and Meeting Streets, named the **Four Corners of Law** for its confluence of federal law (the post office building), state law (the state courthouse), municipal law (city hall), and God's law (St. Michael's Episcopal Church), has been key to Charleston from the beginning. Meeting Street was laid out around 1672 and takes its name from the White Meeting House of early Dissenters, meaning non-Anglicans. Broad Street was also referred to as Cooper Street in the early days. Right in the middle of the street once stood the very first statue in the United States, a figure of William Pitt erected in 1766.

WATERFRONT
The Old Exchange and Provost Dungeon

The **Old Exchange and Provost Dungeon** (122 E. Bay St., 843/727-2165, www.oldexchange.com, daily 9am-5pm, $10 adults, $5 children and students) is brimming with history. The last building erected by the British before the American Revolution, it's also one of the three most historically significant colonial buildings in the United States, along with Philadelphia's Independence Hall and Boston's Faneuil Hall.

The Great Charleston Earthquake

The Charleston peninsula is bordered by three faults: the Woodstock Fault above North Charleston, the Charleston Fault running along the east bank of the Cooper River, and the Ashley Fault to the west of the Ashley River. On August 31, 1886, one of them buckled, causing one of the most damaging earthquakes ever to hit the United States.

The earthquake of 1886 was signaled by foreshocks earlier that week, but Charlestonians remained unconcerned. Then, that Tuesday at 9:50pm, came the big one. With an epicenter somewhere near the Middleton Place Plantation, the Charleston earthquake is estimated to have measured about 7 on the Richter scale. Tremors were felt across half the country, with the ground shaking in Chicago and a church damaged in Indianapolis. A dam 120 miles away in Aiken gave way, washing a train off the tracks. Cracks opened up parallel to the Ashley River, with part of the riverbank falling into the water. Thousands of chimneys all over the state fell or were rendered useless. The quake brought a series of "sand blows," a phenomenon where craters open and spew sand and water into the air. In Charleston's case, some of the craters were 20 feet wide, shooting debris another 20 feet into the air. The whole event lasted less than a minute.

In crowded Charleston, the damage was horrific: over 2,000 buildings destroyed, a quarter of the city's value gone, 27 killed immediately and almost 100 more to die from injuries and disease. Because of the large numbers of newly homeless, tent cities sprang up in every available park and green space. The American Red Cross's first field mission soon brought some relief, but the scarcity of food and especially fresh water made life difficult.

Almost every surviving building had experienced structural damage, in some cases severe. This led to the widespread use of the "earthquake bolt" now seen throughout older Charleston homes. Essentially acting as a very long screw with a washer on each end, the idea of the earthquake bolt is simple: Poke a long iron rod through two walls that need stabilizing, and cap the ends. Charleston being Charleston, the caps were often decorated with a pattern or symbol.

The seismic activity of Charleston's earthquake was so intense that more than 300 aftershocks occurred in the 35 years after the event. Geologists think that most seismic events measured in the region today are probably also aftershocks.

This is actually the former Royal Exchange and Custom House, the cellar of which served as a British prison. The complex was built in 1771 over a portion of the original 1698 seawall, some of which you can see today during the short but fascinating tour of the "dungeon" (actually built as a warehouse). Three of Charleston's four signers of the Declaration of Independence did time downstairs for sedition against the crown. Later, happier times were experienced in the ballroom upstairs, as it was here that the state selected its delegates to the Continental Congress and ratified the U.S. Constitution; it's also where George Washington took a spin on the dance floor during his raucous "Farewell Tour" in 1791.

While the highlight for most is the basement dungeon, or provost, where the infamous "gentleman pirate" Stede Bonnet was imprisoned in 1718 before being hanged, visitors shouldn't miss the sunny upstairs ballroom and its selection of Washington-oriented history.

Waterfront Park

Dubbing it "this generation's gift to the future," Mayor Joe Riley made this eight-acre project another part of his downtown renovation. Situated on Concord Street roughly between Exchange Street and Vendue Range, **Waterfront Park** (Concord St., 843/724-7327, daily dawn-dusk, free) was, like many waterfront locales in Charleston, built on what used to be marsh and water. This particularly massive chunk of "made land" juts about a football field's length farther out than the old waterline. Children will enjoy the large "Vendue" wading fountain at the park's entrance off Vendue Range, while a bit farther south is the large and quite artful Pineapple Fountain with its surrounding wading pool. Contemporary art lovers of all ages will appreciate the nearby **Waterfront Park City Gallery** (34 Prioleau St., www.citygalleryat-waterfrontpark.com, Tues.-Fri. 10am-6pm, Sat.-Sun. noon-5pm, free).

★ South Carolina Aquarium

The **South Carolina Aquarium** (100 Aquarium Wharf, 843/720-1990, www.scaquarium.org, Mar.-Aug. daily 9am-5pm, Sept.-Feb. daily 9am-4pm, $29.95 adults, $22.95 children, 4-D film extra, combo tickets with Fort Sumter tour available) is a great place for the whole family to have some fun while getting educated about the rich aquatic life off the coast and throughout this small but ecologically diverse state.

When you enter you're greeted with the 15,000-gallon Carolina Seas tank, with placid nurse sharks and vicious-looking moray eels. Other exhibits highlight the five key South Carolina ecosystems: beach, salt marsh, coastal plain, piedmont, and mountain forest. Another neat display is the Touch Tank, a hands-on collection of invertebrates found along the coast, such as sea urchins and horseshoe crabs. The pièce de résistance, however, is the three-story Great Ocean Tank with its hundreds of deeper-water marine creatures, including sharks, puffer fish, and sea turtles.

A key part of the aquarium's research and outreach efforts is the Turtle Hospital, which, in partnership with the state of South Carolina, attempts to rehabilitate and save sick and injured specimens. The hospital has saved many sea turtles, the first one being a 270-pound female affectionately known as "Edisto Mama." Tour the hospital or visit the interactive Sea Turtle Recovery exhibit to learn more about these efforts.

★ Fort Sumter National Monument

This is the place that brought about the beginning of the Civil War, a Troy for modern times. Though many historians insist the war would have happened regardless of President Lincoln's decision to keep **Fort Sumter** (843/883-3123, www.nps.gov/fosu, hours seasonal, free) in federal hands, the stated casus belli was Major Robert Anderson's refusal to surrender the fort when requested to do so in the early-morning hours of April 12, 1861. A few hours later came the first shot of the

Fort Sumter National Monument

Mayor Joe's Legacy

the entrance to Joseph P. Riley Jr. Park

Few cities anywhere have been as greatly influenced by one mayor as Charleston has by Joseph P. "Joe" Riley, who finally declined to run for reelection in 2015 after his 10th four-year term. "Mayor Joe," or just "Joe," as he's usually called, is not only responsible for the majority of redevelopment in the city; he also set the bar for its award-winning tourism industry.

Riley won his first mayoral race at the age of 32, the second Irish American mayor of the city. The lawyer, Citadel grad, and former member of the state legislature had a clear vision for his administration: to bring unprecedented numbers of women and minorities into city government, rejuvenate then-seedy King Street, and enlarge the city's tax base by annexing surrounding areas (during Riley's tenure the city grew from 16.7 square miles to over 100).

Here's only a partial list of the major projects and events Mayor Joe has made happen in Charleston:

- Charleston Maritime Center
- Charleston Place
- Children's Museum of the Lowcountry
- Hampton Park rehabilitation
- King Street-Market Street retail district
- Joseph P. Riley Jr. Park (named after the mayor at the insistence of city council)
- MOJA Arts Festival
- Piccolo Spoleto
- South Carolina Aquarium
- Spoleto USA
- Waterfront Park
- West Ashley Bikeway & Greenway

war, fired from Fort Johnson by Confederate captain George James. That 10-inch mortar shell, a signal for the general bombardment to begin, exploded above Fort Sumter. The first return shot from Fort Sumter was fired by none other than Captain Abner Doubleday, the man once credited as the father of baseball. Today the battered but still-standing Fort Sumter remains astride the entrance to Charleston Harbor on an artificial 70,000-ton sandbar, being part of the Third System of fortifications ordered after the War of 1812.

You can only visit by boats run by the approved concessionaire **Fort Sumter Tours** (843/881-7337, www.fortsumtertours.com, $18 adults, $11 ages 6-11, $16 seniors). Once at the fort, there's no charge for admission. Ferries leave from Liberty Square at Aquarium Wharf on the peninsula three times a day during the high season (Apr.-Oct.); call or check the website for times. Make sure to arrive about 30 minutes before the ferry departs. You can also get to Fort Sumter by ferry from Patriots Point at Mount Pleasant through the same concessionaire.

Budget at least 2.5 hours for the whole trip, including an hour at Fort Sumter. At Liberty Square on the peninsula is the **Fort Sumter Visitor Education Center** (340 Concord St., www.nps.gov/fosu, daily 8:30am-5pm, free), so you can learn more about where you're about to go. Once at the fort, you can be enlightened by the regular ranger talks on the fort's history and construction (generally at 11am and 2:30pm), take in the interpretive exhibits throughout the site, and enjoy the view of the spires of the Holy City from afar.

Some visitors are disappointed to find many of the fort's gun embrasures bricked over. This was done during the Spanish-American War, when the old fort was turned into an earthwork and the newer Battery Huger (huge-EE) was built on top of it.

FRENCH QUARTER
★ St. Philip's Episcopal Church
With a pedigree dating back to the colony's fledgling years, **St. Philip's Episcopal Church** (142 Church St., 843/722-7734, www.stphilipschurchsc.org, sanctuary Mon.-Fri. 10am-noon and 2pm-4pm, services Sun. 8:15am) is the oldest Anglican congregation south of Virginia. The first St. Philip's was built in 1680 at the corner of Meeting Street and Broad Street, the present site of St. Michael's Episcopal Church. It was badly damaged by a hurricane in 1710, so the city fathers approved the building of a new sanctuary dedicated to the saint on Church Street. Alas, the second St. Philip's burned to the ground in 1835. Construction immediately began on a replacement, and it's that building you see today. Heavily damaged by Hurricane Hugo in 1989, a $4.5 million renovation kept the church usable.

South Carolina's great statesman John C. Calhoun—who ironically despised Charlestonians for what he saw as their loose morals—was originally buried across Church Street in the former "stranger's churchyard," or West Cemetery, after his death in 1850. (Charles Pinckney and Edward Rutledge are two other notable South Carolinians buried here.) But near the end of the Civil War, Calhoun's body was moved to an unmarked grave closer to the sanctuary in an attempt to hide its location from Union troops.

Circular Congregational Church
The historic **Circular Congregational Church** (150 Meeting St., 843/577-6400, www.circularchurch.org, services fall-spring Sun. 11am, summer Sun. 10:15am, tours Mon.-Fri. 10:30am) has one of the most interesting pedigrees of any house of worship in Charleston. Services were originally held on the site of the "White Meeting House," for which Meeting Street is named; they were moved here beginning in 1681 and catered to a polyglot mix of Congregationalists, Presbyterians, and Huguenots. For that reason it was often called the Church of Dissenters ("dissenter" being the common term at the time for anyone not an Anglican). As with many structures in

town, the 1886 earthquake necessitated a rebuild, and the current edifice dates from 1891.

French Huguenot Church

One of the oldest congregations in town, the **French Huguenot Church** (44 Queen St., 843/722-4385, www.frenchhuguenotchurch. org, liturgy Sun. 10:30am) also has the distinction of being the only remaining independent Huguenot church in the country. Founded around 1681 by French Calvinists, the church had about 450 congregants by 1700. The original sanctuary was built in 1687, but was deliberately destroyed as a firebreak during the great conflagration of 1796. The church was replaced in 1800, but that building was in turn demolished in favor of the picturesque, stucco-coated Gothic Revival sanctuary you see today, which was completed in 1845. Sunday services are conducted in English now, but a single annual service in French is still celebrated in April.

Dock Street Theatre

Any thespian or lover of the stage must pay homage to the first theater built in North America, the **Dock Street Theatre** (135 Church St., 843/720-3968, www.charlestonstage.com, box office Mon.-Fri. 1pm-5pm,

tickets $63-67). The original 1736 Dock Street Theatre burned down, but a second theater opened on the same site in 1754. That building was in turn demolished for a grander edifice in 1773, which, you guessed it, also burned down. The current building dates from 1809, when the Planter's Hotel was built near the site of the original Dock Street Theatre. To mark the theater's centennial, the hotel added a stage facility in 1835, and it's that building you see now. In addition to a very active and well-regarded annual season from the resident Charleston Stage Company, the 464-seat venue has hosted umpteen events of the Spoleto Festival over the past three decades and continues to do so.

Old Powder Magazine

The **Old Powder Magazine** (79 Cumberland St., 843/722-9350, www.powdermag.org, Mon.-Sat. 10am-4pm, Sun. 1pm-4pm, $5 adults, $2 children) may be small, but the building is quite historically significant. The 1713 edifice is the oldest public building in South Carolina and the only one remaining from the days of the Lords Proprietors. As the name indicates, this was where the city's gunpowder was stored during the Revolution. The magazine is designed to implode rather than

the restored Dock Street Theatre

French Huguenots

the French Huguenot Church

A visitor can't spend a few hours in Charleston without coming across many French-sounding names. Some are common surnames, such as Ravenel, Manigault (MAN-i-go), Gaillard, Laurens, or Huger (huge-EE). Some are street or place names, such as Mazyck or Legare (Le-GREE). The Gallic influence in Charleston was of the Calvinist Protestant variety. Known as Huguenots, these French immigrants—refugees from an increasingly intolerant Catholic regime in France—were numerous enough in the settlement by the 1690s that they were granted full citizenship and property rights if they swore allegiance to the British crown.

Unlike other colonies, Carolina never put much of a premium on religious conformity, a trait that exists to this day despite the area's overall conservatism. And unlike many who fled European monarchies to come to the New World, the French Huguenots were far from poverty-stricken. Most arrived already well educated and skilled in one or more useful trades. In Charleston's early days, they were mostly farmers or tar burners (makers of tar and pitch for maritime use). Their pragmatism and work ethic would lead them to higher positions in local society, such as lawyers, judges, and politicians. One of the wealthiest Charlestonians, the merchant Gabriel Manigault, was by some accounts the richest person in the American colonies during the early 1700s. South Carolina's most famous French Huguenot was Francis Marion, the "Swamp Fox" of Revolutionary War fame. Born on the Santee River, Marion grew up in Georgetown and is now interred near Moncks Corner.

The library of the **Huguenot Society of Carolina** (138 Logan St., 843/723-3235, www.huguenotsociety.org, Mon.-Fri. 9am-2pm) is a great research tool for anyone interested in French Protestant history and genealogy.

To this day, the spiritual home of Charleston's Huguenots is the same as always: the French Huguenot Church on Church Street, one of the earliest congregations in the city. The church still holds a liturgy in French every April.

explode in the event of a direct hit. This is another labor of love of the Historic Charleston Foundation, which has leased the building from The Colonial Dames since 1993. It was opened to the public as an attraction in 1997. Next door is the privately owned, circa-1709 **Trott's Cottage,** the first brick dwelling in Charleston.

Old Slave Mart Museum

Slave auctions became big business in the South after 1808, when the United States banned the importation of slaves, thus increasing both price and demand. The auctions generally took place in public buildings where everyone could watch the wrenching spectacle. In the 1850s, public auctions in Charleston were put to a stop when city leaders discovered that visitors from European nations—all of which had banned slavery years before—were horrified at the practice. The slave trade was moved indoors to "marts" near the waterfront, where sales could be conducted out of the public eye. The last remaining such structure is the **Old Slave Mart Museum** (6 Chalmers St., 843/958-6467, www.charleston-sc.gov, Mon.-Sat. 9am-5pm, $7 adults, $5 children, free under age 6). Built in 1859, its last auction was held in November 1863. There are two main areas: the orientation area, where visitors learn about the transatlantic slave trade and the architectural history of the building itself, and the main exhibit area, where visitors can see documents, tools, and displays re-creating what happened inside during this sordid chapter in local history and celebrating the resilience of the area's African American population.

NORTH OF BROAD
Confederate Museum

Located on the 2nd floor of City Market's iconic main building, Market Hall on Meeting Street, the small **Confederate Museum** (188 Meeting St., 843/723-1541, Tues.-Sat. 11am-3:30pm, $5 adults, $3 children, cash only) hosts an interesting collection of Civil War memorabilia, with an emphasis on the military side, and is the local headquarters of the United Daughters of the Confederacy. Perhaps its best contribution, however, is its research library.

Gibbes Museum of Art

The **Gibbes Museum of Art** (135 Meeting St., 843/722-2706, www.gibbesmuseum.org, Tues.-Sat. 10am-5pm, Sun. 1pm-5pm, $9 adults, $7 students, $5 ages 6-12) is one of those rare Southern museums that manages a good blend of the modern and the traditional, the local and the international. Their permanent collection spans a wide range of Southern art from the colonial era on, and they arguably have the most distinctive collection of portrait miniatures in the nation. Begun in 1905 as the Gibbes Art Gallery—the final wish of James Shoolbred Gibbes, who willed $100,000 for its construction—the complex has grown through the years in size and influence. The Gibbes Art School in the early 20th century formed a close association with the Woodstock School in New York, bringing important ties and prestige to the fledgling institution. Georgia O'Keeffe brought an exhibit here in 1955.

Kahal Kadosh Beth Elohim Reform Temple

The birthplace of Reform Judaism in the United States and the oldest continuously active synagogue in the nation is **Kahal Kadosh Beth Elohim Reform Temple** (90 Hasell St., 843/723-1090, www.kkbe.org, services Sat. 11am, tours Mon.-Fri. 10am-noon, Sun. 10am-4pm). The congregation—*Kahal Kadosh* means "holy community" in Hebrew—was founded in 1749, with the current temple dating from 1840 and built in the Greek Revival style. The temple's Reform roots came about indirectly because of the great fire of 1838. In rebuilding, some congregants wanted to bring an organ into the temple, and the Orthodox contingent lost the debate. So the new building became the first home of Reform Judaism in the country, a fitting testament to Charleston's long-standing

The New Charleston Green

Most people know "Charleston green" as a unique local color, the result of adding a few drops of yellow to post-Civil War surplus black paint. But these days the phrase also refers to environmentally friendly development in Charleston.

The most obvious example is the ambitious Navy Yard redevelopment, which seeks to repurpose the closed-down facility. From its inception in 1902 at the command of President Theodore Roosevelt through the end of the Cold War, the Charleston Navy Yard was one of the city's biggest employers. Though the yard was closed in 1995, a 340-acre section now hosts an intriguing mix of green-friendly design firms, small nonprofits, and commercial maritime companies. Clemson University—with the help of a massive federal grant, the largest in the school's history—will oversee one of the world's largest wind turbine research facilities, centered on Building 69.

Also in North Charleston, local retail chain Half Moon Outfitters has a green-friendly warehouse facility in an old grocery store. The first LEED (Leadership in Energy and Environmental Design) Platinum-certified building in South Carolina, the warehouse features solar panels, rainwater reservoirs, and locally harvested or salvaged interiors. There's also the LEED-certified North Charleston Elementary School as well as North Charleston's adoption of a "dark skies" ordinance to cut down on light pollution. On the peninsula, the historic meetinghouse of the Circular Congregational Church has a green addition with geothermal heating and cooling, rainwater cisterns, and Charleston's first vegetative roof.

For many Charlestonians, the green movement manifests in simpler things: the pedestrian and bike lanes on the Ravenel Bridge, the thriving city recycling program, and the Sustainable Seafood Initiative, a partnership of local restaurants, universities, and conservation groups that brings the freshest, most environmentally responsible dishes to your table when you dine out in Charleston.

This forward-thinking mode doesn't just mean enhanced quality of life for Charleston residents. It also pays off in attracting tech businesses and other cutting-edge employers, and the well-educated millennial knowledge workers who founded and staff them.

Charleston's tech economy is among the fastest growing in the nation, 26 percent faster than the national average, faster even than Austin, Texas, and Raleigh/Durham, North Carolina. Nearly 100 firms are part of the public/private Charleston Digital Corridor (www.charlestondigitalcorridor.com). The growth has garnered so much attention that some are using the nickname "Silicon Harbor" for the Charleston region.

---

ecumenical spirit of religious tolerance and inclusiveness.

Old City Jail

If you were to make a movie called *Dracula Meets the Lord of the Rings*, the imposing **Old City Jail** (21 Magazine St., 843/577-5245) might make a great set. Its history is also the stuff from which movies are made. Built in 1802 on a lot set aside for public use since 1680, the edifice was the Charleston County lockup until 1939. Some of the last pirates were jailed here in 1822 while awaiting hanging, as was slave rebellion leader Denmark Vesey. During the Civil War, prisoners of both armies were held here at various times.

The Old City Jail currently houses the American College of the Building Arts. Unless you're a student there, the only way to tour the Old Jail is through **Bulldog Tours** (18 Anson St., 843/722-8687, www.bulldogtours. com). Their Haunted Jail Tour ($20 adults, $10 children) starts daily at 7pm, 8pm, 9pm, and 10pm; all tours are paid for at 40 North Market Street, within a short walk, with jail tours starting at the jail itself.

Old City Market

Part kitschy tourist trap, part glimpse into the Old South, part community gathering place, **Old City Market** (Meeting St. and Market St., 843/973-7236, daily 6am-11:30pm) remains Charleston's most reliable attraction. It is certainly the practical center of the city's tourist trade, not least because so many tours originate nearby. No matter what anyone tries to tell you, Charleston's City Market never hosted a single slave auction. When the Pinckney family donated this land to the city for a "Publick Market," one stipulation was that no slaves were ever to be sold here—or else the property would immediately revert to the family's descendants. A recent multi-million-dollar renovation has prettified the bulk of City Market into more of a big-city air-conditioned pedestrian shopping mall. It's not as shabbily charming as it once was, but it certainly offers a more comfortable stroll during the warmer months.

Philip Simmons Garden

Charleston's most beloved artisan is the late Philip Simmons. Born on nearby Daniel Island in 1912, Simmons became one of the most sought-after decorative ironworkers in the United States. In 1982 the National Endowment for the Arts awarded him its National Heritage Fellowship. His work is on display at the Smithsonian Institution and the Museum of International Folk Art in Santa Fe, New Mexico, among many other places. In 1989, the congregation at Simmons's **St. John's Reformed Episcopal Church** (91 Anson St., 843/722-4241, http://philipsimmons.us) voted to make the church garden a commemoration of the life and work of this legendary African American artisan, who died in 2009 at age 97. Completed in two phases, the Bell Garden and the Heart Garden, the project is a delightful blend of Simmons's signature graceful, sinuous style and fragrant flowers.

Unitarian Church

In a town filled with cool old church cemeteries, the coolest belongs to the **Unitarian Church** (4 Archdale St., 843/723-4617, www.charlestonuu.org, services Sun. 11am, free tours Sat. 10am-1pm). As a nod to the beauty and power of nature, vegetation and shrubbery in the cemetery have been allowed to take their natural course (walkways excepted).

The church itself—the second-oldest such

the cemetery at Unitarian Church

edifice in Charleston and the oldest Unitarian sanctuary in the South—was built in 1776 because of overcrowding at the Circular Congregational Church, but the building saw rough usage by British troops during the Revolution. Repairs were made in 1787 and an extensive modernization took place in 1852. Sadly, the 1886 earthquake toppled the original tower, and the version you see today is a subsequent and less grand design.

To see the sanctuary at times other than weekend mornings, go by the office next door Monday-Friday 9am-2pm and they'll let you take a walk through the interior.

William Rhett House

The oldest standing residence in Charleston is the circa-1713 **William Rhett House** (54 Hasell St.), which once belonged to the colonel who captured the pirate Stede Bonnet. It's now a private residence, but you can admire this excellent prototypical example of a Charleston single house easily from the street and read the nearby historical marker.

UPPER KING
Marion Square

While the Citadel moved lock, stock, and barrel almost a century ago, the college's old home, the South Carolina State Arsenal, still overlooks 6.5-acre **Marion Square** (between King St. and Meeting St. at Calhoun St., 843/965-4104, daily dawn-dusk), a reminder of the days when this was the institute's parade ground, the "Citadel Green" (the old Citadel is now a hotel). Marion Square is named for the "Swamp Fox" himself, Revolutionary War hero and father of modern guerrilla warfare Francis Marion. Marion Square hosts many events, including a farmers market every Saturday early April-late November.

College of Charleston

The oldest college in South Carolina and the first municipal college in the country, the **College of Charleston** (66 George St., 843/805-5507, www.cofc.edu) represents a chunk of the city's history, but its 12,000-plus students bring a modern, youthful touch to many of the city's public activities. Though the college has its share of modernistic buildings, a stroll around the gorgeous campus will uncover some historic gems. The oldest building on campus, the Bishop Robert Smith House, dates from the year of the college's founding, 1770, and is now the president's house; find it on Glebe Street between Wentworth and George. Movies that have had scenes shot on campus include *Cold Mountain, The Patriot,* and *The Notebook.* If you have an iPhone or iPod Touch, you can download a neat self-guided tour, complete with video, from the iTunes App Store (www.apple.com, search "College of Charleston Tour," free).

Emanuel African Methodist Episcopal Church

Known simply as "Mother Emanuel," **Emanuel African Methodist Episcopal Church** (110 Calhoun St., www.emanuela-mechurch.org, services Sun. 9:30am) has a distinguished history as one of the South's oldest African American congregations. Prior to the Civil War, one of the church's founders, Denmark Vesey, was implicated in planning a slave uprising. The edifice was burned as retaliation for Vesey's involvement (and the founding of the Citadel as a military academy nearby was directly related to white unrest over the plot). In the wake of the Nat Turner revolt in 1834, open worship by African Americans was outlawed in Charleston and went underground until after the Civil War. The congregation adopted the "Emanuel" name with the building of a new church in 1872, a wooden structure that unfortunately didn't survive the great earthquake of 1886. The simple, elegant, and deceptively large church you see today dates from 1891, and has hosted luminaries such as Booker T. Washington, Dr. Martin Luther King Jr., and Coretta Scott King. In 2015, the historically black church was the site of the horrific murders of nine worshippers—including its pastor, Clementa Pinckney—by a white racist.

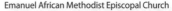

Emanuel African Methodist Episcopal Church

At Pinckney's memorial service, President Barack Obama spoke and led the congregation in singing *Amazing Grace*.

Charleston Museum

During its long history, the **Charleston Museum** (360 Meeting St., 843/722-2996, www.charlestonmuseum.org, Mon.-Sat. 9am-5pm, Sun. noon-5pm, $12 adults, $5 children, combo tickets to Heyward-Washington and Manigault Houses available) has moved literally all over town. It's currently housed in a noticeably modern building, but make no mistake: This is the nation's oldest museum, founded in 1773. It strives to stay as fresh and relevant as any new museum, with a rotating schedule of special exhibits in addition to its very eclectic permanent collection. For a long time this was the only place to get a glimpse of the CSS *Hunley,* albeit just a fanciful replica in front of the main entrance. (Now you can see the real thing at its conservation site in North Charleston, and it's even smaller than the replica would indicate.) Much of the museum's collection focuses on aspects of everyday life of Charlestonians, from the aristocracy to slaves, including items such as utensils, clothing, and furniture. There are quirks as well, such as the Egyptian mummy and the fine lady's fan made out of turkey feathers. A particular and possibly surprising specialty includes work and research by noted regional naturalists like John James Audubon, André Michaux, and Mark Catesby.

Joseph Manigault House

Owned and operated by the nearby Charleston Museum, the **Joseph Manigault House** (350 Meeting St., 843/723-2926, www. charlestonmuseum.org, Mon.-Sat. 10am-5pm, Sun. noon-5pm, last tour 4:30pm, $12 adults, $5 children, combo tickets to Charleston Museum and Heyward-Washington House available) is sometimes called the "Huguenot House." This grand circa-1803 National Historic Landmark was designed by wealthy merchant Gabriel Manigault for his brother, Joseph, a rice planter of local repute. The three-story brick town house is a great example of Adams, or Federal, architecture.

★ Aiken-Rhett House

An acquisition of the Historic Charleston Foundation, the **Aiken-Rhett House** (48 Elizabeth St., 843/723-1159, www.historic-charleston.org, Mon.-Sat. 10am-5pm, Sun. 2pm-5pm, last tour 4:15pm, $12 adults, $5 children) shows another side of the

the Aiken-Rhett House

Family Fun in Charleston

Let's face it: A steady diet of house museums and long-ago history will bore anyone to tears, not just the young folks in your traveling party. Fortunately, Charleston has a range of options to please children of all ages. You just have to know where to look.

- **Children's Museum of the Lowcountry:** Conveniently located in the city's "Museum Row," this indoor playground offers a variety of hands-on activities for kids ages 3 months-12 years.

- **Old Exchange and Provost Dungeon:** For a real-life Pirates of the Caribbean experience, take a guided tour of this spooky spot from colonial times, complete with animatronic-style figures of pirates and scoundrels.

- **Sewee Visitor and Environmental Education Center:** Visit a pack of red wolves (indigenous to the coastal area) at this center devoted to preserving the species and educating people about these magnificent little animals.

- **South Carolina Aquarium:** The closest thing to a zoo, this easily managed and very informative installation features aspects of every habitat in the ecologically diverse Palmetto State—from Lowcountry marshland to Upstate mountain rivers—anchored by an enormous three-floor central observation tank filled with marine life.

- **Waterfront Park:** The park's outdoor fountain sculptures are sure to please any carefree spirit in your group.

organization's mission. Whereas the Historic Charleston-run Nathaniel Russell House seeks to re-create a specific point in time, work at the Aiken-Rhett House emphasizes conservation and research. Built in 1818 and expanded by South Carolina governor William Aiken Jr., after whom we know the house today, parts of this rambling, almost Dickensian house remained sealed from 1918 until 1975, when the family relinquished the property to the Charleston Museum. While the docents are friendly and helpful, the main way to enjoy the Aiken-Rhett House is by way of a self-guided MP3 player audio tour, which is unique in Charleston.

Children's Museum of the Lowcountry

Another example of Charleston's savvy regarding the tourist industry is the **Children's Museum of the Lowcountry** (25 Ann St., 843/853-8962, www.explorecml.org, Tues.-Sat. 9am-5pm, Sun. noon-5pm, $12 non-SC residents). Recognizing that historic homes and Civil War memorabilia aren't enough to keep a family with young children in town for long, the city established this museum in 2005 specifically to give families with kids ages 3 months-12 years a reason to spend more time (and money) downtown.

HAMPTON PARK
The Citadel

The Citadel (171 Moultrie St., 843/953-3294, www.citadel.edu, grounds daily 8am-6pm) was originally sited at the Old State Arsenal at Marion Square, born out of panic over the threat of a slave rebellion organized in 1822 by Denmark Vesey. The school moved to its current 300-acre site farther up the peninsula along the Ashley River in 1922. The Citadel (technically named The Citadel, The Military College of South Carolina) has entered popular consciousness through the works of graduate Pat Conroy, especially his novel *Lords of Discipline,* starring a thinly disguised "Carolina Military Institute."

There's a lot for visitors to see, including **The Citadel Museum** (843/953-6779, daily noon-5pm, free), on your right just as you enter campus; the "Citadel Murals" in the Daniel Library; "Indian Hill," the highest point in Charleston and former site of an Indian trader's home; and the grave of U.S. general Mark Clark of World War II fame, who was Citadel president from 1954 to 1966. Ringing vast Summerall Field—the huge open space where you enter campus—are the many castle-like cadet barracks.

The most interesting single experience for visitors to the Citadel is the Friday afternoon dress parade on Summerall Field, in which cadets pass for review in full dress uniform (the fabled "long gray line") accompanied by a marching band and pipers. Often called "the best free show in Charleston," the parade happens almost every Friday at 3:45pm during the school year; you might want to consult the website before your visit to confirm. Arrive well in advance to avoid parking problems.

WEST ASHLEY
Charles Towne Landing

Any look at West Ashley must start where everything began, with the 600-acre state historic site **Charles Towne Landing** (1500 Old Town Plantation Rd., 843/852-4200, www. southcarolinaparks.com/ctl, daily 9am-5pm, $10 adults, $6 students, free under age 6). This is where Charleston's original settlers first arrived and camped in 1670, remaining only a few years before eventually moving to the more defensible peninsula where the Holy City now resides. A beautiful and fully seaworthy replica of a settlers' ship is the main highlight, docked in the creek on the far side of the long and well-done exploration trail through the site.

★ Drayton Hall

A mecca for historic preservationists from all over the country, **Drayton Hall** (3380 Ashley River Rd., 843/769-2600, www.draytonhall. org, Mon.-Sat. 9am-5pm, Sun. 11am-5pm, tours on the half hour, $22 adults, $10 ages 12-18, $6 ages 6-11, grounds only $10) is remarkable not only for its pedigree, but also for the way in which it has been preserved. This stately redbrick Georgian-Palladian building, the oldest plantation home in the country open to the public, is literally historically preserved—as in no electricity, heat, or running water.

Since its construction in 1738 by John Drayton, son of Magnolia Plantation founder Thomas, Drayton Hall has survived almost completely intact through the ups and downs of Lowcountry history. In its heyday before

Drayton Hall

the American Revolution, Drayton Hall was widely considered the finest home in all the colonies, the very symbol of the extraordinary wealth of the South Carolina aristocracy. John Drayton died while fleeing the British in 1779; subsequently his house served as the headquarters of British generals Henry Clinton and Charles Cornwallis. During the Civil War, Drayton Hall escaped the depredations of the conquering Union army, one of only three area plantation homes to survive.

The guides hold degrees in the field, and a tour of the house, which starts on the half hour, takes every bit of 50 minutes. A separate 45-minute program called "Connections: From Africa to America" chronicles the diaspora of the slaves who originally worked this plantation, from their capture to their eventual freedom. "Connections" is presented at 11:15am, 1:15pm, and 3:15pm.

The site comprises not only the main house, but two self-guided walking trails as well, one along the peaceful Ashley River and another along the marsh. Also on-site is an African American cemetery with at least 33 known graves. It's kept deliberately untended and unlandscaped to honor the final wish of Richmond Bowens (1908-1998), the seventh-generation descendant of some of Drayton Hall's original slaves.

Magnolia Plantation and Gardens

A different legacy of the Drayton family is **Magnolia Plantation and Gardens** (3550 Ashley River Rd., 843/571-1266, www.magnoliaplantation.com, daily 8:30am-4:30pm, $15 adults, $10 children, free under age 6). It claims not only the first garden in the United States, dating back to the 1680s, but also the first public garden, dating to 1872. Thomas Drayton Jr.—scion of Norman aristocracy, son of a wealthy Barbadian planter—came from the Caribbean to build his own fortune; he immediately married the daughter of Stephen Fox, who began this plantation in 1676. Magnolia has stayed in the possession

of an unbroken line of Drayton descendants to this day.

As a privately run attraction, Magnolia has little of the academic veneer of other plantation sites in the area, and there's a slightly kitschy feel here, the opposite of the quiet dignity of Drayton Hall. And unlike Middleton Place a few miles down the road, the gardens here are anything but manicured, with a wild, almost playful feel. That said, Magnolia can claim fame to being one of the earliest bona fide tourist attractions in the United States and the beginning of Charleston's now-booming tourist industry.

While spring remains the best—and the most crowded—time to come, a huge variety of camellias bloom in early winter, a time marked by a yearly Winter Camellia Festival. Children will enjoy finding their way through "the Maze" of manicured camellia and holly bushes, complete with a viewing stand to look within the giant puzzle. Plant lovers will enjoy the themed gardens such as the Biblical Garden, the Barbados Tropical Garden, and the Audubon Swamp Garden, complete with alligators and named after John James Audubon, who visited here in 1851. House tours, the 45-minute Nature Train tour, the 45-minute Nature Boat tour, and a visit to the Audubon Swamp Garden run about $8 per person extra for each offering.

★ Middleton Place

With the first landscaped garden in North America and still one of the most magnificent in the world, **Middleton Place** (4300 Ashley River Rd., 843/556-6020, www.middletonplace.org, daily 9am-5pm, $28 adults, $15 students, $10 children, guided house tour $15 extra) is a sublime, unforgettable combination of history and sheer natural beauty. Nestled along a quiet bend in the Ashley River, the grounds contain a historic restored home, working stables, 60 acres of breathtaking gardens, and the Inn at Middleton Place, a stunning piece of modern architecture.

First granted in 1675, Middleton Place is the culmination of the Lowcountry rice plantation aesthetic. In 1741 the plantation became the family seat of the Middletons, one of the most notable surnames in U.S. history. As the Civil War wound down, on February 22, 1865, the 56th New York Volunteers burned the main house and destroyed the gardens, leaving only the circa-1755 guest wing, which today is the excellently restored **Middleton Place House Museum** (4300 Ashley River Rd., 843/556-6020, www.middletonplace.org, guided tours Mon. 1:30pm-4:30pm, Tues.-Sun. 10am-4:30pm, $15). The 1886 earthquake added its mark, and it wasn't until 1916 that renovation of the property began. In 1971 Middleton Place was named a National Historic Landmark.

A short walk takes you to the **Plantation Stableyards,** where costumed craftspeople work using historically authentic tools and methods, all while surrounded by a happy family of domestic animals. The Stableyards is also home to a pair of magnificent male water buffalo. Henry Middleton originally imported a pair to work the rice fields—the first in North America—but these guys are just there to relax and add atmosphere. Meet them daily 9am-5pm.

The 53-room **Inn at Middleton Place** (www.theinnatmiddletonplace.com) has a bold Frank Lloyd Wright-influenced design, comprising four units joined by walkways. But both inside and outside it manages to blend quite well with the surrounding fields, trees, and riverbanks. The inn also offers kayak tours and instruction—a particularly nice way to enjoy the grounds from the waters of the Ashley—and features its own organic garden and labyrinth, intriguing modern counterpoints to the formal gardens of the plantation itself.

They still grow the exquisite Carolina Gold rice in a field at Middleton Place, harvested in the old style each September. You can sample some of it in many dishes at the **Middleton Place Restaurant** (843/556-6020, www.middletonplace.org, lunch daily 11am-3pm, dinner Tues.-Thurs. 6pm-8pm, Fri.-Sat. 6pm-9pm, Sun. 6pm-8pm, $15-25). You can tour the gardens for free if you arrive for a dinner reservation at 5:30pm or later.

The Coburg Cow

The entire stretch of U.S. 17 (Savannah Hwy.) heading into Charleston from the west is redolent of a particularly Southern brand of retro Americana. The chief example is the famous **Coburg Cow,** a large, rotating dairy cow accompanied by a bottle of chocolate milk. The

Middleton Place

current installation dates from 1959, though a version of it was on this site as far back as the early 1930s, when this area was open countryside. During Hurricane Hugo the Coburg Cow was moved to a safe location. In 2001 the attached dairy closed down, and the city threatened to have the cow moved or demolished. But community outcry preserved the delightful landmark, which is visible today on the south side of U.S. 17 in the 900 block. You can't miss it—it's a big cow on the side of the road!

Caw Caw Interpretive Center

About 10 minutes west of Charleston on U.S. 17 you'll find the unique **Caw Caw Interpretive Center** (5200 Savannah Hwy., Ravenel, 843/889-8898, www.ccprc.com, Tues.-Sun. 9am-5pm, $2), a treasure trove for history buffs and naturalists wanting to learn more about the old rice culture of the South. Most Wednesday and Saturday mornings, guided bird walks are held at 8:30am ($5 pp). You can put in your own canoe for $10 October-April on Saturdays and Sundays. Bikes and dogs aren't allowed on the grounds.

NORTH CHARLESTON
Magnolia Cemetery

Although not technically in North Charleston, historic **Magnolia Cemetery** (Cunnington Ave. at Huguenin Ave., 843/722-8638, Sept.-May daily 8am-5pm, June-Aug. daily 8am-6pm) is well north of the downtown tourist district in the area called "the Neck." This historic burial ground, while not quite the aesthetic equal of Savannah's famed Bonaventure Cemetery, is still a stirring site for its natural beauty and ornate memorials as well as for its historical aspects. Here are buried the crewmen who died aboard the CSS *Hunley,* reinterred after their retrieval from Charleston Harbor. In all, over 2,000 Civil War dead are buried here, including 5 Confederate generals and 84 rebels who fell at Gettysburg and were moved here.

★ CSS *Hunley*

In 1864, the Confederate submarine CSS *Hunley* mysteriously sank right after successfully destroying the USS *Housatonic* with the torpedo attached to its bow, marking the first time a sub ever sank a ship in battle. For the longest time, the only glimpse of the ill-fated Confederate submarine afforded to visitors was a not-quite-accurate replica outside the Charleston Museum. But in 1995, after a 15-year search, maritime novelist and adventurer Clive Cussler and his team finally found the submarine off Sullivan's Island. In 2000, a team comprising the nonprofit **Friends of the Hunley**, the federal government, and private partners successfully implemented a plan to safely raise the vessel.

Today you can view the sub, see the life-size model from the TNT movie *The Hunley,* and look at artifacts such as the "lucky" gold piece of the commander at the **Warren Lasch Conservation Center** (1250 Supply St., Bldg. 255, 866/866-9938, www.hunley.org, Sat. 10am-5pm, Sun. noon-5pm, $16 adults, $8 students, free under age 5). You can even see facial reconstructions of some of the eight sailors who died on board. The remains of the crew lie in Magnolia Cemetery, where they were buried in 2004 with full military honors.

The Lasch Center is only open to the public on weekends so that research and conservation can be performed during the week. Because of this limited window of opportunity and the popularity of the site, reserve tickets ahead of time.

To get to the Warren Lasch Conservation Center from Charleston, take I-26 north to exit 216B. Take a left onto Spruill Avenue and a right onto McMillan Avenue. Once in the Navy Yard, take a right on Hobson Avenue, and after about one mile take a left onto Supply Street. The Lasch Center is the low white building on the left.

Fire Museum

The **North Charleston and American**

LaFrance Fire Museum and Education Center (4975 Centre Pointe Dr., North Charleston, 843/740-5550, www.legacyofheroes.org, Mon.-Sat. 10am-5pm, Sun. 1pm-5pm, last ticket 4pm, $6 adults, free under age 14), which shares a huge 25,000-square-foot space with the North Charleston Convention and Visitors Bureau, is primarily dedicated to maintaining and increasing its collection of antique American LaFrance firefighting vehicles and equipment. The 18 fire engines here date from 1857 to 1969. The museum's exhibits have taken on greater poignancy in the wake of the tragic loss of nine Charleston firefighters killed trying to extinguish a warehouse blaze on U.S. 17 in summer 2007—second only to the 9/11 attacks as the largest single loss of life for a U.S. firefighting department.

SUMMERVILLE

Founded as Pineland Village in 1785, Summerville made its reputation as a place for plantation owners and their families to escape the insects and heat of the swampier areas of the Lowcountry. Summerville boasts a whopping 700 buildings in the National Register of Historic Places. For a walking tour of the historic district, download the map at www.visitsummerville.com or pick up a hard copy at the **Summerville Visitors Center** (402 N. Main St., 843/873-8535, Mon.-Fri. 9am-5pm, Sat. 10am-3pm, Sun. 1pm-4pm).

Azalea Park

Much visitor activity in Summerville centers on **Azalea Park** (S. Main St. and W. 5th St. S., daily dawn-dusk, free), rather obviously named for its most scenic inhabitants. Several fun yearly events take place here, most notably the **Flowertown Festival** (www.flowertownfestival.com, free) each April, a three-day affair heralding the coming of spring and the blooming of the flowers. One of the biggest festivals in South Carolina, 250,000 people usually attend. Another event, **Sculpture in the South** (www.sculpturein-thesouth.com) in May, takes advantage of the extensive public sculpture in the park.

Colonial Dorchester State Historic Site

Just south of Summerville on the way back to Charleston is the interesting **Colonial Dorchester State Historic Site** (300 County Rd. S-18-373, 843/873-1740, www.southcarolinaparks.com, daily 9am-6pm, $2 adults, free under age 16), chronicling a virtually unknown segment of Carolina history. A contingent of Massachusetts Puritans ("Congregationalists" in the parlance of the time) were given special dispensation in 1697 to form a settlement of their own specifically to enhance commercial activity on the Ashley River. Today little is left of old Dorchester but the tabby walls of the 1757 fort overlooking the Ashley. Don't miss the unspectacular but still historically vital remains of the wooden wharf on the walking trail along the river, once the epicenter of a thriving port. The most-photographed thing on-site is the bell tower of the Anglican church of St. George—which actually wasn't where the original settlers worshiped and was in fact quite resented by them since they were forced to pay for its construction.

Summerville-Dorchester Museum

To learn more about Summerville's interesting history, go just off Main Street to the **Summerville-Dorchester Museum** (100 E. Doty Ave., 843/875-9666, www.summervilledorchestermuseum.org, Mon.-Sat. 9am-2pm, donations accepted). Located in the former town police station, the museum has a wealth of good exhibits. The museum opened in 1992 thanks to a group of Summerville citizens who wanted to preserve the region's history.

MOUNT PLEASANT AND EAST COOPER

The main destination in this area on the east bank of the Cooper River is the island of Mount Pleasant, primarily known as a peaceful, fairly affluent suburb of Charleston—a role it has played for about 300 years now.

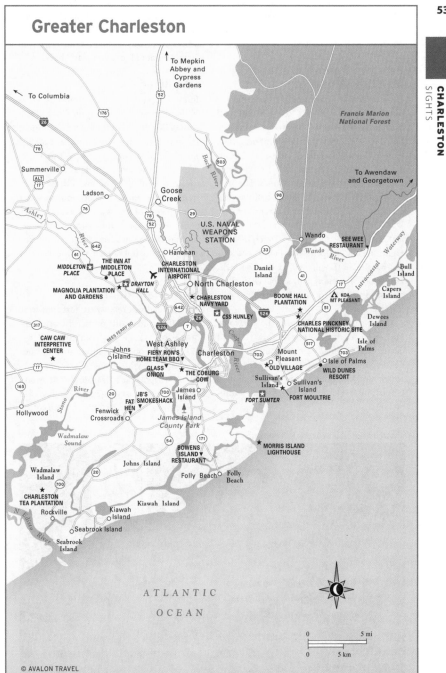

Greater Charleston

To Mepkin
Abbey and
Cypress
Gardens

52

To Columbia

176

26

Francis Marion
National Forest

78

Summerville

ALT
17

Ladson

Ashley

76

642

61

MIDDLETON
PLACE

THE INN AT
MIDDLETON
PLACE

MAGNOLIA PLANTATION
AND GARDENS

DRAYTON
HALL

River

503

Back River

78
52

Goose
Creek

29

U.S. NAVAL
WEAPONS
STATION

Hanahan

CHARLESTON
INTERNATIONAL
AIRPORT

North Charleston

CHARLESTON
NAVY YARD

98

Wando

Wando

33

Daniel
Island

41

Wando River

SEE WEE
RESTAURANT

To Awendaw
and Georgetown

17

KOA
MT PLEASANT

Intracoastal Waterway

Bull
Island

Capers
Island

BOONE HALL
PLANTATION

51

Dewees
Island

317

CAW CAW
INTERPRETIVE
CENTER

165

Hollywood

Stono River

20

642

7

525

26

BEES FERRY RD

Johns
Island

FIERY RON'S
HOME TEAM BBQ

GLASS
ONION

JB'S
SMOKESHACK

FAT
HEN

Fenwick
Crossroads

CSS HUNLEY

West Ashley

THE COBURG
COW

700

James
Island

Charleston

Cooper River

526

CHARLES PINCKNEY
NATIONAL HISTORIC SITE

Isle of
Palms

517

703

Mount
Pleasant

OLD VILLAGE

703

Isle of Palms

WILD DUNES
RESORT

Sullivan's
Island

Sullivan's
Island

FORT SUMTER

FORT MOULTRIE

Wadmalaw
Sound

Wadmalaw
Island

CHARLESTON
TEA PLANTATION

700

Rockville

Seabrook
Island

20

Johns Island

Kiawah
Island

54

171

BOWENS
ISLAND
RESTAURANT

James Island
County Park

MORRIS ISLAND
LIGHTHOUSE

Folly Beach

Folly
Beach

Kiawah Island

Seabrook Island

N Litho River

ATLANTIC

OCEAN

0   5 mi

0   5 km

© AVALON TRAVEL

Through Mount Pleasant is also the only land route to access Sullivan's Island, Isle of Palms, and historic Fort Moultrie.

Patriots Point Naval and Maritime Museum

Directly across Charleston Harbor from the old city lies the **Patriots Point Naval and Maritime Museum** (40 Patriots Point Rd., 843/884-2727, www.patriotspoint.org, daily 9am-6:30pm, $20 adults, $12 ages 6-11, free for active-duty military), one of the first chapters in Charleston's tourism renaissance. The project began in 1975 with what is still its main attraction, the World War II aircraft carrier USS *Yorktown,* named in honor of the carrier lost at the Battle of Midway. Much of "The Fighting Lady" is open to the public, and kids and nautical buffs will thrill to walk the decks and explore the many stations below deck on this massive 900-foot vessel, a veritable floating city.

Other ships moored beside the *Yorktown* and open for tours are the Coast Guard cutter USCG *Ingham,* the submarine USS *Clamagore,* and the destroyer USS *Laffey,* which survived being hit by three Japanese bombs and five kamikaze attacks—all within an hour.

A big plus is the free 90-minute guided tour. If you want to make a family history day out of it, you can hop on the ferry from Patriots Point to Fort Sumter and back.

Old Village

Mount Pleasant's history is almost as old as Charleston's, encapsulated by the **Old Village** (West of Royall Ave. to the waterfront, Mount Pleasant). First settled for farming in 1680, it soon acquired cachet as a great place for planters to spend the hot summers away from the mosquitoes inland. The main drag is Pitt Street, where you can shop and meander among plenty of stores and restaurants (try an ice cream soda at the historic Pitt Street Pharmacy). The huge meeting hall on the waterfront, Alhambra Hall, was the old ferry terminal.

Boone Hall Plantation

Unusual for this area, where fortunes were originally made mostly on rice, **Boone Hall Plantation**'s (1235 Long Point Rd., 843/884-4371, www.boonehallplantation.com, mid-Mar.-Labor Day Mon.-Sat. 8:30am-6:30pm, Sun. noon-5pm, Labor Day.-mid-Mar. Mon.-Sat. 9am-5pm, Sun. noon-5pm, $20 adults, $10 children) main claim to fame was as a cotton

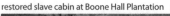
restored slave cabin at Boone Hall Plantation

plantation as well as a noted brickmaking plant. Boone Hall takes the phrase "living history" to its extreme: It's not only an active agricultural facility, it also lets visitors go on "u-pick" walks through its fields, which boast succulent strawberries, peaches, tomatoes, and even pumpkins in October—as well as free hayrides. Keep in mind that the plantation's "big house" is not original; it's a 1935 reconstruction. The most poignant and educational structures by far are the nine humble brick slave cabins from the 1790s, expertly restored and most fitted with interpretive displays. Summers see some serious Civil War reenacting going on. In all, three different tours are available: a 30-minute house tour, a tour of Slave Street, and a garden tour.

Charles Pinckney National Historic Site

The **Charles Pinckney National Historic Site** (1240 Long Point Rd., 843/881-5516, www.nps.gov/chpi, daily 9am-5pm, free) is one of my favorite sights in Charleston, for its uplifting, well-explored subject matter as well as its tastefully maintained house and grounds. Sometimes called "the forgotten founder," Charles Pinckney was not only a hero of the American Revolution and a notable early abolitionist, but also one of the main authors of the U.S. Constitution. His great-aunt Eliza Lucas Pinckney was the first woman agriculturalist in the United States, responsible for opening up the indigo trade. The current main house, doubling as the visitors center, dates from 1828, 11 years after Pinckney sold Snee Farm to pay off debts. That said, it's still a great example of Lowcountry architecture. It replaces Pinckney's original home, where President George Washington slept and had breakfast under a nearby oak tree in 1791 while touring the South.

Isle of Palms

This primarily residential area of about 5,000 people received the state's first "Blue Wave" designation from the Clean Beaches Council for its well-managed and preserved beaches.

Like adjacent Sullivan's Island, there are pockets of great wealth here, but also a laid-back, windswept beach-town vibe. Aside from the whole scene, the main attraction here is the **Isle of Palms County Park** (14th Ave., 843/886-3863, www.ccprc.com, May-Labor Day daily 9am-7pm, Mar.-Apr. and Sept.-Oct. daily 10am-6pm, Nov.-Feb. daily 10am-5pm, $7 per vehicle, free for pedestrians and cyclists), with its oceanfront beach, complete with an umbrella rental front, volleyball court, playground, and lifeguards. The island's other claim to fame is the excellent (and surprisingly affordable) **Wild Dunes Resort** (5757 Palm Blvd., 888/778-1876, www.wilddunes.com), with its two Fazio golf courses and 17 clay tennis courts. Breach Inlet, between Isle of Palms and Sullivan's Island, is where the Confederate sub *Hunley* sortied to do battle with the USS *Housatonic*.

To get here from Mount Pleasant, take the Isle of Palms Connector (Hwy. 517) off U.S. 17 (Johnnie Dodds/Chuck Dawley Blvd.). To get to the county park, go through the light at Palm Boulevard and take the next left at the gate.

Sullivan's Island

Part funky beach town, part ritzy getaway, Sullivan's Island has a certain timeless quality. While much of it was rebuilt after Hurricane Hugo's devastation, plenty of local character remains, as evidenced by some cool little bars in its tiny "business district" on the main drag of Middle Street. There's a ton of history on Sullivan's, but you can also just while the day away on the quiet, windswept beach on the Atlantic or ride a bike all over the island and back. Unless you have a boat, you can only get here from Mount Pleasant. From U.S. 17, follow the signs for Highway 703 and Sullivan's Island. Cross the Ben Sawyer Bridge, and then turn right onto Middle Street; continue for about 1.5 miles.

FORT MOULTRIE

While Fort Sumter gets the bulk of the attention, the older **Fort Moultrie** (1214

Middle St., 843/883-3123, www.nps.gov/fosu, daily 9am-5pm, $3, free under age 16) on Sullivan's Island has a much more sweeping history. Furthering the irony, Major Robert Anderson's detachment at Fort Sumter at the opening of the Civil War was actually the Fort Moultrie garrison, reassigned to Sumter because Moultrie was thought too vulnerable from the landward side. Moultrie's first incarnation, a perimeter of felled palm trees, didn't even have a name when it was unsuccessfully attacked by the British in the summer of 1776, the first victory by the colonists in the Revolution. The redcoat cannonballs bounced off those flexible trunks, and thus was born South Carolina's nickname, "the Palmetto State."

In 1809 a brick fort was built here; it soon gained notoriety as the place where the great chief Osceola was detained after his capture. The chief died at the fort in 1838, and his modest grave site is still here, in front of the fort on the landward side. Other famous people to have trod on Sullivan's Island include Edgar Allan Poe, who was inspired by Sullivan's lonely, evocative environment to write *The Gold Bug* and other works. There's a Gold Bug Avenue and a Poe Avenue here today, and the local library is named after him as well. A young Lieutenant William Tecumseh Sherman was also stationed here during his Charleston stint in the 1830s, well before his encounter with history in the Civil War.

Moultrie's main Civil War role was as a target for Union shot during the long siege of Charleston. It was pounded so hard and for so long that its walls fell below a nearby sand hill and were finally unable to be hit anymore. A full military upgrade happened in the late 1800s, extending over most of Sullivan's Island (some private owners have even bought some of the old batteries and converted them into homes). It's the series of later forts that you'll visit on your trip to the Moultrie site, which is technically part of the Fort Sumter National Monument and administered by the National Park Service.

Most of the outdoor tours are self-guided, but ranger programs typically happen Memorial Day-Labor Day daily at 11am and 2:30pm. There's a bookstore and visitors center across the street offering a 20-minute video on the hour and half hour 9am-4:30pm. Keep in mind there's no regular ferry to Fort Sumter from Fort Moultrie; the closest ferry to Sumter leaves from Patriots Point on Mount Pleasant.

BENCH BY THE ROAD

Scholars say that about half of all African Americans alive today had an ancestor who once set foot on Sullivan's Island. As the first point of entry for at least half of all slaves imported to the United States, the island's "pest houses" acted as quarantine areas so slaves could be checked for communicable diseases before going to auction in Charleston proper. But few people seem to know this. In a 1989 magazine interview, African American author and Nobel laureate Toni Morrison said about historic sites concerning slavery, "There is no suitable memorial, or plaque, or wreath or wall, or park or skyscraper lobby. There's no 300-foot tower, there's no small bench by the road." In 2008, that last item became a reality, as the first of several planned "benches by the road" was installed on Sullivan's Island to mark the sacrifice of enslaved African Americans. It's a simple black steel bench with an attached marker and a nearby plaque. The Bench by the Road is at the Fort Moultrie visitors center (1214 Middle St.).

Awendaw and Points North

This area just north of Charleston along U.S. 17—named for the Sewee Indian village originally located here and known to the world chiefly as the place where Hurricane Hugo made landfall in 1989—is seeing some new growth but still hews to its primarily rural, nature-loving roots.

CAPE ROMAIN NATIONAL WILDLIFE REFUGE

One of the best natural experiences in the area is about a 30-minute drive north of Charleston at **Cape Romain National Wildlife Refuge** (5801 U.S. 17 N., 843/928-3264, www.fws.gov/caperomain, daily dawn-dusk, free). Essentially comprising four barrier islands, the 66,000-acre refuge—almost all of which is marsh—provides a lot of great paddling opportunities, chief among them **Bulls Island** (no overnight camping). A fairly lengthy trek from where you put in is famous Boneyard Beach, where hundreds of downed trees lie on the sand, bleached by sun and salt. Slightly to the south within the refuge, **Capers Island Heritage Preserve** (843/953-9300, www.dnr.sc.gov, daily dawn-dusk, free) is still a popular camping locale despite heavy damage from 1989's Hurricane Hugo. Get permits in advance by calling the South Carolina Department of Natural Resources. You can kayak to the refuge yourself or take the only approved ferry service from **Coastal Expeditions** (514-B Mill St., Mount Pleasant, 843/881-4582, www.coastalexpeditions.com, $40 adults, $20 children, 30 minutes). **Barrier Island Eco Tours** (50 41st Ave., Isle of Palms, 843/886-5000, www.nature-tours.com, 3.5-hour boat excursions $38 adults, $28 children) on Isle of Palms also runs trips to the area.

SEWEE VISITOR AND ENVIRONMENTAL EDUCATION CENTER

Twenty miles north of Charleston is the **Sewee Visitor and Environmental Education Center** (5821 U.S. 17, 843/928-3368, www.fws.gov/seweecenter, Wed.-Sat. 9am-5pm, free). Besides being a gateway of sorts for the almost entirely aquatic Cape Romain National Wildlife Refuge, Sewee is primarily known for housing several rare red wolves, which were part of a unique release program on nearby Bull Island begun in the late 1970s. They're kept at the center to maintain the genetic integrity of the species.

FOLLY BEACH AND THE SOUTHWEST ISLANDS

Folly Beach

A large percentage of the town of **Folly Beach** (south of Charleston via Hwy. 30 and Hwy. 171) was destroyed by Hurricane Hugo in 1989, and erosion since then has increased and hit the beach itself pretty hard. All that said, enough of Folly's funky charm is left to make it worth visiting. Called "the Edge of America" during its heyday as a swinging resort getaway from the 1930s through the 1950s, Folly Beach is now a slightly beaten but enjoyable little getaway on this barrier island. Folly's main claim to larger historical fame is playing host to George Gershwin, who stayed at a cottage on West Arctic Avenue to write the score for *Porgy and Bess,* set across the harbor in downtown Charleston. (Ironically, Gershwin's opera couldn't be performed in its original setting until 1970 because of segregationist Jim Crow laws.) Original *Porgy* author DuBose Heyward stayed around the corner at a summer cottage on West Ashley Avenue that he dubbed "Follywood."

Called Folly Road until it gets to the beach, Center Street is the main drag here, dividing the beach into east and west. In this area you'll find the **Folly Beach Fishing Pier** (101 E. Arctic Ave., 843/588-3474, Apr.-Oct. daily 6am-11pm, Nov. and Mar. daily 7am-7pm, Dec.-Feb. daily 8am-5pm, $5-7 parking, $8 fishing fee), which replaced the grand old wooden pier-and-pavilion structure that burned down in 1960.

To get to Folly Beach from Charleston, go west on Calhoun Street and take the James Island Connector. Take a left on Folly Road (Hwy. 171), which becomes Center Street once in Folly Beach.

At the far east end of Folly Island, about 300 yards offshore, you'll see the **Morris Island Lighthouse,** an 1876 beacon that was once surrounded by lush green landscape, but is now completely surrounded by water after the land eroded around it. Now privately owned, there's an extensive effort to save and preserve the lighthouse (www.savethelight.

org). There's also an effort to keep high-dollar condo development off beautiful bird-friendly Morris Island itself (www.morrisisland.org). To get there while there's still something left to enjoy, take East Ashley Street until it dead-ends. Park in the lot and take a 0.25-mile walk to the beach.

Kiawah Island

The beautiful island of Kiawah—about 45 minutes from downtown Charleston—has as its main attraction the sumptuous **Kiawah Island Golf Resort** (12 Kiawah Beach Dr., 800/654-2924, www.kiawahgolf.com, $600-800), a key location for PGA tournaments. But even if you don't play golf, the resort is an amazing stay. The main component is **The Sanctuary,** an upscale hotel featuring an opulent lobby complete with grand stair-cases, a large pool area overlooking the beach, tasteful Spanish Colonial-style architecture, and 255 smallish but excellently appointed guest rooms. Several smaller private, family-friendly resorts also exist on Kiawah, with fully furnished homes and villas and every amenity you could ask for. Go to www.ex-plorekiawah.com for a full range of options or call 800/877-0837.

Through the efforts of the **Kiawah Island Conservancy** (23 Beachwalker Dr., 843/768-2029, www.kiawahconservancy.org), over 300 acres of the island have been kept as an unde-veloped nature preserve. The island's famous bobcat population has made quite a come-back; the bobcats are vital to the island eco-system, since as top predator they help cull what would otherwise become untenably large populations of deer and rabbit.

The beach at Kiawah is a particular delight, set as it is on such a comparatively undevel-oped island. No matter where you stay on Kiawah, a great thing about the island is the notable lack of light pollution—don't forget to look up at night and enjoy the stars!

Seabrook Island

Like its neighbor Kiawah, **Seabrook Island** is a private resort-dominated island. In ad-dition to offering miles of beautiful beaches, on its 2,200 acres are a wide variety of golf-ing, tennis, equestrian, and swimming facil-ities as well as extensive dining and shopping options. There are a lot of kids' activities as well. For information on lodging options and packages, go to www.seabrook.com or call 866/249-9934. Seabrook Island is about 45 minutes from Charleston. From down-town, take Highway 30 West to Maybank Highway, then take a left onto Cherry Point Road.

Johns Island
ANGEL OAK PARK
The outlying community of Johns Island is where you'll find the inspiring **Angel Oak Park** (3688 Angel Oak Rd., Mon.-Sat. 9am-5pm, Sun. 1pm-5pm, free), home of a mas-sive live oak, 65 feet in circumference, that's over 1,000 years old and commonly consid-ered the oldest tree east of the Mississippi River. As is the case with all live oaks, don't expect impressive height—when oaks age they spread *out*, not up. The sprawling, pic-turesque tree and the park containing it are owned by the city of Charleston, and the scenic grounds are often used for weddings and special events. Angel Oak Park is about 30 minutes from Charleston. Take U.S. 17 over the Ashley River, then Highway 171 to Maybank Highway. Take a left onto Bohicket Road, and then look for signs on the right.

LEGARE FARMS
Legare Farms (2620 Hanscombe Point Rd., 843/559-0763, www.legarefarms.com, hours vary) is open to the public for various activi-ties, including its annual pumpkin patch in October, its "sweet corn" festival in June, and bird walks (Sat. 8:30am, $6 adults, $3 chil-dren) in fall. To make the 20-minute drive from downtown Charleston, take Highway 30 West to Maybank Highway, then make a left onto River Road and a right onto Jenkins Farm Road.

the ancient Angel Oak

Wadmalaw Island

CHARLESTON TEA PLANTATION

Currently owned by the R. C. Bigelow Tea corporation, the **Charleston Tea Plantation** (6617 Maybank Hwy., 843/559-0383, www.charlestonteaplantation.com, Mon.-Sat. 10am-4pm, Sun. noon-4pm, free) is no cute living-history exhibit: It's a big working tea plantation—the only one in the United States—with acre after acre of *Camellia sinensis* being worked by modern farm machinery. Visitors get to see how the tea is brought "from the field to the cup." Factory tours are free, and a trolley tour of the "Back 40" is $10. And, of course, there's a gift shop where you can sample and buy all types of teas and tea-related products. Growing season is April-October. The tea bushes, direct descendants of plants brought over in the 1800s from India and China, "flush up" 2-3 inches every few weeks during growing season. Charleston Tea Plantation is about 30 minutes from Charleston. Take the Ashley River Bridge, stay

left to Folly Road (Hwy. 171), turn right onto Maybank Highway and follow it 18 miles, and look for the sign on the left.

DEEP WATER VINEYARDS

South Carolina has several good wineries, among them Wadmalaw's own **Deep Water Vineyards** (6775 Bears Bluff Rd., 843/559-6867, www.deepwatervineyard.com, Tues.-Sat. 10am-5pm), formerly Irvin House Vineyards, the Charleston area's only vineyard. They make several varieties of muscadine wine here, with $5 tastings and a gift shop. Every Saturday they host a "Wine-Down" party (noon-4pm). Also on the grounds you'll find **Firefly Distillery** (6775 Bears Bluff Rd., 843/559-6867, www.firefly-vodka.com, Tues.-Sat. 10am-5pm), home of their signature Firefly Sweet Tea Vodka. To get here from Charleston, go west on Maybank Highway about 10 miles to Bears Bluff Road, veering right on the latter. The vineyard entrance is on the left after about eight miles.

Entertainment and Events

NIGHTLIFE

Unlike the locals-versus-tourists divide you find so often in other destination cities, in Charleston it's nothing for a couple of visitors to find themselves at a table next to four or five college students enjoying themselves in true Charlestonian fashion: loudly and with lots of good food and strong drink nearby.

Bars close in Charleston at 2am, though there is a movement afoot to make the closing time earlier in some areas of town, mostly the Upper King neighborhood, the youngest and most vibrant nightlife area in Charleston. All hard-liquor sales stop at 7pm, with none at all on Sundays. You can buy beer and wine in grocery stores 24-7.

Pubs and Bars

One of Charleston's favorite neighborhood spots is **Moe's Crosstown Tavern** (714 Rutledge Ave., 843/722-3287, daily 11am-2am) in the Hampton Square area.

In the French Quarter, the Guinness flows freely at touristy **Tommy Condon's Irish Pub** (160 Church St., 843/577-3818, www. tommycondons.com, Sun.-Thurs. 11am-2am, dinner until 10pm, Fri.-Sat. 11am-2am, dinner until 11pm), as do the patriotic Irish songs performed live most nights.

If it's a nice day, a good place to relax and enjoy happy hour outside is **Vickery's Bar and Grill** (15 Beaufain St., 843/577-5300, www.vickerysbarandgrill.com, Mon.-Sat. 11:30am-2am, Sun. 11am-1am, kitchen closes 1am), part of a small regional chain based in Atlanta. Start with the oyster bisque and maybe try the turkey and brie sandwich or crab cakes for your entrée.

The hottest hipster dive bar is the **Recovery Room** (685 King St., 843/727-0999, Mon.-Fri. 4pm-2am, Sat. 3pm-2am, Sun. noon-2am) in Upper King. The drinks are cheap and stiff, and the bar food is addictively tasty (two words: Tater Tots!).

Located not too far over the Ashley River on U.S. 17, Charleston institution **Gene's Haufbrau** (17 Savannah Hwy., 843/225-4363, www.geneshaufbrau.com, daily 11:30am-2am) is worth making a special trip into West Ashley. Boasting the largest beer selection in Charleston—from the Butte Creek Organic Ale from California to a can of PBR—Gene's also claims to be the oldest bar in town, established in 1952.

Though Sullivan's Island has a lot of high-dollar homes, it still has friendly watering holes like **Dunleavy's Pub** (2213-B Middle St., 843/883-9646, Sun.-Thurs. 11:30am-1am, Fri.-Sat. 11:30am-2am). Inside is a great bar festooned with memorabilia, or you can enjoy a patio table.

The other Sullivan's watering hole of note is **Poe's Tavern** (2210 Middle St., 843/883-0083, www.poestavern.com, daily 11am-2am, kitchen closes 10pm) across the street, a nod to Edgar Allan Poe and his service on the island as a clerk in the U.S. Army. It's a lively, mostly local scene, set within a fun but suitably dark interior (though you might opt for one of the outdoor tables on the raised patio). Simply put, no trip to Sullivan's is complete without a stop at one (or possibly both) of these two local landmarks, which are within a stone's throw of each other.

If you're in Folly Beach, enjoy the great views and cocktails at **Blu Restaurant and Bar** (1 Center St., 843/588-6658, www.blu-follybeach.com, daily 7am-10pm) inside the Tides Folly Beach hotel. There's nothing like a Spiked Lemonade on a hot Charleston day at the beach.

Another notable Folly Beach watering hole is the **Sand Dollar Social Club** (7 Center St., 843/588-9498, Sun.-Fri. noon-1am, Sat. noon-2am), the kind of cash-only, mostly local dive you often find in little beach towns. You have to pony up for a "membership" to this private club, but it's only a buck. There's a catch,

Craft Breweries

The craft beer revolution has hit Charleston hard. Here are a few notable places to try:

- **Palmetto Brewing** (289 Huger St., 843/937-0903, www.palmettobrewery.com, tasting room Tues.-Wed. 3pm-7pm, Thurs. 3pm-9pm, Fri. 1pm-10pm, Sat. 1pm-7pm) has roots in Charleston going back before the Civil War and was the city's first post-Prohibition brewery. Known for their nitro beers and their Espresso Porter, among many others, they have an extensive outdoor seating area and often feature live music on weekends.

- **COAST Brewing** (1250 2nd St. N., 843/343-4727, www.coastbrewing.com, Thurs.-Fri. 4pm-7pm, Sat. 11am-4pm) in North Charleston focuses on sustainable and organic ingredients. Try the Blackbeerd Stout if it's available, and any Kölsch. This is more of a casual, all-outdoor tasting experience, so keep weather in mind.

- **Holy City Brewing** (4155C Dorchester Rd., www.holycitybrewing.com, Mon.-Thurs. 11am-8pm, Fri.-Sat. 11am-9pm, Sun. 11am-5pm), also in North Charleston, is known for its porters and stouts. This is also a great choice if you're hungry, as they have a full menu. Try the namesake Holy City Burger.

though: You can't get in until your 24-hour "waiting period" is over.

If you find yourself up in North Charleston, stop by **Madra Rua Irish Pub** (1034 E. Montague Ave., 843/554-2522, daily 11am-1am), an authentic watering hole with a better-than-average pub-food menu that's also a great place to watch a soccer game.

Lounges

On the waterfront, the aptly named **Rooftop Bar and Restaurant** (23 Vendue Range, 843/723-0485, Tues.-Sat. 6pm-2am) at the Vendue is a very popular happy hour spot from which to enjoy the sunset over the Charleston skyline.

If artisan cocktails are your thing, head straight to another waterfront spot, **The Gin Joint** (182 E. Bay St., 843/577-6111, www.theginjoint.com, Thurs.-Fri. 5pm-2am, Sat. 3pm-2am, Sun.-Wed. 5pm-midnight), where you can get drinks with names like Thieve's Tonic (rum, turmeric, lime, coconut, ginger honey) and Studmuffin (Madeira, chicory liqueur, coffee liqueur, and bay leaf ice cubes). With most cocktails running about $11 each, they're actually bargains when you consider the curated ingredients going into each one. Got a big party? Order one of four signature punches to share, prepared tableside (about

$40). Fair warning: These aren't your typical office party punches and pack a commensurately large, well, punch. Thankfully, there is a good little menu of tapas to soak up all the alcohol.

Across the street from Gene's Haufbrau in West Ashley, the retro-chic **Voodoo Lounge** (15 Magnolia Rd., 843/769-0228, Mon.-Fri. 4pm-2am, Sat.-Sun. 5:30pm-2am, kitchen until 1am) is another very popular hangout. It has a wide selection of trendy cocktails and killer gourmet tacos.

Live Music

Charleston's live music scene is hit or miss. With the long-ago passing of the heyday of Hootie & the Blowfish, there's no distinct "Charleston sound" to speak of (though Hootie frontman-turned-country-star Darius Rucker still plays frequently in the area), but the venues do a good job of bringing in well-regarded national and regional touring acts. The best place to find up-to-date music listings is the local free weekly *Charleston City Paper* (www.charlestoncitypaper.com).

The venerable **Music Farm** (32 Ann St., 843/722-8904, www.musicfarm.com) in Upper King isn't much to look at from the outside, but the cavernous space has played host to all sorts of bands over the past two

Doin' the Charleston

It has been called the biggest song-and-dance craze of the 20th century. It first entered the American public consciousness via New York City in a 1923 Harlem musical called *Runnin' Wild,* but the roots of the dance soon to be known as the Charleston were indeed in the Holy City. No one is quite sure of the day and date, but local lore assures us that members of Charleston's legendary Jenkins Orphanage Band were the first to start dancing that crazy "Geechie step," a development that soon became part of the band's act.

The Jenkins Orphanage was started in 1891 by the African American Baptist minister Reverend D. J. Jenkins and was originally housed in the Old Marine Hospital at 20 Franklin Street (which you can see today, although it's not open to the public). To raise money, Reverend Jenkins acquired donated instruments and started a band comprising talented orphans from the house. The orphans traveled as far away as London, where they were a hit with the locals but not with the constabulary, who unceremoniously fined them for stopping traffic. A Charleston attorney who happened to be in London at the time, Augustine Smyth, paid their way back home, becoming a lifelong supporter of the orphanage in the process.

From then on, playing in donated old Citadel uniforms, the Jenkins Orphanage Band frequently took their act on the road. They played at the St. Louis and Buffalo expositions and even at President Taft's inauguration. They also frequently played in New York, and it was there that African American pianist and composer James P. Johnson heard the Charlestonians play and dance to their Gullah rhythms, considered exotic at the time. Johnson would incorporate what he heard into the tune "Charleston," one of many songs in the revue *Runnin' Wild*. The catchy song and its accompanying loose-limbed dance seemed tailor-made for the Roaring '20s and its liberated, hedonistic spirit. Before long the Charleston had swept the nation, becoming a staple of jazz clubs and speakeasies across the country and, indeed, the world.

decades. Recent concerts have included Fitz and the Tantrums, the Dropkick Murphys, and the Drive-By Truckers.

The hippest music spot in town is out on James Island at **The Pour House** (1977 Maybank Hwy., 843/571-4343, www.charlestonpourhouse.com, 9pm-2am on nights with music scheduled), where the local characters are sometimes just as entertaining as the acts onstage.

Dance Clubs

The **Trio Club** (139 Calhoun St., 843/965-5333, Thurs.-Sat. 9pm-2am), right off Marion Square, is a favorite place to make the scene. There's a relaxing outdoor area with piped-in music, an intimate sofa-filled upstairs bar for dancing and chilling, and the dark candlelit downstairs with frequent live music leaning toward hip-hop sounds.

Gay-Friendly

Most gay-oriented nightlife centers on the Upper King area. Charleston's hottest dance spot of any type, gay or straight, is **Cure** (28 Ann St., 843/577-2582, Fri.-Sun. 10pm-2am), on the lower level of the parking garage across from the visitors center (375 Meeting St.). This space was for years known as Club Pantheon but has changed ownership. Cover charges are typically not cheap, but it's worth it for the great DJs, the dancing, and the people watching, not to mention the frequent drag cabaret shows.

Just down the street from Cure—and owned by the same people—is a totally different kind of gay bar, **Dudley's** (42 Ann St., 843/577-6779, daily 4pm-2am). Mellower and more appropriate for conversation or a friendly game of pool, Dudley's is a nice contrast to the thumping club a few doors down.

North of Broad, **Vickery's Bar and Grill** (15 Beaufain St., 843/577-5300, www.vickerysbarandgrill.com, Mon.-Sat. 11:30am-2am, Sun. 11am-1am, kitchen closes 1am) does not market itself as a gay establishment, but it has nonetheless become quite popular with the gay community—not least because of the good reputation its parent tavern in Atlanta has with that city's large and influential gay community.

PERFORMING ARTS
Theater

Unlike the more (literally) puritanical colonies farther up the North American coast, Charleston was an arts-friendly settlement from the beginning. The first theatrical production on the continent happened in Charleston in January 1735, when a nomadic troupe rented a space at Church and Broad Streets to perform Thomas Otway's *The Orphan*. The play's success led to the building of the Dock Street Theatre on what is now Queen Street. Notable thespians performing in town included Edwin Booth, Junius Booth Jr. (brothers of Lincoln's assassin, John Wilkes), and Edgar Allan Poe's mother, Eliza.

Several high-quality troupes continue to keep Charleston's proud theater tradition alive, chief among them **Charleston Stage** (Dock Street Theatre, 135 Church St., 843/577-7183, www.charlestonstage.com), the resident company of the Dock Street Theatre. In addition to its well-received regular season of classics and modern staples, Charleston Stage has debuted more than 30 original scripts over the years, a recent example being *Gershwin at Folly*, recounting the composer's time at Folly Beach working on *Porgy and Bess*.

The Footlight Players (Footlight Players Theatre, 20 Queen St., 843/722-4487, www.footlightplayers.net) make up the oldest continuously active company in town, founded in 1931. This community-based amateur company performs a mix of crowd-pleasers (*Who's Afraid of Virginia Woolf?*) and creative adaptations (*Miracle in Bedford Falls*, a musical based on *It's a Wonderful Life*) at its space at 20 Queen Street.

The players of **PURE Theatre** (477 King St., 843/723-4444, www.puretheatre.org) perform in a black-box space in the heart of the Upper King entertainment/nightlife district.

Their shows emphasize compelling, mature drama, beautifully performed. This is where to catch less glitzy, grittier productions like *Rabbit Hole*, *American Buffalo*, and *Cold Tectonics*, a hit at Piccolo Spoleto.

The city's most unusual players are **The Have Nots!** (Theatre 99, 280 Meeting St., 843/853-6687, www.theatre99.com, Wed. 8pm, Fri.-Sat. 8pm and 10pm, $5-12.50), with a rotating ensemble of dozens of comedians who perform their brand of edgy, adults-only improv at Theatre 99. Friday is the most reliable improve night, while Wednesday and Saturday may feature more sketch comedy.

Music

The **Charleston Symphony Orchestra** (Gaillard Center, 95 Calhoun St., 843/554-6060, www.charlestonsymphony.com) performed for the first time on December 28, 1936, at the Hibernian Hall on Meeting Street. During that first season the CSO accompanied *The Recruiting Officer*, the inaugural show at the renovated Dock Street Theatre. For seven decades, the CSO continued to provide world-class orchestral music, gaining "Metropolitan" status in the 1970s, when it accompanied the first-ever local performance of *Porgy and Bess*, which despite its Charleston setting couldn't be performed locally before then due to segregation laws. Now under the direction of conductor Ken Lam, the CSO performs at the renovated and reimagined Gaillard Center, modeled on European concert halls. Check the website for upcoming concerts.

The excellent music department at the College of Charleston sponsors the annual **Charleston Music Fest** (Simons Center for the Arts, 54 St. Philip St., $25), a series of chamber music concerts at various venues around the beautiful campus, featuring many faculty members of the college as well as visiting guest artists. Other college musical offerings include the **College of Charleston Concert Choir** (www.cofc.edu/music), which performs at various venues, usually churches, around town during the fall; the **College of**

Charleston Opera, which performs at least one full-length production during the school year and often takes the stage at Piccolo Spoleto; and the popular Yuletide Madrigal Singers, who sing in early December at a series of concerts in historic Randolph Hall.

Chamber Music Charleston (various locations, 843/763-4941, www.chambermusiccharleston.org), which relies on many core Charleston Symphony Orchestra musicians, continues to perform around town, including at Piccolo Spoleto. They play a wide variety of picturesque venues, including the Sottile Theatre (44 George St.) and Kiawah Island. They can also be found at private house concerts, which sell out quickly.

CINEMA

The most interesting art-house and indie venue in town is The Terrace (1956D Maybank Hwy., 843/762-4247, www.terracetheater.com), and not only because it offers beer and wine that you can enjoy at your seat. Shows before 5pm are $7. It's west of Charleston on James Island; get there by taking U.S. 17 west from Charleston and going south on Highway 171, after which you take a right on Maybank Highway (Hwy. 700).

FESTIVALS AND EVENTS

Charleston is a festival-mad city, especially in the spring and early fall. And new festivals are being added every year, further enhancing the hedonistic flavor of this city that has also mastered the art of hospitality.

January

Held on a Sunday in late January at historic Boone Hall Plantation in Mount Pleasant, the Lowcountry Oyster Festival (www.charlestonlowcountry.com, Sun. 11am-5pm, $8, food additional) features literal truckloads of the sweet shellfish for your enjoyment. Gates open at 10:30am, and there's plenty of parking. Oysters are sold by the bucket and served with crackers and cocktail sauce. Bring your own shucking knife or glove, or buy them on-site.

February

One of the unique events in town is the Southeastern Wildlife Exposition (various venues, 843/723-1748, www.sewe.com, $12.50 per day, $30 for three days, free under age 13). For the last quarter century, the Wildlife Expo has brought together hundreds of artists and exhibitors to showcase just about any kind of naturally themed art you can think of in over a dozen galleries and venues all over downtown. Kids will enjoy the live animals on hand as well.

North Charleston is home to Brewvival (adjacent to COAST Brewing, 1250 2nd St. N., www.brewvival.com, $75). This daylong craft brew-tasting festival features brewers from the rapidly growing South Carolina craft beer industry. There is live music, and food vendors are available as well.

March

Generally straddling late February and the first days of March, the four-day Charleston Food & Wine Festival (www.charlestonfoodandwine.com, various venues and admission) is a glorious celebration of one of the Holy City's premier draws: its amazing culinary community. While the emphasis is on Lowcountry chefs, guest chefs from New York, New Orleans, and Los Angeles routinely come to show off their skills. Oenophiles, especially of domestic wines, will be in heaven as well. This event has boomed in recent years and downtown gets quite crowded. Tickets aren't cheap—an all-event pass is over $500 per person—but then again, this is one of the nation's great food cities.

Immediately before the Festival of Houses and Gardens is the Charleston International Antiques Show (40 E. Bay St., 843/722-3405, www.historiccharleston.org, admission varies), held at Historic Charleston's headquarters at the Missroon House on the High Battery. It features over 30 of the nation's best-regarded dealers and offers lectures and tours.

Mid-March-April, the perennial favorite Festival of Houses and Gardens

(843/722-3405, www.historiccharleston.org, admission varies) is sponsored by the Historic Charleston Foundation and held at the very peak of the spring blooming season for maximum effect. In all, the festival goes into a dozen historic neighborhoods to view about 150 homes. Each day sees a different three-hour tour of a different area, at about $50 per person. This is a fantastic opportunity to peek inside some amazing old privately owned properties that are inaccessible to visitors at all other times. A highlight is a big oyster roast and picnic at Drayton Hall.

Not to be confused with the above festival, the **Garden Club of Charleston House and Garden Tours** (843/530-5164, www.thegardenclubofcharleston.com, $35) are held over a weekend in late March. Highlights include the Heyward-Washington House and the private garden of the late great Charleston horticulturalist Emily Whaley.

One of Charleston's newest and most fun events, the five-night **Charleston Fashion Week** (www.charlestonfashionweek.com, admission varies) benefits local women's and children's charities. Mimicking New York's Fashion Week events under tenting in Bryant Park, Charleston's version features runway action under big tents in Marion Square—and, yes, past guests have included former contestants on *Project Runway*.

April

The annual **Cooper River Bridge Run** (www.bridgerun.com) happens the first Saturday in April (unless that's Easter weekend, in which case it runs the week before) and features a six-mile jaunt across the massive Arthur Ravenel Bridge over the Cooper River, the longest cable span in the Western Hemisphere. It's not for those with a fear of heights, but it's still one of Charleston's best-attended events—there are well over 30,000 participants.

Previously known as the Family Circle Cup, the **Volvo Car Open** (161 Seven Farms Dr., Daniel Island, 843/856-7900, www.volvocaropen.com, admission varies) is held at

Daniel Island's Family Circle Tennis Center, specifically built for the event. Almost 100,000 people attend the multiple-week event. Individual session tickets go on sale the preceding January.

Mount Pleasant is the home of Charleston's shrimping fleet, and each April sees all the boats parade by the Alhambra Hall and Park for the **Blessing of the Fleet** (843/884-8517, www.townofmountpleasant.com). Family events and lots and lots of seafood are also on tap.

May

Free admission and free parking are not the only draws at the outdoor **North Charleston Arts Festival** (5000 Coliseum Dr., www.northcharleston.org), but let's face it, that's important. Held beside North Charleston's Performing Arts Center and Convention Center, the festival features music, dance, theater, multicultural performers, and storytellers. There are a lot of kids' events as well.

Held over three days at the Holy Trinity Greek Orthodox Church up toward the Neck, the **Charleston Greek Festival** (30 Race St., 843/577-2063, www.charlestongreekfestival.com, $5 admission, food extra) offers a plethora of live entertainment, dancing, Greek wares, and, of course, fantastic Greek cuisine cooked by the congregation. Parking is not a problem, and there's even a shuttle to the church from the lot.

Indisputably Charleston's single biggest and most important event, **Spoleto Festival USA** (843/579-3100, www.spoletousa.org, admission varies) has come a long way since it was a sparkle in the eye of the late Gian Carlo Menotti three decades ago. Though Spoleto long ago broke ties with its founder, his vision remains indelibly stamped on the event from start to finish. There's plenty of music, to be sure, in genres that include orchestral, opera, jazz, and avant-garde, but you'll find something in every other performing art, such as dance, drama, and spoken word, in traditions from Western to African to Southeast Asian. For 17 days from Memorial Day weekend through early June, Charleston hops and hums nearly 24 hours a day to the energy of this vibrant, cutting-edge (yet accessible) artistic celebration.

As if all the hubbub around Spoleto didn't give you enough to do, there's also **Piccolo Spoleto** (843/724-7305, www.piccolospoleto. com, various venues and admission), literally "little Spoleto," running concurrently. The intent of Piccolo Spoleto—begun just a couple of years after the larger festival came to town and run by the city's Office of Cultural Affairs—is to give local and regional performers a time to shine, sharing some of that larger spotlight on the national and international performers at the main event. Of particular interest to visiting families will be Piccolo's children's events, a good counter to some of the decidedly more adult fare at Spoleto USA.

June

Technically part of Piccolo Spoleto but gathering its own following, the **Sweetgrass Cultural Arts Festival** (www.sweetgrass-festival.org) is held the first week in June in Mount Pleasant at the Laing Middle School (2213 U.S. 17 N.). The event celebrates the traditional sweetgrass basket-making skills of African Americans in the historic Christ Church Parish area of Mount Pleasant. If you want to buy some sweetgrass baskets made by the world's foremost experts in the field, this would be the time.

July

Each year over 30,000 people come to see the **Patriots Point Fourth of July Blast** (866/831-1720), featuring a hefty barrage of fireworks shot off the deck of the USS *Yorktown* moored on the Cooper River in the Patriots Point complex. Food, live entertainment, and kids' activities are also featured.

September

From late September into the first week of October, the city-sponsored **MOJA Arts Festival** (843/724-7305, www.mojafestival.com, various venues and admission) highlights the cultural contributions of African Americans and people from the Caribbean with dance, visual art, poetry, cuisine, crafts, and music in genres that include gospel, jazz, reggae, and classical. In existence since 1984, MOJA's name comes from the Swahili word for "one," and its diverse range of offerings in so many media have made it one of the Southeast's premier events. Some events are ticketed, while others, such as the kids' activities and many of the dance and film events, are free.

For five weeks from the last week of September into October, the Preservation Society of Charleston hosts the much-anticipated **Fall Tours of Homes & Gardens** (843/722-4630, www.preservationsociety. org, $45). The tour takes you into more than a dozen local residences and is the nearly 90-year-old organization's biggest fund-raiser. Tickets typically go on sale the previous June, and they tend to sell out very quickly.

Another great food event in this great food city, the **Taste of Charleston** (1235 Long Point Rd., 843/577-4030, www.charleston-restaurantassociation.com, 11am-5pm, $12) is held on a weekend in October at Boone Hall Plantation in Mount Pleasant and sponsored by the Greater Charleston Restaurant Association. Over 50 area chefs and restaurants come together so you can sample their wares, including a wine and food pairing, with proceeds going to charity.

October

Local company **Half Moon Outfitters** (280 King St., 843/853-0990, 425 Coleman Blvd., 843/881-9472, www.halfmoonoutfitters.com, Mon.-Sat. 10am-7pm, Sun. noon-6pm) sponsors an annual six-mile Giant Kayak Race at Isle of Palms Marina in late October benefiting the Coastal Conservation League.

November

Plantation Days at Middleton Place (4300 Ashley River Rd., 843/556-6020, www.middletonplace.org, daily 9am-5pm, last tour 4:30pm, guided tour $10) happen each Saturday in

A Man, a Plan: Spoleto!

People gather in Marion Square to enjoy Piccolo Spoleto.

Sadly, Gian Carlo Menotti is no longer with us, having died in 2007 at the age of 95. But the overwhelming success of the composer's brainchild and labor of love, **Spoleto Festival USA,** lives on, enriching the cultural and social life of Charleston and serving as the city's chief calling card to the world at large.

Menotti began writing music at age seven in his native Italy. As a young man he moved to Philadelphia to study music, where he shared classes—and lifelong connections—with Leonard Bernstein and Samuel Barber. His first full-length opera, *The Consul,* would garner him the Pulitzer Prize, as would 1955's *The Saint of Bleecker Street.* But by far Menotti's best-known work is the beloved Christmas opera *Amahl and the Night Visitors,* composed especially for NBC television in 1951. At the height of his fame in 1958, the charismatic and mercurial genius—fluent and witty in five languages—founded the "Festival of Two Worlds" in Spoleto, Italy, specifically as a forum for young American artists in Europe. But it wasn't until nearly two decades later, in 1977, that Menotti was able to make his long-imagined dream of an American counterpart a reality.

Attracted to Charleston because of its long-standing support of the arts, its undeniable good taste, and its small size—ensuring that his festival would always be the number one activity in town while it was going on—Menotti worked closely with the man who was to become the other key part of the equation: Charleston mayor Joe Riley, then in his first term in office. Since then, the city has built on Spoleto's success by founding its own local version, **Piccolo Spoleto**—literally, "little Spoleto"—which focuses exclusively on local and regional talent.

Things haven't always gone smoothly. Menotti and the stateside festival parted ways in 1993, when he took over the Rome Opera. Making matters more uneasy, the Italian festival—run by Menotti's longtime partner (and later adopted son), Chip—also became estranged from what was intended to be its soul mate in South Carolina. (Chip was later replaced by the Italian Culture Ministry.) But perhaps this kind of creative tension is what Menotti intended all along. Indeed, each spring brings a Spoleto USA that seems to thrive on the inherent conflict between the festival's often cutting-edge offerings and the very traditional city that hosts it. Spoleto still challenges its audiences, just as Menotti intended it to. Depending on the critic and the audience member, that modern opera debut you see may be groundbreaking or gratuitous. The drama you check out may be exhilarating or tiresome.

Each year, a total of about 500,000 people attend both Spoleto and Piccolo Spoleto. Nearly one-third of the attendees are Charleston residents—the final proof that when it comes to supporting the arts, Charleston puts its money where its mouth is.

November, giving visitors a chance to wander the grounds and see artisans at work practicing authentic crafts, as they would have done in antebellum days, with a special emphasis on the contributions of African Americans. A special treat comes on Thanksgiving, when a full meal is offered on the grounds at the Middleton Place Restaurant (843/556-6020, www.middletonplace.org, reservations strongly recommended).

One of Charleston's newest annual events is the **Charleston International Film Festival** (843/817-1617, www.charlestoniff.com, various venues and prices). Despite being a relative latecomer to the film-festival circuit, the event is pulled off with Charleston's usual aplomb.

Though the **Battle of Secessionville** actually took place in June 1862 much farther south, November is the time the battle is reenacted at Boone Hall Plantation (1235 Long Point Rd., 843/884-4371, www.boonehallplantation.

com, $17.50 adults, $7.50 children) in Mount Pleasant. Call for specific dates and times.

December

A yuletide in the Holy City is an experience you'll never forget, as the **Christmas in Charleston** (843/724-3705) events clustered around the first week of the month prove. For some reason—whether it's the old architecture, the friendly people, the churches, the carriages, or all of the above—Charleston feels right at home during Christmas. The festivities begin with the mayor lighting the city's 60-foot Tree of Lights in Marion Square, followed by a parade of brightly lit boats from Mount Pleasant all the way around Charleston up the Ashley River. The key event is the Sunday Christmas Parade through downtown, featuring bands, floats, and performers in the holiday spirit. The Saturday farmers market in the square continues through the middle of the month with a focus on holiday items.

Shopping

Shopping in Charleston centers on King Street, unique not only for the fact that so many national-name stores are lined up so close to each other, but also because there are so many great restaurants of so many different types scattered in and among the retail outlets, ideally positioned for when you need to take a break to rest and refuel. **Lower King** is primarily top-of-the-line antiques stores (most are closed Sundays, so plan your trip accordingly); **Middle King** is where you'll find upscale name-brand outlets such as Banana Republic and American Apparel as well as some excellent shoe stores; and **Upper King,** north of Calhoun Street, is where you'll find funky housewares shops, generally locally owned.

FRENCH QUARTER
Antiques and Vintage

A cute little shop tucked away in an alley,

Curiosity (56½ Queen St., 843/647-7763, www.curiositycharleston.com) is a find even by the standards of antiques/vintage-crazy Charleston. A nice plus is the prices here are a bit lower than in the premier antiques shops on Lower King Street, which would never be accused of being bargain priced.

Art Galleries

While not considered a visual arts mecca, the Holy City has been fertile ground for visual artists since native son Joseph Allen Smith began one of the country's first art collections in Charleston in the late 1700s. For most visitors, the center of gallery activity is in the French Quarter between South Market and Tradd Streets.

Incorporating works from the estate of Charleston legend Elizabeth O'Neill Verner is **Ann Long Fine Art** (54 Broad St., 843/577-0447, www.annlongfineart.com, Mon.-Sat.

Art Walks

11am-5pm), which seeks to combine the painterly aesthetic of the Old World with the edgy vision of the New.

One of the French Quarter's most beloved galleries, the **Corrigan Gallery** (62 Queen St., 843/722-9868, www.corrigangallery.com, daily 10am-5pm) deals in some of the best current local artists, along with a focus on the Charleston Renaissance and the Charleston printmaking tradition.

The **Pink House Gallery** (17 Chalmers St., 843/723-3608, http://pinkhousegallery.tripod.com, Mon.-Sat. 10am-5pm) is housed in the oldest tavern building in the South, built circa 1694. The exhibits here offer a glimpse into old Charleston, including exclusive antique prints.

Robert Lange Studios (2 Queen St., 843/805-8052, www.robertlangestudios.com, daily 11am-5pm) is oriented toward modern art. It hosts not only the work of its owners, Robert and Megan Lange, but also a slate of up-and-coming regional artists. This is a great place to be on the regular first Friday art walks and events.

Books and Music
The great **Shops of Historic Charleston Foundation** (108 Meeting St., 843/724-8484, www.historiccharleston.org) is housed in a beautiful building and has plenty of tasteful Charleston-themed gift ideas, from books to kitchenware.

NORTH OF BROAD
Antiques
Alexandra AD (156 King St., 843/722-4897, Mon.-Sat. 10am-5pm) features great chandeliers, lamps, and fabrics.

Since 1929, **George C. Birlant & Co.** (191 King St., 843/722-3842, Mon.-Sat. 9am-5:30pm) has been importing 18th- and 19th-century furniture, silver, china, and crystal, and it deals in the famous "Charleston Battery Bench."

Art Galleries
For a more modern take from local artists, check out the **Sylvan Gallery** (171 King St., 843/722-2172, www.thesylvangallery.com, Mon.-Fri. 9am-5pm, Sat. 10am-5pm, Sun. 11am-4pm), which specializes in 20th- and 21st-century art and sculpture.

Specializing in original Audubon prints and antique botanical prints is **The Audubon Gallery** (190 King St., 843/853-1100, www.audubonart.com, Mon.-Sat. 10am-5pm), the sister store of the Joel Oppenheimer Gallery in Chicago.

Within City Market is **Gallery Chuma** (188 Meeting St., 843/722-1702, www.gallerychuma.com, daily 9:30am-6pm), which specializes in the art of the Gullah people of the South Carolina coast. They put on lots of cultural and educational events about Gullah culture as well as display art on the subject.

Art Mecca (427 King St., 843/577-0603, www.artmeccaofcharleston.com, Mon.-Fri. 10am-6pm, Sat. 10am-7pm, Sun. 11am-5pm) is an inviting modernist space that specializes in local and regional contemporary artists. It's a great place to get a flavor of what Charleston's younger up-and-coming artists are doing.

Books and Music
The charming **Pauline Books and Media** (243 King St., 843/577-0175, Mon.-Sat. 10am-6pm) is run by the Daughters of Saint Paul and

carries Christian books, Bibles, rosaries, and images from a Roman Catholic perspective.

It's easy to overlook at the far southern end of the retail development on King, but the excellent **Preservation Society of Charleston Book and Gift Shop** (147 King St., 843/722-4630, Mon.-Sat. 10am-5pm) is perhaps the best place in town to pick up books on Charleston lore and history as well as locally themed gift items.

Clothes

A charmingly old-school and notable locally owned clothing store on King Street is the classy **Berlins Men's and Women's** (114-120 King St., 843/722-1665, Mon.-Sat. 9:30am-6pm), dating from 1883. Despite the name, Berlins focuses on men's clothing, offering designs from Canali, Coppley, Jack Victor, and more.

Big companies' losses are your gain at **Oops!** (326 King St., 843/722-7768, Mon.-Fri. 10am-6pm, Sat. 10am-7pm, Sun. noon-6pm), which buys factory mistakes and discontinued lines from major brands at a discount, passing along the savings to you. The range here tends toward colorful and preppy.

The incredible consignment store **The Trunk Show** (281 Meeting St., 843/722-0442, Mon.-Sat. 10am-6pm) offers one-of-a-kind vintage and designer wear and accessories. Some finds are bargains, some not so much, but there's no denying the quality and breadth of the offerings.

For a locally owned clothing shop, try the innovative **Worthwhile** (268 King St., 843/723-4418, www.shopworthwhile.com, Mon.-Sat. 10am-6pm, Sun. noon-5pm), which has lots of organic fashions.

Jewelry

Art Jewelry by Mikhail Smolkin (312 King St., 843/722-3634, www.fineartjewelry.com, Mon.-Sat. 10am-5pm) features one-of-a-kind pieces by this St. Petersburg, Russia, native.

Since 1919, **Croghan's Jewel Box** (308 King St., 843/723-3594, www.

croghansjewelbox.com, Mon.-Fri. 9:30am-5:30pm, Sat. 10am-5pm) has offered amazing locally crafted diamonds, silver, and designer pieces to generations of Charlestonians. An expansion in the late 1990s tripled the size of the historic location.

Joint Venture Estate Jewelers (185 King St., 843/722-6730, www.jventure.com, Mon.-Sat. 10am-5:30pm) specializes in antique, vintage, and modern estate jewelry as well as pre-owned watches, including Rolex, Patek Philippe, and Cartier, with a fairly unique consignment emphasis.

Shoes

A famous locally owned place for footwear is **Bob Ellis Shoe Store** (332 King St., 843/722-2515, www.bobellisshoes.com, Mon.-Sat. 10am-6pm), which has served Charleston's elite with high-end shoes since 1950.

Copper Penny Shooz (317 King St., 843/723-3838, Mon.-Sat. 10am-7pm, Sun. noon-6pm) combines hip and upscale footwear for women, "curated with a Southern eye," as this Charleston-based regional chain's motto goes.

Funky and fun **Phillips Shoes** (320 King St., 843/965-5270, Mon.-Sat. 10am-6pm) deals in Dansko for men, women, and kids (don't miss the awesome painting above the register of Elvis fitting a customer).

Rangoni of Florence (270 King St., 843/577-9554, Mon.-Sat. 9:30am-6pm, Sun. 12:30pm-5:30pm) imports the best women's shoes from Italy, with a few men's designs as well.

Shopping Centers and Malls

Belmond Charleston Place (205 Meeting St., 843/722-4900, www.charlestonplace-shops.com, Mon.-Wed. 10am-6pm, Thurs.-Sat. 10am-8pm, Sun. noon-5pm), usually just called "Charleston Place," is a combined retail-hotel development with highlights such as Gucci, Talbots, Louis Vuitton, Yves Delorme, Everything But Water, and Godiva.

For years dominated by a flea market vibe,

City Market (Meeting St. and Market St., 843/973-7236, daily 9:30am-10:30pm) was recently upgraded and is now chockablock with boutique retail all along its lengthy interior. The humbler crafts tables are toward the back. If you must have one of the handcrafted sweetgrass baskets, try out your haggling skills—the prices have wiggle room built in. In addition to the myriad tourist-oriented shops in the City Market itself, there are a few gems in the surrounding area that also appeal to locals.

Sporting Goods
With retail locations in Charleston and throughout South Carolina and Georgia and a new cutting-edge, eco-friendly warehouse in North Charleston, Half Moon Outfitters (280 King St., 843/853-0990, www.halfmoonoutfitters.com, Mon.-Sat. 10am-7pm, Sun. noon-6pm) is something of a local legend. Here you can find not only top-of-the-line camping and outdoor gear and tips on local recreation, but also some really stylish outdoorsy apparel as well.

UPPER KING
Art Galleries
One of the most important single venues for art, the nonprofit Redux Contemporary Art Center (136 St. Philip St., 843/722-0697, www.reduxstudios.org, Tues.-Fri. 10am-6pm, Sat. noon-5pm) features modernistic work in a variety of media, including illustration, video installation, blueprints, performance art, and graffiti. Outreach is hugely important to this venture and includes lecture series, classes, workshops, and internships.

Books and Music
Housed in an extremely long and narrow storefront, Jonathan Sanchez's funky and friendly Blue Bicycle Books (420 King St., 843/722-2666, www.bluebicyclebooks.com, Mon.-Sat. 10am-7:30pm, Sun. 1pm-6pm) deals primarily in used books and has a particularly nice stock of local and regional titles, art books, and fiction.

Home Goods
Head to Haute Design Studio (489 King St., 843/577-9886, www.hautedesign.com, Mon.-Fri. 9am-5:30pm) for upper-end furnishings with an edgy feel.

WATERFRONT
Art Galleries
The City Gallery at Waterfront (34 Prioleau St., 843/958-6484, www.citygalleryatwaterfrontpark.com, Tues.-Fri. 10am-6pm, Sat.-Sun. noon-5pm) is funded by the city, with exhibits focusing on local and regional culture and folkways. It's mostly an exhibit space, though art is also sold here.

Home Goods
Affiliated with the hip local restaurant chain Maverick Kitchens, Charleston Cooks! (194 E. Bay St., 843/722-1212, www.charlestoncooks.com, Mon.-Sat. 10am-9pm, Sun. 11am-6pm) has an almost overwhelming array of gourmet items and kitchenware, and even offers cooking classes.

Indigo (4 Vendue Range, 800/549-2513, Sun.-Thurs. 10am-6pm, Fri.-Sat. 10am-7pm), a favorite home accessories store, has plenty of one-of-a-kind pieces, many of them by regional artists and rustic in flavor, almost like outsider art.

SOUTH OF BROAD
Art Galleries
Charleston Renaissance Gallery (103 Church St., 843/723-0025, www.fineartsouth.com, Mon.-Sat. 10am-5pm) specializes in 19th- and 20th-century oils and sculpture and features artists from the American South, including some splendid pieces from the Charleston Renaissance.

Helena Fox Fine Art (106-A Church St., 843/723-0073, www.helenafoxfineart.com, Mon.-Sat. 10am-5pm) deals in 20th-century representational art.

WEST ASHLEY
Home Goods
Probably Charleston's best-regarded home

goods store is the nationally recognized **ESD, Elizabeth Stuart Design** (422 Savannah Hwy./U.S. 17, 843/225-6282, www.esdcharleston.com, Mon.-Sat. 10am-6pm), with a wide range of antique and new furnishings, art, lighting, jewelry, and more.

Music

In an age when it's harder and harder to find brick-and-mortar music/movie stores, **Monster Music and Movies** (946 Orleans Rd., 843/571-4657, Mon.-Sat. 10am-9pm, Sun. noon-7pm) is a great discovery. They have new and used vinyl and CDs, and they feature great sales and in-store performances for the annual Record Store Day in April.

NORTH CHARLESTON
Music

Fox Music House (3005 W. Montague Ave., 843/740-7200, Mon.-Fri. 10am-6pm, Sat. 10am-5pm) is a neighborhood favorite, and has been locally owned since 1928. They specialize in pianos and keyboards.

Shopping Centers

The **Tanger Outlet** (4840 Tanger Outlet Blvd., 843/529-3095, www.tangeroutlet.com, Mon.-Sat. 10am-9pm, Sun. 11am-6pm) has factory-priced bargains from stores such as Adidas, Banana Republic, Brooks Brothers,

CorningWare, Old Navy, Timberland, and more.

MOUNT PLEASANT AND EAST COOPER
Antiques

Mount Pleasant boasts a fun antiques and auction spot, **Page's Thieves Market** (1460 Ben Sawyer Blvd., 843/884-9672, www.pagesthievesmarket.com, Mon.-Fri. 9am-5:30pm, Sat. 9am-5pm). Its rambling interior has hosted bargain and vintage shoppers for 50 years, and it's routinely voted Charleston's best antiques store.

Shopping Centers

The most pleasant mall in the area is the retro-themed, pedestrian-friendly **Mount Pleasant Towne Center** (1600 Palmetto Grande Dr., 843/216-9900, www.mtpleasanttownecentre.com, Mon.-Sat. 10am-9pm, Sun. noon-6pm). In addition to national chains you'll find a few cool local stores in here, like Stella Nova spa and day salon and Copper Penny Shooz.

In a Harris Teeter grocery shopping center, **Gwynn's of Mount Pleasant** (916 Houston Northcutt Blvd., 843/884-9518, Mon.-Sat 10am-7pm) is an old-fashioned department store specializing in women's clothing and shoes, with a distinct local and Southern sensibility.

Sports and Recreation

ON THE WATER
Beaches

In addition to the charming town of Folly Beach itself, there's the modest county-run **Folly Beach County Park** (1100 W. Ashley Ave., Folly Beach, 843/588-2426, www.ccprc.com, May-Labor Day 9am-8pm, Mar.-Apr. and Sept.-Oct. 10am-7pm, Nov.-Feb. 10am-6pm, $7 per vehicle, free for pedestrians and cyclists) at the far west end of Folly Island. It has a picnic area, restrooms, outdoor showers, and beach chair and umbrella rentals. Get

there by taking Highway 171 (Folly Rd.) until it turns into Center Street, and then take a right on West Ashley Avenue.

On Isle of Palms you'll find **Isle of Palms County Park** (14th Ave., Isle of Palms, 843/886-3863, www.ccprc.com, fall-spring daily 10am-dark, summer daily 9am-dark, $5 per vehicle, free for pedestrians and cyclists), which has restrooms, showers, a picnic area, a beach volleyball area, and beach chair and umbrella rentals. Get there by taking the Isle of Palms Connector (Hwy. 517) to the island, go through the light at Palm Boulevard, and take the next left at the park gate. There's good public beach access near the Pavilion Shoppes on Ocean Boulevard, accessed via J. C. Long Boulevard.

On the west end of Kiawah Island to the south of Charleston is **Kiawah Island Beachwalker Park** (Kiawah Island, 843/768-2395, www.ccprc.com, Mar.-Apr. and Oct. Sat.-Sun. 10am-6pm, May-Aug. daily 9am-7pm, Sept. daily 10am-6pm, $7 per vehicle, free for pedestrians and cyclists), the only public facility on this mostly private resort island. It has restrooms, showers, a picnic area with grills, and beach chair and umbrella rentals. Get there from downtown Charleston by taking Lockwood Avenue onto the Highway 30 Connector bridge over the Ashley River. Turn right onto Folly Road, then take a left onto Maybank Highway. After about 20 minutes you'll take another left onto Bohicket Road, which leads you to Kiawah in 14 miles. Turn left from Bohicket Road onto the Kiawah Island Parkway. Just before the security gate, turn right on Beachwalker Drive and follow the signs to the park.

For a totally go-it-alone type of beach day, go to the three-mile-long beach on the Atlantic Ocean at **Sullivan's Island.** There are no facilities, no lifeguards, strong offshore currents, and no parking lots on this residential island (park on the side of the street). There's also a lot of dog walking on this beach, since no leash is required November-February. Get there from downtown by crossing the Ravenel Bridge over the Cooper River and bearing right onto Coleman Boulevard, which turns into Ben Sawyer Boulevard. Take the Ben Sawyer Bridge onto Sullivan's Island. Beach access is plentiful and marked.

Diving

Offshore diving centers on a network of **artificial reefs** (see www.dnr.sc.gov for a list and locations), particularly the "Charleston 60" sunken barge and the popular "Train Wreck," comprising 50 deliberately sunk New York City subway cars. Probably Charleston's

best-regarded outfitter and charter operator is **Charleston Scuba** (335 Savannah Hwy., 843/763-3483, www.charlestonscuba.com) in West Ashley. They offer training classes, charters, and offshore diving trips. In addition to Charleston Scuba, you also might want to check out **Cooper River Scuba** (843/572-0459, www.cooperriverdiving.com) and **Atlantic Coast Dive Center** (209 Scott St., 843/884-1500).

Kayaking

Many kayakers put in at the Shem Creek Marina or the public Shem Creek Landing in Mount Pleasant. From here it's a safe, easy paddle—sometimes with appearances by dolphins or manatees—to the Intracoastal Waterway. Another good place to put in is at **Isle of Palms Marina** (50 41st Ave., 843/886-0209) behind the Wild Dunes Resort on Morgan Creek, which empties into the Intracoastal Waterway.

An excellent outfit for guided kayak tours is **Coastal Expeditions** (654 Serotina Ct., 843/881-4582, www.coastalexpeditions.com), which also runs the only approved ferry service to the Cape Romain National Wildlife Refuge. They'll rent you a kayak for roughly $50 per day. Coastal Expeditions also sells an outstanding kayaking, boating, and fishing map of the area (about $12).

The best tour operator close to downtown is **Nature Adventures Outfitters** (Shrimp Boat Ln., 843/568-3222, www.kayakcharlestonsc.com), which puts in on Shem Creek in Mount Pleasant for most of its 2-, 2.5-, 3-, and 3.5-hour and full-day guided trips, with prices from $40 to $85. They also offer blackwater tours out of landings at other locations; see the website for specific directions for those tours.

Fishing and Boating

For casual fishing off a pier, try the well-equipped **Folly Beach Fishing Pier** (101 E. Arctic Ave., Folly Beach, 843/588-3474, daily dawn-dusk, $5-7 parking, $8 fishing fee, rod rentals available) on Folly Beach or the **North Charleston Riverfront Park** (843/745-1087, www.northcharleston.org, daily dawn-dusk) along the Cooper River on the grounds of the old Navy Yard. Get onto the Navy Yard grounds by taking I-26 north to exit 216B. Take a left onto Spruill Avenue and a right onto McMillan Avenue.

Key local marinas include **Shem Creek Marina** (526 Mill St., 843/884-3211, www.shemcreekmarina.com), **Charleston Harbor Marina** (24 Patriots Point Rd., 843/284-7062, www.charlestonharbormarina.com), **Charleston City Marina** (17 Lockwood Dr., 843/722-4968), **Charleston Maritime Center** (10 Wharfside St., 843/853-3625, www.cmcevents.com), and the **Cooper River Marina** (1010 Juneau Ave., 843/554-0790, www.ccprc.com).

Good fishing charter outfits include **Barrier Island Eco Tours** (50 41st Ave., 843/886-5000, www.nature-tours.com, about $80) out of Isle of Palms, **Bohicket Boat Adventure & Tour Co.** (2789 Cherry Point Rd., 843/559-3525, www.bohicketboat.com, $375 per half day for 1-2 passengers) out of the Edisto River, and **Reel Fish Finder Charters** (315 Yellow Jasmine Ct., Moncks Corner, 843/697-2081, www.reelfishfinder.com, $400 per half day for 1-3 passengers), which picks up clients at many different marinas in the area. For a list of all public landings in Charleston County, go to www.ccprc.com.

Surfing and Kiteboarding

The surfing at the famous Washout area on the east side of Folly Beach isn't what it used to be due to storm activity and beach erosion. But diehards still gather at this area when the swell hits. Check out the conditions yourself from the three views of the **Folly Surfcam** (www.follysurfcam.com).

The best local surf shop is undoubtedly the historic **McKevlin's Surf Shop** (8 Center St., Folly Beach, 843/588-2247, www.mckevlins.com, spring-summer daily 10am-6pm, fall-winter daily 10am-5:30pm) on Folly Beach, one of the first surf shops on the East Coast, dating to 1965.

Folly Beach Shaka Surf School (107 E. Indian Ave., Folly Beach, 843/607-9911, www.shakasurfschool.com) offers private and group surf lessons, including youth surf camps throughout summer, women-only weekend outings, and yoga classes geared toward surfers. Surf camps are located on the east end of Folly Beach.

Mount Pleasant is home to **Sol Surfers Surf Camp** (1170 Lazy Ln., Mount Pleasant, 843/881-6700, www.solsurfers.net), which offers surf camps during the summer and private and group lessons throughout the year. The surf camp shuttle picks up students at the Parrot Surf Shop (811 Coleman Blvd.). Surf camps take place on the eastern end of Folly Beach.

Water Parks

During the summer months, Charleston County operates three water parks: **Splash Island Waterpark** (444 Needlerush Pkwy., Mount Pleasant, 843/884-0832); **Whirlin' Waters Adventure Waterpark** (University Blvd., North Charleston, 843/572-7275); and **Splash Zone Waterpark at James Island County Park** (871 Riverland Dr., 843/795-7275), on James Island west of town. Admission runs about $10 per person. Go to www.ccprc.com for more information.

Water Tours

The best all-around tour of Charleston Harbor is the 90-minute ride offered by **Spiritline Cruises** (Charleston Harbor, 800/789-3678, www.spiritlinecruises.com, $22 adults, $12 ages 4-11), which leaves from either Aquarium Wharf or Patriots Point. Allow about 30 minutes for ticketing and boarding. Spiritline also has a three-hour dinner cruise in the evening leaving from Patriots Point (about $50 pp) and a cruise to Fort Sumter.

Sandlapper Water Tours (Charleston Maritime Center, 10 Wharfside St., 843/849-8687, www.sandlappertours.com, Mar.-Aug., $20-27) offers many types of evening and dolphin cruises on a 45-foot catamaran. The company also offers Charleston's only waterborne ghost tour. Most of the tours leave from the Maritime Center near East Bay and Calhoun Streets.

Barrier Island Eco Tours (50 41st Ave., 843/886-5000, www.nature-tours.com, from $40) can take you on a passenger boat ride up to Cape Romain NWR out of Isle of Palms, with a focus on undeveloped Capers Island. Plan on seeing plenty of dolphins!

Coastal Expeditions (514-B Mill St., 843/884-7684, www.coastalexpeditions.com, prices vary) is based on Shem Creek in Mount Pleasant and offers several sea kayak adventures of varying lengths.

ON LAND
Golf

The country's first golf course was constructed in Charleston in 1786, so as you'd expect there's great golfing in the area, generally on the outlying islands. The folks at the nonprofit **Charleston Golf, Inc.** (423 King St., 843/958-3629, www.charlestongolfguide.com) are your best one-stop resource for tee times and packages.

The main public course is the 18-hole, renovated and upgraded **Charleston Municipal Golf Course** (2110 Maybank Hwy., 843/795-6517, www.charleston-sc.gov/golf, $22-24 for 18 holes), affectionately referred to as the Muni. To get there from the peninsula, take U.S. 17 south over the Ashley River, take Highway 171 (Folly Rd.) south, and then take a right onto Maybank Highway.

Probably the most renowned area facilities are at the acclaimed **Kiawah Island Golf Resort** (12 Kiawah Beach Dr., Kiawah Island, 800/654-2924, www.kiawahresort.com/golf, $150-350 for 18 holes, 25 percent discount for resort guests), about 20 miles from Charleston. The resort has five courses in all, the best known of which is the **Kiawah Island Ocean Course,** site of the famous "War by the Shore" 1991 Ryder Cup. This 2.5-mile course, which is walking-only until noon each day, hosted the Senior PGA Championship in 2007 and the PGA Championship in 2012. The resort offers a golf academy and private lessons galore. These are public courses, but be aware that tee times are limited for golfers who aren't guests at the resort.

Two excellent resort-style public courses are at **Wild Dunes Resort** (5757 Palm Blvd., Isle of Palms, 888/845-8932, www.wilddunes.com, $165 for 18 holes) on Isle of Palms. The resort has been named one of the state's best by *Golf Digest.*

The 18-hole **Patriots Point Links** (1 Patriots Point Rd., Mount Pleasant, 843/881-0042, www.patriotspointlinks.com, $100 for 18 holes) on Charleston Harbor, right over the Ravenel Bridge, is one of the most convenient courses in the area, and it boasts some phenomenal views.

In Mount Pleasant you will find perhaps the best course in the area for the money, the award-winning **Rivertowne Golf Course** at the **Rivertowne Country Club** (1700 Rivertowne Country Club Dr., Mount Pleasant, 843/856-9808, www.rivertowne-countryclub.com, $150 for 18 holes). Opened in 2002, the course was designed by Arnold Palmer.

Hiking and Biking

The **West Ashley Greenway** (South Windermere Shopping Center [80 Folly Rd.] to Johns Island, paralleling U.S. 17, dawn-dusk) is an urban walking and biking trail built on a former railbed. The 10-mile trail runs parallel to U.S. 17 and passes parks, schools, and the Clemson Experimental Farm, ending near Johns Island. To get to the trailhead from downtown, drive west on U.S. 17. About 0.5 mile after you cross the bridge, turn left onto Folly Road (Hwy. 171). At the second light, turn right into South Windermere Shopping Center; the trail is behind the center on the right.

The most ambitious trail in South Carolina is the **Palmetto Trail,** begun in 1997 and eventually covering 425 miles from the Atlantic to the Appalachians. The coastal terminus of the Palmetto Trail, the 7-mile **Awendaw Passage,** winds through the Francis Marion National Forest. It begins at the trailhead at the Buck Hall Recreational

Area (McClellanville, 843/887-3257, www.palmettoconservation.org, $5 vehicle fee), which has parking and restroom facilities. Get there by taking U.S. 17 north from Charleston about 20 miles and through the Francis Marion National Forest and then Awendaw. Take a right onto Buck Hall Landing Road.

Charleston-area beaches are perfect for a leisurely bike ride on the sand. Sullivan's Island is a particular favorite, and you might be surprised at how long you can ride in one direction on these beaches. Those desiring a more demanding use of their legs can walk or ride their bike in the dedicated pedestrian and bike lane on the massive **Arthur Ravenel Jr. Bridge** over the Cooper River, the longest cable-stayed bridge in the Western Hemisphere.

Tennis

Tennis fans are in for a treat at the **Family Circle Tennis Center** (161 Seven Farms Dr., 800/677-2293, www.volvocaropen.com, Mon.-Thurs. 8am-8pm, Fri. 8am-7pm, Sat. 8am-5pm, Sun. 9am-5pm, $15/hour) on Daniel Island. This multimillion-dollar facility is owned by the city of Charleston and was built in 2001 specifically to host the annual Family Circle Cup women's competition, which is now known as the Volvo Car Open. But it's also open to the public year-round (except when the Volvo Car Open is on) with 17 courts.

The best resort tennis activity is at the **Kiawah Island Golf Resort** (12 Kiawah Beach Dr., Kiawah Island, 800/654-2924, www.kiawahresort.com, $44 per hour for nonguests). The resort's Roy Barth Tennis Center has nine clay and three hard courts, while the West Beach Tennis Club has 10 Har-Tru courts and 2 lighted hard courts.

There are four free, public, city-funded facilities on the peninsula: **Moultrie Playground** (Broad St. and Ashley Ave., 843/769-8258, www.charlestoncity.info, six lighted hard courts), **Jack Adams Tennis Center** (290 Congress St., six lighted hard courts), **Hazel Parker Playground** (70 E. Bay St., on the Cooper River, one hard court),

and **Corrine Jones Playground** (Marlowe St. and Peachtree St., two hard courts).

Bird-Watching

Right in Charleston Harbor is the little **Crab Bank Seabird Sanctuary** (803/734-3886, www.dnr.sc.gov, Oct. 16-Mar. 14 daily dawn-dusk), where thousands of migratory birds can be seen, depending on the season. The sanctuary has been designated an Important Bird Area by Audubon. Mid-October-mid-March you can either kayak there yourself or take a charter with **Nature Adventures Outfitters** (1900 Iron Swamp Rd., Awendaw Island, 800/673-0679). During nesting season, mid-March-mid-October, the sanctuary is closed to the public.

On Johns Island southwest of Charleston is **Legare Farms** (2620 Hanscombe Point Rd., Johns Island, 843/559-0788, www.legare-farms.com, farm hours vary), which holds migratory bird walks ($6 adults, $3 children) in the fall each Saturday at 8:30am.

Once part of a rice plantation, the **I'on Swamp Trail** (15 miles northeast of Charleston via U.S. 17, 843/928-3368, www. fs.fed.us, daily dawn-dusk, free) is one of the premier bird-watching sites in South Carolina, particularly during spring and fall migrations. The rare Bachman's warbler, commonly considered one of the most elusive birds in North America, has been seen here. To get here, make the 10-minute drive to Mount Pleasant, then head north on U.S. 17 and take a left onto I'on Swamp Road (Forest Service Rd. 228). The parking area is 2.5 miles ahead on the left.

Ice-Skating

Ice-skating in South Carolina? Yep, 100,000 square feet of it, year-round at the two NHL-size rinks of the **Carolina Ice Palace** (7665 Northwoods Blvd., North Charleston, 843/572-2717, www.carolinaicepalace.com, daily public sessions, $7 adults, $6 children). This is also the practice facility for the local hockey team, the Stingrays, as well as where the Citadel's hockey team plays.

SPECTATOR SPORTS

A New York Yankees Class A affiliate in the South Atlantic League, the **Charleston River Dogs** play April-August at **Joseph P. Riley Jr. Park** (360 Fishburne St., 843/577-3647, www.riverdogs.com, $8-11 general admission), aka "the Joe." There are a lot of fun promotions to keep things interesting should the play on the field be less than stimulating. Expect to pay $5 for parking.

The professional USL Pro soccer team **Charleston Battery** plays April-July at **MUSC Health Stadium** (MUSC Health Stadium, 1990 Daniel Island Dr., 843/971-4625, www.charlestonbattery.com, about $10) on Daniel Island, north of Charleston.

An ECHL professional hockey team, the **South Carolina Stingrays** get a good crowd out to their rink at the **North Charleston Coliseum** (5001 Coliseum Dr., 843/744-2248, www.stingrayshockey.com, $15), playing October-April.

The Citadel (171 Moultrie St., 843/953-3294, www.citadelsports.com, ticket prices vary) plays Southern Conference football home games at **Johnson Hagood Stadium,** next to the campus on the Ashley River near Hampton Park. The basketball team plays home games at **McAlister Field House** on campus. The school's ice hockey team has its home games at the **Carolina Ice Palace** (7665 Northwoods Blvd., North Charleston).

Food

Charleston's long history of good taste and livability combines with an affluent and sophisticated population to attract some of the brightest chefs and restaurateurs in the country. A long list of James Beard Award nominees each year confirms the city's role as perhaps the preeminent hub of culinary excellence in the American South.

Kitchens here eschew fickle trends, instead emphasizing quality, professionalism, and, most of all, freshness of ingredients. The farm-to-table movement is as strong here as anywhere in the country and drives the menus of most of the premier establishments.

If you come here in the first week or two of the New Year, keep in mind that is usually the time when Charleston's more popular restaurants might close briefly for renovations.

WATERFRONT
New Southern

Few restaurants in Charleston have inspired such impassioned advocates as legendary chef Sean Brock's flagship restaurant, ★ **McCrady's** (2 Unity Alley and 155 Bay St., www.mccradysrestaurant.com, Wed.-Thurs. and Sun. 7pm seating, Fri.-Sat. seatings at 6:30pm and 8:45pm, $125 pp, $85 pp wine pairing). In the restaurant's early days, Brock's then-groundbreaking sous vide (or vacuum cooking technique) was spoken of in reverent tones by his clientele. In an expansion and reimagining, Brock moved the original McCrady's to a spot right next door, where it continues to offer the sophisticated, almost frighteningly delicious tasting-menu experience for which it is renowned. Brock repurposed the former McCrady's space as **McCrady's Tavern,** a return to the original use of the building as a watering hole and community gathering spot back in the 1770s. In a nod to a more egalitarian dining experience, the tavern has a more casual New Southern menu. Either spot is a core stop of any Charleston foodie pilgrimage.

Magnolias (185 E. Bay St., 843/577-7771, www.magnoliascharleston.com, Mon.-Sat. 11:30am-10pm, Sun. 3:45pm-10pm, $25-35) began life as one of Charleston's first serious eating spots. While the interior has since been given a warm renovation, the menu remains as attractive as ever, with a delightful take on Southern classics like the lump crab cakes, the shellfish over grits, and the rainbow trout. The appetizers are particularly strong—start with the famous fried green tomatoes or maybe the boiled peanut hummus.

Slightly North of Broad (192 E. Bay St., 843/723-3424, www.snobcharleston.com, daily 11:30am-2:30pm and 5pm-10pm, $25-35), or "SNOB," is an ironic play on the often pejorative reference to the insular South of Broad neighborhood. This hot spot, routinely voted best restaurant in town in such contests, is anything but snobby. Hopping with happy foodies for lunch and dinner, the fun is enhanced by the long, open kitchen with its own counter area. The dynamic but comforting menu here is practically a bible of the new wave of Lowcountry cuisine, with dishes like beef tenderloin, jumbo lump crab cakes, grilled barbecue tuna—and, of course, the pan-seared flounder. An interesting twist at SNOB is the selection of "medium plates," dishes that are a little more generous than an appetizer but with the same adventurous spirit.

For many visitors to Charleston, there comes a point when they just get tired of stuffing themselves with seafood. If you find yourself in that situation, the perfect antidote is **High Cotton** (199 E. Bay St., 843/724-3815, www.mavericksouthernkitchens.com, Mon.-Thurs. 5:30pm-10pm, Fri. 5:30pm-11pm, Sat. 11:30am-2:30pm and 5:30pm-11pm, Sun. 10am-2pm and 5:30pm-10pm, $35-45), a meat lover's paradise offering some of the best steaks in town as well as a creative menu of assorted lamb and pork dishes. Chef Anthony Gray places heavy emphasis on using fresh local ingredients, both veggies and game, and the rotating menu always reflects that. None of this comes particularly cheap, but splurges rarely do. In the woody (and popular) bar area there's usually a solo live pianist or sax player after 6pm.

NORTH OF BROAD
Classic Southern

Executive chef Sean Brock of McCrady's fame already had a reputation as one of the country's leading purveyors of the farm-to-table fine-dining movement, but he cemented that reputation with **Husk** (76 Queen St., 843/577-2500, www.huskrestaurant.com, Mon.-Thurs. 11:30am-2pm and 5:30pm-10pm, Fri.-Sat. 11:30am-2pm and 5:30pm-11pm, Sun. 10am-2:30pm and 5:30pm-10pm, $25-35), voted "Best New Restaurant in the U.S." by *Bon Appétit* magazine soon after its 2011 opening. Brock says of his ingredients, "If it doesn't come from the South, it's not coming through the door." The spare, focused menu is constantly changing with the seasons. On a recent lunch visit my party enjoyed two types of catfish (a fried catfish BLT on Texas toast and a lightly cornmeal-dusted broiled catfish with local vegetables), Husk's signature cheeseburger, and—wait for it—lamb barbecue. Reservations are strongly recommended.

In business for over 40 years now, **Poogan's Porch** (72 Queen St., 843/577-2337, www.poogansporch.com, Mon.-Fri. 11:30am-2:30pm and 5pm-9:30pm, Sat.-Sun. 9am-3pm and 5pm-9:30pm, $25-30) is the prototype of a classic Charleston restaurant: lovingly restored old home, professional but unpretentious service, great fried green tomatoes, and rich, calorie-laden Lowcountry classics like crab cakes and shrimp and grits. Brunch is the big thing here, a bustling affair with ample portions, Bloody Marys, mimosas, and soft sunlight.

Walk through the gaslit courtyard of the Planter's Inn at Market and Meeting Streets into the intimate dining room of the ★ **Peninsula Grill** (112 N. Market St., 843/723-0700, www.peninsulagrill.com, daily from 5:30pm, $35-50) and begin an epicurean journey you'll not soon forget. Peninsula Grill might be Charleston's quintessential purveyor of high-style Lowcountry cuisine. You'll want to start with the sampler trio of soups and finish with the legendary coconut cake. Reservations are strongly recommended.

Follow Rachael Ray's lead and wait in the long lines outside **Jestine's Kitchen** (251 Meeting St., 843/722-7224, Tues.-Thurs. 11am-9:30pm, Fri.-Sat. 11am-10pm, $15-20) to enjoy a simple Southern take on such meat-and-three comfort food classics as meat loaf, pecan-fried fish, and fried green tomatoes. Most of the recipes are handed down from the restaurant's namesake, Jestine Matthews, the African American woman who raised owner Dana Berlin.

New Southern

Cru Café (18 Pinckney St., 843/534-2434, www.crucafe.com, Tues.-Thurs. 11am-3pm and 5pm-10pm, Fri.-Sat. 11am-3pm and 5pm-11pm, $20-30) boasts an adventurous menu within a traditional-looking Charleston single house just around the corner from the main stable for the city's carriage tours, with a choice of interior or exterior seating. Sample entrées include poblano and mozzarella fried chicken and seared maple leaf duck breast.

The intimate bistro and stylish bar ★ **FIG** (232 Meeting St., 843/805-5900, www.eatatfig.com, Mon.-Thurs. 6pm-11pm, Fri.-Sat. 6pm-midnight, $30-35) has a passion for fresh, simple ingredients. FIG—short for "Food Is Good"—attracts young professional scenesters as well as die-hard foodies. Chef Mike Lata won James Beard's Best Chef of the Southeast award in 2009. FIG is one of Charleston's great champions of the Sustainable Seafood Initiative, and the kitchen staff strives to work as closely as possible with local farmers and anglers in determining its seasonal menu.

Inside the plush Charleston Place Hotel you'll find **Charleston Grill** (224 King St., 843/577-4522, www.charlestongrill.com, dinner daily from 6pm, $30-60), one of the city's favorite (and priciest) fine-dining spots for locals and visitors alike. The menu specializes in French-influenced Lowcountry cuisine, with dishes like the niçoise vegetable tart. There are a lot of great fusion dishes as well, such as the tuna and *hamachi* sashimi topped with pomegranate molasses and lemongrass oil. Reservations are a must.

Focusing on purely seasonal offerings that never stay on the menu longer than three months, ★ **Circa 1886** (149 Wentworth St., 843/853-7828, www.circa1886.com,

Mon.-Sat. 5:30pm-9:30pm, $30-35) combines the best old-world tradition of Charleston with the vibrancy of its more adventurous kitchens. The restaurant—surprisingly little known despite its four-star Mobil rating—is located in the former carriage house of the grand Wentworth Mansion B&B just west of the main College of Charleston campus. The menu has featured such entrées as robust beef au poivre and shrimp-and-crab-stuffed flounder. Be sure to check the daily prix fixe offerings; they can be a great deal.

Coffee, Tea, and Sweets

Considered the best coffeehouse in town, **Black Tap Coffee** (70½ Beaufain St., 843/793-4402, Mon.-Fri. 7am-7pm, Sat.-Sun. 8am-6pm) features an array of Counter Culture beans roasted and served to perfection by skilled baristas. Cold brew and pour-over cups are specialties of the house, as is their signature Lavender Latte. It's smallish and a bit off the beaten King Street path but still well within walking distance of that shopping thoroughfare.

If you find yourself needing a quick pick-me-up while shopping on King Street, avoid the lines at the two Starbucks locations on the avenue and instead turn east on Market Street and duck inside **City Lights Coffeehouse** (141 Market St., 843/853-7067, Mon.-Thurs. 7am-9pm, Fri.-Sat. 7am-10pm, Sun. 8am-6pm). The sweet goodies are delectable in this cozy little Euro-style place, and the Counter Culture organic coffee is to die for. If you're lucky, they'll have some of their Ethiopian Sidamo brewed.

Routinely voted as having the best desserts in the city, the cakes alone at **Kaminsky's** (78 N. Market St., 843/853-8270, daily noon-2am) are worth the trip to the City Market area. The fresh fruit torte, the red velvet, and the "Mountain of Chocolate" are the three best sellers.

French

On the north side of Broad Street you'll find **Gaulart & Maliclet** (98 Broad St.,

843/577-9797, www.fastandfrenchcharleston.com, Mon. 8am-4pm, Tues.-Thurs. 8am-10pm, Fri.-Sat. 8am-10:30pm, $20-25), subtitled "Fast and French." This is a gourmet bistro with a strong takeout component. Prices are especially reasonable for this area of town, with great lunch specials under $10, Thursday night Fondue for Two specials at about $20, and breakfast all day.

Queen Street Grocery (133 Queen St., 843/723-4121, www.queenstreetgrocerycafe.com, kitchen Mon.-Sat. 10am-5pm, Sun. 11am-3pm, $10, store Mon.-Sat. 8am-8:30pm) is the kind of place frequented almost exclusively by locals. At this corner store you can load up on some of the tastiest made-to-order crepes this side of France—as well as light groceries, beer, wine, and cigarettes.

Mediterranean

The cuisine of northern Italy comes alive in the bustling, dimly lit room of **Fulton Five** (5 Fulton St., 843/853-5555, www.fultonfive.com, Mon.-Sat. 5:30pm-close, $30-40), from the *insalata de funghi* to the sublime risotto. It's not cheap, and the portions aren't necessarily the largest, but with these tasty, non-tomato-based dishes and this romantic, gusto-filled atmosphere, you'll be satiated with life itself.

Seafood

Hyman's Seafood (215 Meeting St., 843/723-6000, www.hymanseafood.com, Mon.-Thurs. 11am-9pm, Fri.-Sun. 11am-11pm, $20-40) is thought by many locals to border on a tourist trap, and it's mostly tourists who line up for hours to get in. To keep things manageable, Hyman's offers the same menu and prices for both lunch and dinner. After asking for some complimentary fresh boiled peanuts in lieu of bread, start with the Carolina Delight, a delicious appetizer (also available as an entrée) involving a lightly fried cake of grits topped with your choice of delectable seafood, or maybe a half-dozen oysters from the Half Shell oyster bar. Definitely try the she-crab soup, one of the best you'll find anywhere. As for entrées, the ubiquitous Lowcountry crispy scored flounder is always a good bet.

UPPER KING
Classic Southern

One of a comparatively few great Charleston restaurants with an equally expert focus on breakfast as on the other meals, **Virginia's on King** (412 King St., 912/735-5800, www.holycityhospitality.com, Mon.-Fri. 7am-10pm, Sat. 8am-10pm, Sun. 10am-3pm, $15-25) is a great place to enjoy Southern classics like fried green tomatoes, tomato pie, and their signature she-crab soup. The salmon BLT lunch dish (or in their old Southern parlance, "dinner," with "supper" being the name of the last meal of the day) is one of the best seafood dishes I've had anywhere. As for breakfast, the omelets are solid and most of the lunch menu is also available.

Rapidly gaining a reputation as one of the best brunch scenes in town, **The Macintosh** (479 King St., 843/789-4299, www.themacintoshcharleston.com, Mon.-Sat. 6:30am-7pm, Sun. 9am-6pm, $25-40) combines the best of Charleston's Classic/New South style with a gastropub sensibility, complete with an extensive craft beer menu. The chef is three-time James Beard semifinalist Jeremiah Bacon, which means you can't really go wrong. But for brunch I'd suggest the baked chorizo, and from the small but artfully curated dinner menu, any seafood dish is good. Happy hour (Mon.-Fri. 5pm-7pm) is also a big draw here, with its own special $5 small-plate bar food menu.

American

Charleston's fave rave is ★ **Edmund's Oast** (1081 Morrison Dr., 843/727-1145, www.edmundsoast.com, Mon.-Thurs. 5:30pm-10pm, Fri.-Sat. 5:30pm-11pm, Sun. 10am-2:30pm and 5:30pm-10pm, $25-40), a boisterous beer garden/brewpub on the Upper Peninsula, boasting a 40-tap array, several brews made

Lowcountry Locavores

Charleston has merged its own indigenous and abiding culinary tradition with the "new" idea that you should grow your food as naturally as possible and purchase it as close to home as you can. From bacon and snapper to sweet potatoes, the typical Charleston dish of today harkens back to its soulful Southern roots, before the days of factory food.

Spurred in part by an influx of trained chefs after the establishment of the Spoleto Festival in the 1970s, the locavore movement in Charleston came from the efforts of epicureans committed to sustainability and the principles of community-supported agriculture (CSA). Spearheaded by visionaries like the James Beard Award-winning Mike Lata of the bistro FIG and Sean Brock of Mc-Crady's, sustainable food initiatives have sprung up in Charleston and the Lowcountry, such as the South Carolina Aquarium's Sustainable Seafood Initiative (http://scaquarium.org), partnering with local restaurants to ensure a sustainable wild-caught harvest; Certified South Carolina (www.certifiedsc.com), guaranteeing that the food you eat was grown in the Palmetto State; and a local chapter of the Slow Food Movement (http://slowfoodcharleston.org).

The list of Holy City restaurants relying almost exclusively on local and sustainable sources is long, but here are a few notable examples:

· **Husk** (76 Queen St., 843/577-2500, www.huskrestaurant.com)

· **Charleston Grill** (224 King St., 843/577-4522, www.charlestongrill.com)

· **FIG** (232 Meeting St., 843/805-5900, www.eatatfig.com)

· **Al Di La** (25 Magnolia Rd., 843/571-2321, www.aldilarestaurant.com)

· **Queen Street Grocery** (133 Queen St., 843/723-4121, www.queenstreetgrocerycafe.com)

· **Middleton Place Restaurant** (4300 Ashley River Rd., 843/556-6020, www.middleton-place.org)

· **Circa 1886** (149 Wentworth St., 843/853-7828, www.circa1886.com)

· **COAST Bar and Grill** (39D John St., 843/722-8838, www.coastbarandgrill.com)

· **Cru Café** (18 Pinckney St., 843/534-2434, www.crucafe.com)

· **Hominy Grill** (207 Rutledge Ave., 912/937-0930, www.hominygrill.com)

· **Peninsula Grill** (112 N. Market St., 843/723-0700, www.peninsulagrill.com)

on-site, and, perhaps surprisingly, an excellent cocktail menu. The small plates, though, might be what stay with you. Expressive, excellent charcuterie and pitch-perfect sliders are the highlights. If you sit at the bar, the $4 per plate happy hour items (4:30pm-6:30pm) are a must-try; I suggest the smoked wings.

Asian

There's usually a long wait to get a table at the great Thai place **Basil** (460 King St., 843/724-3490, www.basilthairestaurant.com, Mon.-Thurs. 11:30am-2:30pm and 5pm-10:30pm,

Fri.-Sat. 5pm-11pm, Sun. 5pm-10pm, $15-20) on Upper King, since they don't take reservations. But Basil also has one of the hippest, most happening bar scenes in the area, so you won't necessarily mind. Revelers enjoy fresh, succulent takes on Thai classics like cashew chicken and pad thai. The signature dish is the basil duck.

Barbecue

The Downtown/Upper Peninsula outpost of Charleston's favorite barbecue chain, **Fiery Ron's Home Team BBQ** (126 Williman St.,

843/225-7427, www.hometeambbq.com, daily 11am-10pm, $10-20), boasts a bit of an upscale feel from the original West Ashley location and the Sullivan's Island version. But don't be deceived by the excellent artisanal cocktail menu; the barbecue here is just as good.

Coffee, Tea, and Sweets

One of the best java joints in Charleston is **Kudu Coffee** (4 Vanderhorst St., 843/853-7186, Mon.-Sat. 6:30am-7pm, Sun. 9am-6pm). A kudu is an African antelope, and the Africa theme extends to the beans, which all have an African pedigree. Poetry readings and occasional live music add to the mix. A lot of green-friendly, left-of-center community activism goes on here as well.

French

The best mussels I've ever had were at ★ **39 Rue de Jean** (39 John St., 843/722-8881, www.holycityhospitality.com, Mon.-Thurs. 11:30am-11pm, Fri.-Sat. 11:30am-1am, Sun. 10am-11pm, $20-30). But anything off the bistro-style menu is unbelievably tasty, from the foie gras to the confit to the coq au vin to the steak frites. There are incredible Prohibition-style cocktails to go along with the extensive wine list.

Italian

One of Upper King's "it" restaurants, **Indaco** (525 King St., 843/727-1218, www.indaco-charleston.com, Sun.-Thurs. 5pm-10pm, Fri.-Sat. 5pm-midnight, $15-25) features a small but well-curated menu of antipasti, custom wood-fired gourmet pizzas, and delicious Italian specialties like black pepper tagliatelle. Yes, there's brussels sprout pizza, and it's quite delicious! Indaco is set in a stylish, bustling restored warehouse.

Mexican

The quesadillas at **Juanita Greenberg's Nacho Royale** (439 King St., 843/723-6224, www.juanitagreenbergs.com, daily 11am-11pm, $10-15) are perfectly packed with jack cheese, spicy sausage, and a delightful *pico de gallo*. This modest Mexican joint caters primarily to a college crowd, as you can tell from the reasonable prices, the large patio out back, the extensive tequila list, and the bar that stays open until 2am on weekends.

Seafood

Near 39 Rue de Jean you'll find the affiliated **COAST Bar and Grill** (39D John St., 843/722-8838, www.coastbarandgrill.com, daily 5:30pm-close, $20-25), which makes the most of its loud, hip setting in a former warehouse. The raw bar is satisfying, with a particularly nice selection of ceviche. COAST is a strong local advocate of the Sustainable Seafood Initiative, whereby restaurants work directly with the local fishing industry.

HAMPTON PARK
Classic Southern

With a motto like "Grits are good for you," you know what you're in store for at **Hominy Grill** (207 Rutledge Ave., 912/937-0930, www.hominygrill.com, Mon.-Fri. 7:30am-8:30pm, Sat.-Sun. 9am-8:30pm, $15-20), set in a renovated barbershop at Rutledge Avenue and Cannon Street near the Medical University of South Carolina. Primarily revered for his Sunday brunch, chef Robert Stehling has fun—almost mischievously so—breathing new life into American and Southern classics. Because this is largely a locals' place, you can impress your friends back home by saying you had the rare pleasure of the Hominy's sautéed shad roe with bacon and mushrooms—when the shad are running, that is.

Moe's Crosstown Tavern (714 Rutledge Ave., 843/722-3287, Mon.-Sat. 11am-midnight, bar until 2am, $10-15) is not only one of the classic Southern dives, but also has one of the best kitchens on this side of town, known for hand-cut fries, great wings, and, most of all, excellent burgers. On Tuesdays, the burgers are half price at happy hour—one of Charleston's best deals.

Italian

A rave of Charleston foodies is the

Tuscan-inspired fare of chef Ken Vedrinski at **Trattoria Lucca** (41 Bogard St., 843/973-3323, www.luccacharleston.com, Mon.-Sat. 6pm-10pm, $25-30). The menu is simple but perfectly focused, featuring handmade pasta and signature items like the pork chop or the fresh cheese plate. You'll be surprised at how much food your money gets you here. Monday evenings see a family-style prix fixe communal dinner.

WEST ASHLEY
Classic Southern
Tucked away on the grounds of the Middleton Place Plantation is the romantic **Middleton Place Restaurant** (4300 Ashley River Rd., 843/556-6020, www.middletonplace.org, Tues.-Thurs. and Sun. 11am-3pm and 6pm-8pm, Fri.-Sat. 11am-3pm and 6pm-9pm, $25-30). Theirs is a respectful take on traditional plantation fare like hoppin' John, gumbo, she-crab soup, and collards. The special annual Thanksgiving buffet is a real treat. Reservations are required for dinner. A nice plus is being able to wander the gorgeous landscaped gardens before dusk if you arrive at 5:30pm or later with a dinner reservation.

New Southern
One of the more unassuming advocates of farm-to-table dining, ★ **The Glass Onion** (1219 Savannah Hwy., 843/225-1717, www.ilovetheglassonion.com, Mon.-Thurs. 11am-9pm, Fri. 11am-10pm, Sat. 10am-3pm and 4pm-10pm, $20-30) is in an equally unassuming location on U.S. 17 (Savannah Hwy.) on the western approach to town. That said, their food is right in the thick of the sustainable food movement and is incredibly tasty to boot (not to mention that there is more parking there than there is downtown). The interior says "diner," and indeed the emphasis here is on Southern soul and comfort-food classics. The Glass Onion also boasts a good variety of specialty craft brews to wash it all down. Another plus: In this town full of Sunday brunches, Glass Onion's specialty is a Saturday brunch!

American
Gene's Haufbrau (17 Savannah Hwy., 843/225-4363, www.genes-haufbrau.com, daily 11:30am-2am, $10) is worth making a special trip into West Ashley. Claiming to be the oldest bar in continuous operation in town (1952), Gene's complements its fairly typical bar-food menu with some good wraps. Start with the "Drunken Trio" (beer-battered cheese sticks, mushrooms, and onion rings) and follow with a portobello wrap or a good old-fashioned crawfish po'boy. One of the best meals in town for the money is Gene's $8.50 blue plate special, a rotating comfort food entrée like country-fried steak or pot roast, offered Monday-Friday 11:30am-4pm. The late-night kitchen hours, until 1am, are a big plus.

If you're any kind of fan of fried chicken, whether good old-fashioned Southern fried or the type of sandwich you might get at Chick-fil-A, you will want to check out **Boxcar Betty's** (1922 Savannah Hwy., 843/225-7470, www.boxcarbetty.com, daily 11am-9pm, $10). Be warned, these juicy, incredibly tasty flour-breaded fried chicken sandwiches are addictive.

Barbecue
My favorite barbecue joint, the rowdy and always hopping ★ **Fiery Ron's Home Team BBQ** (1205 Ashley River Rd., 843/225-7427, www.hometeambbq.com, Mon.-Sat. 11am-9pm, Sun. 11:30am-9pm, $10-20) has pulled pork and ribs that rank with the best I've had anywhere in the country. Even the sides are amazing here, including perfect collards and tasty mac and cheese. Pitmaster Madison Ruckel provides an array of tableside sauces, including hot sauce, indigenous South Carolina mustard sauce, and his own "Alabama white," a light and delicious mayonnaise-based sauce. As if that weren't enough, the owners' close ties to the regional jam-band community mean there's great live blues and indie rock after 10pm most nights (Thursday is bluegrass night) to spice up the bar action, which goes until 2am.

Fiery Ron's Home Team BBQ is one of the state's best.

Mediterranean

Anything on this northern Italian-themed menu is good, but the risotto—a legacy of original chef John Marshall—is the specialty dish at **Al Di La** (25 Magnolia Rd., 843/571-2321, www.aldilarestaurant.com, Tues.-Sat. 6pm-10pm, $15-20), a very popular West Ashley fine-dining spot. Reservations are recommended.

NORTH CHARLESTON
Pizza

If you have a hankering for pizza in North Charleston, don't miss **EVO Pizzeria** (1075 E. Montague Ave., 843/225-1796, www.evo-pizza.com, Tues.-Fri. 11am-2:30pm and 5pm-10pm, Sat. 6pm-10pm, $15) in the Olde North Charleston area at Park Circle. They specialize in a small but rich menu of unusual gourmet pizza toppings, like pistachio pesto.

SUMMERVILLE
American

For a down-home-style pancakes-and-sandwich place that's popular with the locals at all hours of the day, try **Alex's Restaurant** (120 E. 5th N. St., 843/871-3202, daily 24 hours, $10).

A popular local landmark is **Guerin's Pharmacy** (140 S. Main St., 843/873-2531, Mon.-Fri. 9am-6pm, Sat. 9am-5pm, $5), which claims to be the state's oldest pharmacy. Complete with an old-fashioned soda fountain, they offer malted milk shakes and lemonade.

MOUNT PLEASANT AND EAST COOPER

In Mount Pleasant, most of the restaurant action centers on the picturesque shrimping village of Shem Creek, which is dotted on both banks with bars and restaurants, most dealing in fresh local seafood. As with Murrells Inlet up the coast, some spots on Shem Creek border on tourist traps. Don't be afraid to go where the lines aren't.

American

For a burger and an adult beverage or two, go straight to friendly **Poe's Tavern** (2210 Middle St., Sullivan's Island, 843/883-0083, www.poestavern.com, daily 11am-2am, kitchen until 10pm, $10-15), a nod to Edgar Allan Poe's stint at nearby Fort Moultrie.

Seafood

At the **Red Drum Gastropub** (803 Coleman Blvd., 843/849-0313, www.reddrumrestaurant.com, daily 5:30pm-10pm, lunch/brunch

To Market, to Market

A fun and favorite local fixture April-mid-December, the **Charleston Farmers Market** (843/724-7309, www.charlestoncity.info, Sat. 8am-2pm) rings beautiful Marion Square with stalls of local produce, street eats, local arts and crafts, and kids' activities.

Running April-October, East Cooper has its own version in the **Mount Pleasant Farmers Market** (843/884-8517, http://townofmountpleasant.com, Tues. 3pm-dark) at the Moultrie Middle School on Coleman Boulevard.

Sat.-Sun. 10:30am-2pm, $20-40), the food is just as important as the drink. While you're likely to need reservations for the dining room, where you can enjoy Lowcountry-Tex-Mex fusion-style cuisine with a typically Mount Pleasant-like emphasis on seafood, the bar scene is very hopping and fun, with live music every Wednesday-Thursday night.

A must-stop roadside diner in the Awendaw area is ★ **See Wee Restaurant** (4808 U.S. 17 N., 843/928-3609, Mon.-Thurs. 11am-8:30pm, Fri.-Sat. 11am-9:30pm, Sun. 11am-8pm, $15-25), about 20 minutes north of Charleston by car. Housed in a humble former general store on the west side of U.S. 17 (the restrooms are still outside), this diner draws folks from far and wide to enjoy signature menu items like the grouper and the unreal she-crab soup, considered by some epicures to be the best in the world. You can't miss with any of their seafood entrées. Occasionally the crowds can get thick, but rest assured it's worth any wait.

A popular spot, especially for the younger crowd, **Vickery's Shem Creek Bar and Grill** (1313 Shrimp Boat Ln., 843/884-4440, daily 11:30am-1am, $15-20) has a similar menu to its partner location on the peninsula, but this Vickery's has the pleasant added bonus of a beautiful view overlooking the creek. You'll get more of the Vickery's Cuban flair here, with a great black bean soup and an awesome Cuban sandwich.

A well-regarded spot on Shem Creek is **Water's Edge** (1407 Shrimp Boat Ln., 843/884-4074, daily 11am-11pm, $20-35), which consistently takes home a *Wine* *Spectator* Award of Excellence for its great selection of vintages. Native Charlestonian Jimmy Purcell concentrates on fresh seafood with a slightly more upscale flair than many Shem Creek places.

Vegetarian

For a real change of pace, try **The Sprout Cafe** (629 Johnnie Dodds Blvd., 843/849-8554, www.thehealthysprout.com, Mon.-Fri. 6am-8pm, Sat. 9am-3pm, Sun. 11am-3pm, $10) on U.S. 17. Dealing totally in raw foods, the restaurant emphasizes healthy and fresh ingredients. You might be surprised at the inventiveness of their breakfast-through-dinner seasonal menu, which might include a tasty crepe topped with a pear-and-nut puree and maple syrup, or a raw squash and zucchini "pasta" dish topped with walnut "meatballs."

FOLLY BEACH AND THE SOUTHWEST ISLANDS

American

Three words: duck fat fries. The **Tattooed Moose** (3328 Maybank Hwy., 843/277-2990, www.tattooedmoose.com, daily 11:30am-1am, $10-15) is a dive bar sensation on Johns Island, combining classic bar food with a typically Charlestonian touch of Old South culinary bravado. While the fries—served straight up with roasted garlic and blue cheese or with gravy—are the signature menu item, the sandwiches are simply fantastic. Try the duck confit sandwich or the pork belly sandwich. Brunch is becoming huge here, too, and live music is featured most nights.

Barbecue

If barbecue is your thing, head straight to **JB's Smokeshack** (3406 Maybank Hwy., 843/557-0426, www.jbssmokeshack.com, Wed.-Sat. 11am-8:30pm, $8-18), considered one of the better 'cue joints in the Lowcountry. True connoisseurs will tell you it's the chicken that's really awesome, however. JB's offers a buffet for $8.88 per person ($5 under age 11), or you can opt for a barbecue plate, including hash, rice, and two sides. In a nice twist, the plates include a three-meat option: pork, chicken, ribs, or brisket.

Breakfast and Brunch

The closest thing to a taste of old Folly is the **Lost Dog Café** (106 W. Huron Ave., 843/588-9669, daily 6:30am-3pm, $10-15), so named for its bulletin board stacked with alerts about lost pets, pets for adoption, and new pups and kittens for sale or giveaway. It opens early to offer a tasty, healthy breakfast to the surfing crowd. It's a great place to pick up a quick, inexpensive, and tasty meal while you're near the beach.

For a hearty and delicious breakfast, go to **Sunrise Bistro** (1797 Main Rd., 843/718-1858, www.sunrise-bistro.com, Tues.-Thurs. 7am-2:30pm, Fri.-Sat. 7am-2:30pm and 5pm-9pm, Sun. 9am-1pm, $10-15), one of those unassuming diners that always seems to have an eager crowd. Everything, from the omelets to the pancakes down to the simplest bagel with coffee, is spot-on, and a great value to boot. The best offerings here are during the day.

French

★ **Fat Hen** (3140 Maybank Hwy., 843/559-9090, Tues.-Sat. 11:30am-3pm and 5:30pm-10pm, Sun. 10am-3pm, $20-40) is a self-styled "country French bistro" begun by a couple of old Charleston restaurant hands. The fried oysters are a particular specialty. There's also a bar menu (4pm-10pm).

Mexican

Taco Boy (15 Center St., 843/588-9761, Sun.-Thurs. 11am-10pm, Fri.-Sat. 11am-11pm, $10) is a fun place to get a fish taco, have a margarita, and take a walk on the nearby beach afterward. Though no one is under any illusions that this is an authentic Mexican restaurant, the fresh guacamole is particularly rave-worthy, and there's a good selection of tequilas and beers *hecho en México*, with the bar staying open until 2am on weekends.

Seafood

Set within the trendy Tides Folly Beach boutique hotel, **Blu** (1 Center St., 843/588-6658, www.blufollybeach.com, breakfast daily 7am-11am, lunch daily 11am-5pm, dinner Sun.-Thurs. 5pm-9pm, Fri.-Sat. 5pm-10pm, $15-30) offers an equally high standard of food and decor, along with some amazing views of the ocean. The menu isn't particularly pretentious, but it does offer high-quality Sustainable Seafood Initiative options, all of which are recommended.

Fans of the legendary **Bowens Island Restaurant** (1870 Bowens Island Rd., 843/795-2757, Tues.-Sat. 5pm-10pm, $15-20, cash only) on James Island went into mourning when it burned to the ground in 2006. But you can't keep a good oysterman down, and owner Robert Barber rebuilt. A universe removed from the Lexus-and-khaki scene downtown, Bowens Island isn't the place for the uptight. This is the spot to go when you want shovels of oysters literally thrown onto your table, freshly steamed and delicious and all-you-can-eat.

To get to Bowens Island from the peninsula, take Calhoun Street west onto the James Island Connector (Hwy. 30). Take exit 3 onto Highway 171 south and look for Bowens Island Road on the right. The restaurant will be on the left in a short while, after passing by several ritzy McMansions that in no way resemble the restaurant you're about to experience.

Accommodations

Due to the city's long-standing tradition of hospitality and the high standards it has set for itself, hotels and bed-and-breakfasts are generally well maintained and have a high level of service.

The price differential is not that much between the peninsula and the outskirts. You'll pay more to stay in the tourist areas, but not *that* much more, with the bonus of being able to walk to most places you want to see. The farther south you go on the peninsula, the quieter and more affluent it tends to be. Folks looking for a more wild and woolly good time will be drawn to the Upper King area farther north.

SOUTH OF BROAD
$150-300

On the south side of Broad Street is a great old Charleston lodging, **Governor's House Inn** (117 Broad St., 843/720-2070, www.governorshouse.com, $200-350). This circa-1760 building, a National Historic Landmark, is associated with Edward Rutledge, signer of the Declaration of Independence. Though most of its 11 guest rooms—all with four-poster beds, period furnishings, and high ceilings—go for around $300, some of the smaller guest rooms can be had for closer to $200 in the off-season.

The nine guest rooms of ★ **Two Meeting Street Inn** (2 Meeting St., 843/723-7322, www.twomeetingstreet.com, $200-450) down by the Battery are individually appointed, with themes like "the Music Room" and the "the Spell Room." The decor in this 1892 Queen Anne bed-and-breakfast is very traditional, with lots of floral patterns and hunt club-style pieces and artwork. It's considered by many to be the most romantic lodging in town, and you won't soon forget the experience of sitting on the veranda enjoying the sights, sounds, and breezes. Three of the guest rooms—the Canton, Granite, and Roberts—can be had for not much over $200.

WATERFRONT
$150-300

The guest rooms and the thoroughly hospitable service are the focus at nearby ★ **The Vendue** (19 Vendue Range, 800/845-7900, www.thevendue.com, $250-450). All guest rooms are sumptuously appointed in boutique style, with lots of warm, rich fabrics, unique pieces, and high-end bath amenities. That said, the public spaces are cool as well, with a focus on featuring quality art that essentially turns the property into one huge exhibition space. The inn gets a lot of traffic in the evenings because of the popular and hopping Rooftop Bar, which has amazing views.

Over $300

About as close to the Cooper River as a hotel gets, the **Harbourview Inn** (2 Vendue Range, 843/853-8439, www.harbourviewcharleston.com, $300-500) comprises a "historic wing" and a larger, newer, but still tastefully done main building. For the best of those eponymous harbor views, try to get a room on the 3rd floor or you might have some obstructions. It's the little touches that keep guests happy here, with wine, cheese, coffee, tea, and cookies galore and an emphasis on smiling, personalized service. The guest rooms are quite spacious, with big baths and 14-foot ceilings. You can take your complimentary breakfast—good but not great—in your room or eat it on the nice rooftop terrace.

FRENCH QUARTER
Over $300

A great place in this part of town is the **French Quarter Inn** (166 Church St., 843/722-1900, www.fqicharleston.com, $350-500). The decor in the 50 surprisingly spacious guest rooms is suitably high-period French, with low-style noncanopied beds and crisp fresh linens. Many guest rooms feature fireplaces, whirlpool baths, and private balconies.

NORTH OF BROAD
$150-300

It calls itself a boutique hotel, perhaps because each room is unique and sumptuously appointed. But the charming ★ **Andrew Pinckney Inn** (199 Church St., 843/937-8800, www.andrewpinckneyinn.com, $250-350) is very nearly in a class by itself in Charleston not only for its great rates but for its casual West Indies-style decor, charming courtyard, gorgeous three-story atrium, and rooftop terrace on which you can enjoy your complimentary (and delicious) breakfast. For the money and the amenities, it's possibly the single best lodging package in town.

If you plan on some serious shopping, you might want to stay right on the city's main shopping thoroughfare at the **Kings Courtyard Inn** (198 King St., 866/720-2949, www.kingscourtyardinn.com, $200-300). This 1853 Greek Revival building houses a lot more guest rooms—more than 40—than meets the eye, and it can get a little crowded at times. Still, its charming courtyard and awesome location on King Street are big bonuses, as is the convenient but cramped parking lot right next door (about $12 per day, a bargain for this part of town), with free in-and-out privileges.

Affiliated with the Kings Courtyard—and right next door, in fact—is the smaller, cozier **Fulton Lane Inn** (202 King St., 866/720-2940, www.fultonlaneinn.com, $240-350), with its lobby entrance on tiny Fulton Lane between the two inns. Small, simple guest rooms—some with fireplaces—have comfortable beds and spacious baths. This is the kind of place for active people who plan to spend most of their days out and about but want a cozy place to come back to at night. You mark down your continental breakfast order at night, leave it on your doorknob, and it shows up at the *exact* time you requested the next morning. Then when you're ready to shop and walk, just go down the stairs and take the exit right out onto busy King Street. Also nice is the $12-per-day parking with free in-and-out privileges.

Although it is a newer building by Charleston standards, the **Mills House Hotel** (115 Meeting St., 843/577-2400, www.millshouse.com, $250-400) boasts an important pedigree. Dating to 1853, the first incarnation was a grand edifice that hosted luminaries such as Robert E. Lee. Through the years, fire and restoration wrought their changes, and the modern version basically dates from an extensive renovation in the 1970s. The hotel

Andrew Pinckney Inn

has a very good restaurant and lounge inside, the Barbadoes Room (breakfast, lunch, dinner, and Sunday brunch), as well as a healthy banquet and event schedule. So this isn't the place to go for peace and quiet. Rather, this Wyndham-affiliated property is where you go to feel the bustle of downtown Charleston and to be conveniently close to its main sightseeing and shopping attractions. Some of the upper floors of this seven-story building offer spectacular views.

Over $300

Considered Charleston's premier hotel, Charleston Place maintains a surprisingly high level of service and decor for its massive 440-room size. Currently owned by the London-based Orient-Express Hotels, ★ **Belmond Charleston Place** (205 Meeting St., 843/722-4900, www.charlestonplace.com, $300-500) is routinely rated as one of the best hotels in North America by *Condé Nast Traveler* and other publications. The guest rooms aren't especially large, but they are well appointed, featuring Italian marble baths, high-speed Internet, and voice messaging—and, of course, there's a pool available. A series of suite offerings—Junior, Junior Executive, Parlor, and the 800-square-foot Senior—feature enlarged living areas and multiple TVs and phones. The on-site **spa** (843/937-8522) offers all kinds of massages, including couples and "mommy to be" sessions. Diners and tipplers have three fine options to choose from: the famous **Charleston Grill** (843/577-4522, daily 6pm-close, $27-65) for fine dining; the breakfast, lunch, and brunch hot spot **Palmetto Cafe** (843/722-4900, daily 6:30am-3pm, $24-31); and the **Thoroughbred Club** (daily 11am-midnight) for cocktails and, for groups of 10 or more, afternoon tea.

On the north side of Broad Street, the magnificent ★ **John Rutledge House Inn** (116 Broad St., 843/723-7999, www.johnrutledgehouseinn.com, $300-400) is very close to the old South of Broad neighborhood not only in geography but in feel. Known as "America's most historic inn," the Rutledge House boasts a fine old pedigree indeed: Built for Constitution signer John Rutledge in 1763, it's one of only 15 homes belonging to the original signers to survive. George Washington breakfasted here with Mrs. Rutledge in 1791. The interior is stunning: Italian marble fireplaces, original plaster moldings, and masterful ironwork abound in the public spaces. The inn's 19 guest rooms are divided among the original mansion and two carriage houses.

UPPER KING
$150-300

Stretching the bounds of the "Upper King" definition, the **Ashley Inn** (201 Ashley Ave., 843/723-1848, www.charleston-sc-inns.com, $200-300) is located well northwest of Marion Square, almost in the Citadel area. Although it's too far to walk from here to most any historical attraction in Charleston, the Ashley Inn does provide free bikes to its guests as well as free off-street parking, a particularly nice touch. It also deserves a special mention not only because of the romantic, well-appointed nature of its six guest rooms, suite, and carriage house but for its outstanding breakfasts. You get to pick a main dish, such as Carolina sausage pie, stuffed waffles, or cheese blintzes.

In a renovated 1924 building overlooking beautiful Marion Square, the **Francis Marion Hotel** (387 King St., 843/722-0600, www.francismarionhotel.com, $200-300) offers quality accommodations in the hippest, most bustling area of the peninsula—but be aware that it's quite a walk down to the Battery from here. The guest rooms are plush and big, though the baths can be cramped. The hotel's parking garage costs a reasonable $12 per day, with valet parking available until about 8pm. A Starbucks in the lobby pleases many guests on their way out or in. Most rooms hover around $300, but some are a real steal.

HAMPTON PARK
Under $150

Downtown Charleston's least-expensive lodging is also its most unique: the **Not So Hostel** (156 Spring St., 843/722-8383, www.

notsohostel.com, $30-70). The already-reasonable prices also include a make-your-own bagel breakfast, off-street parking, bikes, high-speed Internet access in the common room, and even an airport, train, and bus shuttle. The inn actually comprises three 1840s Charleston single houses, all with the obligatory piazzas. (However, unlike some hostels, there's air-conditioning in all the rooms.) Because the free bike usage makes up for its off-the-beaten-path location, a stay at the Not So Hostel is a fantastic way to enjoy the Holy City on a budget. They now have an annex at 33 Cannon Street with all-private rooms ($75-85).

WEST ASHLEY
$150-300

Looking like Frank Lloyd Wright parachuted into a 300-year-old plantation and got to work, ★ **The Inn at Middleton Place** (4290 Ashley River Rd., 843/556-0500, www.theinnatmiddletonplace.com, $200-300) is one of Charleston's unique lodgings—and not only because it's on the grounds of the historic and beautiful Middleton Place Plantation. The four connected buildings, comprising over 50 guest rooms, are modern yet deliberately blend in with the forested, neutral-colored surroundings. The spacious guest rooms have that same woodsy minimalism, with excellent fireplaces, spacious Euro-style baths, and huge floor-to-ceiling windows overlooking the grounds and the river. Guests also have full access to the rest of the gorgeous Middleton grounds. The only downside is that you're a lengthy drive from the peninsula and all its attractions, restaurants, and nightlife. But don't worry about food—the excellent Middleton Place Restaurant is open for lunch and dinner. There are nightly happy hours at the lodge, a great way to meet some of your fellow lodging mates and relax.

SUMMERVILLE
Over $300

The renowned **Woodlands Resort & Inn** (125 Parsons Rd., 843/875-2600, www.

woodlandsmansion.com, $500 and up) is one of a handful of inns in the United States with a five-star rating both for lodging and dining. Its 18 guest rooms within the 1906 great house are decorated in a mix of old-fashioned plantation high style and contemporary designer aesthetics, with modern, luxurious baths. There's also a freestanding guest cottage ($950) that seeks to replicate a hunting lodge vibe. There's a full day spa on the premises; the most basic offering, a one-hour massage, will run you about $120. Within Woodlands is its award-winning world-class restaurant, simply called **The Dining Room** (Mon.-Sat. 11am-2pm and 6pm-9pm, brunch Sun. 11:30am-2pm, $40-50). The 900-entry wine list and sommelier are collectively fantastic, as are the desserts. Jackets are required, and reservations are strongly advised.

MOUNT PLEASANT AND EAST COOPER
$150-300

One of the more accessible and enjoyable resort-type stays in the Charleston area is on the Isle of Palms at **Wild Dunes Resort** (5757 Palm Blvd., 888/778-1876, www.wilddunes.com, $275-350). This is the place to go for relaxing, beach-oriented vacation fun in your choice of a traditional hotel room, a house, or a villa. Bustling Mount Pleasant is only a couple of minutes away, and Charleston proper not much farther.

FOLLY BEACH AND THE SOUTHWEST ISLANDS
$150-300

The upbeat but still cozy **Tides Folly Beach** (1 Center St., 843/588-6464, www.tidesfollybeach.com, $200-300) boutique hotel has a combination of attentive staff, great oceanfront views, and an excellent on-site restaurant, Blu.

Over $300

The beautiful island of Kiawah—about 45 minutes from downtown Charleston—has as its main attraction the sumptuous

★ **Kiawah Island Golf Resort** (1 Sanctuary Beach Dr., 800/654-2924, www.kiawahgolf. com, $500-1000), a frequent venue for PGA tournaments. But even if you don't play golf, the resort is an amazing stay. The main component is The Sanctuary, an upscale hotel featuring an opulent lobby complete with grand staircases, a large pool area overlooking the beach, tasteful Spanish Colonial-style architecture, and 255 smallish but excellently appointed guest rooms.

CAMPING

Charleston County runs a family-friendly, fairly boisterous campground at **James Island County Park** (871 Riverland Dr., 843/795-7275, www.ccprc.com, $31 tent site, $37 pull-through site). A neat feature here is the $5-per-person round-trip shuttle to the visitors center downtown, Folly Beach Pier, and Folly Beach County Park. The park also has 10 furnished cottages (843/795-4386, $138) for rent, sleeping up to eight people. Reservations are recommended. For more commercial camping in Mount Pleasant, try the **KOA of Mount Pleasant** (3157 U.S. 17 N., 843/849-5177, www.koa.com, from $30 tent sites, from $50 pull-through sites).

Transportation and Services

AIR

Way up in North Charleston is **Charleston International Airport** (CHS, 5500 International Blvd., 843/767-1100, www.chs-airport.com), served by American (www. aa.com), Delta (www.delta.com), JetBlue (www.jetblue.com), and Southwest (www. southwest.com).

It'll take about 20 minutes to make the 12-mile drive from the airport to downtown, and vice versa. The airport is conveniently located just off the I-526/Mark Clark Expressway perimeter highway off I-26. As in most cities, taxi service from the airport is regulated. This translates to about $30 for two people from the airport to Charleston Place downtown.

CAR

There are two main routes into Charleston: I-26 from the west-northwest (which dead-ends downtown) and U.S. 17 from the west (called Savannah Highway when it gets close to Charleston proper), which continues east over the Ravenel Bridge into Mount Pleasant and beyond. There's a fairly new perimeter highway, I-526 (Mark Clark Expressway), which loops around the city from West Ashley to North Charleston to Daniel Island and into Mount Pleasant. It's accessible both from I-26 and U.S. 17.

Keep in mind that I-95, while certainly a gateway to the region, is actually a good ways out of Charleston, about 30 miles west of the city. Charleston is almost exactly two hours from Savannah by car, and about an hour's drive from Beaufort and Hilton Head.

Car Rentals

Charleston International Airport has rental kiosks for **Avis** (843/767-7031), **Budget** (843/767-7051), **Dollar** (843/767-1130), **Enterprise** (843/767-1109), **Hertz** (843/767-4550), **National** (843/767-3078), and **Thrifty** (843/647-4389). There are a couple of rental locations downtown: **Budget** (390 Meeting St., 843/577-5195) and **Enterprise** (398 Meeting St., 843/723-6215). **Hertz** has a location in West Ashley (3025 Ashley Town Center Dr., 843/573-2147), as does **Enterprise** (2004 Savannah Hwy., 843/556-7889).

BUS

Public transportation by **Charleston Area Regional Transit Authority** (CARTA, 843/724-7420, www.ridecarta.com) is a convenient and inexpensive way to enjoy Charleston without the more structured nature of an organized tour. There's a wide variety of routes, but most visitors will limit their acquaintance to the tidy, trolley-like **DASH** (Downtown Area Shuttle, free) buses run by CARTA primarily for visitors. Keep in mind that DASH only stops at designated places.

TAXI

The South is generally not big on taxis, and Charleston is no exception. The best bet is simply to call rather than try to flag one down. Charleston's most fun service is **Charleston Black Cabs** (843/216-2627, www.charlestonblackcabcompany.com), using Americanized versions of the classic British taxi. A one-way ride anywhere on the peninsula below the bridges is about $10 per person, and rates go up from there. They're very popular, so call as far ahead as you can or try to get one at their stand at Charleston Place. Two other good services are **Safety Cab** (843/722-4066) and **Yellow Cab** (843/577-6565).

You can also try a human-powered taxi service from **Charleston Rickshaw** (843/723-5685). A cheerful (and energetic) young cyclist will pull you and a friend to most points on the Lower Peninsula for about $10-15. Call 'em or find one by City Market. They work late on Friday and Saturday nights too.

PARKING

As you'll quickly see, parking is at a premium in downtown Charleston. An exception seems to be the large number of free spaces all along the Battery, but unless you're an exceptionally strong walker, that's too far south to use as a reliable base from which to explore the whole peninsula.

Metered spaces are enforced 8am-6pm Monday-Saturday. Most metered parking downtown is on and around Calhoun Street, Meeting Street, King Street, Market Street, and East Bay Street.

The city has several conveniently located and comparatively inexpensive parking garages. I strongly suggest that you make use of them. They're located at the aquarium,

Camden and Exchange Streets, Charleston Place, Concord and Cumberland Streets, East Bay and Prioleau Streets, Marion Square, Gaillard Auditorium, Liberty and St. Philip Streets, Majestic Square, the Charleston Visitor Reception and Transportation Center, and Wentworth Street.

The city's website (www.charlestoncity. info) has a good interactive map of parking.

TOURIST INFORMATION
Visitors Centers

I highly recommend a stop at the **Charleston Visitor Reception and Transportation Center** (375 Meeting St., 800/774-0006, www.charlestoncvb.com, Mon.-Fri. 8:30am-5pm). I also recommend using the attached parking garage not only for your stop at the center but also anytime you want to see the many sights this part of town has to offer, such as the Charleston Museum, the Manigault and Aiken-Rhett Houses, and the Children's Museum. Go to the center to take advantage of the great deal offered by the **Charleston Heritage Passport** (www. heritagefederation.org), which gives you 40 percent off admission to all of Charleston's key historic homes, the Charleston Museum, and the two awesome plantation sites on the Ashley River: Drayton Hall and Middleton Place. You can get the Heritage Passport *only* at the Charleston Visitor Reception and Transportation Center on Meeting Street.

Other area visitors centers include the **Mount Pleasant-Isle of Palms Visitors Center** (99 Harry M. Hallman Jr. Blvd., 800/774-0006, daily 9am-5pm) and the **North Charleston Visitors Center** (4975B Centre Pointe Dr., 843/853-8000, Mon.-Sat. 10am-5pm).

Hospitals

If there's a silver lining in getting sick or injured in Charleston, it's that there are plenty of high-quality medical facilities available. The premier institution is the **Medical University of South Carolina** (171 Ashley Ave., 843/792-2300, www.muschealth.com)

in the northwest part of the peninsula. Two notable facilities are near each other downtown: **Roper Hospital** (316 Calhoun St., 843/402-2273, www.roperhospital.com) and **Charleston Memorial Hospital** (326 Calhoun St., 843/792-2300). In Mount Pleasant there's **East Cooper Regional Medical Center** (1200 Johnnie Dodds Blvd., www.eastcoopermedctr.com). In West Ashley there's **Bon Secours St. Francis Hospital** (2095 Henry Tecklenburg Ave., 843/402-2273, www.ropersaintfrancis.com).

Police

For nonemergencies in Charleston, West Ashley, and James Island, contact the **Charleston Police Department** (843/577-7434, www.charlestoncity.info). You can also contact the police department in Mount Pleasant (843/884-4176). North Charleston is a separate municipality with its own police department (843/308-4718, www.northcharleston.org). Of course, for emergencies always call **911.**

Media

The daily newspaper of record is the *Post and Courier* (www.charleston.net). Its entertainment insert, *Preview,* comes out on Thursdays. The free alternative weekly is the *Charleston City Paper* (www.charlestoncity-paper.com), which comes out on Wednesdays and is the best place to find local music and arts listings. A particularly well-done and lively metro glossy is *Charleston* magazine (www.charlestonmag.com), which comes out once a month.

The National Public Radio affiliate is the South Carolina ETV radio station WSCI at 89.3 FM. South Carolina ETV is on television at WITV. The local NBC affiliate is WCBD, the CBS affiliate is WCSC, the ABC affiliate is WCIV, and the Fox affiliate is WTAT.

Libraries

The main branch of the **Charleston County Public Library** (68 Calhoun St., 843/805-6801, www.ccpl.org, Mon.-Thurs. 9am-9pm, Fri.-Sat. 9am-6pm, Sun. 2pm-5pm) has been at its current site since 1998. Named for Sullivan's Island's most famous visitor, the **Edgar Allan Poe Library** (1921 I'on Ave., 843/883-3914, www.ccpl.org, Mon. and Fri. 2pm-6pm, Tues., Thurs., and Sat. 10am-2pm) has been housed in Battery Gadsden, a former Spanish-American War gun emplacement, since 1977.

The College of Charleston's main library is the **Marlene and Nathan Addlestone Library** (205 Calhoun St., 843/953-5530, www.cofc.edu), home to special collections, the Center for Student Learning, the main computer lab, the media collection, and even a café. The college's **Avery Research Center for African American History and Culture** (125 Bull St., 843/953-7609, www.cofc.edu/avery, Mon.-Fri. 10am-5pm, Sat. noon-5pm) houses documents relating to the history and culture of African Americans in the Lowcountry.

For other historical research on the area, check out the collections of the **South Carolina Historical Society** (100 Meeting St., 843/723-3225, www.southcarolinahistoricalsociety.org, Mon.-Fri. 9am-4pm, Sat. 9am-2pm). There's a $5 research fee for nonmembers.

LGBTQ Resources

Contrary to many media portrayals of the region, Charleston is quite open to the LGBTQ community, which plays a major role in arts, culture, and business. As with any other place in the South, however, it's generally expected that people—straights as well—will keep personal matters and politics to themselves in public settings. A key local advocacy group is the **Alliance for Full Acceptance** (29 Leinbach Dr., Ste. D-3, 843/883-0343, www.affa-sc.org). The **Lowcountry Gay and Lesbian Alliance** (843/720-8088) holds a potluck the last Sunday of each month. For the most up-to-date happenings, try the *Charleston City Paper.*

Myrtle Beach and the Grand Strand

The West has Las Vegas, Florida has Orlando, and South Carolina has Myrtle Beach.

There's no Bellagio Resort or Magic Kingdom here, but Myrtle Beach remains the number one travel destination in the state, with even more visitors than Charleston. Unlike Charleston, you'll find little history here. With several theme parks, 100 golf courses, 50 miniature golf courses, over 2,000 restaurants—not to mention miles of beautiful shoreline—Myrtle Beach is built for all-out vacation enjoyment. The hot, hazy height of the summer marks the busy season on the Strand, when its long main drag, Kings Highway (aka Business U.S. 17), is packed full of families eager for more swimming, more shopping, more eating, and just plain more.

While to many people the name Myrtle Beach conjures an image of tacky, downscale people doing tacky, downscale things, that's an outmoded stereotype. Tacky is certainly still in vogue here, but an influx of higher-quality development, both in accommodations and entertainment value, has lifted the bar significantly. Rather than slumming in a beat-up motel, quaffing PBR on the beach, and loading up on $2 T-shirts like in the "good old days," a typical Myrtle Beach vacation now involves a stay in a large condo apartment with flat-screen TVs, a full kitchen, and a sumptuous palmetto-lined pool; dining at the House of Blues; having drinks at the Hard Rock Café; stops at high-profile attractions like Ripley's Aquarium; and shopping at trendy retailers like Anthropologie and Abercrombie & Fitch.

The Grand Strand on which Myrtle Beach sits—a long, sandy peninsula stretching 60 miles from Winyah Bay to the North Carolina border—has been a vacation playground for generations of South Carolinians. Unlike Hilton Head, where New York and Midwestern accents are more common than Lowcountry drawls, Myrtle Beach and the Grand Strand remain largely homegrown passions, with many visitors living within a few hours' drive. Despite the steady increase of money and high-dollar development in the area, its strongly regional nature works to your advantage in that prices are generally lower than in Vegas or Orlando.

To the south of Myrtle proper lies the understated, affluent, and relaxing Pawleys Island, with nearby Murrells Inlet and its

Previous: family fun at Myrtle Beach; Ripley's Aquarium at Broadway at the Beach. **Above:** lounging chairs on Myrtle Beach.

Look for ★ to find recommended sights, activities, dining, and lodging.

Highlights

★ **Broadway at the Beach:** You'll find good cheesy fun along with tons of interesting shops, theme restaurants, and, of course, miniature golf (page 100).

★ **Barefoot Landing:** This commercial hub is North Myrtle Beach's answer to Broadway at the Beach, with the Alabama Theatre and the House of Blues nearby (page 102).

★ **Ocean Drive Beach:** The still-beating, still-shuffling heart of the Grand Strand is also the center of shag dancing culture (page 104).

★ **Carolina Opry:** This popular show offers corny but high quality family entertainment in an intimate, friendly setting (page 106).

★ **Brookgreen Gardens:** Enjoy the country's largest collection of outdoor sculptures, set amid a fine collection of formal gardens (page 126).

★ **Huntington Beach State Park:** The scenic beach combines with one-of-a-kind Atalaya Castle to make a unique getaway (page 126).

★ **Hampton Plantation:** This historic Georgian mansion on the scenic Wambaw Creek inspired a South Carolina poet laureate to give it to the state for posterity (page 132).

Myrtle Beach and the Grand Strand

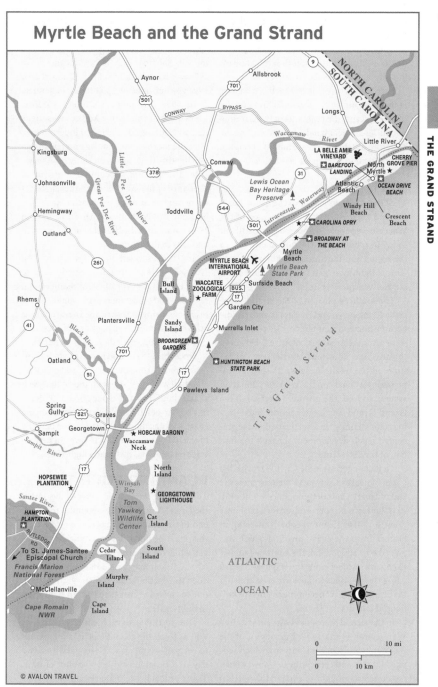

© AVALON TRAVEL

great seafood restaurants. Unique, eclectic Brookgreen Gardens hosts the largest collection of outdoor sculpture in the country, with one-of-a-kind Huntington Beach State Park literally right across the street.

Even farther south, in the northern quarter of the Lowcountry proper, you'll find a totally different scene: the remnants of the Carolina rice culture in quaint old Georgetown, and the haunting antebellum mansions at Hampton Plantation and Hopsewee Plantation.

HISTORY

The Grand Strand was once the happy hunting and shellfish-gathering grounds of the Waccamaw people, whose legacy is still felt today in the name of the dominant river in the region and the Strand's main drag itself, Kings Highway, which is actually built on an old Native American trail.

The southern portion of the Strand, especially Georgetown and Pawleys Island, rapidly became home to a number of rice plantations soon after the area was colonized. However, the area now known as Myrtle Beach didn't share in the wealth because its soil and topography weren't conducive to the plantation system. Indeed, the northern portion of the Grand Strand was largely uninhabited during colonial times, and hurricane damage prevented much development through the first half of the 19th century.

That changed after the Civil War with the boom of nearby Conway to the west, now the seat of Horry County (pronounced "OR-ee"). As Conway's lumber and export economy grew, a railroad spur was built to bring in lumber from the coast, much of which was owned by a single firm, the Conway Lumber Company. Lumber company employees began using the rail lines to take vacation time on the Strand, in effect becoming the first of millions of tourists to the area.

In the second half of the 19th century, Civil War veteran Franklin G. Burroughs, of the Burroughs and Collins Company, which supplied lumber and turpentine to Conway business interests, sought to expand the tourism profitability of the coastal area. He died in 1897, but his heirs continued his dream, inaugurated by the opening of the Seaside Inn in 1901. The first bona fide resort came in the 1920s with the building of the Arcady resort, which included the first golf course in the area.

In 1938 Burroughs's widow, Adeline, known locally as "Miss Addie," was credited with giving the town its modern name, after the locally abundant wax myrtle shrub. During this time, locals on the Strand originated the shagging subculture, built around the dance of the same name and celebrated at numerous pavilions and "beach clubs." The building of Myrtle Beach Air Force Base in 1940—now closed—brought further growth and jobs to the area.

Tourism, especially, grew apace here until Hurricane Hazel virtually wiped the slate clean in 1954. In typical Carolinian fashion, residents and landowners made lemonade out of lemons, using the hurricane's devastation as an excuse to build even bigger resort developments, including a plethora of golf courses.

Since then, the Strand has grown to encompass about 250,000 permanent residents, with about 10 million visitors on top of that each year. A huge influx of money in the 1990s led to a higher-dollar form of development on the coast, sadly leading to the demolition of many of the old beach pavilions in favor of new attractions and massive condo high-rises.

PLANNING YOUR TIME

The most important thing to remember is that the Grand Strand is *long*—60 miles from one end to the other. This has real-world effects that must be taken into account. For example, while the separate municipality of North Myrtle Beach may sound like it is right next door to Myrtle Beach proper, getting from one to the other can take half an hour even in light traffic.

Due to this geographical stretching, as well as to all the attractions, it is impossible to cover this area in a single day, and even two days is a ridiculously short amount of time. That's probably the main reason many folks indulge in a weekly rental. Not only does it give you enough time to see everything, but it enables you to relax, slow down, and enjoy the beaches and the general laid-back attitude.

In May, Memorial Day weekend and Bike Week have traditionally signaled the beginning of the tourism season in Myrtle Beach. The busy season exactly corresponds with the hottest months of the year, July and August. This is when crowds are at their peak, restaurants are most crowded, and the two spurs of U.S. 17 are at their most gridlocked.

Springtime in Myrtle Beach is quite nice, but keep in mind that water temperatures are still chilly through April. There is almost always one last cold snap in March that augurs the spring.

Personally, I recommend hitting Myrtle Beach just as the busy season wanes, right after Labor Day. Rooms are significantly cheaper, but most everything is still fully open and adequately staffed, with the added benefit of the biggest crush of visitors being absent. Similarly, for some really inexpensive room rates, try to hit town in late February.

Winter on the Grand Strand is very slow, as befitting this very seasonal locale. Many restaurants, especially down the Strand near Murrells Inlet, close entirely through February.

ORIENTATION

This part of the Strand comprises several municipalities, from Surfside Beach to the south up to Little River near the North Carolina border, but for all intents and purposes it's one big place all its own. As a general rule, development (read: money) is moving more quickly to the North Myrtle Beach area rather than the older Myrtle Beach proper to the south.

North Myrtle is actually a recent aggregation of several historic beachfront communities: Windy Hill, Crescent Beach, Cherry Grove, and Ocean Drive. You'll see numerous signs announcing the entrance or exit into or out of these communities, but keep in mind you're still technically in North Myrtle Beach.

The **Grand Strand grid** is based on a system of east-west avenues beginning just north of Myrtle Beach State Park. Confusingly, these are separated into "North" and "South" avenues. Perhaps even more confusing, North Myrtle Beach also uses its own distinct north-and-south avenue system, also for roads running east-west. Got it?

It goes like this: Myrtle Beach starts with 29th Avenue South at the Myrtle Beach International Airport and goes up to 1st Avenue South just past Family Kingdom Amusement Park. From here, the avenues are labeled as "North" from 1st Avenue North up to 82nd Avenue North, which concludes Myrtle Beach proper. North Myrtle Beach begins at 48th Avenue South near Barefoot Landing and goes up to Main Street (the center of the shag culture). It continues with 1st Avenue North, goes up to 24th Avenue North (Cherry Grove Beach), and finally concludes at 61st Avenue North, near the North Carolina state line.

Sights

TOP EXPERIENCE

★ BROADWAY AT THE BEACH

Love it or hate it, **Broadway at the Beach** (1325 Celebrity Circle, 800/386-4662, www. broadwayatthebeach.com, summer daily 10am-11pm, winter daily 10am-6pm), between 21st and 29th Avenues, is one of Myrtle's biggest and flashiest attractions—which is saying a lot. Opened in the late 1990s and expanded significantly since then, this collection of three hotels, over two dozen restaurants, about 50 shops, and a dozen kid-oriented activities sprawls over 350 acres with several other major attractions, restaurants, and clubs (such as the Hard Rock Café) on its periphery.

Just like the Magic Kingdom that many of Myrtle's attractions seek to emulate, Broadway at the Beach has at its center a large lagoon, around which everything else is situated. Needless to say, there's also a massive parking lot. Activity goes on all day and well into the wee hours, with the weekly Tuesday-night fireworks a big draw. While there's plenty to do, what with the great shops, tasty treats, and piped-in music following you everywhere, it's also fun just to walk around.

The biggest attraction at Broadway—and it's really big—is **Wonderworks** (1313 Celebrity Circle, 843/626-9962, www.wonderworksonline.com, Sun.-Thurs. 10am-8pm, Fri.-Sat. 10am-9pm, $23 adults, $15 children). You can't miss it—look for the thing that looks exactly like a massive, crumbling, upside-down creepy mansion. Inside you'll find a wide and quite varied assortment of interactive experiences designed to let you know what it's like to be upside down, or on a bed of nails, or in a hurricane, or freezing after the *Titanic* sank, and things of that nature. Think Ripley's Believe It or Not updated for a modern age, complete with laser tag.

Adjacent to the main Wonderworks building is the **Soar and Explore Zipline and Ropes Course** (daily noon-dusk, hours vary seasonally, zip line $19.95, ropes course $11.99, combo $26.99), where you can strap in and zip 1,000 feet overwater across the large lagoon around which Broadway at the Beach is constructed.

Medieval Times (2904 Fantasy Way, 843/236-4635, www.medievaltimes.com, $51 adults, $31 ages 3-12, free under age 3) is a combination dinner theater and medieval tournament reenactment. If the ticket prices sound high, keep in mind you're getting a three-course meal and a professional show done largely on horseback. Ask around for coupons to get a discount.

Now that almost all of the old-fashioned amusement parks at Myrtle Beach are gone, victims of "modernization," you can find a

Wonderworks is an upside-down mansion!

facsimile of sorts at **Pavilion Nostalgia Park** (843/913-9400, www.pavilionnostalgiapark.com, summer daily 11am-11pm, hours vary in other seasons, rides $3 each), which seeks to simulate the days of Myrtle gone by.

Of course, nowhere in Myrtle is really complete without miniature golf, and Broadway at the Beach's version is **Dragon's Lair Fantasy Golf** (1197 Celebrity Circle, 843/913-9301, $9), with two medieval-themed 18-hole courses boasting a fire-breathing dragon.

Ripley's Aquarium

If you've been to Boston's New England Aquarium, don't expect something similar at **Ripley's Aquarium** (1110 Celebrity Circle, 800/734-8888, www.ripleysaquarium.com, Sun.-Thurs. 9am-9pm, Fri.-Sat. 9am-10pm, $22 adults, $11 ages 6-11, $4 ages 2-5, free under age 2) at Broadway at the Beach. This is a smaller but quite delightful aquarium built primarily for entertainment purposes rather than education. Calming music plays throughout, and a moving sidewalk takes you around and under a huge main tank filled with various marine creatures. There's even the requisite stingray-petting touch tank.

You might see the garish billboards for the aquarium up and down U.S. 17, featuring massive sharks baring rows of scary teeth. But don't expect an over-the-top shark exhibit—the truth is that most of the sharks in the aquarium are smaller and much more peaceful.

Broadway Grand Prix

Just outside Broadway at the Beach you'll find the **Broadway Grand Prix** (1820 21st Ave. N., 843/839-4080, www.broadwaygrandprix.com, summer daily 10am-midnight, shorter hours in other seasons, from $20), where can you speed around in little go-karts on your choice of seven tracks, organized according to speed, age, and skill level. This being Myrtle Beach, there's other family-oriented entertainment offered here, including a rock-climbing wall and, of course, miniature golf.

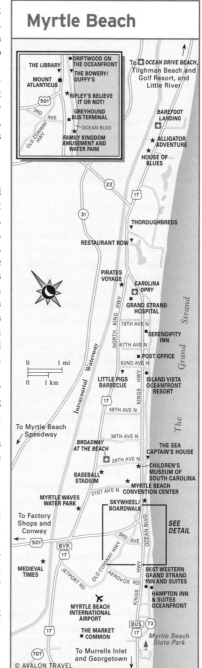

Myrtle Beach

© AVALON TRAVEL

THE GRAND STRAND
SIGHTS

Myrtle Waves Water Park

Billed as South Carolina's largest water park, **Myrtle Waves Water Park** (U.S. 17 Bypass and 10th Ave. N., 843/913-9260, www.myrtlewaves.com, May-Labor Day 10am-dusk, $25 ages 7 and over, $23 ages 3-6, free under age 3) is right across the street from Broadway at the Beach, covers 20 acres, and features all kinds of safe, fun "rides," such as the Ocean in Motion Wave Pool, the Layzee River, and the Saturation Station, where a huge water volcano absolutely soaks everybody in proximity every five minutes or so. That's just to name a few.

As you would expect, there are plenty of lifeguards on hand at all the rides. Food is plentiful if unremarkable, and there are shaded areas for the less adventurous to chill while the kids splash around. With one admission price covering all rides all day, this is one of the better deals in Myrtle Beach, which has more than its share of confusingly (and occasionally exorbitantly) priced attractions.

MYRTLE BEACH BOARDWALK AND PROMENADE

The **Boardwalk** (www.visitmyrtlebeach.com, daily 24 hours, free) is the new pride of old Myrtle, greatly improving civic life and morale. The fun, meandering 1.2-mile jaunt from the 2nd Avenue Pier to the 14th Avenue Pier is built in three distinct sections, not only leading you through the commercial areas of the waterfront, but also allowing easy pedestrian beach access. One section provides a nice peaceful walking experience amid the dunes.

Skywheel

You can't miss spotting the **Skywheel** (1110 N. Ocean Blvd., 843/839-9200, http://myrtlebeachskywheel.com, summer daily noon-midnight, $13 adults, $9 children), a huge Ferris wheel dominating the skyline at the Boardwalk. The cars are family-size and fully enclosed, and offer a great view of the ocean and surrounding area during the approximately 10-minute, three-rotation trip.

★ BAREFOOT LANDING

Before the arrival of Broadway at the Beach, the Strand's original high-concept retail and dining complex was **Barefoot Landing** (4898 U.S. 17 S., 843/272-8349, www.bflanding.com, hours vary). It's less flashy on the surface and certainly more tasteful, but just as commercial.

The centerpiece of the two-decade-old entertainment and shopping complex is **The Alabama Theatre** (4750 U.S. 17 S., 843/272-5758, www.alabama-theatre.com, ticket prices vary), a project of the famed country-and-western band of the same name, who despite their eponymous roots actually got their start gigging in juke joints in the Grand Strand. A stone's throw away is the **House of Blues** (4640 U.S. 17 S., 843/272-3000, www.hob.com, ticket prices vary), bringing in name acts on an almost nightly basis as well as diners to its excellent restaurant. On some nights you can pose for a picture with a real live tiger cub on your lap at **T.I.G.E.R.S. Preservation Station** (843/361-4552, www.tigerfriends.com, hours vary, free). Shopping is mostly the name of the game here, though.

Alligator Adventure

One of the most popular attractions within Barefoot Landing is **Alligator Adventure** (843/361-0789, www.alligatoradventure.com, daily 9am-7pm, $21.99 adults, $16.99 ages 4-12, free under age 4). They have hundreds of alligators, yes, but also plenty of turtles, tortoises, snakes, and birds. The otters are a big hit as well. The highlight, though, comes during the daily alligator feedings, when you get a chance to see the real power and barely controlled aggression of these magnificent indigenous beasts. Keep in mind that due to the cold-blooded reptiles' dormant winter nature, the feedings are not held in the colder months.

CHILDREN'S MUSEUM OF SOUTH CAROLINA

A less-expensive form of entertainment with an added educational component at Myrtle is the **Children's Museum of South Carolina**

(2501 N. Kings Hwy., 843/946-9469, www. cmsckids.org, summer Mon.-Sat. 9am-5pm, Sun. noon-5pm, $8). This facility tries hard to compete with the splashier attractions in town but still manages to keep a reasonably strong educational focus with programs like "Crime Lab Chemistry," "World of Art," and "Space Adventures."

FAMILY KINGDOM AMUSEMENT AND WATER PARK

For a taste of old-time beachfront amusement park fun, try the **Family Kingdom** (300 4th Ave. S., 843/626-3471, www.family-kingdom. com, free admission, cost of rides varies) overlooking the Atlantic Ocean. It boasts several good old-school rides, such as the Sling Shot, the Yo-Yo, and everyone's favorite, the wooden Swamp Fox roller coaster with a crazy 110-foot free fall. The attached water park, though not a match to the one at Broadway at the Beach, is a lot of fun, with the requisite slides and a long "lazy river" floating ride.

There is no admission charge—you pay by the ride (although all-inclusive wristbands are available starting at $27). This means parents and grandparents without the stomach for the

rides don't have to pay through the nose just to chauffeur the little ones who do.

RIPLEY'S BELIEVE IT OR NOT!

Distinct in all but name from Ripley's Aquarium at Broadway at the Beach, this combo attraction down in the older area of Myrtle Beach—but very close to the brand-new Boardwalk—features several separate, though more or less adjacent, offerings from the venerable Ripley's franchise.

The **Ripley's Believe It or Not! Odditorium** (901 N. Ocean Blvd., 843/448-2331, www.ripleys.com, Sun.-Thurs. 10am-10pm, Fri.-Sat. 10am-11pm, $15 adults, $10 ages 6-11, free under age 6) is a repository of strange artifacts from around the world, updated with video and computer graphics for the new generation. It's fun and easy and takes no more than a half hour.

Ripley's Haunted Adventure (915 N. Ocean Blvd., 843/448-2331, www.ripleys.com, Sun.-Thurs. noon-10pm, Fri.-Sat. noon-11pm, $15 adults, $10 ages 6-11, free under age 6) is a sort of scaled-down version of Disney's famous Haunted House ride, with live actors scaring you through three floors.

Ripley's Believe It or Not!

Ripley's Moving Theater (917 N. Ocean Blvd., 843/448-2331, www.ripleys.com, Sun.-Thurs. 10am-10pm, Fri.-Sat. 10am-11pm, $15 adults, $10 ages 6-11, free under age 6) is a combined ride and movie theater featuring two motion-oriented films screened on a self-contained human conveyor belt, with a sort of kinetic IMAX effect.

★ OCEAN DRIVE BEACH

Less an actual place than a state of mind, the "OD" up in North Myrtle Beach is notable for its role in spawning one of America's great musical genres, beach music. Don't confuse beach music with the Beach Boys or Dick Dale—that's surf music. Beach music, simply put, is music to dance the shag to. Think the Drifters, the Platters, and the Swingin' Medallions.

To experience the OD, go to the intersection of Ocean Boulevard and Main Street and take in the vibe. There's still major shag action going on up here, specifically at several clubs specializing in the genre. If you don't want to shag, don't worry—this is still a charming, laid-back area that's a lot of fun simply to stroll around and enjoy a hot dog or ice cream cone.

CHERRY GROVE PIER

One of the few grand old pavilions left on the Southeast coast, North Myrtle's **Cherry Grove Pier** (3500 N. Ocean Blvd., 843/249-1625, www.cherrygrovepier.com, Sun.-Thurs. 6am-midnight, Fri.-Sat. 6am-2am, free) was built in the 1950s. Despite renovations in the late 1990s, it still retains that nostalgic feel, with anglers casting into the waters and kids eating ice cream cones. There's a neat two-story observation deck, and on a clear day you can see North Carolina.

Unusually, this is a privately owned pier. It's particularly popular with anglers, who have their state licensing needs covered by the pier. Get bait or rent a fishing rod ($20 per day plus refundable $50 deposit) at the **Tackle and Gift Shop** (843/249-1625). They'll also sell you a crab net to cast off the pier ($6, licenses and permits included).

TOURS

The number of tours offered in Myrtle Beach is nothing compared to Charleston, this being much more of a "doing" place than a "seeing" place. The most fun and comprehensive tour in the area is **Coastal Safari Jeep Tours** (843/497-5330, www.carolinasafari.com, $38 adults, $20 children), which takes you on a guided tour in a super-size Jeep (holding 12-14 people). You'll go well off the commercial path to see such sights on the Waccamaw Neck as old plantations, Civil War sites, and slave cabins, as well as hear lots of ghost stories. They'll pick you up at most area hotels.

Entertainment and Events

NIGHTLIFE

Any discussion of Myrtle Beach nightlife must begin with a nod to **The Bowery** (110 9th Ave. N., 843/626-3445, www.theborerybar. com, daily 11am-2am), a country-and-western and Southern-rock spot right off the beach, which has survived several hurricanes since opening in 1944. Its roadhouse-style decor hasn't changed a whole lot since then, other than some cheesy marketing to play up its role in history as the place where the country band Alabama got its start playing for tips in 1973 under the name Wildcountry. They were still playing gigs here when their first big single, "Tennessee River," hit the charts in 1980.

Bands usually crank up here around 9pm, and there is a nominal cover charge. There's only one type of draft beer served at The Bowery, at $2.50 per mug, and there is no real dance floor to speak of. If the proud display of Confederate flags doesn't bother you, it's usually a lot of fun. Next door is The Bowery's

The Bowery

"sister bar," **Duffy's** (110 9th Ave. N., 843/626-3445, daily 11am-2am), owned by the same folks and with a similarly down-home vibe, except without the live music.

For a more upscale if definitely less personal and unique experience, Broadway at the Beach hosts the high-profile **Hard Rock Café** (1304 Celebrity Circle, 843/946-0007, www.hardrock.com, daily 11am-midnight). This is a new location as of 2016, the previous landmark pyramid having been demolished.

You don't have to be a Parrothead to enjoy **Jimmy Buffett's Margaritaville** (1114 Celebrity Circle, 843/448-5455, www.margaritavillemyrtlebeach.com, daily 11am-midnight) at Broadway at the Beach, actually a pretty enjoyable experience considering it's a national chain. The eponymous margaritas are, of course, the beverage highlight, but they also serve Jimmy's signature LandShark Lager on tap for beer lovers.

In addition to its attached live performance space, the **House of Blues** (4640 U.S. 17 S., 843/272-3000, www.hob.com) at Barefoot Landing features a hopping bar in its dining area, situated amid a plethora of folk art reminiscent of the Mississippi Delta. Most nights feature live entertainment starting at about 10pm, with one of the best-mixed sound systems you're likely to hear.

SHAG DANCING

North Myrtle Beach is the nexus of that Carolina-based dance known as the shag. There are several clubs in town that have made a name for themselves as the unofficial "shag clubs" of South Carolina. The two main ones are **Duck's** (229 Main St., 843/249-3858, www.ducksatoceandrive.com) and **Fat Harold's** (210 Main St., 843/249-5779, www.fatharolds.com). There's also **The Pirate's Cove** (205 Main St., 843/249-8942).

Another fondly regarded spot is the **OD Pavilion** (91 S. Ocean Blvd., 843/280-0715), aka the Sunset Grill or "Pam's Palace," on the same site as the old Roberts Pavilion that was destroyed by 1954's Hurricane Hazel. Legend has it this was where the shag was born. Also in North Myrtle, the **Ocean Drive Beach Club** (98 N. Ocean Blvd., 843/249-6460), aka "the OD Lounge," inside the Ocean Drive Beach and Golf Resort, specializes in shag dancing most days after 4pm. The resort is a focal point of local shag conventions and is

The Story of the Shag

Duck's is one of the oldest shag emporiums.

In South Carolina, the shag is neither a type of rug nor what Austin Powers does in his spare time. It's a dance—a smooth, laid-back, happy dance done to that equally smooth, laid-back, happy kind of rhythm and blues called beach music (not to be confused with surf music such as the Beach Boys). The boys twirl the girls while their feet kick and slide around with a minimum of upper-body movement—the better to stay cool in the Carolina heat.

Descended from the Charleston, another indigenous Palmetto State dance, the shag originated on the Strand sometime in the 1930s, when the popular Collegiate Shag was slowed down to

even home to the **Shaggers Hall of Fame.** Also inside the Ocean Drive Resort is another popular shag club, **The Spanish Galleon** (100 N. Ocean Blvd., 843/249-1047), aka "the Galleon."

Key local shag events, which are quite well attended, include the **National Shag Dance Championships** (www.shagnationals.com, Jan.-Mar.), the **Spring Safari** (www.shagdance.com, Apr.), and the **Fall Migration** (www.shagdance.com, mid-Sept.).

SHOWS
★ Carolina Opry

Nothing can duplicate the experience of the Grand Ole Opry in Nashville, but don't

snicker at Myrtle's **Carolina Opry** (8901-A Business U.S. 17, 800/843-6779, www.thecarolinaopry.com, showtimes and ticket prices vary). Since 1986 this well-respected stage show, begun by legendary promoter Calvin Gilmore, has packed 'em in at the Grand Strand. It is a hoot for country music fans and city slickers alike.

The main focus is the regular Opry show, done in the classic, freewheeling, fast-moving variety format known to generations of old-school country fans from the original Opry. Some of the humor is corny, and the brief but open displays of patriotic and faith-based music aren't necessarily for everyone. But there's no arguing the high energy and the subgenre now called the Carolina Shag. While shag scholars differ as to the exact spawning ground, there's a consensus that North Myrtle Beach's Ocean Drive, or "OD" in local patois, became the home of the modern shag sometime in the mid-1940s.

Legend has it that the real shag was born when white teenagers, "jumping the Jim Crow rope" by watching dancers at black nightclubs in the segregated South, brought those moves back to the beach and added their own twists. Indeed, while the shag has always been primarily practiced by white people, many of the leading beach music bands were (and still are) African American.

By the mid-late 1950s, the shag, often called simply "the basic" or "the fas' dance," was all the rage with the Strand's young people, who gathered at beachfront pavilions and in local juke joints called beach clubs, courting each other to the sounds of early beach music greats like the Drifters, the Clovers, and Maurice Williams and the Zodiacs. This is the time period most fondly remembered by today's shaggers, a time of penny loafers (no socks!), poodle skirts, and 45-rpm records, when the sea breeze was the only air-conditioning.

The shag is practiced today by a graying but devoted cadre of older fans, with a vanguard of younger practitioners keeping the art form alive. A coterie of North Myrtle clubs specializes in the dance, while the area hosts several large-scale gatherings of shag aficionados each year.

To immerse yourself in shag culture, head on up to Ocean Drive Beach in North Myrtle at the intersection of Ocean Boulevard and Main Street and look down at the platters in the sidewalk marking the **Shaggers Walk of Fame.** Walk a couple of blocks up to the corner of Main Street and Hillside Drive and visit the mecca of beach music stores, **Judy's House of Oldies** (300 Main St., 843/249-8649, www.judyshouseofoldies.com, Mon.-Sat. 9am-6pm). They also sell instructional DVDs.

To get a taste of the dance itself, stop by the **OD Pavilion** (91 S. Ocean Blvd., 843/280-0715), **Duck's** (229 Main St., 843/249-3858, www.ducksatoceandrive.com), or **Fat Harold's** (210 Main St., 843/249-5779, www.fatharolds.com), or visit **The Spanish Galleon** (100 N. Ocean Blvd., 843/249-1047) inside the Ocean Drive Beach Resort. If you're interested, don't be shy; shaggers are notoriously gregarious and eager to show off their stock-in-trade. It's easy to learn, it's family-friendly, and there will be no shortage of pleasant young-at-heart shaggers around who will be happy to teach you the steps.

vocal and instrumental abilities of these very professional singers, instrumentalists, and dancers, who gamely take on hits through the generations ranging from bluegrass to Motown, pop, and modern country.

The Carolina Opry augments its regular music, comedy, and dance show with a seasonal Christmas special, which is extremely popular and sells out even faster than the regular shows, often six or more months in advance.

Legends in Concert

Way down in Surfside Beach, where the big buildup on the Strand begins, you'll find *Legends in Concert* (301 Business U.S. 17, 843/238-7827, www.legendsinconcert.com,

ticket prices vary), a popular rotating show of celebrity impersonators from Elvis to Barbra Streisand. As cheesy as that sounds, the resemblances can be quite uncanny, and the shows are really entertaining.

House of Blues

Besides being a great place for dinner, on the other side of the restaurant is the stage for the **House of Blues** (4640 U.S. 17 S., 843/272-3000, www.hob.com, ticket prices vary) at Barefoot Landing in North Myrtle Beach. They bring some pretty happening names in R&B, straight blues, and rock-and-roll to this fun venue dedicated to preserving old-school music and live performance, with a professional sound mix.

the Carolina Opry

Medieval Times

Oh, come on—what's not to like about bountiful feasts, juggling jesters, skillful falconers, fetching maidens, and brave jousting knights? At **Medieval Times** (2904 Fantasy Way, 843/236-4635, www.medievaltimes.com, $51 adults, $31 under age 13) you'll get all that and more. The kitsch quotient is high at this Renaissance Faire on steroids, a live-action story line featuring plenty of stage combat, music, and a steady stream of culinary items for your enjoyment (and yes, there's a full bar for those of drinking age). The price may seem high at first glance, but keep in mind you're getting a hearty full dinner plus a two-hour stage and equestrian show.

Pirate's Voyage

Sharing a parking lot with the Carolina Opry is **Pirate's Voyage** (8901-B N. Kings Hwy., 843/497-9700, www.piratesvoyage.com, from $44.99 adults, $26.99 ages 4-11, free under age 4), one of the newer entertainment attractions to hit Myrtle Beach. Affiliated with Dolly Parton's entertainment empire—her "Dixie Stampede" originally occupied this

the House of Blues

building—Pirate's Voyage takes you on a rollicking two-hour trip into the world of buccaneers, with fighting, lost treasure, dancing, acrobatics, mermaids, and assorted high-seas drama, all with photographers on hand to document your experience . . . for a price, me hearties. Like Medieval Times, this is essentially dinner theater, with three shows a day in the high season of late summer.

The Alabama Theatre

The Alabama Theatre (4750 U.S. 17, 843/272-5758, www.alabama-theatre.com, ticket prices vary) at Barefoot Landing in North Myrtle Beach focuses on the long-running song-and-dance revue *One: The Show* as well as big-name acts who may be past their prime but are still able to fill seats, such as the Oak Ridge Boys, Kenny Rogers, and, of course, the eponymous troubadours Alabama, who got their big break while playing at Myrtle Beach. It's not all country, though—Motown and beach music acts like the Temptations and the Platters are often featured as well. As with the Carolina Opry, Barefoot Landing has its own Christmas special, and as with the Opry's offering, this one sells out well in advance.

Palace Theatre

The **Palace Theatre** (1420 Celebrity Circle, 800/905-4228, www.palacetheatremyrtlebeach.com, ticket prices vary) at Broadway at the Beach offers a variety of toned-down Vegas-style entertainment. Recent shows included tributes to the Beatles and Queen.

CINEMA

At Broadway at the Beach, there's a multiplex, Carmike's **Broadway Cinema 16** (843/445-1600, www.carmike.com). Other movie theaters include the **Cinemark** (2100 Coastal Grand Circle, 843/839-3221, www.cinemark.com) at the Coastal Grand Mall and the massive **Grand 14 at the Market Common** (4002 Deville St., 843/282-0550), part of a multiuse development on a repurposed Air Force base.

FESTIVALS AND EVENTS

Interestingly, most events in Myrtle Beach don't happen during the three-month high season of June-August, mostly because it's so darn hot that all anyone wants to do is get in the water.

Winter

The Grand Strand is the birthplace of the dance called the shag, and each winter for the last 25 years the **National Shag Dance Championships** (2000 N. Kings Hwy., 843/497-7369, www.shagnationals.com, from $15 per night) have been the pinnacle of the art form. Beginning with preliminaries in January, contestants in five age ranges compete for a variety of awards, culminating in the finals the first week in March. The level of professionalism might amaze you—for such a lazy-looking dance, these are serious competitors.

Spring

You might not automatically associate our colder neighbor to the north with Myrtle Beach, but **Canadian American Days** (various venues, www.myrtlebeachinfo.com, free), or "Can Am," brings tens of thousands of visitors of both nationalities to sites all over the Strand each March to enjoy a variety of musical and cultural events. Always on top of marketing opportunities, the Myrtle Beach Chamber of Commerce makes sure this happens during Ontario's spring holidays to ensure maximum north-of-the-border attendance. While most of the events have little or nothing to do with Canada itself, this is basically a great excuse for Canucks to get some Carolina sunshine.

The **Spring Games and Kite Flying Contest** (843/448-7881, free) brings an exciting array of airborne craft to the Strand in front of Broadway at the Beach on an April weekend as the springtime winds peak.

Also in April is the area's second-largest shag event, the **Society of Stranders Spring Safari** (www.shagdance.com). Several clubs

Motorcycle Madness

Growling engines? Spinning tires? Patriotic colors? Polished chrome? Bikini car washes? Erotic bull-riding contests? That is the spectacle known as **Myrtle Beach Bike Week,** one of the largest gatherings of Harley-Davidson enthusiasts on the East Coast and one of the oldest, at about 75 years.

The event has historically happened each May on the week and weekend before Memorial Day weekend, bringing over 250,000 motorcyclists and their entourages to town for 10 days of riding, bragging, and carousing. South Carolina's lack of a helmet law is a particular draw to these freedom-cherishing motorcyclists. A few days later, on Memorial Day weekend, there's another bike rally, this one simply called Black Bike Week. Nearly as large as the regular Bike Week, the focus is on African American riders and their machines.

Contrary to stereotype, there's not much of an increase in crime during either Bike Week. Regardless, they are widely known as a particularly bad time to bring families to the area, and therein lies the controversy. Joining other municipalities around the nation in discouraging motorcycle rallies, the city of Myrtle Beach has enacted tough measures to force the bike rallies to leave town and make the area more family-friendly during that time. Most controversial among recent measures was a municipal helmet law, enforceable only within Myrtle Beach city limits, that was later struck down by the South Carolina Supreme Court. Other still-standing measures include stringent noise ordinances designed to include the roaring, rattling tailpipes of pretty much every Harley ever made. The separate municipality of North Myrtle Beach, however, has made it clear that bikers are welcome there even if they're non grata a few miles to the south.

As of now, it seems that the rallies will remain on the Strand rather than gun their collective throttle and head elsewhere, as they occasionally threaten to do when relations with local municipalities and police departments get too tense. The upshot for the nonmotorcyclist visitor? Bikers are somewhat less of a factor than in years past, and certainly local police are taking them more seriously. But the time around Memorial Day is still as crowded as ever.

in North Myrtle Beach host shag dancers from all over for a week of, well, shagging.

The biggest single event in Myrtle Beach happens in May with the **Spring Bike Rally** (various venues, www.myrtlebeachbikeweek.com, free), always known simply as "Bike Week." In this 75-year-old event, over 250,000 Harley-Davidson riders and their entourages gather to cruise around the place, admire each other's custom rides, and generally party their patooties off. While the typical Harley dude these days is getting on in years and is probably a mild-mannered store manager in regular life, young or old they all do their best to let their hair down at this festive event. Dozens of related events go on throughout the week at venues all over the Strand, from tough-man contests to "foxy boxing" matches to wet T-shirt contests. You get the picture—it's not for the politically correct or for young children.

Summer

Right after the Spring Bike Rally, on Memorial Day weekend, is the **Atlantic Beach Bikefest** (various venues), much more commonly referred to as "Black Bike Week." This event started in the 1980s and is spiritually based in Atlantic Beach, formerly the area's "black beach" during the days of segregation. It sees over 200,000 African American motorcycle enthusiasts gather in Myrtle Beach for a similar menu of partying, bikini contests, cruising, and the like. While the existence of separate events often reminds some people of the state's unfortunate history of segregation, supporters of both Bike Week and Black Bike Week insist it's not a big deal, and that bikers of either race are welcome at either event.

Kicking off with a festive parade, the 50-year-old **Sun Fun Festival** (various venues, www.grandstrandevents.com), generally held the weekend after Memorial Day weekend, signals the real beginning of the summer season with bikini contests, Jet Ski races, parades, air shows, and concerts galore.

The **City of Myrtle Beach Independence Day Celebration** (www.cityofmyrtlebeach.com, free) is held each July 4 weekend, when the largest number of visitors is in Myrtle Beach. It's fun, it's hot, there's fireworks aplenty, and boy, is it crowded.

Fall

For a week in mid-September, North Myrtle Beach hosts one of the world's largest shag dancing celebrations, the **Society of Stranders Fall Migration** (www.shagdance.com, free). Head up to the intersection of Ocean Drive and Main Street to hear the sounds of this unique genre, and party with the shaggers at various local clubs. If you don't know the steps, don't worry—instructors are usually on hand.

There's another, smaller Harley riders' rally the first week in October, the **Fall Motorcycle Rally** (various venues, www.myrtlebeachbikeweek.com, free).

Thanksgiving weekend, when the beaches are much less crowded and the hotels much cheaper, is the **South Carolina Bluegrass Festival** (2101 N. Oak St., 706/864-7203, www.aandabluegrass.com, $30 adults, $20 ages 6-13, free under age 6), a delightful and well-attended event at the Myrtle Beach Convention Center, celebrating the Appalachian music tradition. It attracts some of the biggest names in the genre.

Shopping

Shopping on the Grand Strand is strongly destination-oriented. You tend to find shops of similar price points and merchandise types clustered together in convenient locations: Upscale shops are in one place and discount and outlet stores in another. Here's a rundown of the main retail areas on the Strand with some of the standout shops.

BROADWAY AT THE BEACH

The sprawling **Broadway at the Beach** (U.S. 17 Bypass and 21st Ave. N., www.broadwayatthebeach.com, hours vary) complex has scads of stores, some of which are quite interesting and rise well beyond tourist schlock. There are maps and directories of the site available at various kiosks around the area.

One of my favorite stores is **Retroactive** (843/916-1218, www.shopretroactive.com), a shop specializing in 1970s and 1980s styles and kitsch, with some of the best (and wittiest) pop-culture T-shirts I've seen. The owners are frank about their continuing obsession with '80s hair bands. Another awesome T-shirt and trinket shop that the kids and teens will particularly enjoy is **Stupid Factory** (843/448-1100). The kids—and those with a sweet tooth—will go crazy in the aptly named **It'SUGAR** (843/916-1300, www.itsugar.com), a store dedicated to just about any kind of candy and candy-themed merchandise you can think of, from modern brands to retro favorites. If the packaged or bulk varieties don't float your boat, you can design your own massive chocolate bar. And, of course, this being Myrtle Beach, there's a **Harley Davidson** (843/293-5555) gift store with Hog-oriented merch galore.

The bottom line on Broadway at the Beach, though, is that it's made for walking around and browsing. Just bring your walking shoes—the place is huge—and keep in mind that there's not a lot of shade.

BAREFOOT LANDING

There are over 100 shops at **Barefoot Landing** (4898 U.S. 17 S., 843/272-8349, www.bflanding.com, hours vary) in North Myrtle Beach—as well as one cool old-fashioned carousel—but perhaps the most unique spot is **T.I.G.E.R.S. Preservation Station** (843/361-4552, www.tigerfriends.com, hours vary), where you get the opportunity to have your picture taken with a live tiger or lion cub. This is the fund-raising arm of a local organization for conservation of the big cats as well as gorillas and monkeys. Portraits begin at $100 to pose with a single critter and go up from there depending on the number of people you want to pose with in the shot. It's a lot of money, but this is truly a once-in-a-lifetime experience.

Relocated to the Strand from its grape yards in Chester, South Carolina, is **Carolina Vineyards Winery** (843/361-9181, www.carolinavineyards.com). Buy wine as a gift, or taste any seven of its labels for only $3.

There are magic shops, and then there are *magic shops*. **Trickmaster Magic Shop** (843/281-0705, http://trickmastermagicshop.com) is definitely the latter. Packed in this relatively small space is just about every legendary trick and trick deck known to the magician's art, along with a cool variety of magic books teaching you, in deadly serious fashion, the innermost secrets of the trade.

THE MARKET COMMON

The Market Common (4017 Deville St., www.marketcommonmb.com, hours vary) is an ambitious residential-retail mixed-use development opened for business on the site of the decommissioned Myrtle Beach Air Force Base. While its location near the Myrtle Beach International Airport means it's not exactly amid the sun-and-fun action (possibly a good thing, depending on the season), the very pedestrian-friendly development style and tasteful shops might provide a refreshing change of pace.

There are three dozen (and counting) stores, including Anthropologie, Williams-Sonoma, Copper Penny, Chico's, Brooks Brothers, Fossil, Banana Republic, Barnes & Noble, and Jake and Company ("Life Is Good"). There are plenty of restaurants,

including Ultimate California Pizza and P. F. Chang's, and a large multiplex movie theater.

For those interested in how the sprawling old base was closed in the 1990s and repurposed so completely, there's interpretive signage all around the pedestrian mall and along the roadways leading to it. At The Market Common's entrance is Warbird Park, a well-done veterans memorial featuring an Air Force A-10 attack aircraft, an F-100 Super Sabre, and a Corsair II.

MALLS

The premier mall in the area is **Coastal Grand Mall** (2000 Coastal Grand Circle, 843/839-9100, www.coastalgrand.com, Mon.-Sat. 10am-9pm, Sun. noon-6pm) at the U.S. 17 Bypass and U.S. 501. It's anchored by Belk, J. C. Penney, Sears, Dillard's, and Dick's Sporting Goods.

Your basic meat-and-potatoes mall, **Myrtle Beach Mall** (10177 N. Kings Hwy., 843/272-4040, http://shopmyrtlebeachmall.com, Mon.-Sat. 10am-9pm, Sun. noon-6pm) is anchored by Belk, J. C. Penney, and Bass Pro Shops.

DISCOUNT BEACHWEAR

Literally dozens of cavernous, tacky, deep-discount T-shirt-and-towel-type places are spread up and down Kings Highway like mushrooms after a rain. The vast majority of them belong to one of several well-established chains: **Eagles Beachwear** (www.eaglesbeachwear.net), **Whales** (www.whalesnauticalgifts.com), **Wing's Beachwear** (www.wingsbeachwear.com), and **Bargain Beachwear** (www.bargainbeachwear.com). These are the kinds of places to get assorted bric-a-brac and items for your beach visit. The quality isn't that bad, and the prices are uniformly low.

OUTLET MALLS

There are two massive **Tanger Outlets** (www.tangeroutlet.com) at Myrtle Beach: **Tanger Outlet North** (10835 Kings Rd., 843/449-0491), off Kings Road/U.S. 17, and **Tanger Outlet South** (4635 Factory Stores

Blvd., 843/236-5100), off U.S. 501. Both offer over 100 factory outlet stores of almost every imaginable segment, from Fossil to Disney, OshKosh B'gosh to Timberland. Full food courts are available, and many folks easily spend an entire day here.

For years, busloads of hard-core shoppers from throughout the South have taken organized trips to the Grand Strand specifically to shop at **Waccamaw Factory Shoppes** (3071 Waccamaw Blvd., 843/236-8200). Their passion hasn't abated, as new generations of shopaholics get the fever to come here and browse the often deeply discounted offerings at row after row of outlet stores. There are actually two locations, the Factory Shoppes themselves and the nearby **Waccamaw Pottery** (3200 Pottery Dr., 843/236-6152). Bring your walking shoes (or buy some new ones at one of the many shoe stores), but don't worry about getting from one mall to the other—there's a free shuttle.

Sports and Recreation

Myrtle Beach's middle name might as well be recreation. While some of the local variety tends toward overkill—I personally loathe Jet Skis, for example—there's no denying that if it involves outdoor activity, it's probably offered here. For general info, visit www.grandstrandevents.com. For municipal recreation info, visit www.cityofmyrtlebeach.com.

ON THE WATER
Beaches

The center of activity is the Strand itself, with its miles of user-friendly beaches. They're not the most beautiful in the world, but they're nice enough, and access is certainly no problem. In Myrtle Beach and North Myrtle Beach, you'll find clearly designated public access points off Ocean Boulevard, some with parking and some without. Both municipalities run well-marked public parking lots at various points, some of which are free during the off-season.

Dog owners will be pleased to know that May 15-September 15, dogs are allowed on the beach before 9am and after 5pm. September 15-May 15, dogs are allowed on the beach at any time of day.

Restrict your swimming to within 150 feet of shore. Surfside Beach to the south is a no-smoking beach with access points at 16th Avenue North, 6th Avenue North, 3rd Avenue North, Surfside Pier, 3rd Avenue South, 4th Avenue South, 13th Avenue South, and Melody Lane.

Surfing

There's a steady, if low-key, surf scene in Myrtle Beach, despite the fact that the waves are not really that good and the sport is restricted to certain areas during the busy summer season. The rules are a little complicated.

In **Myrtle Beach proper,** surfing is only allowed April 15-September 15 daily 10am-5pm in the following zones:

- 29th Avenue South to the southern city limits
- 37th Avenue North to 47th Avenue North
- 62nd Avenue North to 68th Avenue North

82nd Avenue North to the northern city limits Up in **North Myrtle Beach,** surfers must stay in the following zones May 15-September 15 daily 9am-4pm:

- Cherry Grove Pier
- 6th Avenue North
- 13th Avenue South
- 28th Avenue South

38th Avenue South Down at **Surfside Beach,** surfing is restricted to the following zones, year-round daily 10am-5pm:

- 12th Avenue North to 14th Avenue North
- Melody Lane to 13th Avenue South

The oldest surf shop in the area, south of Myrtle Beach in Garden City Beach, is the

Village Surf Shoppe (500 Atlantic Ave., 843/651-6396, www.villagesurf.com), which has catered to the Strand's growing surf scene since 1969. Nearly as old is the **Surf City Surf Shop** (1758 U.S. 17 S., 843/272-1090; 3001 N. Kings Hwy., 843/626-5412, www.surfcitysurf-shop.com) franchise in Myrtle proper.

Diving

Diving is popular on the Strand. As with fishing, many trips depart from Little River just above North Myrtle Beach. Offshore features include many historic wrecks, including the post-Civil War wreck of the **USS *Sherman*** offshore of Little River, and artificial reefs such as the famed **"Barracuda Alley,"** teeming with marine life, off Myrtle Beach.

Coastal Scuba (1901 U.S. 17 S., 843/361-3323, www.coastalscuba.com) in North Myrtle is a large operator, offering several different dive tours.

Parasailing, Windsurfing, and Jet Skis

Ocean Watersports (405 S. Ocean Blvd., 843/445-7777, www.parasailmyrtlebeach.com) takes groups of up to six people on well-supervised, well-equipped parasailing adventures (about $50 pp), with tandem and triple flights available. Observers can go out on the boat for about $20. They also rent Jet Skis and offer "banana boat" rides ($15) in which a long—yes, banana-shaped—raft, straddled by several riders, is towed by a boat up and down the beach.

Downwind Watersports (2915 S. Ocean Blvd., 843/448-7245, www.downwindsails-myrtlebeach.com) has similar offerings, with the addition of good old-fashioned sailboat lessons and rentals ($16). Parasailing is about $65 per person for a single ride, banana boats are $16 for 20 minutes, and Jet Ski rentals are about $100 per hour.

Farther up the Strand in North Myrtle, between Cherry Grove Beach and Little River, you'll find **Thomas Outdoors Watersports** (2200 Little River Neck Rd., 843/280-2448, www.mbjetski.com), which rents kayaks in addition to Jet Skis and pontoon boats. They offer several Jet Ski tours ($75-125), including a dolphin-watching trip, as well as all-day kayak rental ($45 pp).

Fishing

Most fishing on the Strand is saltwater, with charters, most based in Little River, taking anglers well into Atlantic waters. Tuna, wahoo, mackerel, and dolphin (not the mammal!) are big in the hot months, while snapper and grouper are caught year-round but are best in the colder months.

A good operator up in Little River is **Longway Fishing Charters** (843/249-7813, www.longwaycharters.com), which specializes in offshore fishing. Another in the same area is **Capt. Smiley's Inshore Fishing** (843/361-7445, www.captainsmiley-fishingcharters.com). **Fish Hook Charters** (2200 Little River Neck Rd., 843/283-7692, www.fishhookcharters.com) takes a 34-foot boat out from North Myrtle Beach.

For surf fishing on the beach, you do not need a license of any type. All other types of fishing require a valid South Carolina fishing license, available for a nominal fee online (http://dnr.sc.gov) or at any tackle shop and most grocery stores.

Cruises

Except in the winter months, there are plenty of places to cruise in the Strand, from Little River down to Murrells Inlet, and from the Waccamaw River to the Intracoastal Waterway. The **Great American Riverboat Company** (8496 Enterprise Rd., 843/650-6600, www.mbriverboat.com) offers sightseeing and dinner cruises along the Intracoastal Waterway. **Island Song Charters** (4374 Landing Rd., 843/467-7088, www.sailingmyr-tlebeach.com) out of Little River takes you on sunset and dolphin cruises on the 32-foot sailboat *Island Song.*

Up in North Myrtle, **Getaway Adventures** (843/663-1100, www.myrtle-beachboatcruises.com) specializes in dolphin tours. Also in North Myrtle, **Thomas**

Outdoors Watersports (2200 Little River Neck Rd., 843/280-2448, www.mbjetski.com) runs dolphin cruises.

ON LAND
Golf

The Grand Strand in general, and Myrtle Beach in particular, is world golf central. There are over 120 courses in this comparatively small area, and if golfers can't find something they like here, they need to sell their clubs. While the number of truly great courses is few—the best courses are farther down the Strand near Pawleys Island—the quality overall is still quite high.

A great bonus is affordability. Partially because of dramatically increased competition due to the glut of courses, and partially because of savvy regional marketing, greens fees here are significantly lower than you might expect, in many cases under $100. For even more savings, finding a golf-lodging package deal in Myrtle Beach is like finding sand on the beach—almost too easy. Check with your hotel to see if they offer any golf packages. At any time of year, some good one-stop shops on the Internet are at www.mbn.com and www.myrtlebeachgolf.com.

Some highlights of area golf include the Davis Love III-designed course at **Barefoot Resort** (4980 Barefoot Resort Ridge Rd., 843/390-3200, www.barefootgolf.com, $105-185) in North Myrtle, maybe the best in the Strand outside Pawleys Island. Or would that be the Greg Norman course, or the Tom Fazio course, or the Pete Dye course, all also at Barefoot? You get the picture.

Also up near North Myrtle is a favorite with visitors and locals alike, the challenging **Glen Dornoch Golf Club** (4840 Glen Dornoch Way, 800/717-8784, www.glensgolfgroup.com, from $100), on 260 beautiful acres. Affiliated with Glen Dornoch are the 27 holes at Little River's **Heather Glen** (4650 Heather Glen Way, 800/868-4536, www.glensgolfgroup.com, $130), which are divided into Red, White, and Blue courses. They combine for what's consistently rated one of the best public courses in the United States.

And no list of area golf is complete without a nod to **Myrtle Beach National** (4900 National Dr., 843/347-4298, www.mbn.com, from $80). With three distinct courses—King's North, West, and South Creek, with its South Carolina-shaped sand trap at hole 3—the National is one of the state's legendary courses, not to mention a heck of a deal.

Miniature Golf

Don't scoff—miniature golf, or "putt-putt" to an older generation, is a big deal in Myrtle Beach. If you thought there were a lot of regular golf courses here, the 50 miniature golf courses will also blow your mind. Sadly, almost all of the classic old-school miniature golf courses are no more, victims of the demand for increased production values and modernized gimmick holes. But here are some of the standouts, including the best of the North Myrtle courses as well.

Down near the older section of Myrtle, the completely over-the-top **Mount Atlanticus Minotaur Goff** (707 N. Kings Hwy., 843/444-1008, $10 for 18 holes) is garish yet wonderful. And yes, that's how it's spelled—get it? Legend has it that this one course cost $3 million to build. Literally the stuff of dreams—or maybe hallucinations—this sprawling course mixes the mythological with the nautical to wonderful effect. You don't actually encounter the Minotaur until the bonus 19th hole, a fiendish water trap. If you get a hole in one, you get free golf here for life.

My favorite course is a bit farther north on the main drag. **Captain Hook's Miniature Golf** (2205 N. Kings Hwy., www.captainhooksminigolf.com, $10 for 18 holes) has two courses depicting the world of Peter Pan and Neverland, including a hole entirely on board the eponymous captain's pirate ship! I wouldn't call it particularly difficult, but it's a lot of fun.

Hawaiian Rumble (3210 U.S. 17, 843/458-2585, www.prominigolf.com) in North Myrtle is not only a heck of a fun, attractive course,

Mount Atlanticus Minotaur Goff

it's also the official training center for the U.S. Professional Miniature Golf Association (the folks who generally get a hole in one on every hole). The Rumble's sister course is **Hawaiian Village** (4205 U.S. 17, 843/361-9629, www. prominigolf.com) in North Myrtle, which is also the home of serious professional miniature golf competitions.

For a bit of retro action, try **Rainbow Falls** (9550 Kings Hwy., 843/497-2557). It's not as garish as some of the newer courses, but fans of old-school putt-putt will love it.

While at Broadway at the Beach, you might want to try the popular medieval-themed **Dragon's Lair** (1197 Celebrity Circle, 843/913-9301). Yep, it has a 30-foot fire-breathing dragon, Sir Alfred, that you have to make your way around. While the dinosaur craze has cooled somewhat, the golf at **Jurassic Golf** (445 29th Ave., 843/448-2116), festooned with dozens of velociraptors and the like, certainly has stayed hot. There is a similarly themed site in North Myrtle, the **Dinosaur Adventure** (700 7th Ave., 843/272-8041).

Tennis

There are over 200 tennis courts in the Myrtle Beach area. The main municipal site is the

Myrtle Beach Tennis Center (3302 Robert Grissom Pkwy., 843/918-2440, www.myrtle-beachtennis.com, $2 pp per hour), which has 10 courts, 8 of them lighted. The city also runs six lighted courts at **Midway Park** (U.S. 17 and 19th Ave. S.).

The privately owned **Kingston Plantation** (843/497-2444, www.kingston-plantation.com) specializes in tennis vacations, and you don't even have to be a guest. They have a pro on staff and offer lessons. Down in Pawleys Island, the **Litchfield Beach and Golf Resort** (14276 Ocean Hwy., 866/538-0187, www.litchfieldbeach.com) has two dozen nice courts.

Cycling

In Myrtle Beach, when they say "biker," they mean a Harley dude. Bicycling—or safe bicycling, anyway—is largely limited to fat-tire riding along the beach and easy pedaling through the quiet residential neighborhoods near Little River. There is a bike lane on North Ocean Boulevard from about 29th Avenue North to about 82nd Avenue North. Riding on the sidewalk is strictly prohibited.

As for bike rentals, a good operator is **Beach Bike Shop** (711 Broadway St., 843/448-5335, www.beachbikeshop.com). In North Myrtle, try **Wheel Fun Rentals** (91 S. Ocean Blvd., 843/280-7900, www.wheelfunrentals.com).

Horseback Riding

A horse ride along the surf is a nearly iconic image of South Carolina, combining two of the state's chief pursuits: equestrian sports and hanging out on the beach. A great way to enjoy a horseback ride along the Grand Strand without having to bring your own equine is to check out **Horseback Riding of Myrtle Beach** (843/294-1712, www.myrtlebeachhorserides. com). They offer a variety of group rides, each with a guide, going to nature-preserve or beach locales. While they'll take you out any day of the week, advance reservations are required. Ninety minutes on a nature preserve costs about $50 per person, while a 90-minute ride on the beach is about $75 per person.

You can go horseback riding on Myrtle Beach from the third Saturday in November until the end of February, with these conditions: You must access the beach from Myrtle Beach State Park, you cannot ride over sand dunes in any way, and you must clean up after your horse.

SPECTATOR SPORTS

Playing April-early September in a large stadium near Broadway at the Beach are the **Myrtle Beach Pelicans** (1251 21st Ave. N., 843/918-6000, www.myrtlebeachpelicans. com, $8-11), a single-A affiliate of the Chicago Cubs.

NASCAR fans already know of the **Myrtle Beach Speedway** (455 Hospitality Ln., www.myrtlebeachspeedway.com, $12, free under age 10) off U.S. 501, one of the more vintage tracks in the country, dating back to 1958 (it was actually a dirt track well into the 1970s). Currently the main draws are the NASCAR Whelen All-American Series races (Apr.-Nov. Sat. 7:30pm).

Other spectator sports in the area tend to revolve around the Chanticleer teams of **Coastal Carolina University** (132 Chanticleer Dr. W., 843/347-8499, www. goccusports.com), just inland from Myrtle Beach in Conway. The baseball team won the school's first national title in 2016. By the way, *chanticleer* is an old name for a rooster, and in this case is a self-conscious derivative of the mascot of the University of South Carolina, the gamecock.

Food

There are about 2,000 restaurants in the Myrtle Beach area, not counting hotel room service and buffets. You can find any dining option that floats your boat at almost any price level. Seafood, of course, is heartily recommended, but there are steak houses, rib joints, pizza places, and vegetarian restaurants galore as well. We can only explore a small fraction here, but following are some of the unique and tasty experiences on the bustling Grand Strand.

Food is never far away, with the biggest concentration of restaurants—including the gigantic seafood buffet places—on "Restaurant Row," a stretch of Kings Highway/U.S. 17

between Myrtle Beach and North Myrtle Beach, from about the merge of U.S. 17 Bypass and U.S. 17 Business in the south and the Tanger Outlets to the north.

BREAKFAST

Pancakes are big on the Strand, with many flapjack places open daily 24 hours to accommodate partiers and night owls. A prime purveyor of pancakes is **Harry's Breakfast Pancakes** (2306 N. Kings Hwy., 843/448-8013, www.harryspancake.com, daily 5:30am-2pm, $4-10). They're not open all day, but there's enough time to enjoy their fluffy stacks and rich omelets.

BARBECUE, BURGERS, AND STEAKS

The best barbecue in town—and a delightfully low-key experience in this often too-flashy area—is at ★ **Little Pigs Barbecue** (6102 Frontage Rd., 843/692-9774, Mon.-Sat. 11am-8pm, $8-12). This is a local-heavy place dealing in no-frills pulled pork, piled high at the counter and reasonably priced with a selection of sauces. The lack of atmosphere *is* the atmosphere, and they prefer to let the barbecue (and the hush puppies and onion rings) do the talking.

Since opening 30 years ago, ★ **Thoroughbreds** (9706 N. Kings Hwy., 843/497-2636, www.thoroughbredsrestaurant.com, Sun.-Thurs. 5pm-10pm, Fri.-Sat. 5pm-11pm, $20), on the old Restaurant Row, has been considered the premier fine-dining place in Myrtle Beach, dealing in the kind of wood-heavy, clubby, Old World-meets-New World ambience you'd expect to see in Palm Beach, Florida. That said, the prices are definitely more Myrtle Beach; you can easily have a romantic dinner for two for under $100. The menu is a carnivore's delight: Beef includes the signature prime rib, a great steak au poivre, and a nod to cowboy machismo, the 22-ounce bone-in rib eye.

The darling of the steak-loving set is **Rioz Brazilian Steakhouse** (2920 Hollywood Dr., 843/839-0777, www.rioz.com, daily 4pm-10pm, $20-40). It's not cheap—the recommended 15-item meat sampler is about $35 per person—but then again, an experience this awesome shouldn't be cheap (a big plus is that kids under age 7 eat for free). The meats are fresh and vibrant, slow-cooked over a wood fire in the simple but succulent style typical of the gaucho *churrascaria* tradition. The service is widely considered to be the best in the area. But the biggest surprise may turn out to be the salad and seafood bar, which even has sushi.

There is no dearth of places to nosh at Barefoot Landing, but meat lovers (not to mention golfers) will probably enjoy **Greg Norman's Australian Grille** (4930 Kings Hwy. S., 843/361-0000, www.gregnormansaustraliangrille.com, lunch daily 11am-3pm, dinner daily 5pm-10pm, $20-30), which, despite the chain-sounding name, is the only restaurant of its kind. It's the place to enjoy a cocktail by the lake and a premium entrée like the lobster-crusted swordfish.

I normally shy away from mentioning national chain-type places, but I'll make an exception for Myrtle Beach, where you expect things to be a little cheesy. **Jimmy Buffett's Margaritaville** (1114 Celebrity Circle, 843/448-5455, www.margaritavillemyrtlebeach.com, Sun.-Thurs. 11am-10pm, Fri.-Sat. 11am-midnight, $13-22) at Broadway at the Beach is widely regarded as the best single location of the national chain. The signature Cheeseburger in Paradise is the obvious big hit. You get a lot of entertainment for your money as well, with balloon-twisting performers coming to your table and a bizarre whirling "hurricane" that acts up in the main dining area every now and then. As you'd expect, the margaritas are good, if expensive.

Many locals insist the better burger is at another Buffett-owned chain, the succinctly titled **Cheeseburger in Paradise** (7211 N. Kings Hwy., 843/497-3891, www.cheeseburgerinparadise.com, Sun.-Thurs. 11:30am-11pm, Fri.-Sat. 11:30am-midnight, $10-15), which offers a range of burgers on the menu with sweet potato chips on the side, all served up in a less flashy but still very boisterous atmosphere than the flagship restaurant.

CLASSIC SOUTHERN

If you've got a hankering for some spicy Cajun-Creole food, go no farther than the **House of Blues** (4640 U.S. 17 S., 843/272-3000, www.hob.com, Mon.-Fri. 4pm-9pm, Sat. 8am-9pm, Sun. 9am-2pm and 3pm-9pm, $10-25) at Barefoot Landing in North Myrtle Beach. With 11 similarly themed locations around North America, this particular venue deals in the same kind of retro delta vibe, with specially commissioned folk art festooning the walls and live music cranking up at about 10pm. At your table, a gregarious server will walk you through the limited but intense menu, which includes such tasty bits as buffalo tenders (boneless chicken wings in a perfectly spicy sauce) and a couple of excellent jambalaya-type dishes. All portions are enormous and richly spiced. It's a loud, clanging room, so keep in mind that this is less a romantic experience than an exuberant, earthy one.

A special experience at House of Blues is the weekly **Gospel Brunch** (Sun. 9am-2pm, $20 adults, $10 ages 6-12, free under age 6), an opportunity not only to enjoy some tasty Southern-style brunch treats like cheese grits, jambalaya, and catfish tenders but to enjoy some outstanding gospel entertainment at the same time. The Gospel Brunch is served in seatings, and reservations are recommended.

CONTINENTAL

In Myrtle Beach it can be difficult to find a good meal that's not fried or smothered or both. For a highbrow change of pace, try **The Library** (1212 N. Kings Hwy., 843/448-4527, www.thelibraryrestaurantsc.com, Mon.-Sat. 5pm-10pm, $20-50), which is hands-down the most romantic dining experience in Myrtle proper. It's not cheap, but then again, nothing about this place is pedestrian, from the very attentive European-style service to the savvy wine list and the signature dishes (many of them prepared tableside), like she-crab soup, Caesar salads, steak Diane, and the ultimate splurge, steak and lobster.

Like art? Like food? Try the **Collector's Café** (7726 N. Kings Hwy., 843/449-9370, www.collectorscafeandgallery.com, $10-20), which, as the name implies, is a combined gallery and dining space. Don't be daunted by the strip mall setting—inside is a totally different ball game with a trendy open kitchen and plush, eclectic furniture awaiting you amid the original artwork. As for the menu, you may as well go for what's widely regarded as the best single dish, the scallop cakes. Make sure you save room for dessert.

ITALIAN

The best-regarded Italian place in Myrtle Beach—though it could just as easily go in the *Steaks* category, since that's its specialty—is **Angelo's** (2011 S. Kings Hwy., 843/626-2800, www.angelosteakandpasta.com, Sun.-Thurs. 4pm-8:30pm, Fri.-Sat. 4pm-9pm, $12-25). The signature dishes are intriguingly spiced cuts of steak (request beforehand if you don't want them seasoned), cooked medium and under for an exquisite tenderness. You can get spaghetti as a side with the steaks, or just go with the classic baked potato. Don't forget to check out the Italian buffet, including lasagna, Italian sausage, chicken cacciatore, ravioli, and, of course, pizza.

MEXICAN

If you need a fix of absolutely authentic Mexican food, head straight to ★ **La Poblanita** (311 Hwy. 15, 843/448-3150, daily 11am-10pm, $7-10). Don't be put off by the humble exterior in a small strip mall; the food is simply amazing—and amazingly inexpensive. Eighty percent of the diners are Mexican American families, which attests to the authenticity of the cuisine. Everything on the menu is handmade, including the tortillas. The empanadas and burritos are quite simply the best I've eaten anywhere. Even the rice melts in your mouth. Don't forget the Mexican Coke!

SEAFOOD

The grandest old Calabash seafood joint in town, **Original Benjamin's** (9593 N. Kings Hwy., 843/449-0821, daily 3:30pm-10pm, buffet $25 adults, $12 children), on the old Restaurant Row, is one of the more unique dining experiences in Myrtle Beach. With themed rooms overlooking the Intracoastal Waterway, including the concisely named Bus Room—yes, it has an old school bus in it—you'll find yourself in the mood to devour copious amounts of fresh seafood at its humongous 170-item buffet line.

Closer to Broadway at the Beach, try **George's** (1401 29th Ave. N., 843/916-2278, www.captaingeorges.com, Mon.-Sat. 3pm-10pm, Sun. noon-9pm, buffet $31, $16 ages 5-12, free under age 5). Despite the usual kitschy nautical decor, this is the kind of place even locals will admit going to for the enormous seafood buffet, widely considered a cut above the norm.

With old reliables like crab cakes and sea scallops as well as signature house dishes like pecan-encrusted grouper and stuffed flounder, you can't go wrong at **The Sea Captain's House** (3002 N. Ocean Blvd., 843/448-8082, daily 6am-10:30am, 11:30am-2:30pm, and 5pm-10pm, $10-20), one of Myrtle Beach's better seafood restaurants. This opinion is widely held, however, so prepare to wait—often up to two hours. Luckily, you can sip a cocktail and gaze out over the Atlantic Ocean as you do so. Old hands will tell you it's not as good as back in the day, but it's still a cut above.

When you're at Ocean Drive Beach up in North Myrtle, check out another venerable old name, the **Duffy Street Seafood Shack** (202 Main St., 843/281-9840, www.duffyst.com, daily noon-10pm, $10). This is a humble, unkempt roadside affair dealing in the kind of down-home treats Myrtle Beach seems to love ("pigskin" shrimp, fried pickles, and the like). Overall, it's a good place to get a tasty bite and soak in the flavor of this Cherry Grove neighborhood at the heart of the old shag culture.

Accommodations

There is no dearth of lodging in the Myrtle Beach area, from the typical high-rise "resorts" (think condos on steroids) to chain hotels, vacation villas, house rentals, and camping. Because of the plethora of options, prices are generally reasonable, and competition to provide more and more on-site amenities—free breakfasts, "lazy river" pools, washers and dryers, hot tubs, poolside grills, and so on—has only increased. You are the beneficiary, so you might as well take advantage of it.

Note that the stated price range may be very broad because so many Myrtle Beach lodgings offer several room options, from one-bed guest rooms to full three-bedroom suites. Here are a few general tips to consider when booking a room:

• The larger suites are generally "condo apartments," meaning they're privately owned. While they're usually immaculately clean for your arrival, it means that housekeeping is minimal and you won't get lots of complimentary goodies whenever you call the front desk.

• The entire Myrtle Beach area is undergoing growth, and that includes the accommodations. This means that many properties have older sections and newer ones. Ask beforehand which section you're being booked in.

• Check www.myrtlebeachhotels.com for last-minute deals and specials at 11 well-run local resorts.

• By the end of September, prices drop dramatically.

• Almost all area lodgings, especially the high-rises, feature on-site pools galore; lounge chairs and tables are at a premium and go very quickly during high season when the sun's out.

• Always keep in mind that summer is the high season here, unlike the rest of South Carolina, and guest rooms, especially at beachfront places, get snapped up very early.

UNDER $150

For 75 years, ★ **Driftwood on the Oceanfront** (1600 N. Ocean Blvd., 843/448-1544, www.driftwoodlodge.com, $100-120) has been a favorite place to stay. Upgraded over the years, but not *too* upgraded, this five-story, 90-room complex is family-owned and takes pride in delivering personalized service that is simply impossible to attain in the larger high-rises nearby. As you'd expect, the guest rooms and suites are a bit on the small side by modern Myrtle Beach standards—with none of the increasingly popular three-bedroom suites available—but most everyone is impressed by the value.

Probably the best-regarded bed-and-breakfast in Myrtle Beach (yes, there are a precious few) is the ★ **Serendipity Inn** (407 71st Ave. N., 843/449-5268, www.serendipityinn.com, $90-150). A short walk from the beach but sometimes seemingly light-years away from the typical Myrtle sprawl, this 15-room gem features a simple but elegant pool, an attractive courtyard, and sumptuous guest rooms. The full breakfast is simple but hearty. There's free Wi-Fi throughout the property.

If you're looking for a basic, inexpensive, one-bed hotel experience on the beach, ask for a room at the new oceanfront section of the **Best Western Grand Strand Inn and Suites** (1804 S. Ocean Blvd., 843/448-1461, $80-140), a smallish but clean and attentively run chain hotel. The property's other buildings are significantly older and are located across busy Ocean Boulevard, and the walk across the street to the beach can be difficult, especially if you have small kids. That said, this is a great value and a quality property.

If water park-style entertainment is your thing, try **Dunes Village Resort** (5200 N. Ocean Blvd., 877/828-2237, www.dunesvillage.com, $140-300), also one of the better values in Myrtle. Its huge indoor water park has copious waterslides, including several for adults, and various other aquatic diversions. The buildings themselves—the property comprises two high-rise towers—are modern and well equipped, although since this is a time-share-style property, housekeeping is minimal.

$150-300

My favorite place to stay at Myrtle Beach is the ★ **Island Vista Oceanfront Resort** (6000 N. Ocean Blvd., 855/732-6250, www.islandvista.com). While not the flashiest or heaviest in amenities by any means, Island Vista's location in a quiet residential area overlooking a mile of the Strand's best and least-traveled beach makes it a standout alternative to the often crowded and logistically challenging environment you'll find in the more built-up high-rise blocks farther south on the beach. In the high season you'll pay about $300 for a one-bedroom suite, but the prices on the spacious and very well equipped two- and three-bedroom suites are competitive. They have the usual multiple-pool option, including an indoor heated pool area. A big plus is the fact that the in-house fine-dining restaurant, the **Cypress Room,** is a definite cut above most area hotel kitchens.

Consistently one of the best-regarded properties in Myrtle proper, the **Hampton Inn & Suites Oceanfront** (1803 S. Ocean Blvd., 843/946-6400, www.hamptoninnoceanfront.com, $169-259) has been made even better by a thorough upgrade. This is a classic beachfront high-rise (not to be confused with the Hampton Inn at Broadway at the Beach), clean inside and out, with elegant, tasteful guest rooms in various sizes. Guest rooms range from typical one-bed, one-bath hotel-style rooms to larger condo-style suites with a fridge.

Situated more toward North Myrtle, the **Sea Watch Resort** (161 Sea Watch Blvd., $171-395) is a good choice for those who want the full-on condo high-rise Myrtle Beach experience but not necessarily the crowds that usually go with it. Guest rooms are clean and well equipped.

One of the better-quality stays for the price in Myrtle is the **Roxanne Towers** (1604 N. Ocean Blvd., 843/839-1016, www.theroxanne.com, $150-250). Known for attentive service, this is a busy property in a busy area. Parking is historically something of a problem. Keep in mind that room size is capped at two bedrooms, so there are none of the sprawling three-bedroom suites that many other local places have.

For a quality stay in the heart of Myrtle's beach bustle, go for the **Sandy Beach Resort** (201 S. Ocean Blvd., 800/844-6534, www. sandybeachoceanfrontresort. com, $200-300). The guest rooms are top-notch, and the service is professional. As is the case with many local properties, there is a newer section, the Palmetto Tower, and an "old" section, the venerable Magnolia Tower. There are one-, two-, and three-bedroom units available, the latter a particularly good value.

Considered one of the major remaining centers of the shag subculture on the Strand, the **Ocean Drive Beach and Golf Resort** (98 N. Ocean Blvd., $200-350) up in North Myrtle Beach hosts many events surrounding the notable regional dance, including the Shaggers Hall of Fame. Its on-site lounge, **The Spanish Galleon,** specializes in beach music. It's also just a great place to stay, with amenities such as a "lazy river," a whirlpool, full galley-style kitchens, and, of course, proximity to the beach.

Also up in North Myrtle is the ★ **Tilghman Beach and Golf Resort** (1819 Ocean Blvd., 843/280-0913, www.tilghmanresort.com, $200-350), owned by the same company as the Ocean Drive Beach Resort. It's not directly on the beach, but since the buildings in front of it are pretty low, you can still get awesome ocean views. Even the views from the back of the building aren't bad, since they overlook a golf course. But you don't have to be a duffer to enjoy the Tilghman—the pool scene is great, the balconies are roomy, and the suites are huge and well enough equipped (a flat-screen TV in every room) to make you feel right at home.

VACATION RENTALS

There are hundreds, probably thousands, of privately rented condo-style lodgings at Myrtle Beach, in all shapes and forms. Most, however, do a great job of catering to what vacationers here really seem to want: space, convenience, and a working kitchen. All rental agencies basically work with the same listings, so looking for and finding a rental is easier than you might think.

Some of the key brokers are **Myrtle Beach Vacation Rentals** (800/845-0833, www. mb-vacationrentals.com), **Beach Vacations** (866/453-4818, www.beachvacationsmb.com), **Barefoot Vacations** (800/845-0837, www. barefootvacations.info), **Elliott Realty and Beach Rentals** (www.elliottrealty.com), and **Atlantic Dunes Vacation Rentals** (866/544-2568, www.atlanticdunesvacations. com).

BEACH CAMPING

Myrtle Beach is not where you go for a pristine, quiet camping experience. For that, I suggest Huntington State Park down near Murrells Inlet. However, there is plenty of camping, almost all of it heavily RV-oriented, if you want it. For more info, visit www.campmyrtlebeach.com.

The closest thing to a real live campground is good old **Myrtle Beach State Park** (4401 S. Kings Hwy., 843/238-5325, www.southcarolinaparks.com, daily 6am-10pm, $4 adults, $1.50 ages 6-15, free under age 6), which despite being only a short drive from the rest of the beachfront sprawl is still a fairly relaxing place to stay, complete with its own scenic fishing pier (daily fishing fee $4.50). There's even a nature center with a little aquarium and exhibits.

The park's charming and educational atmosphere is largely due to the fact that this is one of the 17 Civilian Conservation Corps parks built during the Great Depression. There are four cabins ($54-125) available, all fully furnished and about 200 yards from the beach. The main campground is about 300 yards from the beach and comprises 300 sites with electricity and water ($23-25) and a 45-site tent and overflow campground ($17-19) that is only open during the summer high season.

The **Myrtle Beach KOA** (613 6th Ave. S., 800/562-7790, www.myrtlebeachkoa. com), though not at all cheap ($40-50 even for tenters), offers the usual safe, dependable amenities of that well-known chain, including rental "kabins" and activities for kids.

Willow Tree RV Resort and Campground (520 Southern Sights Dr., 843/756-4334, www.willowtreervr.com) is set inland on a well-wooded 300-acre tract with large sites well away from the sprawl, and it offers lakeside fishing and bike trails. In the summer high season, basic sites are $50-82, and the one- and two-bedroom cabins range $120-190.

Information and Services

The main visitors center for Myrtle Beach is the **Myrtle Beach Area Chamber of Commerce and Visitor Center** (1200 N. Oak St., 843/626-7444, www.visitmybeach.com, Mon.-Fri. 8:30am-5pm, Sat. 10am-2pm). There's an **Airport Welcome Center** (1180 Jetport Rd., 843/626-7444) as well, and a visitors center in North Myrtle Beach, the **North Myrtle Beach Chamber of Commerce and Convention & Visitors Bureau** (270 U.S. 17 N., 843/281-2662, www.northmyrtlebeachchamber.com).

The main health care facility in the Myrtle Beach area is **Grand Strand Regional Medical Center** (809 82nd Pkwy., 843/692-1000, www.grandstrandmed.com). Myrtle Beach is served by the **Myrtle Beach Police Department** (1101 N. Oak St., 843/918-1382, www.cityofmyrtlebeach.com). The separate municipality of North Myrtle Beach is served by the **North Myrtle Beach Police Department** (843/280-5555, www.nmb.us).

Transportation

GETTING THERE

The Myrtle Beach area is served by the fast-growing **Myrtle Beach International Airport** (MYR, 1100 Jetport Rd., 843/448-1589, www.flymyrtlebeach.com), which hosts Allegiant (www.allegiantair.com), American (www.aa.com), Delta (www.delta.com), Porter Airlines (www.flyporter.com), Spirit (www.spiritair.com), United (www.ual.com), and WestJet (www.westjet.com).

Unusual for South Carolina, a state that is exceptionally well served by the interstate highway system, the main route into the area is the smaller U.S. 17, which runs north-south, with a parallel business spur, from Georgetown up to the North Carolina border. The approach from the west is by U.S. 501, called Black Skimmer Trail as it approaches Myrtle Beach.

The local **Greyhound Bus Terminal** (511 7th Ave. N., 843/231-2222, www.greyhound.com) is in "downtown" Myrtle Beach.

GETTING AROUND

In practice, the Myrtle Beach municipalities blend and blur into each other in one long sprawl parallel to the main north-south route, U.S. 17. However, always keep this in mind: Just north of Murrells Inlet, U.S. 17 divides into two distinct portions. There's the U.S. 17 Bypass, which continues to the west of much of the coastal growth, and there's Business U.S. 17, also known as Kings Highway, the main drag along which most key attractions and places of interest are located.

The other key north-south route, Ocean Boulevard, runs along the beach. This is a two-lane road that can get pretty congested in the summer.

Thankfully, area planners have provided a

great safety valve for some of this often horrendous traffic. Highway 31, the Carolina Bays Parkway, begins inland from Myrtle Beach at about 16th Avenue. This wide and modern highway roughly parallels the Intracoastal Waterway and takes you on a straight shot, with a 65 mph speed limit, all the way to Highway 22 (the Conway Bypass) or all the way to Highway 9 at Cherry Grove Beach, the farthest extent of North Myrtle Beach. If time is of the essence, you should use Highway 31 whenever possible.

Rental Car, Taxi, and Bus

You will need a vehicle to make the most of this area. Rental cars are available at the airport. Rental options outside the airport include **Enterprise** (1377 U.S. 501, 843/626-4277; 3401 U.S. 17 S., 843/361-4410, www.enterprise.com), **Hertz** (851 Jason Blvd., 843/839-9530, www.hertz.com), and the unique **Rent-a-Wreck** (901 3rd Ave. S., 843/626-9393).

Taxi service on the Strand is plentiful but fairly expensive. Look in the local Yellow Pages for full listings; a couple of good services are **Yellow Cab** (917 Oak St., 843/448-5555) and **Beach Checker Cab** (843/272-6212) in North Myrtle.

The area is served by the **Coastal Rapid Public Transit Authority** (1418 3rd Ave., 843/248-7277), which runs several bus routes up and down the Strand. Ask for information at a visitors center or call for a schedule.

Bicycle

Bicyclists in Myrtle Beach can take advantage of some completed segments of the South Carolina portion of the **East Coast Greenway** (www.greenway.org), which, generally speaking, is Ocean Boulevard. You can actually ride Ocean Boulevard all the way from 82nd Avenue North down to the southern city limit.

In North Myrtle Beach, from Sea Mountain Highway in Cherry Grove, you can bike Ocean Boulevard clear down to 46th Avenue South, with a detour from 28th to 33rd Avenues. A right on 46th Avenue South takes you to Barefoot Landing. And, of course, for a scenic ride, you can pedal on the beach itself for miles. But remember: Bicycling on the sidewalk is strictly prohibited.

For bike rentals, try **Beach Bike Shop** (711 Broadway St., 843/448-5335, www.beachbikeshop.com). In North Myrtle, try **Wheel Fun Rentals** (91 S. Ocean Blvd., 843/280-7900, www.wheelfunrentals.com).

Points Inland

CONWAY

A nice day trip west of Myrtle Beach—and a nice change from that area's intense development—is to the charming town of Conway, just northwest of Myrtle Beach on U.S. 501 and the Waccamaw River. Founded in 1733 with the name Kingston, it originally marked the frontier of the colony. It was later renamed Conwayborough, soon shortened to Conway, in honor of local leader Robert Conway, and now serves as the seat of Horry County.

Conway's heyday was during Reconstruction, when it became a major trade center for timber products and naval stores from the

interior. The railroad came through town in 1887 (later being extended to Myrtle Beach), and most remaining buildings date from this period or later. The most notable Conway native is perhaps an unexpected name: William Gibson, originator of the cyberpunk genre of science fiction, was born here in 1948.

Conway is small and easily explored. Make your first stop the **Conway Visitors Center** (903 3rd Ave., 843/248-1700, www.cityofconway.com, Mon.-Fri. 9am-5pm), where you can pick up maps. It also offers guided tours ($2 pp) that depart from City Hall (3rd Ave. and Main St.); call for a schedule. You can also visit the **Conway Chamber of Commerce** (203 Main St.) for maps and information.

Sights

Conway's chief attraction is the 850-foot **Riverwalk** (843/248-2273, www.conwayscchamber.com, daily dawn-dusk) along the blackwater Waccamaw River, a calming location with shops and restaurants nearby. Waterborne tours on the *Kingston Lady* leave from the Conway Marina at the end of the Riverwalk.

Another key stop is the **Horry County Museum** (428 Main St., 843/248-1542, www.horrycountymuseum.org, Tues.-Sat. 9am-4pm, free), which tells the story of this rather large South Carolina county from prehistory to the present. It holds an annual Quilt Gala in February, which features some great regional examples of the art.

Across from the campus of Coastal Carolina University is the circa-1972 Traveler's Chapel, aka **The Littlest Church in South Carolina** (U.S. 501 and Cox Ferry Rd.). At 12 by 24 feet, it seats no more than a dozen people. Weddings are held here throughout the year. Admission is free, but donations are accepted.

Accommodations

The best stay in town is at the four-star

Cypress Inn (16 Elm St., 843/248-8199, www.acypressinn.com, $145-235), a beautiful and well-appointed 12-room B&B right on the Waccamaw River.

LEWIS OCEAN BAY HERITAGE PRESERVE

The humongous (over 9,000 acres) **Lewis Ocean Bay Heritage Preserve** (803/734-3886, www.dnr.sc.gov, daily dawn-dusk, free) is one of the more impressive phenomena in the Palmetto State, from a naturalist's viewpoint, made all the more special by its location a short drive from heavily developed Myrtle Beach. Managed by the state, it contains an amazing 23 Carolina bays, by far the largest concentration in South Carolina. These elliptical depressions, scattered throughout the Carolinas and all oriented in a northwest-southeast direction, are typified by a cypress-tupelo bog environment.

To get here from Myrtle Beach, take U.S. 501 north to Highway 90 and head east. After about seven miles, turn east onto the unpaved International Drive across from the Wild Horse subdivision. After about 1.5 miles on International Drive, veer left onto Old Kingston Road. The preserve is shortly ahead on both sides of the road; park along the shoulder.

The Lower Grand Strand

Tiny **Pawleys Island** (year-round population about 200) likes to call itself "America's first resort" because of its early role, in the late 1700s, as a place for planters to go with their families to escape the mosquito-infested rice and cotton fields. It's still a vacation getaway and still has a certain elite understatement, an attitude the locals call "arrogantly shabby." While you can visit casually, most people who enjoy the famous Pawleys Island beaches do so from one of the many vacation rental properties.

Shabby arrogance does have its upside,

however—there is a ban on further commercial development in the community, allowing Pawleys to remain slow and peaceful. For generations, Pawleys was famous for its cypress cottages, many on stilts. Sadly, 1989's Hurricane Hugo destroyed a great many of these iconic structures—27 out of 29 on the south end alone, most of which have been replaced by far less aesthetically pleasing homes. Hurricane Matthew in 2016, while nowhere near as catastrophic, caused extensive damage to the beach itself and surrounding dunes.

Directly adjacent to Pawleys, **Litchfield**

Beach offers similar low-key enjoyment along with a world-class golf resort. **Murrells Inlet** is chiefly known for a single block of seafood restaurants on its eponymous waterway.

SIGHTS
★ Brookgreen Gardens

One of the unique—and most unlikely—sights in the developed Grand Strand area is bucolic **Brookgreen Gardens** (1931 Brookgreen Dr., 843/235-6000, www.brookgreen.org, May-Mar. daily 9:30am-5pm, Apr. daily 9:30am-8pm, $15 adults, $7 ages 6-12, free under age 6), directly across U.S. 17 from Huntington Beach State Park. Once one of several massive contiguous plantations in the Pawleys Island area, the modern Brookgreen is a result of the charity and passion of Archer Milton Huntington and his wife, Anna. Quite the sculptor in her own right, Anna Huntington saw to it that Brookgreen's 9,000 acres would host by far the largest single collection of outdoor sculpture in the United States. To learn more, visit the on-site **Carroll A. Campbell Jr. Center for American Sculpture,** which offers seminars and workshops throughout the year. A highlight of the year is the **Night of a Thousand Candles** in early December. It's actually closer to 6,000 candles, lit all across the grounds to gorgeous seasonal effect.

On the other end of the grounds opposite the gardens is the **E. Craig Wall Jr. Lowcountry Nature Center,** which includes a small enclosed cypress swamp with a boardwalk, herons and egrets, and a delightful river otter exhibit.

To add an extra layer of enjoyment to your visit, you can explore this massive preserve much more deeply by taking one of several tours offered on Brookgreen's pontoon boat ($7 adults, $4 children, on top of regular admission); check the website for a schedule.

★ Huntington Beach State Park

Right across the street from Brookgreen is **Huntington Beach State Park** (16148 Ocean Hwy., 843/237-4440, www.southcarolinaparks.com, daily 6am-10pm, $5 adults, $3 ages 6-15, free under age 6), probably the best of South Carolina's state parks not built by the Civilian Conservation Corps. Once a part of the same vast parcel of land owned by Archer Huntington and his wife, Anna, the state has leased it from the trustees of their estate since the 1960s.

You can tour the "castle" on the beach,

salt marsh at Huntington Beach State Park

Atalaya, former home of the Huntingtons and now the yearly site of the Atalaya Arts and Crafts Festival. This evocative Moorish-style National Historic Landmark is open to the public for free guided tours (Memorial Day-Sept. daily noon-1pm, Oct. Sun.-Mon. noon-1pm, Tues.-Sat. noon-2pm). You can stroll three miles of beach, view birds and wildlife from boardwalks into the marsh, hike several nature trails, and visit the well-done **Environmental Education Center** (843/235-8755, Tues.-Sun. 10am-5pm), which features a saltwater touch tank and a baby alligator.

While Hurricane Matthew in 2016 felled many trees at the park, thankfully it avoided major long-term damage.

Pawleys Island Historic District

Although many of the island's homes were leveled by Hurricane Hugo, the **Pawleys Island Historic District** (843/237-1698, www.townofpawleysisland.com), in the central portion of the island, still has a dozen contributing structures, almost all on Myrtle Avenue. Among them are the **Weston House** (506 Myrtle Ave.), or Pelican Inn, and the **Ward House** (520 Myrtle Ave.), or Liberty Lodge. As you view the structures, many with their own historical markers, note the architecture. Because these were intended to be lived in May-November, they resemble open and airy Caribbean homes, with extensive porches and plenty of windows.

EVENTS

The highlight of the lower Grand Strand calendar is the annual **Atalaya Arts and Crafts Festival** (www.atalayafestival.com, $6 adults, free under age 16), which takes place on the grounds of Huntington Beach State Park each September. There's music, food, and about 100 vendors who show their art and wares within the exotic Atalaya home. Admission to the park is free during the festival.

Also in September is the **Pawleys Island Festival of Music and Art** (www.

pawleysmusic.com, prices vary), which happens outdoors, across U.S. 17 under the stars in Brookgreen Gardens, with a few performances at nearby Litchfield Plantation.

A main event in Murrells Inlet is the annual **Fourth of July Boat Parade** (843/651-0900, free), which celebrates American independence with a patriotically themed procession of all kinds of streamer- and flag-bedecked watercraft down the inlet. It begins at about 6pm and ends, of course, with a big fireworks display.

Another big deal in Murrells Inlet is the annual **Blessing of the Inlet** (843/651-5099, www.belinumc.org), always held the first Saturday in May and sponsored by a local Methodist church. Enjoy food vendors, goods baked by local women, and a great family atmosphere.

SHOPPING

The shopping scene revolves around the famous Pawleys Island hammock, a beautiful and practical bit of local handiwork sold primarily at the **Hammock Shops Village** (10880 Ocean Hwy., 843/237-8448, Mon.-Sat. 10am-6pm, Sun. 1pm-5pm). To purchase a Pawleys Island hammock, go to **The Original Hammock Shop** (843/237-9122, www.the-hammockshop.com), housed in a century-old cottage. Next door is the affiliated **Hammock Shop General Store,** which, as the name implies, sells a variety of other goods such as beachwear, books, and a notable style of local fudge. The actual hammocks are handcrafted in the shed next door, the way they have been since 1889.

SPORTS AND RECREATION
Beaches

Public access to the beach that remains after 2016's Hurricane Matthew is very limited. The best way to enjoy the beach is to rent one of the many private beach homes for a week or so. Beach access with parking at Pawleys Island includes a fairly large lot at the south end of the island and parking areas off Atlantic

Avenue at Hazard, 1st, Pearce, 2nd, and 3rd Streets, and Shell Road.

Kayaking and Canoeing

The Waccamaw River and associated inlets and creeks are peaceful and scenic places to kayak, with plenty of bird-watching opportunities to boot. For a two-hour guided tour of the area salt marsh, reserve a spot on the kayak trips sponsored by the **Environmental Education Center** (Huntington Beach State Park, 843/235-8755, office Tues.-Sun. 10am-5pm, $30 pp). Call for tour days and times. Or you can put in yourself at Oyster Landing, about one mile from the entrance to the state park.

Golf

Home to some of the best links in the Carolinas, the lower part of the Grand Strand recently organized its courses under the umbrella moniker **Waccamaw Golf Trail** (www. waccamawgolftrail.com), chiefly for marketing purposes. No matter, the courses are still as superb as ever, if generally pricier than their counterparts up the coast.

The best course in the area, and one of the best in the country, is the **Caledonia Golf and Fish Club** (369 Caledonia Dr., 843/237-3675, www.fishclub.com, $195). While the course itself is almost ridiculously young—it opened in 1995—this masterpiece is built, as so many area courses are, on the grounds of a former rice plantation. The clubhouse, in fact, dates from before the Civil War. Packages (800/449-4005, www.myrtlebeachcondo-rentals.com) are available. Affiliated with Caledonia is the fine **True Blue Golf Club** (900 Blue Stem Dr., 843/235-0900, www.fishclub.com, $100), considered perhaps the most challenging single course on the Strand.

Another excellent Pawleys course is the **Litchfield Country Club** (U.S. 17 and Magnolia Dr., 843/237-3411, www.litchcc.com, $60), one of the Grand Strand's oldest. The facilities are self-consciously dated—this is a country club, after all—setting it apart from the flashier, newer courses sprouting like mushrooms farther up the Strand. It's a deceptive course that's short on yards but heavy on doglegs.

The Jack Nicklaus-designed **Pawleys Plantation Golf and Country Club** (70 Tanglewood Dr., 843/237-6100, www.pawleysplantation.com, $150) has set a tough example for the last 20 years. The front nine is a traditional layout, while the back nine melts into the marsh.

FOOD
Breakfast and Brunch

The high-end strip mall setting isn't the most romantic, but by broad consensus the best breakfast on the entire Strand is at **Applewood House of Pancakes** (14361 Ocean Hwy., 843/979-1022, daily 6am-2pm, $5-10) in Pawleys. Eggs Benedict, specialty omelets, crepes, waffles, and pancakes abound in this roomy, unpretentious dining room. Do it; you won't regret it.

Seafood

Murrells Inlet has several good places clustered together along the marsh on U.S. 17. The best is ★ **Lee's Inlet Kitchen** (4460 Business U.S. 17, 843/651-2881, www.leesinletkitchen.com, Mar.-Nov. Mon.-Sat. 4:30pm-10pm, $20-40), the only joint still in the original family—in this case the Lee family, who started the place in the mid-1940s. The seafood is simply but delectably prepared (your choice of fried or broiled). They close down December-February.

Everything from the fried green tomatoes to the crab cakes is fresh, hot, and tasty at **Flo's Place Restaurant** (3797 Business U.S. 17, 843/651-7222, www.flosplace.com, daily 11am-10pm, $15-25). Flo is sadly no longer with us, but her place still eschews schlock for a humble, down-home feel. In recent years the menu has added more New Orleans-style Creole seafood dishes.

On the other end of the spectrum stylewise is **Divine Fish House** (3993 Business U.S. 17, 843/651-5800, www.divinefishhouse.com, daily 5pm-10pm, $20-33), which offers more adventurous high-end cuisine like the fine San Antonio salmon (smothered with pepper-jack cheese and bacon) and the Asian-flavored banana leaf mangrove grouper.

ACCOMMODATIONS
Under $150

Similarly named but not to be confused with Litchfield Plantation is the nearby **Litchfield Beach and Golf Resort** (14276 Ocean Hwy., 866/538-0187, www.litchfieldbeach.com, $100-170). In typical Grand Strand fashion, this property delivers a lot of service for a surprisingly low price and offers a wide range of lodging choices, from a basic room at the Seaside Inn on the low end to four-bedroom villas ($230) on the other. A regular free shuttle takes you to the beach. There are also lots of water activities right on the premises, including a "lazy river" tube course.

$150-300

The premier B&B-style lodging on the entire Grand Strand is ★ **Litchfield Plantation** (Kings River Rd., 843/237-9121, www.litchfieldplantation.com, $230-275) on Pawleys Island, built, as you've probably come to expect by now, on an old plantation. There is a host of lodging choices, all of them absolutely splendid. The Plantation House has four sumptuous suites, all impeccably decorated. The humbly named Guest House—actually an old mansion—has six bedrooms, and the entire 2nd floor is an executive suite. Lastly, the newer outparcel villas contain an assortment of two- and three-bedroom suites.

Vacation Rentals

Many who enjoy the Pawleys area do so using a vacation rental as a home base rather than a traditional hotel or B&B. **Pawleys Island Realty** (88 N. Causeway Rd., 800/937-7352, www.pawleysislandrealty.com) can hook you up.

Camping

At **Huntington Beach State Park** (16148 Ocean Hwy., 843/237-4440, www.southcarolinaparks.com, daily 6am-10pm, $5 adults, $3 ages 6-15, free under age 6), the beach is beautiful, there are trails and an education center, and the bird-watching is known as some of the best on the East Coast. While there are 131 RV-suitable sites ($23-28), tenters should go to one of the six walk-in tent sites ($17-19).

INFORMATION AND SERVICES

On Pawleys Island is the **Georgetown County Visitors Bureau** (95-A Centermarsh Ln., 843/235-6595, www.visitgeorgetowncountysc.com). The **Myrtle Beach Area Chamber of Commerce** (1200 N. Oak St., 843/626-7444, www.visitmybeach.com) and the **Waccamaw Community Hospital** (4070 U.S. 17 Bypass, 843/652-1000, www.georgetownhospitalsystem.org) are in Murrells Inlet. Pawleys Island is served by the **Pawleys Island Police Department** (321 Myrtle Ave., 843/237-3008, www.townofpawleysisland.com).

Georgetown and Vicinity

Think of Georgetown as Beaufort's lesser-known cousin. Like Beaufort, it's an hour away from Charleston, it boasts a tidy historic downtown, and it was once a major center of Lowcountry plantation culture. However, Georgetown gets significantly less attention and less traffic. The fact that the entrance to town is dominated by the sprawling, ominous-looking Georgetown Steel mill on one side of the road and the massive International Paper plant on the other has something to do with it. Making matters worse was a disastrous fire in September 2013, which destroyed seven historic waterfront buildings.

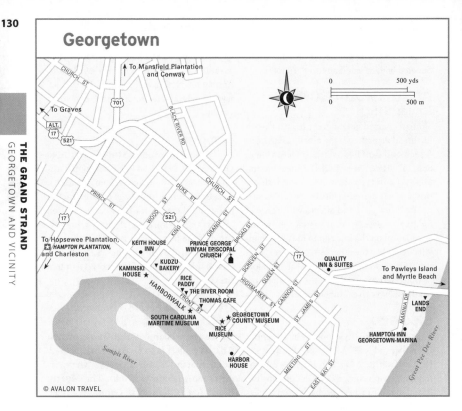

Georgetown

To Mansfield Plantation and Conway

CHURCH ST.

To Graves

ALT. 17 · 521

701

BLACK RIVER RD.

CHURCH ST.

DUKE ST.

CHURCH ST.

PRINCE ST.

WOOD ST.

KING ST.

521

17

ORANGE ST.

BROAD ST.

SCREVEN ST.

QUEEN ST.

CANNON ST.

17

HIGHMARKET ST.

ST. JAMES ST.

MEETING ST.

EAST BAY ST.

MARINA DR.

To Hopsewee Plantation, **HAMPTON PLANTATION,** and Charleston

KEITH HOUSE INN

PRINCE GEORGE WINYAH EPISCOPAL CHURCH

QUALITY INN & SUITES

To Pawleys Island and Myrtle Beach

KAMINSKI HOUSE

KUDZU BAKERY

RICE PADDY

THE RIVER ROOM

THOMAS CAFE

GEORGETOWN COUNTY MUSEUM

LANDS END

HARBORWALK

FRONT ST.

SOUTH CAROLINA MARITIME MUSEUM

RICE MUSEUM

HAMPTON INN GEORGETOWN-MARINA

HARBOR HOUSE

Sampit River

Great Pee Dee River

500 yds
500 m

© AVALON TRAVEL

HISTORY

The third-oldest city in South Carolina, after Charleston and Beaufort, Georgetown was founded in 1729 on a four- by eight-block grid, most of which still exists today, complete with original street names. The Revolutionary War hero Francis Marion, the "Swamp Fox," was born in nearby Berkeley County and conducted operations in and around the area throughout the war.

While Charleston-area plantations get most of the attention, the truth is that by 1840 about 150 rice plantations on the Sampit and Little Pee Dee Rivers were producing half of the entire national output of the staple crop. After the Civil War, the collapse of the slave-based economy (at its height, 90 percent of Georgetown's population were enslaved) meant the collapse of the rice economy as well.

In 1905, Bernard Baruch—native South

Carolinian, Wall Street mover and shaker, and adviser to presidents—came to town, purchasing Hobcaw Barony, a former plantation. It became his winter residence and hunting ground, and his legacy of conservation lives on there today in an education center on the site.

On the national level Georgetown is perhaps best known for being the hometown of comedian Chris Rock. Although he moved away long ago, many members of his family continue to live here.

SIGHTS
Kaminski House

The city of Georgetown owns and operates the historic **Kaminski House** (1003 Front St., 843/546-7706, www.kaminskimuseum.org, Mon.-Sat. 9am-5pm, $7 adults, $3 ages 6-12, free under age 6). Not to be confused with the

the Old Market building, part of the Rice Museum

1842 timepiece, hosts the bulk of the archival information on the impact of rice growing on the region's history and economy. The adjacent **Kaminski Hardware Building** includes a 17-minute video on the rice industry, a good Gullah-Geechee cultural exhibit, and a gift shop.

Most visitors to the Rice Museum take a one-hour **guided tour,** included in the price of admission. The highlight is the "Browns Ferry Vessel," the remains of a wrecked local colonial-era boat, circa 1730, which has its own listing in the National Register of Historic Places.

South Carolina Maritime Museum

As the Palmetto State's second-largest port, Georgetown has more than its share of nautical history. Check it out at the burgeoning **South Carolina Maritime Museum** (729 Front St., 843/520-0111, www.scmaritimemuseum.org, Mon.-Sat. 11am-5pm, free). The 2013 downtown fire caused a bit of damage to the building, but the museum is still humming. It sponsors the fun Wooden Boat Show each October on the waterfront.

Georgetown County Museum

For a more complete look at various aspects of local history, check out the **Georgetown County Museum** (632 Prince St., 843/545-7020, Tues.-Fri. 10am-5pm, Sat. 10am-3pm, $4 adults, $2 ages 6-18, free under age 6). The highlight is a recently discovered letter written by Revolutionary War hero Francis Marion.

Prince George Winyah Episcopal Church

It has seen better days—the British partially burned it during the Revolutionary War—but **Prince George Winyah Episcopal Church** (301 Broad St., 843/546-4358, www.pgwinyah.org, Mon.-Fri. 11:30am-4:30pm, services Sun. 8am, 9am, and 11am) is still a fine example of the Anglican tradition of the Lowcountry rice culture. Built in 1750 out

Kaminski Hardware Building down the block, this grand home was built in 1769 and was the executive residence of several city mayors. It is furnished with a particularly exquisite selection of 18th- and 19th-century antiques.

The grounds are beautiful as well, overlooking the Sampit River and lined with Spanish moss-covered oaks. Take the free 45-minute **guided tour** departing Monday-Saturday at 11am, 1pm, and 3pm; call ahead to confirm tour times.

Rice Museum

The succinctly named **Rice Museum** (633 Front St., 843/546-7423, www.ricemuseum.org, Mon.-Sat. 10am-4:30pm, $7 adults, $3 ages 6-21, free under age 6) is a look back at the all-important staple crop and its massive effects on Georgetown, which at one point accounted for half of the country's rice production.

There are actually two parts of the museum. The **Old Market building,** often simply called "the Town Clock" because of its

The Swamp Fox and the Coming of Guerrilla Warfare

Short, bowlegged, and moody, Francis Marion was as far away from the template of the war hero as his tactics were from the storybook exploits of military literature. The father of modern guerrilla warfare was born an unimpressively small and sickly baby, the youngest of seven, somewhere in Berkeley County, South Carolina, in 1732 to hardworking French Huguenot parents. Soon his family would move near Georgetown on the coast, and the teenage Marion became enamored with the sea. While his infatuation with maritime life lasted exactly one voyage—a whale rammed and sank his ship—a taste for adventure remained.

During the French and Indian War, Marion fought local Cherokee people, using irregular tactics that would resurface during the Revolutionary War. His first experience in the Revolutionary War was in more textbook engagements, such as the defenses of Fort Moultrie and Fort Sullivan and the siege of Savannah. But with the fall of Charleston in 1780, a vengeful Marion and his ragged band of volunteer fighters—who, unusual for the time, included African Americans—vanished into the bogs of the Pee Dee and took up a different way of warfare: ambush and retreat, harass and vanish. In a foreshadowing of the revolutionary movements of the 20th century, "Marion's Men" provisioned themselves with food and supplies from a sympathetic local populace, offering receipts for reimbursement after the war.

Astride small agile mounts called Marsh Tackies, descendants of horses originally left by the

---

of ballast stones (the parish itself dates from substantially earlier, 1721), the sanctuary features classic box pews, expert stained glass, and ornate woodwork on the inside. The bell tower dates from 1824.

Hopsewee Plantation

Beautiful in an understated way, **Hopsewee Plantation** (494 Hopsewee Rd., 843/546-7891, www.hopsewee.com, Feb.-Nov. Tues.-Fri. 10am-4pm, Sat. 11am-4pm, Dec.-Jan. by appointment only, $17.50 adults, $10.50 ages 12-17, $7.50 ages 5-11, free under age 5), on the Santee River 12 miles south of Georgetown, was the birthplace of Thomas Lynch Jr., one of South Carolina's signers of the Declaration of Independence. Some key archaeological work is going on at the former slave village on this old indigo plantation; you can visit two of the original slave cabins on the tour. The 1740 main house is a masterpiece of colonial architecture, and all the more impressive because it's very nearly original, with the black cypress exterior largely intact. There's a fairly active calendar of events throughout the year, including sweetgrass basket-weaving classes.

★ Hampton Plantation

Tucked away three miles off U.S. 17 on the South Santee River is **Hampton Plantation State Historic Site** (1950 Rutledge Rd., 843/546-9361, www.southcarolinaparks.com, grounds daily 9am-5pm, free, house tours Sat.-Tues. 1pm, 2pm, and 3pm, $7.50 adults, $3.50 ages 6-15, free under age 6). This Georgian gem, one of the grandest of the antebellum Lowcountry homes, hosted George Washington in 1791. Supposedly the grand "Washington Oak" nearby provided shade for a picnic at which our first president dined. It was also the home of South Carolina poet laureate Archibald Rutledge, who sold it to the state in 1971. Because it's now a state-run project, admission fees are significantly lower than at most of the private plantation homes in the area. The imposing antebellum main house, built in 1735 and expanded in 1757, is magnificent both inside and out. If you want to skip the house tour, visiting the scenic grounds is free.

St. James-Santee Episcopal Church

This redbrick church doesn't look that old,

Spanish, the Patriots rode where bigger British cavalry horses balked. Marion's nocturnal cunning and his superior intelligence network frustrated the British army and their Loyalist supporters to no end, leading to his nickname, "the Swamp Fox."

British colonel Banastre Tarleton, himself known as "the Butcher" for atrocities committed against civilians, was dispatched to neutralize Marion. The savage cat-and-mouse game between the two formed the basis for the storyline of Mel Gibson's *The Patriot* (Gibson's character was reportedly a composite of Marion and several other South Carolina irregulars). Filmed entirely in South Carolina—including at Middleton Plantation, Cypress Gardens, and Historic Brattonsville— *The Patriot* is far from an exact chronicle, but it does accurately portray the nature of the war in the Southern theater, in which quarter was rarely asked or given, and little distinction was made between combatant and civilian.

While certainly the most famous, the Swamp Fox was merely first among equals in a veritable menagerie of hit-and-run fighters. Thomas Sumter, a Virginian by birth, became known as "the Carolina Gamecock" for his ferocity on the battlefield; Andrew Pickens, "the Wizard Owl," and his militiamen played a key role in the Battle of Cowpens in the Upstate.

After the war, Marion served in elected office, married, and settled down at his Pine Bluff Plantation, now submerged under the lake that bears his name. He died in 1795 at the age of 63.

but the sanctuary of **St. James-Santee Episcopal Church** (Old Georgetown Rd., 843/887-4386), south of Georgetown near Hampton Plantation State Historic Site, dates from before the Revolutionary War. Known locally as "the Old Brick Church," this building dates from 1768, but the St. James-Santee parish it serves was actually the second in the colony after St. Michael's in Charleston. The parish was notable for incorporating large numbers of French Huguenots. The interior is nearly as Spartan as the exterior, featuring the rare sight of old-fashioned family box pews. While the brick was imported from Britain, the columns are made of cypress. Today, only one official service is held each year in the Old

Hampton Plantation

Brick Church, during Easter. You can have a look at the exterior and walk through the cemetery during daylight hours anytime, though. You get here by following the signs via a very long dirt road, not recommended in rainy weather unless you have a good four-wheel-drive vehicle.

McClellanville

The almost unbearably cute little fishing village of McClellanville is nestled among the woods of Francis Marion National Forest and is known mostly for the annual **Lowcountry Shrimp Festival and Blessing of the Fleet** (http://lowcountryshrimpfestival.com), held on the waterfront in early May. This is the place to go for any kind of delectable fresh shrimp dish you might want, from fried shrimp to shrimp kebabs and shrimp tacos. The event culminates with the colorful and touching Blessing of the Fleet ceremony.

Hobcaw Barony

Once a plantation, then a winter home for a Wall Street investor, **Hobcaw Barony** (22 Hobcaw Rd., 843/546-4623, www.hobcaw-barony.org, hours and prices vary) is now an environmental education center. Hobcaw entered its modern period when 11 former plantations were purchased en masse in 1905 by Wall Street investor Bernard Baruch, a South Carolina native who wanted a winter residence to escape the brutal Manhattan winters. Presidents and prime ministers came to hunt and relax on its nearly 18,000 acres. Fifty years later, Baruch died, and his progressive-minded daughter Belle took over, immediately wanting to open the grounds to universities for scientific research.

Still privately owned by the Belle W. Baruch Foundation, much of Hobcaw Barony is open only to researchers, but the **Hobcaw Barony Discovery Center** (843/546-4623, www.hobcawbarony.org, Mon.-Fri. 9am-5pm, free) has various exhibits on local history and culture, including Native American artifacts and a modest but fun aquarium with a touch tank. To experience the rest of Hobcaw Barony, you must take one of the various themed guided tours (call for days and times). The basic Hobcaw tour ($20) takes you on a three-hour van ride all around the grounds, including the main Hobcaw House, the historic stables, and the old slave quarters, with an emphasis on the natural as well as human history of the area. Other special tours include Birding on the Barony ($30), Christmas in the Quarters ($20), and a catch-and-release fly-fishing tour ($250) of local waters.

Georgetown Lighthouse

While you can't access the state-owned **Georgetown Lighthouse,** you can indeed take a trip to the beach on North Island, where the lighthouse stands. The 1811 structure, repaired after heavy damage in the Civil War, is still an active beacon, now entirely automated.

North Island was part of lands bequeathed to the state by former Boston Red Sox owner Tom Yawkey; North Island is now part of a wildlife preserve bearing Yawkey's name. In 2001, the Georgetown Lighthouse, listed in the National Register of Historic Places, was added to the preserve.

Tours and Cruises

One of the most sought-after tour tickets in the Georgetown area is for the annual **Plantation Home Tour** (843/545-8291). Sponsored by the Episcopal Church Women of Prince George Winyah Parish, this event, generally happening the first week in April, brings visitors onto many local private antebellum estates that are not open to the public at any other time. Each ticket is for either the Friday or Saturday tour, both of which feature a different set of homes. Tickets include tea at the Winyah Indigo Society Hall each afternoon.

For a standard downtown tour, get on one of the blue-and-white trams of **Swamp Fox Historic District Tours** (1001 Front St., 843/527-6469, $10 pp), which leave daily on the hour starting at 10am near the Harborwalk.

The best walking tour of Georgetown is

Miss Nell's Tours (843/546-3975, Tues. and Thurs. 10:30am and 2:30pm, other times by appointment, $7-24 depending on length of tour). Leaving from the Harborwalk Bookstore (723 Front St.), Miss Nell, who's been doing this for over 20 years, takes you on a delightful trek through Georgetown's charming downtown waterfront.

One of the more interesting local waterborne tours is on board the *Jolly Rover* and *Carolina Rover* (735 Front St., 843/546-8822, www.rovertours.com, Mon.-Sat., times and prices vary). The *Jolly Rover* is an honest-to-goodness tall ship that takes you on a two-hour tour of beautiful Winyah Bay and the Intracoastal Waterway, all with a crew in period dress. The *Carolina Rover* takes you on a three-hour ecotour to nearby North Island, site of the historic Georgetown Lighthouse. You can't tour the lighthouse itself, but you can get pretty darn close to it on this tour.

ENTERTAINMENT AND EVENTS

The **Winyah Bay Heritage Festival** (632 Prince St., 843/833-9919, www.winyahbay.org, free) happens each January at various venues and benefits the local historical society. The focus is on wooden decoys and waterfowl paintings, similar to Charleston's well-known Southeast Wildlife Exposition.

Each October brings the delightful **Wooden Boat Show** (843/545-0015, www.woodenboatshow.com, free) to the waterfront, a celebration of, you guessed it, wooden boats. These aren't toys but the real thing—sleek, classic, and beautiful in the water. There are kids' activities, canoe-making demonstrations, a boat contest, and the highlight, a boatbuilding challenge involving two teams working to build a skiff in four hours.

SPORTS AND RECREATION
Kayaking and Canoeing

Kayakers and canoeists will find a lot to do in the Georgetown area, which includes the confluence of five rivers and the Atlantic Ocean.

A good trip for more advanced paddlers is to go out on **Winyah Bay** to undeveloped North Island. With advance permission from the state's Department of Natural Resources (803/734-3888), you can camp here. Any paddling in Winyah Bay is pleasant, whether you camp or not.

Another long trip is on the nine-mile blackwater **Wambaw Creek Wilderness Canoe Trail** in the Francis Marion National Forest, which takes you through some beautiful cypress and tupelo habitats. Launch sites are at the Wambaw Creek Boat Ramp and a bridge landing. Other good trips in the national forest are on the Santee River and Echaw Creek.

For rentals and guided tours, contact **Nature Adventures Outfitters** (800/673-0679), which runs daylong paddles (about $85 pp); and **Black River Outdoors Center and Expeditions** (21 Garden Ave., 843/546-4840, www.blackriveroutdoors.com), which runs a good half-day tour ($55 adults, $35 under age 13). For those who want to explore the intricate matrix of creeks and tidal canals that made up the Georgetown rice plantation empire, a guided tour is essential.

Occasional kayak ecotours leave from the **Hobcaw Barony Discovery Center** (22 Hobcaw Rd., 843/546-4623, www.hobcawbarony.org, Mon.-Fri. 9am-5pm, $50) under the auspices of the **North Inlet Winyah Bay National Estuarine Research Reserve** (843/546-6219, www.northinlet.sc.edu).

Hiking

The **Francis Marion National Forest** (www.fs.fed.us) hosts a number of great hiking opportunities, chief among them the Swamp Fox passage of the **Palmetto Trail** (www.palmettoconservation.org). This 47-mile route winds through longleaf pine forests, cypress swamps, bottomland hardwood swamps, and various bogs, much of the way along an old logging railbed. The main entrance to the trail is near Steed Creek Road off U.S. 17; the entrance is clearly marked on the west side of the highway.

Another way to access the Swamp

Fox passage is at **Buck Hall Recreation Area** (843/887-3257) on the Intracoastal Waterway. This actually marks the trailhead of the Awendaw Connector of that part of the Palmetto Trail, a more maritime environment. Another trailhead from which to explore Francis Marion hiking trails is farther down U.S. 17 at the **Sewee Visitor Center** (5821 U.S. 17, 843/928-3368, www.fws.gov/seweecenter, Tues.-Sat. 9am-5pm).

Golf

The closest really good links to Georgetown are the courses of the **Waccamaw Golf Trail** (www.waccamawgolftrail.com), a short drive north on U.S. 17. The best public course close to Georgetown is the **Wedgefield Plantation Golf Club** (129 Clubhouse Ln., 843/546-8587, www.wedgefield.com, $69), on the grounds of an old rice plantation on the Black River about four miles west of town.

FOOD

Don't be fooled by Georgetown's small size—there's often a wait for tables at the better restaurants.

Breakfast and Brunch

The *Southern Living*-recommended **Thomas Cafe** (703 Front St., 843/546-7776, www.thomascafe.net, Mon.-Fri. 7am-2pm, Sat. 7am-1pm, $5-9) offers awesome omelets and pancakes in addition to more Lowcountry-flavored lunch dishes like crab cake sandwiches and fried green tomatoes.

Classic Southern

Georgetown's best-known fine-dining establishment is **The Rice Paddy** (732 Front St., 843/546-2021, www.ricepaddyrestaurant.com, lunch Mon.-Sat. 11:30am-2pm, dinner Mon.-Sat. 6pm-10pm, $20-30), with the name implying not an Asian menu but rather a nod to the town's Lowcountry culture. The seafood is strong, but they do a mean veal scaloppine and rack of lamb as well. Reservations are strongly recommended.

Coffee, Tea, and Sweets

A perennial favorite is ★ **Kudzu Bakery** (120 King St., 843/546-1847, Mon.-Fri. 9am-5:30pm, Sat. 9am-2pm), renowned for its fresh-baked goodies such as delectable breakfast muffins, velvety chocolate cakes, and seasonal pies with fresh ingredients like strawberries, peaches, and pecans.

Seafood

Find the best shrimp and grits in town at **The River Room** (801 Front St., 843/527-4110, www.riverroomgeorgetown.com, Mon.-Sat. 11:30am-2:30pm and 5pm-10pm, $15-25), which combines a gourmet attitude in the kitchen with a casual attitude on the floor. However, dishes like the herb-encrusted grouper or the signature crab cakes taste like fine dining all the way. Reservations are not accepted, and dress is casual. Literally right on the waterfront, the dining room in this former hardware store extends 50 feet over the Sampit River, adjacent to a public dock where many diners arrive by boat. There's even a large aquarium inside to complete the atmosphere.

ACCOMMODATIONS
Under $150

Close to the historic district is **Quality Inn & Suites** (210 Church St., 843/546-5656, www.qualityinn.com, $90-140), which has an outdoor pool and an included breakfast. On the north side of town on U.S. 17 you'll find the **Hampton Inn Georgetown-Marina** (420 Marina Dr., 843/545-5000, www.hamptoninn.com, $140-170), which also offers a pool and complimentary breakfast.

$150-300

By far the most impressive lodging near Georgetown—and indeed among the most impressive in the Southeast—is ★ **Mansfield Plantation** (1776 Mansfield Rd., 843/546-6961, www.mansfieldplantation.com, $150-200), a bona fide antebellum estate dating from a 1718 king's grant. It is so evocative and so authentic that Mel Gibson shot part of his film *The Patriot* here, and renovation was recently completed on a historic slave chapel and cabin. You can stay in one of nine guest rooms situated in three guesthouses on the grounds, each within easy walking distance of the public areas in the main house, which include a 16-seat dining room.

With the closing of two longtime favorite B&Bs, the Dupre House and the Harbour House Inn, it's left to another B&B, the **Keith House Inn** (1012 Front St., 843/485-4324, www.thekeithhouseinn.com, $149-169), to carry on the tradition. Its four 2nd-floor suites, with balconies, each have a different theme. The public areas are wonderfully and whimsically furnished.

INFORMATION AND SERVICES

In the historic waterfront area, you'll find the **Georgetown County Chamber of Commerce and Visitor Center** (531 Front St., 843/546-8436, www.georgetownchamber.

com). **Georgetown Memorial Hospital** (606 Black River Rd., 843/527-7000, www. georgetownhospitalsystem.org) is the main medical center in the area. If you need non-emergency law-enforcement help, call the **Georgetown Police** (2222 Highmarket St., 843/545-4300, www.cityofgeorgetownsc. com).

GETTING THERE AND AROUND

Georgetown is at the extreme southern tip of the Grand Strand, accessible by U.S. 17 from the east and south and U.S. 521 (called Highmarket St. in town) from the west. Very centrally located for a tour of the coast, it's about an hour north of Charleston and slightly less than an hour from Myrtle Beach.

Although there's no public transportation in Georgetown, its small size makes touring fairly simple. Metered parking is available downtown.

Hilton Head and the Lowcountry

For many people around the world, the Lowcountry is the first image that comes to mind when they think of the American South.

History hangs in the humid air where first the Spanish and French came to interrupt the native tribes' ancient reverie, followed by the English. Although time, erosion, and development have erased most traces of these various occupants, you can almost hear their ghosts in the rustle of the branches in a sudden sea breeze or in the piercing call of a heron over the marsh.

The defining characteristic of the Lowcountry is its liquid nature—not only literally, in the creeks and waterways that dominate every vista and the seafood cooked in all manner of ways, but figuratively too, in the slow but deep quality of life here. Not so very long ago, before the influx of resort development, retirement subdivisions, and tourism, much of the Lowcountry was like a flatter, more humid Appalachia—poverty-stricken and desperately underserved. While the archetypal South has been marketed in any number of ways to the rest of the world, here you get a sense that this is the real thing—timeless, endlessly alluring, but somehow very familiar.

South of Beaufort is the historically significant Port Royal area and the East Coast Marine Corps Recruit Depot of Parris Island. East of Beaufort is the center of Gullah culture, St. Helena Island, and the scenic gem of Hunting Island. To the south is the scenic but entirely developed golf and tennis mecca, Hilton Head Island, and Hilton Head's close neighbor but diametrical opposite in every other way, Daufuskie Island, another important Gullah center. Nestled between is the close-knit and gossipy little village of Bluffton on the gossamer May River.

PLANNING YOUR TIME

A commonsense game plan is to use centrally located Beaufort as a home base and spend **three days** exploring the region. Take at least half a day of leisure to walk all over Beaufort, a delightfully walkable place. If you're in the mood for a road trip, dedicate a full day to tour the area to the north and northeast, with

---

Previous: yoga on the beach; the Harbour Town Lighthouse. **Above:** Old Town Bluffton.

Look for ★ to find recommended sights, activities, dining, and lodging.

Highlights

★ **Henry C. Chambers Waterfront Park:** While away the time on a porch swing at this clean and inviting gathering place on the serene Beaufort River (page 143).

★ **St. Helena's Episcopal Church:** To walk through this Beaufort sanctuary and its walled graveyard is to walk through history (page 145).

★ **Penn Center:** Visit the center of modern Gullah culture and education—and a key site in the history of the civil rights movement (page 154).

★ **Hunting Island State Park:** One of the most peaceful natural getaways on the East Coast is only minutes away from the civilized temptations of Beaufort (page 157).

★ **ACE Basin:** You can take a lifetime to learn your way around this massive, marshy estuary—or just a few hours to soak in its lush beauty (page 157).

★ **Edisto Beach State Park:** Relax at this quiet, friendly, and relatively undeveloped park on Sea Island, a mecca for shell collectors (page 161).

★ **Pinckney Island National Wildlife Refuge:** This well-maintained sanctuary is a major birding location and a great getaway from nearby Hilton Head (page 164).

★ **Coastal Discovery Museum at Honey Horn:** This beautifully repurposed plantation house with spacious grounds is a great place to learn about Hilton Head history, both human and natural (page 165).

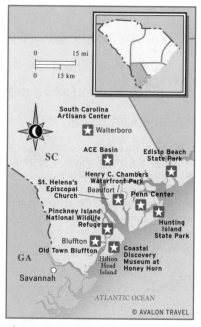
© AVALON TRAVEL

★ **Old Town Bluffton:** By turns gossipy and gorgeous, the charming "Old Town" on the May River centers on a thriving artist colony (page 176).

★ **South Carolina Artisans Center:** Visual artists and fine craftspeople from all over the state contribute work to this high-quality collective in Walterboro (page 181).

Hilton Head and the Lowcountry

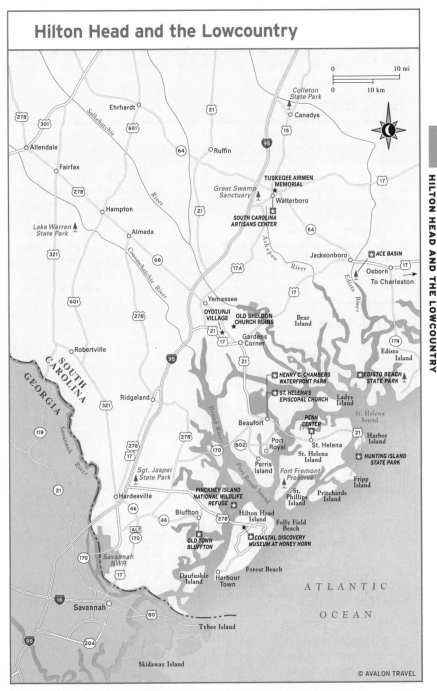

© AVALON TRAVEL

a jaunt to the ACE Basin National Wildlife Refuge. While the New York accents fly fast and furious on Hilton Head Island, that's no reason for you to rush. Plan on at least half a day just to enjoy the fine broad beaches alone. I recommend another half day to tour the island itself, maybe including a stop in Sea Pines for a late lunch or dinner.

Beaufort

Sandwiched halfway between the prouder, louder cities of Charleston and Savannah, Beaufort is in many ways a more authentic slice of life from the past than either of those two. If you want to party, stay in those two cities. If you want to relax in a similar environment, Beaufort's your ticket.

Long a staple of movie crews seeking to portray some archetypal aspect of the Old South (*The Prince of Tides, The Great Santini, Forrest Gump*) or just to film beautiful scenery for its own sake (*Jungle Book, Last Dance*), Beaufort—pronounced "BYOO-fert," by the way, not "BO-fort"—features many well-preserved examples of Southern architecture, most all of them in idyllic, family-friendly neighborhoods.

While you'll run into plenty of charming and gracious locals during your time here, you might be surprised at the number of transplanted Northerners. That's due not only to the high volume of retirees who've moved

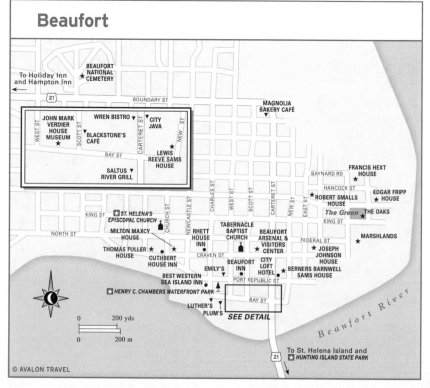

to the area, but also to the active presence of three major U.S. Navy facilities: the Marine Corps Air Station Beaufort, the Marine Corps Recruit Depot on nearby Parris Island, and the Beaufort Naval Hospital.

The two main avenues to remember are Bay Street, along the Beaufort River and the real center of downtown; and Boundary Street, which becomes Carteret Street as you arrive into downtown proper.

HISTORY

This was the site of the second landing by the Spanish on the North American continent, the expedition of Captain Pedro de Salazar in 1514 (Ponce de León's more famous landing at St. Augustine was but a year earlier). A Spanish slaver made a brief stop in 1521, long enough to name the area Santa Elena. Port Royal Sound didn't get its modern name until the first serious attempt at a permanent settlement, Jean Ribault's exploration in 1562. Though ultimately disastrous, Ribault's base of Charlesfort was the first French settlement in America.

In 1776, Beaufort planter Thomas Heyward Jr. was a signer of the Declaration of Independence. After independence, Lowcountry planters turned to cotton as the main cash crop, since England had been their prime customer for indigo. The gambit paid off, and Beaufort soon became one of the wealthiest towns in the new nation. In 1861, only seven months after secessionists fired on Fort Sumter in nearby Charleston, a Union fleet sailed into Port Royal and occupied the Lowcountry for the duration of the war.

Gradually developing their own distinct dialect and culture, much of it linked to their West African roots, isolated Lowcountry African Americans became known as the Gullah. Evolving from an effort by abolitionist missionaries early in the Civil War, in 1864 the Penn School was formed on St. Helena Island specifically to teach the children of the Gullah communities. Now known as the Penn Center, the facility has been a beacon for the study of this aspect of African American culture ever since.

SIGHTS
★ Henry C. Chambers Waterfront Park

A tastefully designed, well-maintained, and user-friendly mix of walkways, bandstands, and patios, **Henry C. Chambers Waterfront Park** (843/525-7054, www. cityofbeaufort.org, daily 24 hours) is a favorite gathering place for locals and visitors

the Henry C. Chambers Waterfront Park

Pat Conroy's Lowcountry

No person was as closely associated with the South Carolina Lowcountry as beloved author Pat Conroy, who passed away in 2016. After moving around as a child in a military family, he began high school in Beaufort. His painful teen years there formed the basis of his first novel, a brutal portrait of his domineering Marine pilot father, Colonel Donald Conroy, aka Colonel Bull Meecham of *The Great Santini* (1976). Many scenes from the 1979 film adaptation were filmed at the famous Tidalholm, the Edgar Fripp House (1 Laurens St.) in Beaufort. (The house was also front and center in *The Big Chill*.)

Conroy's pattern of thinly veiled autobiography actually began with his first book, the self-published *The Boo*, a tribute to a teacher at the Citadel in Charleston while Conroy was still a student there. His second work, *The Water is Wide* (1972), is a chronicle of his experiences teaching in a one-room African American school on Daufuskie Island. Though ostensibly a straightforward first-person journalistic effort, Conroy changed the location to the fictional Yamacraw Island, supposedly to protect Daufuskie's fragile culture from curious outsiders. The 1974 film adaptation starring Jon Voight was titled *Conrack* after the way his students mispronounced his name. You can visit that same one-room school today on Daufuskie. Known as the Mary Field School, the building is now a local community center.

Conroy would go on to publish in 1980 *The Lords of Discipline*, a reading of his real-life experience with the often-savage environment faced by cadets at the Citadel—though Conroy would change the name, calling it the Carolina Military Institute. Still, when it came time to make a film adaptation in 1983, the Citadel refused to allow it to be shot there, so the "Carolina Military Institute" was filmed in England instead. Conroy also wrote the foreword to the cookbook *Gullah Home Cooking the Daufuskie Way: Smokin' Joe Butter Beans, Ol' 'Fuskie Fried Crab Rice, Sticky-Bush Blackberry Dumpling, and Other Sea Island Favorites* by Daufuskie native and current Savannah resident Sallie Ann Robinson.

For many of his fans, Conroy's *The Prince of Tides* is his ultimate homage to the Lowcountry. Surely, the 1991 film version starring Barbra Streisand and Nick Nolte—shot on location and awash in gorgeous shots of the Beaufort River marsh—did much to implant an idyllic image of the area with audiences around the world. According to local legend, Streisand originally didn't intend to make the film in Beaufort, but a behind-the-scenes lobbying effort allegedly coordinated by Conroy himself, and including a stay at the Rhett House Inn, convinced her.

The Bay Street Inn (601 Bay St.) in Beaufort was seen in the film, as was the football field at the old Beaufort High School. The beach scenes were shot on nearby Fripp Island. Interestingly, some scenes set in a Manhattan apartment were actually shot within the old Beaufort Arsenal (713 Craven St.), now a visitors center. Similarly, the Beaufort Naval Hospital doubled as New York's Bellevue.

Despite the many personal tribulations he faced in the area, to the end Conroy never gave up on the Lowcountry. He is interred in the old Gullah Cemetery on St. Helena Island, near the historic Penn Center, beside civil rights heroine Agnes Sherman. As for the "Great Santini" himself, you can visit the final resting place of Colonel Conroy in the Beaufort National Cemetery—Section 62, Grave 182.

alike, beckoning one and all with its open green space and wonderful marsh-front views.

John Mark Verdier House Museum

A smallish but stately Federalist building on the busiest downtown corner, the **John Mark Verdier House Museum** (801 Bay St., 843/379-6335, www.historicbeaufort.org, tours on the half hour Mon.-Sat. 10:30am-3:30pm, $5) is the only historic Beaufort planter's home open to regular tours. Built in 1805 for John Mark Verdier, its main claims to fame are acting as the Union headquarters during the long occupation of Beaufort during the Civil War and hosting Revolutionary War

Helena's Episcopal Church (505 Church St., 843/522-1712, Tues.-Fri. 10am-4pm, Sat. 10am-1pm) has witnessed some of Beaufort's most compelling tales. Built in 1724, this was the parish church of Thomas Heyward, one of South Carolina's signers of the Declaration of Independence. John "Tuscarora Jack" Barnwell, one of Beaufort's founders, is buried on the grounds.

While the cemetery and sanctuary interior are likely to be your focus, take a close look at the church exterior—many of the bricks are actually ships' ballast stones. Also be aware that you're not looking at the church's original footprint; the building has been expanded several times since its construction (a hurricane in 1896 destroyed the entire east end). A nearly $3 million restoration, mostly for structural repairs, was completed in 2000.

Reconstruction Era National Monument

One of Barack Obama's last acts as president was the creation of the **Reconstruction Era National Monument** (www.nps.gov/reer, hours vary, free). Encompassing several sites in the Beaufort area, this isn't a single park you visit but rather a collection of locations that were important in the years immediately following the Civil War.

The easiest site to visit is the Beaufort Firehouse (706 Craven St.) downtown across from the Beaufort Arsenal/Museum. Once home to private businesses and now deeded to the National Park Service, the firehouse marks the site of community gatherings in the post-Civil War occupation era. As the national monument takes shape, it is likely to be a visitors center of some sort.

Two key sites on St. Helena Island are Darrah Hall on the Penn Center campus (for which there's a separate listing in this chapter) and the Brick Baptist Church, just across the street from the Penn Center. Darrah Hall is the epicenter of one of the nation's first schools for emancipated slaves. The Brick Baptist Church was built by slaves in 1855 and is the oldest church on St. Helena Island.

St. Helena's Episcopal Church

hero the Marquis de Lafayette, who stayed at the Verdier House on his 1825 U.S. tour. In 2011 the Verdier House was extensively and professionally restored, with exterior paint reflecting the home's authentic 1863 look.

Beaufort Arsenal Visitors Center and History Museum

The imposing yellow-gray tabby facade of the 1852 **Beaufort Arsenal** (713 Craven St.) houses the **Beaufort Visitors Center** (843/986-5400, www.beaufortsc.org, Mon.-Sat. 9am-5pm, Sun. noon-5pm) and **Beaufort History Museum** (www.beauforthistorymuseum.com, Mon.-Sat. 10am-4pm, $5). The visitors center is a great place to purchase various tour tickets, and the adjacent museum is a small but informative stop to learn more about the area's long and important history. There are also public restrooms.

★ St. Helena's Episcopal Church

Nestled within a low brick wall surrounding this historic church and cemetery, **St.**

The Camp Saxton/Emancipation Oak site is on the grounds of the Beaufort Naval Hospital. While currently not open to the public, that will likely change at some point in the future.

Tabernacle Baptist Church

Built in 1845, the handsome **Tabernacle Baptist Church** (911 Craven St., 843/524-0376) had a congregation of over 3,000 before the Civil War. Slaves made up most of the congregation, and during the war freed slaves purchased the church. A congregant was the war hero Robert Smalls, who seized the Confederate steamer he was forced to serve on and delivered it to Union forces. He is buried in the church cemetery and has a nice memorial dedicated to him facing the street.

Beaufort National Cemetery

Begun by order of Abraham Lincoln in 1863, **Beaufort National Cemetery** (1601 Boundary St., daily 8am-sunset) is one of the few cemeteries containing the graves of both Union and Confederate troops. This national cemetery is where 19 soldiers of the all-black 54th and 55th Massachusetts Infantries were reinterred after being found on Folly Island near Charleston. Also buried here is "the Great Santini" himself, novelist Pat Conroy's father, Donald.

Santa Elena History Center

The actual historic site is on nearby Parris Island, but in downtown Beaufort you'll find the **Santa Elena History Center** (1501 Bay St., 843/379-1550, www.santa-elena.org, Tues.-Sat. 10am-4pm, Sun. 1pm-4pm, free), detailing the Spanish occupation of the area beginning 450 years ago, long before English-speaking settlers arrived. This is a new and growing venture, and exhibits and resources will be added as funds become available.

A Walking Tour of Beaufort Homes

Here's a walking tour of some of Beaufort's fine historic homes in private hands. You won't be taking any tours of the interiors, but these homes are part of the legacy of the area and are locally valued as such. Be sure to respect the privacy of the inhabitants by keeping the noise level down and not trespassing on private property to take photos.

- **Thomas Fuller House:** Begin at the corner of Harrington and Bay Streets and view the 1796 Thomas Fuller House (1211 Bay St.), one of the oldest in Beaufort and unique in that much of the building material is tabby (hence the home's other name, the Tabby Manse).

- **Milton Maxcy House:** Walk east on Bay Street one block and take a left on Church Street; walk up to the corner of Church and Craven Streets. Otherwise known as the Secession House (113 Craven St.), this 1813 home was built on a tabby foundation dating from 1743. In 1860, when it was the residence of attorney Edmund Rhett, the first Ordinance of Secession was signed here, and the rest, as they say, is history.

- **Lewis Reeve Sams House:** Resume the walking tour on the other side of the historic district at the foot of the bridge in the old neighborhood simply called "the Point." The beautiful Lewis Reeve Sams House (601 Bay St.) at the corner of Bay and New Streets, with its double-decker veranda, dates from 1852 and like many Beaufort mansions served as a Union hospital during the Civil War.

- **Berners Barnwell Sams House:** Continue up New Street, where shortly ahead on the left you'll find the 1818 Berners Barnwell Sams House (310 New St.), which served as the African American hospital during the Union occupation. Harriet Tubman of Underground Railroad fame worked here for a time as a nurse.

- **Joseph Johnson House:** Continue up New Street and take a right on Craven Street. Cross East Street to find the 1850 Joseph Johnson House (411 Craven St.), with the massive live oak in the front yard.

Legend has it that when the Yankees occupied Hilton Head, Mr. Johnson buried his valuables under an outhouse. After the war he returned to find his home for sale due to unpaid back taxes. He dug up his valuables, paid the taxes, and resumed living in the home. You might recognize the home from the film *Forces of Nature*.

- **Marshlands:** Backtrack to East Street, walk north to Federal Street, and go to its end. Built by James R. Verdier, Marshlands (501 Pinckney St.) was used as a hospital during the Civil War, as many Beaufort homes were, and is now a National Historic Landmark. It was the setting of Francis Griswold's 1931 novel *A Sea Island Lady*.

- **The Oaks:** Walk up to King Street and take a right. Soon after you pass a large open park on the left, King Street dead-ends at Short Street. The Oaks (100 Laurens St.) at this corner was owned by the Hamilton family, who lost a son who served with General Wade Hampton's cavalry in the Civil War. After the conflict, the family couldn't afford the back taxes; neighbors paid the debts and returned the deed to the Hamiltons.

- **Edgar Fripp House:** Continue east on Laurens Street toward the water to find this handsome Lowcountry mansion, sometimes called Tidalholm (1 Laurens St.). Built in 1856 by the wealthy planter for whom nearby Fripp Island is named, this house was a key setting in *The Big Chill* and *The Great Santini*.

- **Francis Hext House:** Go back to Short Street, walk north to Hancock Street, and take a left. A short way ahead on the right, the handsome red-roofed estate known as Riverview (207 Hancock St.) is one of the oldest structures in Beaufort; it was built in 1720.

- **Robert Smalls House:** Continue west on Hancock Street, take a short left on East Street, and then a quick right on Prince Street. The 1834 Robert Smalls House (511 Prince St.) was the birthplace of Robert Smalls, a former slave and Beaufort native who stole the Confederate ship *Planter* from Charleston Harbor while serving as helmsman and delivered it to Union troops in Hilton Head. Smalls and a few compatriots commandeered the ship while the officers were at a party at Fort Sumter. Smalls used the bounty he earned for the act of bravery to buy his boyhood home. After the war, Smalls was a longtime U.S. congressman.

ENTERTAINMENT AND NIGHTLIFE
Performing Arts
Beaufort's fine arts scene is small but professional in outlook. Most performances are based in the nice Performing Arts Center on the oak-lined campus of the **University of South Carolina Beaufort** (USCB, 801 Carteret St., 843/521-4100, www.uscb.edu). A prime mover of the local performing arts scene is **Beaufort Performing Arts Inc.**, formed by a mayoral task force in 2003 specifically to encourage arts and cultural development within the area. Ticket prices typically range $12-40.

Perhaps surprising for such a small place, Beaufort boasts its own full orchestra, the **Beaufort Orchestra** (1106 Carteret St., 843/986-5400, www.beaufortorchestra.org), which plays in the Performing Arts Center.

Cinema
One of only two functional drive-ins in the state, the **Highway 21 Drive In** (55 Parker Dr., 843/846-4500, www.hwy21drivein.com) has two screens, great sound, movies Friday-Sunday, and awesome concessions that include Angus beef hamburgers. All you need to provide is the car and the company.

Festivals and Events
Surprising for a town so prominent in so many films, Beaufort didn't have its own film festival until 2007. The **Beaufort Film Festival** (843/986-5400, www.beaufortfilmfestival.com) is held in February. It's small in scale but growing steadily each year and

boasts a diverse range of high-quality, cutting-edge entries, including shorts and animation. Most events are held at the University of South Carolina Beaufort campus.

Now over 20 years old, the **Gullah Festival of South Carolina** (www.theoriginalgullahfestival.org) celebrates Gullah history and culture on Memorial Day weekend at various locations throughout town, mostly focusing on Waterfront Park.

By far the biggest single event on the local festival calendar is the over 50-year-old **Beaufort Water Festival** (www.bftwaterfestival.com), held over two weeks in June or July each year, centering on the Waterfront Park area.

Fall in the Lowcountry means shrimping season, and early October brings the **Beaufort Shrimp Festival** (www.beaufortsc.org). Various cooking competitions are held, obviously centering on the versatile crustaceans that are the raison d'être of the shrimp fleet.

St. Helena Island hosts the three-day **Penn Center Heritage Days** (www.penncenter.com) each November, without a doubt the Beaufort area's second-biggest celebration after the Water Festival. Focusing on Gullah culture, history, and delicious food, Heritage Days does a great job of combining fun with education.

SHOPS

The recently renovated Old Bay Marketplace, with a facade so bright red you can't miss it, hosts a few cute shops, most notably the stylish **Lulu Burgess** (917 Bay St., 843/524-5858, Mon.-Sat. 10am-6pm, Sun. noon-5pm), an eclectic store that brings a rich, quirky sense of humor to its otherwise tasteful assortment of gift items for the whole family.

A great women's clothing store nearby is **Go Fish** (719 Bay St., 843/379-8448, www.shopgofish.com, Mon.-Thurs. 10am-6pm, Fri.-Sat. 10am-8pm), a regional chain with particularly high-quality but affordable garments, jewelry, and shoes.

At the far end of Bay Street is **Bay Street Treasures** (1001 Bay St., 843/379-4488, Mon.-Sat. 10am-5pm), an eclectic home goods/furnishings store, strong with regional and Lowcountry appeal.

My favorite shop in Beaufort is **Nevermore Books** (201 Carteret St., 843/812-9460, www.nevermorebooks.com, Tues.-Fri. 10am-5pm, Sat. 11am-4pm), a very short walk off Bay Street around the corner on Carteret. While Edgar Allan Poe is the ostensible theme of this locally owned shop—check out the awesome window display!—they specialize in fiction of all types and have a range of regional books as well.

Art Galleries

A complete art experience blending the traditional with the cutting edge is at the **I. Pinckney Simons Art Gallery** (711 Bay St., 843/379-4774, www.ipinckneysimonsgallery.com, Tues.-Fri. 11am-5pm, Sat. 11am-3pm), which is pronounced "Simmons" despite the spelling.

For a taste of Gullah-themed art, head to **LyBenson's Gallery & Studio** (211 Charles St., 843/525-9006, www.lybensons.com). Not just a place to enjoy and purchase art, they have some small exhibits on local history and culture, including a room dedicated to local African American hero Robert Smalls.

Right on the water is a fun local favorite, the **Longo Gallery** (103 Charles St., 843/522-8933, Mon.-Sat. 11am-5pm). Owners Suzanne and Eric Longo provide a whimsical assortment of less traditional art than you might find in the more touristy waterfront area. Take Charles Street as it works its way toward the waterfront, and the gallery is right behind a storefront on the corner of Charles and Bay Streets.

You'll find perhaps the area's best-known gallery over the bridge on St. Helena Island. Known regionally as one of the best places to find Gullah folk art, **Red Piano Too** (870 Sea Island Pkwy., 843/838-2241, www.redpianotoo.com, Mon.-Sat. 10am-5pm) is on the corner before you turn onto the road to the historic Penn Center. Over 150 artists from a diverse range of traditions and styles are represented in this charming little 1940 building with a red tin awning.

SPORTS AND ACTIVITIES

Beaufort County comprises over 60 islands, so it's no surprise that nearly all recreation in the area revolves around the water, which dominates so many aspects of life in the Lowcountry. The closer to the ocean you get, the more it's a salt marsh environment. But as you explore more inland, including the sprawling ACE Basin, you'll encounter primarily blackwater.

Kayaking

The Lowcountry is tailor-made for kayaking. Most kayakers put in at the public landings in nearby **Port Royal** (1 Port Royal Landing Dr., 843/525-6664) or **Lady's Island** (73 Sea Island Pkwy., 843/522-0430), across the river from downtown Beaufort. If you don't feel comfortable with your navigation skills, it's a good idea to contact Kim and David at **Beaufort Kayak Tours** (843/525-0810, www.beaufortkayaktours.com), who rent kayaks and can guide you on a number of excellent tours. They charge about $40 for adults and $30 for children for a two-hour trip. A tour with Beaufort Kayak Tours is also the best (and nearly the only) way to access the historically significant ruins of the early British tabby Fort Frederick, now located on the grounds of the Beaufort Naval Hospital and inaccessible by car.

Fishing and Boating

Key marinas in the area are the **Downtown Marina** (1006 Bay St., 843/524-4422) in Beaufort, the **Lady's Island Marina** (73 Sea Island Pkwy., 843/522-0430), and the **Port Royal Landing Marina** (1 Port Royal Landing Dr., 843/525-6664). Hunting Island has a popular 1,000-foot fishing pier at its south end. A good local fishing charter service is Captain Josh Utsey's **Lowcountry Guide Service** (843/812-4919, www.

beaufortscfishing.com). Captain Ed Hardee (843/441-6880) offers good inshore charters.

Biking

Despite the Lowcountry's, well, lowness, biking opportunities abound. It might not get your heart rate up like a ride in the Rockies, but the area lends itself to laid-back two-wheeled enjoyment. Many local B&Bs provide bikes free for guests, and you can rent your own just across the river from Beaufort in Lady's Island at **Lowcountry Bikes** (102 Sea Island Pkwy., 843/524-9585, Mon.-Tues. and Thurs.-Fri. 10am-6pm, Wed. 10am-1pm, Sat. 10am-3pm, about $5 per hour). They can also hook you up with some good routes around the area.

Tours

Colorful character Jon Sharp has retired from his popular walking tours, but filling his shoes is Janet Matlock, who took over the venture and now runs the equally popular **Janet's Walking History Tour** (843/226-4412, www.janetswalkinghistory.com, $25). This highly recommended two-hour jaunt begins and ends at the Downtown Marina (1006 Bay St.) and takes you all through the downtown area. Tours leave at 12:30pm Monday and 11am Tuesday-Saturday; during the hot months of June-September they leave at 10am Monday-Saturday.

The Spirit of Old Beaufort (103 West St. Extension, 843/525-0459, www.thespiritofoldbeaufort.com, Mon.-Sat. 10:30am, 2pm, and 7pm, $18) runs a good year-round series of themed walking tours, roughly two hours long, with guides usually in period dress. If you don't want to walk, you can hire one of their guides to join you in your own vehicle (from $50).

As you might expect, few things could be more Lowcountry than an easygoing carriage ride through the historic neighborhoods. **Southurn Rose Buggy Tours** (843/524-2900, www.southurnrose.com, daily 10am-5pm, $18 adults, $7 children)—yes, that's how they spell it—offers 50-minute narrated

Lowcountry Boil or Frogmore Stew?

Near Beaufort it's called Frogmore stew after the township (now named St. Helena) just over the river. Closer to Savannah it's simply called Lowcountry boil. Supposedly the first pot of this delectable, hearty concoction was made by Richard Gay of the Gay Fish Company. As with any vernacular dish, dozens of local and family variants abound. The key ingredient that makes Lowcountry boil/Frogmore stew what it is—a well-blended mélange with a character all its own rather than just a bunch of stuff thrown together in a pot of boiling water—is some type of crab-boil seasoning. You'll find Zatarain's seasoning suggested on a lot of websites, but Old Bay is far more common in the eponymous Lowcountry where the dish originated.

In any case, here's a simple six-serving recipe to get you started. The only downside is that it's pretty much impossible to make it for just a few people. The dish is intended for large gatherings, whether a football tailgate party on a Saturday or a family afternoon after church on Sunday. Note the typical ratio of one ear of corn and 0.5 pound each of meat and shrimp per person.

- 6 ears fresh corn on the cob, cut into 3-inch sections
- 3 pounds smoked pork sausage, cut into 3-inch sections
- 3 pounds fresh shrimp, shells on
- 5 pounds new potatoes, halved or quartered
- 3 ounces Old Bay Seasoning

Put the sausage and potato pieces, along with the Old Bay, in two gallons of boiling water. When the potatoes are about halfway done, about 15 minutes in, add the corn and boil for about half that time, 7 minutes. Add the shrimp and boil for another 3 minutes, until they just turn pink. Do not overcook the shrimp. Take the pot off the heat and drain; serve immediately. If you cook the shrimp just right, the oil from the sausage will cause those shells to slip right off.

This is but one of dozens of recipes. Some cooks add some lemon juice and beer in the water as it's coming to a boil; others add onion, garlic, or green peppers.

carriage rides of the Point, including movie locations, embarking and disembarking near the Downtown Marina about every 40 minutes.

An important specialty bus tour in the area is **Gullah-N-Geechie Man Tours** (843/838-7516, www.gullahngeechietours.net, $20 adults, $18 children), focusing on the rich Gullah history and culture of the St. Helena Island area, including the historic Penn Center. Call for pickup information.

FOOD

Because of Beaufort's small size and insular nature, many of its restaurants double as nightlife hot spots, with hopping bar scenes—or as hopping as it gets here, anyway—at dinner hours and beyond, often with a crowd of regulars. That said, those looking for a rowdy late-night time will be happier seeking it in the notorious party towns of Charleston and Savannah.

New Southern

The stylishly appointed **Wren Bistro, Bar and Market** (210 Carteret St., 843/524-9463, www.wrenbistroandbar.com, Mon.-Sat. 11am-11pm, $15-25) is known for any of its chicken dishes. While the food is great, the interior is particularly well done, simultaneously warm and classy. As seems to be typical of Beaufort, the lunches are as good as the dinners, and the bar scene is quite active.

Breakfast and Brunch

One of the best breakfasts I've had anywhere was a humble two-egg plate for five bucks at Beaufort's most popular morning

Common Ground Coffeehouse and Market Cafe

well-kept little modernist space next to the similarly modernist City Loft Hotel. Their espresso is big-city quality, their periodicals are timely, and their pastries and sandwiches are good for tiding you over when you need some quick energy for more walking around town.

A few blocks across downtown is a great coffee place, **Common Ground Coffeehouse and Market Cafe** (102 West St., 843/524-2326, daily 7:30am-10pm). Located in a historic building facing the river, this is not just a serenely pleasant and convenient place to enjoy your coffee, but the cakes, cookies, light sandwiches, and fresh Italian gelatos are all delightfully delicious. Get here by strolling down Bay Street; it's at the end of an alley between two blocks, and is right on the Waterfront Park. There's an open mike every Friday night.

Seafood
The hottest dinner table in town is at the ★ **Saltus River Grill** (802 Bay St., 843/379-3474, Sun.-Thurs. 5pm-9pm, Fri.-Sat. 5pm-10pm, $10-39), famous throughout the state for its raw bar. Other specialties include she-crab bisque, lump crab cakes, and the ubiquitous shrimp and grits. The Saltus River Grill is more upscale in feel and in price than most Lowcountry places, with a very see-and-be-seen attitude and a hopping bar. Reservations are recommended.

The short and focused menu at **Plum's** (904½ Bay St., 843/525-1946, lunch daily 11am-4pm, dinner daily 5pm-10pm, $15-25) keys in on entrées highlighting local ingredients, such as the shrimp penne *all'amatriciana* and fresh black mussel pasta. An outstanding microbrew selection makes Plum's a big nightlife hangout as well.

Steaks
★ **Luther's Rare & Well Done** (910 Bay St., 843/521-1888, daily 10am-midnight, from $8) on the waterfront is the kind of meat-lover's place where even the French onion soup has a morsel of rib eye in it. While the patented

hangout, ★ **Blackstone's Café** (205 Scott St., 843/524-4330, Mon.-Sat. 7:30am-2:30pm, Sun. 7:30am-2pm, under $10). The dish is complete with tasty hash browns, a comparative rarity in this part of the country, where grits rule as the breakfast starch of choice.

Burgers and Sandwiches
A lunch favorite is **Magnolia Bakery Café** (703 Congress St., 843/524-1961, Mon.-Sat. 9am-5pm, under $10). Lump crab cakes are a specialty item, but you can't go wrong with any of the sandwiches. Vegetarian diners are particularly well taken care of with a large selection of black bean burger plates. As the name indicates, the range of desserts here is tantalizing, with the added bonus of a serious espresso bar.

Coffee, Tea, and Sweets
The closest thing to a hipster coffeehouse in Beaufort is **City Java and News** (301 Carteret St., 843/379-5282, Mon.-Sat. 6am-6:30pm, Sun. 7am-6:30pm), a sunny and

succulent rubbed steaks are a no-brainer here, the handcrafted specialty pizzas are also quite popular. Housed in a historic pharmacy building, Luther's is also a great place for late eats after many other places in this quiet town have rolled up the sidewalk. A limited menu of appetizers and bar food to nosh on at the inviting and popular bar is available after 10pm.

Tapas

Emily's (906 Port Republic St., 843/522-1866, www.emilysrestaurantandtapasbar.com, dinner Mon.-Sat. 4pm-10pm, bar until 2am, $10-20) is a very popular fine-dining spot that specializes in a more traditional brand of rich, tasty tapas and is known for its active bar scene.

ACCOMMODATIONS

Beaufort's historic district is blessed with an abundance of high-quality accommodations that blend well with their surroundings.

Under $150

The **Best Western Sea Island Inn** (1015 Bay St., 843/522-2090, www.bestwestern.

com, $135-170) is a good value for those for whom the B&B experience is not paramount. Anchoring the southern end of the historic district in a tasteful low brick building, the Best Western offers decent service, basic amenities, and surprisingly attractive rates for the location on Beaufort's busiest street.

$150-300

Any list of upscale Beaufort lodging must highlight the ★ **Beaufort Inn** (809 Port Republic St., 843/379-4667, www.beaufortinn. com, $152-425), consistently voted one of the best B&Bs in the nation. It's sort of a hybrid in that it comprises not only the 1897 historic central home, but also a cluster of freestanding historic cottages, each with a charming little porch and rocking chairs.

The 18-room circa-1820 **Rhett House Inn** (1009 Craven St., 843/524-9030, www. rhetthouseinn.com, $175-320) is the local vacation getaway for the stars. Such arts and entertainment luminaries as Robert Redford, Julia Roberts, Ben Affleck, Barbra Streisand, Dennis Quaid, and Demi Moore have all stayed here at one time or another.

the Beaufort Inn

There's nothing like enjoying the view of the Beaufort River from the expansive porches of the ★ **Cuthbert House Inn** (1203 Bay St., 843/521-1315, www.cuthberthouseinn.com, $205-250). This grand old circa-1790 Federal mansion was once the home of the wealthy Cuthbert family of rice and indigo planters. Some of the king rooms have fireplaces and claw-foot tubs. Of course you get a full Southern breakfast in addition to sunset hors d'oeuvres on the veranda.

While a stay at a B&B is the classic way to enjoy Beaufort, many travelers swear by the **City Loft Hotel** (301 Carteret St., 843/379-5638, www.citylofthotel.com, $200). Housed in a former motel, City Loft represents a total modernist makeover, gleaming from stem to stern with chrome and various art deco touches.

TRANSPORTATION AND SERVICES

The **Beaufort Visitors Information Center** (713 Craven St., 843/986-5400, www.beaufortsc.org, Mon.-Sat. 9am-5pm, Sun. noon-5pm), the headquarters of the Beaufort Chamber of Commerce and Convention and Visitors Bureau, has relocated from its old Carteret Street location and can now be found within the Beaufort Arsenal.

Air

While the Marines can fly their F-18s directly into Beaufort Naval Air Station, you won't have that luxury. The closest major airport to Beaufort is the **Savannah/ Hilton Head International Airport** (SAV, 400 Airways Ave., 912/964-0514, www.savannahairport.com) off I-95 outside Savannah. From there it's about an hour to Beaufort. If you're not going into Savannah for any reason, the easiest route to the Beaufort area from the airport is to take I-95's exit 8, and from there take U.S. 278 east to Highway 170.

Alternatively, you could fly into **Charleston International Airport** (CHS, 5500 International Blvd., www.chs-airport.com), but because that facility is on the far north side of Charleston, it will take a bit longer (about an hour and 20 minutes) to get to Beaufort. From the Charleston Airport the best route south to Beaufort is U.S. 17 south, exiting onto U.S. 21 at Gardens Corner and then into Beaufort.

Car

If you're coming into the region by car, I-95 will be your likely primary route, with your main point of entry being exit 8 off I-95 connecting to U.S. 278 east to Highway 170. Beaufort is a little over an hour from Charleston.

Don't be discouraged by the big-box sprawl that assaults you on the approaches to Beaufort on Boundary Street, lined with the usual discount megastores, fast-food outlets, and budget motels. After you make the big 90-degree bend where Boundary turns into Carteret Street—known locally as the "Bellamy Curve"—it's like entering a whole new world of slow-paced, Spanish moss-lined avenues, friendly people, gentle breezes, and inviting storefronts.

Outside Beaufort

The areas outside tourist-traveled Beaufort can take you even further back into sepia-toned Americana, into a time of sharecropper homesteads, sturdy oystermen, and an altogether variable and subjective sense of time.

About 15 minutes east of Beaufort is the center of Gullah culture, St. Helena Island, and the scenic gem of Hunting Island. Just a few minutes south of Beaufort is the East Coast Marine Corps Recruit Depot of Parris Island. About 10 minutes away is the little community of Port Royal.

SIGHTS
★ Penn Center

By going across the Richard V. Woods Memorial Bridge over the Beaufort River on the Sea Island Parkway (which turns into U.S. 21), you'll pass through Lady's Island and reach St. Helena Island. Known to old-timers as Frogmore, the area took back its old Spanish-derived place name in the 1980s. Today St. Helena Island is most famous for the **Penn Center** (16 Martin Luther King Jr. Dr., 843/838-2474, www.penncenter.com, Mon.-Sat. 11am-4pm, $4 adults, $2 seniors and children), the spiritual home of Gullah culture and history. When you visit here among the live oaks and humble but well-preserved buildings, you'll instantly see why Martin Luther King Jr. chose this as one of his major retreat and planning sites during the civil rights era. The Penn Center continues to serve an important civil rights role by providing legal counsel to African American homeowners in St. Helena. Because clear title is difficult to acquire in the area due to the fact that so much of the land has stayed in the families of former slaves, developers are constantly making shady offers so that ancestral land can be opened up to upscale development.

The 50-acre campus is part of the Penn School Historic District, a National Historic Landmark comprising 19 buildings, most of historical significance. The Retreat House was intended for Dr. King to continue his strategy meetings, but he was assassinated before being able to stay there. The museum and bookshop

Penn Center played an important role during the civil rights movement.

are housed in the Cope Building, now called the York W. Bailey Museum, situated right along MLK Jr. Drive.

To get to the Penn Center from Beaufort (about 10 miles), proceed over the bridge until you get to St. Helena Island. Take a right onto MLK Jr. Drive when you see the Red Piano Too Art Gallery. The Penn Center is a few hundred yards down on your right. If you drive past the Penn Center and continue a few hundred yards down MLK Jr. Drive, look for the ancient tabby ruins on the left side of the road. This is the **Chapel of Ease,** the remnant of a 1740 church destroyed by forest fire in the late 1800s.

Fort Fremont Preserve

Military historians and sightseers of a particularly adventurous type will want to drive several miles past the Penn Center on St. Helena Island to visit **Fort Fremont Preserve** (Lands End Rd., www.fortfremont. org, daily 9am-dusk, free). Two artillery batteries remain of this Spanish-American War-era coastal defense fort (an adjacent private residence is actually the old army hospital). The fort was active until 1921, but now the big guns are long gone. Their heavy concrete emplacements, however—along with many dark tunnels and small rooms—are still here and make for a very interesting visit. Guided docent tours happen the fourth Saturday of the month starting at 10:30am at the St. Helena Branch of the Beaufort County Library (6355 Jonathan Francis Senior Rd.). The two-hour tours are free, and reservations aren't required.

Old Sheldon Church

About 20 minutes north of Beaufort are the poignantly desolate ruins of the once-magnificent **Old Sheldon Church** (Old Sheldon Church Rd., off U.S. 17 just past Gardens Corner, daily dawn-dusk, free). One of the first Greek Revival structures in the United States, the house of worship held its first service in 1757. The sanctuary was first burned by the British in 1779. After being rebuilt in 1826, the sanctuary survived until General Sherman's arrival in 1865, whereupon Union troops razed it once more. Nothing remains now but these towering walls and columns made of red brick instead of the tabby often seen in similar ruins on the coast. It's now owned by the nearby St. Helena's Episcopal Church in Beaufort, which holds outdoor services here the second Sunday after Easter.

the ruins of Old Sheldon Church

Port Royal

This sleepy hamlet between Beaufort and Parris Island touts itself as a leader in "small-town New Urbanism," with an emphasis on livability, retro-themed shopping areas, and relaxing walking trails. However, **Port Royal** is still pretty sleepy—but not without very real charms, not the least of which is the fact that everything is within easy walking distance of everything else. The highlight of the year is the annual Softshell Crab Festival, held each April to mark the short-lived harvesting season for that favorite crustacean.

While much of the tiny historic district has a scrubbed, tidy feel, the main historic structure is the charming little **Union Church** (11th St., 843/524-4333, Mon.-Fri. 10am-4pm, donation), one of the oldest buildings in town, with guided docent tours.

Don't miss the boardwalk and observation tower at **The Sands** municipal beach and boat ramp. The 50-foot-tall structure provides a commanding view of Battery Creek. The little beach is artificial (made from dredged material) but still somewhat unusual in this area. To get to The Sands, head east onto 7th Street off the main drag of Parris Avenue. Seventh Street turns into Sands Beach Road for a brief stretch and then merges with 6th Street, taking you directly to The Sands.

A must-stop for families is the **Port Royal Maritime Center** (310 Okatie Hwy., 843/645-7774, www.portroyalsoundfoundation.org, Tues.-Sat. 10am-5pm, free), a new venture that is a great resource for learning about the area's ecological history. Another environmentally oriented point of pride is the **Lowcountry Estuarium** (1402 Parris Ave., 843/524-6600, www.lowcountryestuarium.org, Wed.-Sat. 10am-5pm, feedings at 11:30am and 3pm, $5 adults, $3 children).

If you get hungry in Port Royal, try the waterfront seafood haven **11th Street Dockside** (1699 11th St., 843/524-7433, daily 4:30pm-10pm, $17-27). The Dockside Dinner is a great sampler plate with lobster tail, scallops, crab legs, and shrimp. The views of the waterfront and the adjoining shrimp-boat docks are relaxing and beautiful.

Parris Island

Though more commonly known as the home of the legendary **Marine Corps Recruit Depot Parris Island** (283 Blvd. de France, 843/228-3650, www.mcrdpi.marines.mil, free), the island is also of historical significance as the site of some of the earliest European presence in the New World. Today it's where all female U.S. Marine recruits and most male recruits east of the Mississippi River go through the Corps' grueling 13-week boot camp. Almost every Friday during the year marks the graduation of a company of newly minted Marines. That's why you might notice an influx of visitors to the area each Thursday, aka "Family Day," with the requisite amount of celebration on Fridays after that morning's ceremony.

Unlike many military facilities in the post-9/11 era, Parris Island still hosts plenty of visitors. Just check in with the sentry at the gate and show your valid driver's license, registration, and proof of insurance. Rental car drivers must show a copy of the rental agreement. On your way to the depot proper, there are a couple of beautiful picnic areas. Once inside, stop first at the **Douglas Visitor Center** (Bldg. 283, Blvd. de France, 843/228-3650, Mon. 7:30am-noon, Tues.-Wed. 7:30am-4:30pm, Thurs. 6:30am-7pm, Fri. 7:30am-3pm), a great place to find maps and information. As you go by the big parade ground, or "deck," be sure to check out the beautiful sculpture re-creating the famous photo of Marines raising the flag on Iwo Jima. A short way ahead is the **Parris Island Museum** (Bldg. 111, 111 Panama St., 843/228-2951, www.mcrdpimuseum.com, daily 10am-4:30pm, free), detailing the proud history of the Corps with a particular focus on this Recruit Depot.

The Spanish built Santa Elena nearby the original French settlement, Charlesfort. They then built two other settlements, San Felipe and San Marcos. The Santa Elena site, now on the circa-1950s Parris Island Depot golf course, is a National Historic Landmark. So far, archaeologists have found a residence of a wealthy family in the town and have identified two of Santa Elena's five forts. Many artifacts are viewable at the nearby **clubhouse-interpretive center** (daily 7am-5pm, free). You can take a self-guided tour; to get to the site from the museum, continue on Panama Street and take a right on Cuba Street. Follow the signs to the golf course and continue through the main parking lot of the course.

★ Hunting Island State Park

Rumored to be a hideaway for Blackbeard himself, the aptly named Hunting Island was indeed for many years a notable hunting preserve, and its abundance of wildlife remains to this day. The island is one of the East Coast's best birding spots and also hosts dolphins, loggerheads, alligators, and deer. A true family-friendly outdoor adventure spot, **Hunting Island State Park** (2555 Sea Island Pkwy., 866/345-7275, www.huntingisland.com, winter daily 6am-6pm, during daylight saving time daily 6am-9pm, $5 adults, $3 children) has something for everyone—kids, parents, and newlyweds. Yet it still retains a certain sense of lush wildness—so much so that it doubled as Vietnam in the movie *Forrest Gump*.

At the north end past the campground is the island's main landmark, the historic **Hunting Island Light**, which dates from 1875. Although the lighthouse ceased operations in 1933, a rotating light—not strong enough to serve as an actual navigational aid—is turned on at night. While the 167-step trek to the top (donation $2 pp) is strenuous, the view is stunning.

★ ACE Basin

Occupying pretty much the entire area between Beaufort and Charleston, the **ACE Basin**—the acronym signifies its role as the collective estuary of the Ashepoo, Combahee, and Edisto Rivers—is one of the most enriching natural experiences the country has to offer. The ACE Basin's three core rivers, the Edisto being the largest, are the framework for a matrix of waterways crisscrossing its approximately 350,000 acres of salt marsh. While the ACE Basin can in no way be called "pristine," it's a testament to the power of nature that after 6,000 years of human presence and often intense cultivation, the basin manages to retain much of its untamed feel.

About 12,000 acres of the ACE Basin Project comprise the **Ernest F. Hollings ACE Basin National Wildlife Refuge** (8675

the view from the Hunting Island Light

The Lost Art of Tabby

Tabby is a unique construction technique combining oyster shells, lime, water, and sand found along the South Carolina and Georgia coasts.

Contrary to popular belief, it did not originate with Native Americans. The confusion is due to the fact that the native population left behind many middens, or trash heaps, of oyster shells. While these middens indeed provided the bulk of the shells for tabby buildings to come, Native Americans had little else to do with it. Also contrary to lore, although the Spanish were responsible for the first use of tabby in the Americas, almost all remaining tabby in the area dates from later English settlement. The British first fell in love with tabby after the siege of Spanish-held St. Augustine, Florida, and quickly began building with it in their colonies to the north.

Scholars are divided as to whether tabby was invented by West Africans or its use spread to Africa from Spain and Portugal, circuitously coming to the United States through the knowledge of imported slaves. The origin of the word itself is also unclear, as similar words exist in Spanish, Portuguese, Gullah, and Arabic to describe various types of wall.

We do know for sure how tabby is made: The primary technique was to burn alternating layers of oyster shells and logs in a deep hole in the ground, thus creating lime. The lime was then mixed with oyster shells, sand, and freshwater and poured into wooden molds, or "forms," to dry and then be used as building blocks, much like large bricks. Tabby walls were usually plastered with stucco. Tabby is remarkably strong and resilient, able to survive the hurricanes that often batter the area. It also stays cool in the summer and is insect-resistant, two enormous advantages down here.

Following are some great examples of true tabby you can see today on the South Carolina and Georgia coasts, from north to south:

- **Dorchester State Historic Site** in Summerville, north of Charleston, contains a well-preserved tabby fort.

- Several younger tabby buildings still exist in downtown Beaufort: the **Barnwell-Gough House** (705 Washington St.); the Thomas Fuller House, or **"Tabby Manse"** (1211 Bay St.); and the **Saltus House** (800 block of Bay St.), perhaps the tallest surviving tabby structure.

- The **Chapel of Ease** on St. Helena Island dates from the 1740s. If someone tells you Sherman burned it down, don't believe it; the culprit was a forest fire.

Willtown Rd., 843/889-3084, www.fws.gov/acebasin, grounds year-round daily dawn-dusk, office Mon.-Fri. 7:30am-4pm, free), run by the U.S. Fish and Wildlife Service. The historic 1828 **Grove Plantation House** is in this portion of the basin and houses the refuge's headquarters. Sometimes featured on local tours of homes, it's one of only three antebellum homes left in the ACE Basin. Surrounded by lush, ancient oak trees, it's really a sight in and of itself.

This section of the refuge, the **Edisto Unit,** is about an hour's drive from Beaufort. To get to the Edisto Unit of the Hollings/ACE Basin National Wildlife Refuge, take U.S. 17 to Highway 174 (going all the way down this route takes you to Edisto Island) and turn right onto Willtown Road. The unpaved entrance road is about two miles ahead on the left. There are restrooms and a few picnic tables.

You can also visit the two parts of the **Combahee Unit** of the refuge, which offers a similar scene of trails among impounded wetlands along the Combahee River, with parking; it's farther west near Yemassee. The Combahee Unit is about 30 minutes from Beaufort. Get here by taking a left off U.S. 17 onto Highway 33. The larger portion of the Combahee Unit is soon after the turnoff, and the smaller, more northerly portion is about five miles up the road.

the Chapel of Ease on St. Helena Island

- The **Stoney-Baynard Ruins** in Sea Pines Plantation on Hilton Head are all that's left of the home of the old Braddock's Point Plantation. Foundations of a slave quarters are nearby.

- **Wormsloe Plantation** near Savannah has the remains of Noble Jones's fortification on the Skidaway Narrows.

- **St. Cyprian's Episcopal Church** in Darien is one of the largest tabby structures still in use.

- **Fort Frederica** on St. Simons Island has not only the remains of a tabby fort but many foundations of tabby houses in the surrounding settlement.

- The remarkably intact walls of the **Horton-DuBignon House** on Jekyll Island, Georgia, date from 1738, and the house was occupied into the 1850s.

Recreation
KAYAKING

A good service for rentals and knowledgeable guided tours of the ACE Basin is **Outpost Moe's** (843/844-2514, www.geocities.ws/outpostmoe), where the basic 2.5-hour tour costs $40 per person, and an all-day extravaganza through the basin is $80. Moe's provides lunch for most of its tours. Another premier local outfitter for ACE Basin tours is **Carolina Heritage Outfitters** (U.S. 15 in Canadys, 843/563-5051, www.canoesc.com), which focuses on the Edisto River trail. In addition to guided tours ($30) and rentals, you can camp overnight in their cute tree houses ($125) along the kayak routes. They load you up with your gear and drive you 22 miles upriver, then you paddle downriver to the tree house for the evening. The next day, you paddle yourself the rest of the way downriver back to home base.

To have a drier experience of the ACE Basin from the deck of a larger vessel, try **ACE Basin Tours** (1 Coosaw River Dr., Beaufort, 843/521-3099, www.acebasintours.com, Mar.-Nov. Wed. and Sat. 10am, $35 adults, $15 children), which will take you on a three-hour tour in the 40-passenger *Dixie Lady*. To get to their dock from Beaufort, take Carteret Street over the bridge to St. Helena Island, and then take a left on Highway 802 east (Sam's Point Rd.). Continue until you cross Lucy Point Creek;

the ACE Basin Tours marina is on your immediate left after you cross the bridge.

The state of South Carolina has conveniently gathered some of the best self-guided kayak trips at www.acebasin.net/canoe.html.

GOLF

Golf is much bigger in Hilton Head than in the Beaufort area, but there are some local highlights. The best-regarded public course in the area, and indeed one of the best military courses in the world, is **Legends at Parris Island** (Bldg. 299, Parris Island, 843/228-2240, www.mccssc.com, $30). Call in advance for a tee time.

Another popular public course is **South Carolina National Golf Club** (8 Waveland Ave., Cat Island, 843/524-0300, www.sc-national.com, $70). Get to secluded Cat Island by taking the Sea Island Parkway onto Lady's Island and continuing south as it turns into Lady's Island Drive. Turn onto

Island Causeway and continue for about three miles.

CAMPING

Hunting Island State Park (2555 Sea Island Pkwy., 866/345-7275, www.huntingisland. com, winter daily 6am-6pm, during daylight saving time daily 6am-9pm, $5 adults, $3 children, $25 RV sites, $19 tent sites, $87-172 cabin) has 200 campsites with individual water and electric hookups on the north end of the island. There used to be plenty of cabins for rent, but beach erosion has sadly made the ones near the water uninhabitable. One cabin near the lighthouse is still available for rent, and it is in such high demand that the park encourages you to camp instead.

Another neat place to camp is **Tuck in the Wood** (22 Tuc In De Wood Ln., St. Helena, 843/838-2267, $25), a very well-maintained 74-site private campground just past the Penn Center on St. Helena Island.

Edisto Island

One of the last truly unspoiled places in the Lowcountry, Edisto Island has been highly regarded as a getaway spot since the Edisto people first started coming here for shellfish. In fact, locals here swear that the island was settled by English-speaking colonists even before Charleston was settled in 1670.

There are rental homes galore on Edisto Island. Because of the lack of hotels, this is the most popular option for most vacationers here—indeed, it's just about the only option. Contact **Edisto Sales and Rentals Realty** (1405 Palmetto Blvd., 800/868-5398, www.edistorealty.com).

SIGHTS

The **Edisto Museum** (8123 Chisolm Plantation Rd., 843/869-1954, www.edistomuseum.org, Tues.-Sat. noon-5pm, $4 adults, $2 children, free under age 10), a project of the Edisto Island Historic Preservation Society,

has recently expanded and incorporated a nearby slave cabin. Its well-done exhibits of local lore and history are complemented by a gift shop. The Edisto Museum is before you get to the main part of the island, off Highway 174.

Opened in 1999 by local snake hunters the Clamp brothers, the **Edisto Island Serpentarium** (1374 Hwy. 174, 843/869-1171, www.edistoserpentarium.com, hours vary, $14.95 adults, $10.95 ages 4-12, free age 3 and younger) is educational and fun, taking you up close and personal with a variety of reptilian creatures native to the area. They usually close Labor Day-April 30.

The **Botany Bay Wildlife Management Area** (www.preserveedisto.org, Wed.-Mon. dawn-dusk, free) is a great way to enjoy the unspoiled nature of Edisto Island. On the grounds of two former rice and indigo plantations comprising 4,000 acres, Botany Bay features several remains of the old plantations and a small, wonderful beach. There are no facilities to speak of, so pack and plan accordingly. Botany Bay is closed on hunt days, which vary depending on the hunting season but are fairly rare.

SPORTS AND ACTIVITIES

As the largest river of the ACE (Ashepoo, Combahee, Edisto) Basin complex, the Edisto River figures large in the lifestyle of residents and visitors. A good public landing is at Steamboat Creek off Highway 174 on the way down to the island. Take Steamboat Landing Road (Hwy. 968) from Highway 174 near the James Edwards School. Live Oak Landing is farther up Big Bay Creek near the interpretive center at the state park. The **Edisto Marina** (3702 Docksite Rd., 843/869-3504) is on the far west side of the island.

Captain Ron Elliott of **Edisto Island Tours** (843/869-1937) offers various ecotours and fishing trips as well as canoe and kayak rentals for about $25 per day. A typical kayak tour runs about $35 per person for a 1.5-2-hour trip, and he offers a "beachcombing" trip for $15 per person. Riding a bike on Edisto

Beach and all around the island is a great and relaxing way to get some exercise and enjoy its scenic, laid-back beauty. The best place to rent a bike—or a kayak or canoe, for that matter—is **Island Bikes and Outfitters** (140 Jungle Rd., 843/869-4444, Mon.-Sat. 9am-4pm). Bike rentals run about $16 per day; single kayaks are about $60 per day.

★ Edisto Beach State Park

Edisto Beach State Park (8377 State Cabin Rd., 843/869-2156, www.southcarolinaparks. com, Nov.-mid-Mar. daily 8am-6pm, mid-Mar.-Oct. daily 6am-10pm, $5 adults, $3 children, free under age 6) is one of the world's foremost destinations for shell collectors. Largely because of fresh loads of silt from the adjacent ACE Basin, there are always new specimens, many of them fossils, washing ashore. The park stretches almost three miles and features the state's longest system of fully accessible hiking and biking trails, including one leading to a 4,000-year-old shell midden, now much eroded from past millennia. The particularly well-done **interpretive center** (Tues.-Sat. 9am-4pm) has plenty of interesting exhibits about the nature and history of the park as well as the surrounding ACE Basin.

Edisto Island

CAMPING

A great thing about Edisto Island is the total absence of ugly chain lodging or beachfront condo development. My recommended option is staying at **Edisto Beach State Park** (843/869-2156, www.southcarolinaparks.com, $25 tent sites, $75-100 cabins) itself, either at a campsite on the Atlantic side or in a marsh-front cabin on the northern edge. During high season (Apr.-Nov.), there's a minimum week-long stay in the cabins; during the off-season, the minimum stay is two days. You can book cabins up to 11 months in advance.

FOOD

One of the all-time great barbecue places in South Carolina is on Edisto: ★ **Po Pigs Bo-B-Q** (2410 Hwy. 174, 843/869-9003, Wed.-Sat. 11:30am-9pm, $4-10), on the way into town. This is the real thing, the full pig cooked in all its many ways: white meat, dark meat, crack-lin's, and hash, served in the local style of "all you care to eat." Unlike many barbecue spots, they do serve beer and wine.

Another popular joint on the island is **Whaley's** (2801 Myrtle St., 843/869-2161, Tues.-Sat. 11:30am-2pm and 5pm-9pm, bar daily 5pm-2am, $5-15), a down-home place in an old gas station a few blocks off the beach. This is a good place for casual seafood like boiled shrimp, washed down with a lot of beer. The bar is open seven days a week.

The legendary ★ **Old Post Office** (1442 Hwy. 174, 843/869-2339, www.theoldpost-officerestaurant.com, Tues.-Sun. 5:30pm-10pm, $20), a Lowcountry-style fine-dining spot, served a devoted clientele for 20 years. It recently reopened with a bang and thank-fully kept its old-school mystique intact. Specialties include fine crab cakes drizzled with mousseline sauce, the pecan-encrusted Veal Edistonian, and a Carolina rib eye topped with a pimiento cheese sauce.

TRANSPORTATION

Edisto Island is basically halfway between Beaufort and Charleston. There's one main land route here, south on Highway 174 off U.S. 17. It's a long way down from U.S. 17 to Edisto, but the 20- to 30-minute drive is scenic and enjoyable. Most activity on the island centers on the township of Edisto Beach, which voted to align itself with Colleton County for its lower taxes (the rest of Edisto Island is part of Charleston County).

Tours

Edisto has many beautiful plantation homes, relics of the island's longtime role as host to cotton plantations. While all are in private hands and therefore off-limits to the public, an exception is offered through **Edisto Island Tours & T'ings** (843/869-9092, $20 adults, $10 under age 13). You'll take a van tour around Edisto's beautiful churches and old plantations.

Hilton Head Island

Literally the prototype of the modern planned resort community, Hilton Head Island is also a case study in how a landscape can change when money is introduced. From Reconstruction until the post-World War II era, the island consisted almost entirely of African Americans with deep roots in the area. In the mid-1950s Hilton Head began its transformation into an almost all-white, upscale golf, tennis, and shopping mecca populated largely by Northern transplants and retirees. As you can imagine, the flavor here is now quite different from surrounding areas of the Lowcountry, to say the least, with an emphasis on material excellence, top prices, get-it-done-yesterday punctuality, and the attendant aggressive traffic.

These days, Hilton Head gets the most national media attention for the RBC Heritage golf tournament each April, when the entire

Hilton Head Island

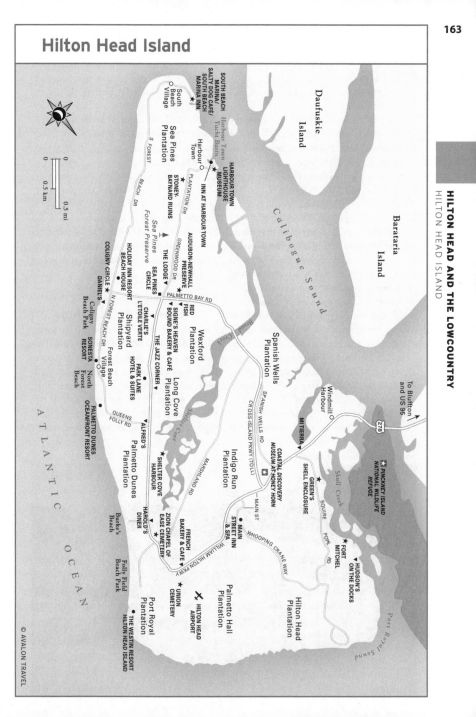

island is packed with golf fans for this extremely popular PGA event.

HISTORY

The second-largest barrier island on the East Coast was named in 1663 by adventurer Sir William Hilton, who thoughtfully named the island—with its notable headland or "Head"—after himself. Later it gained fame as the first growing location of the legendary Sea Island cotton, a long-grain variety that, following its introduction in 1790 by William Elliott II of the Myrtle Bank Plantation, would soon be the dominant version of the cash crop.

Though it seems unlikely given the island's modern demographics, Hilton Head was almost entirely African American through much of the 20th century. When Union troops occupied the island at the outbreak of the Civil War, freed and escaped slaves flocked to the island, and many of the dwindling number of African Americans on the island today are descendants of this original Gullah population.

In the 1950s the Fraser family bought 19,000 of the island's 25,000 acres with the intent to continue forestry on them. But in 1956—not at all coincidentally the same year the first bridge to the island was built—Charles Fraser convinced his father to sell him the southern tip. Fraser's brainchild and decades-long labor of love—some said his obsession—Sea Pines Plantation became the prototype for the golf-oriented resort communities so common today on both U.S. coasts. Fraser himself was killed in a boating accident in 2002 and is buried under the famous Liberty Oak in Harbour Town.

SIGHTS

Contrary to what many think, there are things to do on Hilton Head that don't involve swinging a club at a little white ball or shopping for designer labels, but instead celebrate the area's history and natural setting. The following are some of those attractions, arranged in geographical order from where you first access the island.

★ Pinckney Island National Wildlife Refuge

Consisting of many islands and hammocks, **Pinckney Island National Wildlife Refuge** (912/652-4415, daily dawn-dusk, free) is the only part of this small but very well-managed 4,000-acre refuge that's open to the public. Almost 70 percent of the former rice plantation is salt marsh and tidal creeks, making it a perfect microcosm for the Lowcountry

Pinckney Island National Wildlife Refuge

as a whole, as well as a great place to kayak or canoe. Some of the state's richest birding opportunities abound here.

Green's Shell Enclosure

Less known than the larger Native American shell ring farther south at Sea Pines, **Green's Shell Enclosure** (803/734-3886, daily dawn-dusk) is certainly easier to find, and you don't have to pay $5 to enter the area, as with Sea Pines. This three-acre heritage preserve dates back to at least the 1300s. The heart of the site comprises a low embankment, part of the original fortified village. To get here, take a left at the intersection of U.S. 278 and Squire Pope Road. Turn left into Green's Park, pass the office on the left, and park. The entrance to the shell enclosure is on the left behind a fence.

★ Coastal Discovery Museum at Honey Horn

With the acquisition of Honey Horn's 70-acre spread of historic plantation land, Hilton Head finally has a full-fledged museum worthy of the name, and the magnificent **Coastal Discovery Museum** (70 Honey Horn Dr., 843/689-6767, www.coastaldiscovery.org, Mon.-Sat. 9am-4:30pm, Sun. 11am-3pm, free)

is a must-see, even for those who came to the island mostly to golf and soak up sun.

The facility centers on the expertly restored Discovery House, the only antebellum house still existing on Hilton Head, with exhibits and displays devoted to the history of the island. The museum is also a great one-stop place to sign up for a variety of specialty on-site and off-site guided tours, such as birding and Gullah history tours. The cost for most on-site tours is a reasonable $10 adults and $5 children.

But the real draw is the 0.5-mile trail through the Honey Horn grounds, including several boardwalk viewpoints over the marsh, a neat little butterfly habitat, a few gardens, and a stable and pasture that host Honey Horn May and Tadpole, the museum's two Marsh Tackies—short, tough little ponies descended from Spanish horses and used to great effect by Francis "Swamp Fox" Marion and his freedom fighters in the American Revolution.

While a glance at a map and area signage might convince you that you must pay the $1.25 toll on the Cross Island Parkway to get to Honey Horn, that isn't so. The exit to Honey Horn on the parkway is actually before you get to the toll plaza; therefore access is free.

one of the Coastal Discovery Museum's Marsh Tackies

Union Cemetery

A modest but key aspect of African American history on Hilton Head is at **Union Cemetery** (Union Cemetery Rd.), a small burial ground featuring several graves of black Union Army troops (you can tell by the designation "USCI" on the tombstone, for "United States Colored Infantry"). Also of interest are the charming hand-carved cement tombstones of nonveterans. To get here, turn north off William Hilton Parkway onto Union Cemetery Road. The cemetery is a short way ahead on the left. There is no signage or site interpretation.

Zion Chapel of Ease Cemetery

More like one of the gloriously desolate scenes common to the rest of the Lowcountry, this little cemetery in full view of the William Hilton Parkway at Folly Field Road is all that remains of one of the "Chapels of Ease," a string of chapels set up in the 1700s. The **Zion Chapel of Ease Cemetery** (daily dawn-dusk, free) is said to be haunted by the ghost of William Baynard, whose final resting place is in a mausoleum on the site (the remains of his ancestral home are farther south at Sea Pines Plantation).

Audubon-Newhall Preserve

Plant lovers shouldn't miss this small but very well-maintained 50-acre wooded tract in the south-central part of the island on Palmetto Bay Road between the Cross Island Parkway and the Sea Pines Circle. Almost all plant life, even that in the water, is helpfully marked and identified. The **Audubon-Newhall Preserve** (year-round dawn-dusk, free) is open to the public, but you can't camp here. For more information, call the **Hilton Head Audubon Society** (843/842-9246).

Sea Pines Plantation

This private residential resort development at the extreme west end of the island—the first on Hilton Head and the prototype for every other such development in the country—hosts several attractions that collectively are well worth the $5 per vehicle "road use" fee, which you pay at the main entrance gate.

HARBOUR TOWN

It's not particularly historic and not all that natural, but **Harbour Town** is still pretty cool. The dominant element is the squat, colorful **Harbour Town Lighthouse Museum** (149 Lighthouse Rd., 843/671-2810, www.harbourtownlighthouse.com, daily 10am-dusk, $4.25, free age 5 and under), which has never really helped a ship navigate its way near the island. The 90-foot structure was built in 1970 purely to give visitors a little atmosphere, and that it does, as kids especially love climbing the stairs to the top and looking out over the island's expanse.

STONEY-BAYNARD RUINS

The **Stoney-Baynard ruins** (Plantation Dr., dawn-dusk, free), tabby ruins in a residential neighborhood, are what remains of the circa-1790 central building of the old Braddock's Point Plantation, first owned by patriot and raconteur Captain "Saucy Jack" Stoney and later by the Baynard family. Active during the island's heyday as a cotton center, the plantation was destroyed after the Civil War.

SEA PINES FOREST PRESERVE

The **Sea Pines Forest Preserve** (175 Greenwood Dr., 843/363-4530, free) is set amid the Sea Pines Plantation golf resort development, but you don't need a bag of clubs to enjoy this 600-acre preserve, which is built on the site of an old rice plantation (dikes and logging trails are still visible). Here you can ride a horse, fish, or just take a walk on the eight miles of trails (dawn-dusk) and enjoy the natural beauty around you. No bike riding is allowed on the trails, however.

In addition to the Native American shell ring farther north off Squire Pope Road, the Sea Pines Forest Preserve also boasts a shell ring set within a canopy of tall pines.

Tours and Cruises

Most guided tours on Hilton Head focus on

the water. **Harbour Town Cruises** (843/363-9023, www.vagabondcruise.com, $30-60) offers several sightseeing tours as well as excursions to Daufuskie and Savannah. They also offer a tour on a former America's Cup racing yacht.

"Dolphin tours" are extremely popular on Hilton Head, and there is no shortage of operators. **Dolphin Watch Nature Cruises** (843/785-4558, $25 adults, $10 children) departs from Shelter Cove, as does **Lowcountry Nature Tours** (843/683-0187, www.lowcountrynaturetours.com, $40 adults, $35 children, free under age 3). **Outside Hilton Head** (843/686-6996, www.outsidehiltonhead.com) runs a variety of water ecotours and dolphin tours as well as a guided day-trip excursion to Daufuskie, complete with golf cart rental.

There is a notable land-based tour by **Gullah Heritage Trail Tours** (leaves from Coastal Discovery Museum at Honey Horn, 843/681-7066, www.gullahheritage.com, $32 adults, $15 children) delving into the island's rich, if poorly preserved, African American history from slavery through the time of the freedmen.

ENTERTAINMENT AND NIGHTLIFE
Nightlife

The highest-quality live entertainment on the island is at **The Jazz Corner** (1000 William Hilton Pkwy., 843/842-8620, www.thejazzcorner.com, dinner daily 6pm-9pm, late-night menu after 9pm, dinner $15-20, cover varies), which brings in big names in the genre to perform in this space in the unlikely setting of a boutique mall, the Village at Wexford. The dinners are actually quite good, but the attraction is definitely the music. Reservations are recommended. Live music starts around 7pm.

For years islanders jokingly referred to the "Barmuda Triangle," an area named for the preponderance of bars within vague walking distance of Sea Pines Circle. While some of the names have changed over the years, the long-time anchor of the Barmuda Triangle is the **Tiki Hut** (1 S. Forest Beach Dr., 843/785-5126,

Sun.-Thurs. 11am-8pm, Fri.-Sat. 11am-10pm, bar until 2am), actually part of The Beach House hotel at the entrance to Sea Pines. This popular watering hole is the only beachfront bar on the island, which technically makes it the only place you can legally drink alcohol on a Hilton Head beach. Another Triangle fave is **The Lodge** (7 Greenwood Dr., 843/842-8966, www.hiltonheadlodge.com, daily 11:30am-midnight). After the martini-and-cigar craze waned, this popular spot successfully remade itself into a beer-centric place with 36 rotating taps.

Despite its location in the upscale strip mall of the Village at Wexford, the **British Open Pub** (1000 William Hilton Pkwy./Hwy. 278, 843/686-6736, daily 11am-10pm) offers a fairly convincing English vibe with, as the name suggests, a heavy golf theme. The fish-and-chips and shepherd's pie are both magnificent.

Inside Sea Pines is the **Quarterdeck Lounge and Patio** (843/842-1999, www.seapines.com, Sun.-Thurs. 5:30pm-10pm, Fri.-Sat. 5:30pm-midnight) at the base of the Harbour Town Lighthouse. This is where the party's at after a long day on the fairways during the Heritage golf tournament. Within Sea Pines at the South Beach Marina is also where you'll find **The Salty Dog Cafe** (232 S. Sea Pines Dr., 843/671-2233, www.saltydog.com, lunch daily 11am-3pm, dinner daily 5pm-10pm, bar daily until 2am), one of the area's most popular institutions (some might even call it a tourist trap) and something akin to an island empire, with popular T-shirts, a gift shop, books, and an ice cream shop, all overlooking the marina. My suggestion, however, is to make the short walk to the affiliated **Wreck of the Salty Dog** (843/671-7327, daily until 2am), where the marsh views are better and the atmosphere not quite so tacky.

A gay-friendly bar on Hilton Head is **Cool Cats Lounge** (32 Palmetto Bay Rd., Mon.-Fri. 8pm-3am, Sat. 8pm-2am), with a welcoming dive-bar atmosphere and a small but lively dance floor.

Performing Arts

Because so many residents migrated here from art-savvy metropolitan areas in the Northeast, Hilton Head maintains a very high standard of top-quality entertainment. Much of the activity centers on the multimillion-dollar **Arts Center of Coastal Carolina** (14 Shelter Cove Ln., 843/842-2787, www.artshhi.com), which hosts touring shows, resident companies, musical concerts, dance performances, and visual arts exhibits.

Under the direction of maestro John Morris Russell, the **Hilton Head Symphony Orchestra** (843/842-2055, www.hhso.org) performs a year-round season of masterworks and pops programs at various venues, primarily the First Presbyterian Church (540 William Hilton Pkwy./Hwy. 278). They also take their show on the road with several concerts in Bluffton and even perform several "Symphony Under the Stars" programs at Shelter Cove. **Chamber Music Hilton Head** (www.cmhh.org) performs throughout the year with selections ranging from Brahms to Smetana at All Saints Episcopal Church (3001 Meeting St.).

Cinema

There's an art house on Hilton Head, the charming **Coligny Theatre** (843/686-3500, www.colignytheatre.com) in the Coligny Plaza shopping center before you get to Sea Pines. For years this was the only movie theater for miles around, but it has reincarnated as a primarily indie film venue. Look for the entertaining murals by local artist Ralph Sutton. Showtimes are Monday 11:30am and 4pm, Tuesday and Friday 11:30am, 4pm, and 7pm, Wednesday-Thursday and Saturday-Sunday 4pm and 7pm.

Festivals and Events

Late February-early March brings the **Hilton Head Wine and Food Festival** (www.hiltonheadhospitality.org), culminating in what they call "the East Coast's Largest Outdoor Public Tasting and Auction," which is generally held at the Coastal Discovery Museum at Honey Horn. Some events charge admission.

Without question, Hilton Head's premier event is the **RBC Heritage Golf Tournament** (843/671-2248, http://theheritagegolfsc.com), held each April (usually the week after the Masters) at the Harbour Town Golf Links on Sea Pines Plantation. Formerly known as the Verizon Heritage Classic, the event is South Carolina's only PGA Tour event and brings thousands of visitors to town. The entire island gets *quite* crowded during this time, so be aware.

A fun and fondly anticipated yearly event is the **Kiwanis Club Chili Cookoff** (www.hiltonheadkiwanis.org), held each October at Honey Horn on the south end. A low admission price gets you all the chili you can eat plus free antacids. All funds go to charity, and all excess chili goes to a local food bank.

Every November brings Hilton Head's second-largest event, the **Hilton Head Concours d'Elegance & Motoring Festival** (www.hhiconcours.com), a multiday affair bringing together vintage car clubs from throughout the nation and culminating in a prestigious "Best of Show" competition. It started as a fund-raiser for the Hilton Head Symphony, but now people come from all over the country to see these fine vintage cars in a beautiful setting.

SHOPS

As you'd expect, Hilton Head is a shopper's delight, with an emphasis on upscale stores and prices to match. Keep in mind that hours may be shortened in the off-season (Nov.-Mar.). Here's a rundown of the main island shopping areas in the order you'll encounter them as you enter the island.

Shelter Cove

Shelter Cove Towne Centre (40 Shelter Cove Ln., www.sheltercovetownecentre), a repurposed former mall space, centers on a Belk anchor store and a Kroger. New retail locations are steadily opening there. The nearby **Plaza at Shelter Cove** (50 Shelter Cove Ln., www.theplazaatsheltercove.com) features a Whole Foods and the flagship location of **Outside Hilton Head** (843/686-6996, www.outsidehiltonhead.com, Mon.-Sat. 10am-5:30pm, Sun. 11am-5:30pm), a complete outdoor outfitter with a knowledgeable staff.

Village at Wexford

Easily my favorite place to shop on Hilton Head, this well-shaded shopping center on William Hilton Parkway (Hwy. 278) hosts plenty of well-tended shops, including the foodie equipment store **Le Cookery** (843/785-7171, Mon.-Sat. 10am-6pm), the Lily Pulitzer signature women's store **S. M. Bradford Co.** (843/686-6161, Mon.-Sat. 10am-6pm), and the aromatic **Scents of Hilton Head** (843/842-7866, Mon.-Fri. 10am-6pm, Sat. 10am-5pm).

My favorite shop on all Hilton Head is at Wexford, **The Oilerie** (843/681-2722, www.oilerie.com, Mon.-Sat. 10am-7pm, Sun. noon-5pm). This franchise provides free samples of all its high-quality Italian olive oils and vinegars. After you taste around awhile, you pick what you want and the friendly staff bottles it for you in souvenir-quality glassware. They also have a selection of spices, soaps, and other goodies.

Coligny Circle

This is the closest Hilton Head comes to funkier beach towns like Tybee Island or Folly Beach, although it doesn't really come that close. You'll find dozens of delightful and somewhat quirky stores here, many keeping long hours in the summer, like the self-explanatory **Coligny Kite & Flag Co.** (843/785-5483, Mon.-Sat. 10am-9pm, Sun. 11am-6pm), the comprehensive and stylish **Quiet Storm Surf Shop** (843/671-2551, daily 10am-9pm), and **Fresh Produce** (843/842-3410, www.freshproduceclothes.com, Mon.-Sat. 10am-10pm, Sun. 10am-9pm), actually a very cute women's clothing store. Kids will love both **The Shell Shop** (843/785-4900, Mon.-Sat. 10am-9pm, Sun. noon-9pm) and **Black Market Minerals** (843/785-7090, Mon.-Sat. 10am-10pm, Sun. 11am-8pm).

Harbour Town

The **Shoppes at Harbour Town** (www.

seapines.com) are a collection of about 20 mostly boutique stores along Lighthouse Road in Sea Pines Plantation. At **Planet Hilton Head** (843/363-5177, www.planethiltonhead.com, daily 10am-9pm) you'll find some cute, eclectic gifts and home goods. Other clothing highlights include **Knickers Men's Store** (843/671-2291, daily 10am-9pm) and **Radiance** (843/363-5176, Mon.-Tues. 10am-5pm, Wed.-Sat. 10am-9pm, Sun. 11am-9pm), a very cute and fashion-forward women's store.

The **Top of the Lighthouse Shoppe** (843/671-2810, www.harbourtownlighthouse.com, daily 10am-9pm) is where many a climbing visitor has been coaxed to part with some of their disposable income. And, of course, as you'd expect being near the legendary Harbour Town links, there's the **Harbour Town Pro Shop** (843/671-4485, daily 7am-5pm), routinely voted one of the best pro shops in the nation.

South Beach Marina

On South Sea Pines Drive at the marina you'll find several worthwhile shops, including a good marine store and all-around grocery dealer **South Beach General Store** (843/671-6784, daily 8am-10pm). I like to stop in **Blue Water Bait and Tackle** (843/671-3060, daily 7am-8pm) and check out the cool nautical stuff. They can also hook you up with a variety of kayak trips and fishing charters. And, of course, right on the water there's the ever-popular **Salty Dog Cafe** (843/671-2233, www.saltydog.com, lunch daily 11am-3pm, dinner daily 5pm-10pm), whose ubiquitous T-shirts seem to adorn every other person on the island.

Art Galleries

Despite the abundant wealth apparent in some quarters here, there's no freestanding art museum in the area, that role being filled by independent galleries. A good representative example is **Morris & Whiteside Galleries** (220 Cordillo Pkwy., 843/842-4433, www.morris-whiteside.com, Mon.-Fri. 9am-5pm,

Sat. 10am-4pm), located in the historic Red Piano Too Art Gallery building, which features a variety of paintings and sculpture, heavy on landscapes but also showing some fine figurative work. The nonprofit **Art League of Hilton Head** (14 Shelter Cove Ln., 843/681-5060, Mon.-Sat. 10am-6pm) is located in the Walter Greer Art Gallery within the Arts Center of Coastal Carolina and displays work by member artists in all media. The **Nash Gallery** (13 Harbourside Ln., 843/785-6424, Mon.-Fri. 10am-9pm, Sat. 10am-8pm, Sun. 11am-5pm) in Shelter Cove Harbour deals more in North American craft styles. Hilton Head art isn't exactly known for its avant-garde nature, but you can find some whimsical stuff at **Picture This** (78D Arrow Rd., 843/842-5299, Mon.-Fri. 9:30am-5:30pm, Sat. 9:30am-12:30pm), including a selection of Gullah craft items.

SPORTS AND ACTIVITIES
Beaches

First, the good news: Hilton Head Island has 12 miles of some of the most beautiful, safe beaches you'll find anywhere. The bad news is that there are only a few ways to gain access, generally at locations referred to as "beach parks." Don't just drive into a residential neighborhood and think you'll be able to park and find your way to the beach.

Driessen Beach Park has 207 long-term parking spaces, costing $0.25 for 30 minutes. There's free parking but fewer spaces at the Coligny Beach Park entrance and at Fish Haul Creek Park. Also, there are 22 metered spaces at Alder Lane Beach Access, 51 at Folly Field Beach Park, and 13 at Burkes Beach Road. Most other beach parks have permit parking only. Clean, well-maintained public restrooms are available at all the beach parks. You can find **beach information** at 843/342-4580 and www.hiltonheadislandsc. gov. Beach park hours vary: Coligny Beach Park is open daily 24 hours; all other beach parks are open March-September daily 6am-8pm and October-February daily 6am-5pm. Alcohol is strictly prohibited on Hilton Head's beaches.

Kayaking

Kayakers will enjoy Hilton Head Island, which offers several gorgeous routes, including Calibogue Sound to the south and west and Port Royal Sound to the north. For particularly good views of life on the salt marsh, try Broad Creek, which nearly bisects Hilton Head Island, and Skull Creek, which separates Hilton Head from the natural beauty of Pinckney Island. Broad Creek Marina is a good place to put in.

If you want a guided tour, there are plenty of great kayak tour outfits to choose from in the area. Chief among them is **Outside Hilton Head** (32 Shelter Cove Ln., 800/686-6996, www.outsidehiltonhead.com).

Biking

Although the very flat terrain is not challenging, Hilton Head provides some scenic and relaxing cycling opportunities. Thanks to wise planning and foresight, the island has an extensive and award-winning 50-mile network of biking trails that does a great job of keeping cyclists out of traffic. A big plus is the long bike path paralleling the William Hilton Parkway, enabling cyclists to use that key artery without braving its traffic. There is even an underground bike path beneath the parkway to facilitate crossing that busy road. In addition, there are also routes along Pope Avenue as well as North and South Forest Beach Drive. Go to www.hiltonheadisland. org/biking to download a map of the island's entire bike path network.

Palmetto Dunes Oceanfront Resort (4 Queens Folly Rd., 800/827-3006, www. palmettodunes.com) has a particularly nice 25-mile network of bike paths that all link up to the island's larger framework. Within the resort is **Palmetto Dunes Outfitters**

Hilton Head is a great place to golf.

(843/785-2449, www.pdoutfitters.com, daily 9am-5pm), which will rent you any type of bike you might need. Sea Pines Plantation also has an extensive 17-mile network of bike trails; you can pick up a map at most information kiosks within the plantation.

There's a plethora of bike rental facilities on Hilton Head with competitive rates. Be sure to ask if they offer free pickup and delivery. Try **Hilton Head Bicycle Company** (112 Arrow Rd., 843/686-6888, daily 9am-5pm, $16 per day).

Horseback Riding

Within the Sea Pines Forest Preserve is **Lawton Stables** (190 Greenwood Dr., 843/671-2586, www.lawtonstableshhi.com), which features pony rides, a small-animal farm, and guided horseback rides through the preserve. You don't need any riding experience, but you do need reservations.

Bird-Watching

The premier birding locale in the area is the **Pinckney Island National Wildlife Refuge** (U.S. 278 east, just before Hilton Head, 912/652-4415, www.fws.gov, free). You can see bald eagles, ibis, wood storks, painted buntings, and many more species. Birding is best in spring and fall. The refuge has several freshwater ponds that serve as wading bird rookeries. During migration season, so many beautiful birds make such a ruckus that you'll think you've wandered onto an Animal Planet shoot.

Golf

Hilton Head is one of the world's great golf centers, with no fewer than 23 courses, and one could easily write a book about nothing but that. This, however, is not that book. Perhaps contrary to what you might expect, most courses on the island are public, and some are downright affordable. All courses are 18 holes unless otherwise described; greens fees are averages and vary with season and tee time.

The best-regarded course, with prices to match, is **Harbour Town Golf Links** (Sea Pines Plantation, 843/363-4485, www.

seapines.com, $239). It's on the island's south end at Sea Pines and is the home of the annual RBC Heritage Classic, far and away the island's number one tourist draw.

There are two Arthur Hills-designed courses on the island, **Arthur Hills at Palmetto Dunes Resort** (843/785-1140, www.palmettodunes.com, $125) and **Arthur Hills at Palmetto Hall** (Palmetto Hall Plantation, 843/689-4100, www.palmetto-hallgolf.com, $130), both of which now offer the use of Segway vehicles on the fairways. The reasonably priced **Barony Course** at Port Royal Plantation (843/686-8801, www.portroyalgolfclub.com, $98) also boasts some of the toughest greens on the island. Another challenging and affordable course is the **George Fazio at Palmetto Dunes** Resort (843/785-1130, www.palmettodunes.com, $105).

It's wise to book tee times through the **Golf Island Call Center** (888/465-3475, www.golfisland.com), which can also hook you up with good packages.

Tennis

One of the top tennis destinations in the country, Hilton Head has over 20 tennis clubs, some of which offer court time to the public (walk-on rates vary; call for information). They are: **Palmetto Dunes Tennis Center** (Palmetto Dunes Resort, 843/785-1152, www.palmettodunes.com, $30 per hour), **Port Royal Racquet Club** (Port Royal Plantation, 843/686-8803, www.portroyalgolfclub.com, $25 per hour), **Sea Pines Racquet Club** (Sea Pines Plantation, 843/363-4495, www.seapines.com, $25 per hour), **South Beach Racquet Club** (Sea Pines Plantation, 843/671-2215, www.seapines.com, $25 per hour), and **Shipyard Racquet Club** (Shipyard Plantation, 843/686-8804, $25 per hour).

Free, first-come, first-served play is available at the following public courts, maintained by the Island Recreation Association (www.islandreccenter.org): **Chaplin Community**

Park (Singleton Beach Rd., four courts, lighted), **Cordillo Courts** (Cordillo Pkwy., four courts, lighted), **Fairfield Square** (Adrianna Ln., two courts), **Hilton Head High School** (School Rd., six courts), and **Hilton Head Middle School** (Wilborn Rd., four courts).

Zip Line

Billing itself as the only zip line experience within 250 miles, the **Zip Line Hilton Head** (33 Broad Creek Marina Way, 843/682-6000, www.ziplinehiltonhead.com) offers an extensive canopy tour making great use of the area's natural scenery and features. You generally "fly" in groups of about eight. Reservations are strongly encouraged. The latest offering is "Aerial Adventure," a challenging two-hour trip ($50) with about 50 obstacles.

FOOD

Because of the cosmopolitan nature of the population, with so many transplants from the northeastern United States and Europe, there is uniformly high quality in Hilton Head restaurants. Hilton Head has shed its reputation as a somewhat stodgy food town and does offer some fun, cutting-edge, big-city-style spots to enjoy.

Bistro

Combining rib-sticking comfort food with hearty European-style cuisine is ★ **Lucky Rooster** (841 William Hilton Pkwy., 843/681-3474, www.luckyroosterhhi.com, daily 5pm-10pm, $15). This really is one of the most vibrant and satisfying menus on the island, from the fried green tomatoes to the pan-fried sweetbread starters, to the short rib and shrimp and grits and mushroom lasagna entrées. A lively full bar complements the bistro-style scene.

An upgrade of a longtime island favorite called simply Daniel's, **Crave by Daniel's** (2 N. Forest Beach Dr., 843/341-9379, http://danielshhi.com, daily 4pm-2am, $25) is now an upscale steak house with a twist. In addition to offering gorgeous cuts of meat like a center-cut filet mignon, they specialize in what they call "big small plates." Try a sizzling cinnamon steak kebab or a gyro pizzetta.

Breakfast and Brunch

There are a couple of great diner-style places on the island. Though known more for its hamburgers and Philly cheesesteaks, **Harold's Diner** (641 William Hilton Pkwy., 843/842-9292, Mon.-Sat. 7am-3pm, $4-6) has great pancakes as well as its trademark brand of sarcastic service. The place is small, popular, and does not take reservations.

If you need a bite in the Coligny Plaza area, go to **Skillets** (1 N. Forest Beach Dr., 843/785-3131, www.skilletscafe.com, breakfast daily 7am-5pm, dinner daily 5pm-9pm, $5-23) in Coligny Plaza. Their eponymous stock-in-trade is a layered breakfast dish of sautéed ingredients served in a porcelain skillet, like the "Kitchen Sink" (pancakes ringed with potatoes, sausage, and bacon, topped with two poached eggs).

A great all-day breakfast place with a twist is ★ **Signe's Heaven Bound Bakery & Café** (93 Arrow Rd., 843/785-9118, www.signesbakery.com, Mon.-Fri. 8am-4pm, Sat. 9am-2pm, $5-10). Breakfast is tasty dishes like frittatas and breakfast polenta, while the twist is the extensive artisanal bakery, with delicious specialties like the signature key lime pound cake. Expect a wait during peak periods.

German

I'm pretty sure you didn't come all the way to South Carolina to eat traditional German food, but while you're here, check out ★ **Alfred's** (807 William Hilton Pkwy./Hwy. 278, 843/341-3117, wwww.alfredshiltonhead.com, Mon.-Sat. 5pm-11pm, $20-30), one of the more unique spots on Hilton Head and a big favorite with the locals. Expect a wait. Bratwurst, veal cordon bleu, and of course Wiener schnitzel are all standouts. I recommend the German Mix Platter ($25), which features a brat, some sauerbraten, and a schnitzel.

Seafood and Southern

Honest-to-goodness Southern cookin' isn't always that easy to come by on this island full of transplants from outside the South. But a great place to find it is **A Lowcountry Backyard** (32 Palmetto Bay Rd., #4A, www.hhbackyard.com, Mon.-Sat. 11am-3pm and 4:30pm-9pm, Sat. brunch 9am-noon, Sun. brunch 9am-3pm, $15). As the name implies, this is regional cuisine served in a relaxed and casual atmosphere fitting for island life. As with many Hilton Head establishments, it's located within a strip mall setting, the Village Exchange.

Not to be confused with Charley's Crab House next door to Hudson's, seafood lovers will enjoy the experience down near Sea Pines at ★ **Charlie's L'Etoile Verte** (8 New Orleans Rd., 843/785-9277, http://charliesgreenstar.com, lunch Tues.-Sat. 11:30am-2pm, dinner Mon.-Sat. 5:30pm-10pm, $25-40), which is considered by many connoisseurs to be Hilton Head's single best restaurant. The emphasis here is on "French country kitchen" cuisine—think Provence, not Paris. In keeping with that theme, each day's menu is concocted from scratch and handwritten. Reservations are essential.

A longtime Hilton Head favorite is **Red Fish** (8 Archer Rd., 843/686-3388, www.redfishofhiltonhead.com, lunch Mon.-Sat. 11:30am-2pm, dinner daily beginning with early-bird specials at 5pm, $20-37). Strongly Caribbean in decor as well as menu, with romanticism and panache to match, this is a great place for couples. Reservations are essential.

Fresh seafood lovers will enjoy one of Hilton Head's staples, the huge **Hudson's on the Docks** (1 Hudson Rd., 843/681-2772, www.hudsonsonthedocks.com, lunch daily 11am-4pm, dinner daily from 5pm, $14-23) on Skull Creek just off Squire Pope Road on the less-developed north side. Much of the catch—though not all of it, by any means—comes directly off the boats you'll see dockside. Try the stuffed shrimp filled with crabmeat. Leave room for one of the homemade desserts crafted by Ms. Bessie, a 30-year veteran employee of Hudson's.

ACCOMMODATIONS

Generally speaking, accommodations on Hilton Head are often surprisingly affordable given their overall high quality and the breadth of their amenities.

Under $150

You can't beat the price at **Park Lane Hotel and Suites** (12 Park Ln., 843/686-5700, www.hiltonheadparklanehotel.com, $130). This is your basic suite-type hotel (formerly a Residence Inn) with kitchens, laundry, a pool, and a tennis court. The allure here is the price, hard to find anywhere these days at a resort location. For a nonrefundable fee, you can bring your pet. The one drawback is that the beach is a good distance away. The hotel does offer a free shuttle, however, so it would be wise to take advantage of that and avoid the usual beach-parking hassles. As you'd expect given the price, rooms here tend to go quickly; reserve early.

$150-300

A great place for the price is the **South Beach Inn** (232 S. Sea Pines Dr., 843/671-6498, www.sbinn.com, $186) in Sea Pines. Located near the famous Salty Dog Cafe and outfitted in a similar nautical theme, the inn not only has some pretty large guest rooms for the price, it offers a lovely view of the marina and has a very friendly feel. As with all Sea Pines accommodations, staying on the plantation means you don't have to wait in line with other visitors to pay the $5-per-day "road fee." Sea Pines also offers a free trolley to get around the plantation.

One of Hilton Head's favorite hotels for beach lovers is **The Beach House** (1 S. Forest Beach Dr., 855/474-2882, www.beachhousehhi.com, $200), formerly the Holiday Inn Oceanfront and home of the famed Tiki Hut bar on the beach. Staff turnover is less frequent here than at other local accommodations, and while it's no Ritz-Carlton and

occasionally shows signs of wear, it's a good value in a bustling area of the island.

One of the better resort-type places for those who prefer the putter and the racquet to the Frisbee and the surfboard is the **Inn and Club at Harbour Town** (7 Lighthouse Ln., 843/363-8100, www.seapines.com, $199) in Sea Pines. The big draw here is the impeccable service, delivered by a staff of "butlers" in kilts, mostly Europeans who take the venerable trade quite seriously. While it's not on the beach, you can take advantage of the free Sea Pines Trolley every 20 minutes.

Recently rated the number one family resort in the United States by *Travel + Leisure*, the well-run ★ **Palmetto Dunes Oceanfront Resort** (4 Queens Folly Rd., 800/827-3006, www.palmettodunes.com, $150-300) offers something for everybody in terms of lodging. There are small, cozy condos by the beach or larger villas overlooking the golf course, and pretty much everything in between. The prices are perhaps disarmingly affordable considering the relative luxury and copious recreational amenities, which include 25 miles of very well-done bike trails, 11 miles of kayak and canoe trails, and, of course, three signature links. As with most developments of this type on Hilton Head, the majority of the condos are privately owned, and therefore each has its own particular set of guidelines and cleaning schedules.

A little farther down the island you'll find the **Sonesta Resort** (130 Shipyard Dr., 843/842-2400, www.sonesta.com/hiltonhead-island, $160-200), which styles itself as Hilton Head's only green-certified accommodations. The guest rooms are indeed state-of-the-art, and the expansive, shaded grounds near the beach are great for relaxation. No on-site golf here, but immediately adjacent is a well-regarded tennis facility with 20 courts.

Another good resort-style experience heavy on the golf is on the grounds of the Port Royal Plantation on the island's north side, **The Westin Resort Hilton Head Island** (2 Grasslawn Ave., 843/681-4000, www.westin.com/hiltonhead, from $200), which hosts three PGA-caliber links. The beach is also but a short walk away. This AAA four diamond-winning Westin offers a mix of suites and larger villas.

Vacation Rentals

Many visitors to Hilton Head choose to rent a home or villa for an extended stay, and there is no scarcity of availability. Try **Resort Rentals of Hilton Head** (www.hhivacations. com) or **Destination Vacation** (www.destinationvacationhhi.com).

TRANSPORTATION AND SERVICES

The best place to get information on Hilton Head, book a room, or secure a tee time is just as you come onto the island at the **Hilton Head Island Chamber of Commerce Welcome Center** (100 William Hilton Pkwy., 843/785-3673, www.hiltonheadisland. org, daily 9am-6pm).

Air

A few years back, the **Savannah/Hilton Head International Airport** (SAV, 400 Airways Ave., Savannah, 912/964-0514, www.savannahairport.com) added Hilton Head to its name specifically to identify itself with that lucrative market. Keep in mind that when your plane touches down in Savannah, you're still about a 45-minute drive to Hilton Head proper. From the airport, go north on I-95 into South Carolina, and take exit 8 onto U.S. 278 east.

There is a local regional airport as well, the **Hilton Head Island Airport** (HXD, 120 Beach City Rd., 843/689-5400, www.bcgov. net). While attractive and convenient, keep in mind that it only hosts propeller-driven commuter planes because of the runway length and concerns about noise.

Getting Around

Hilton Head Islanders have long referred to their island as the "shoe" and speak of driving to the toe or going to the heel. If you take a look at a map, you'll see why: Hilton Head bears an uncanny resemblance to a running shoe pointed toward the southwest, with the aptly named Broad Creek forming a near facsimile of the Nike "swoosh" symbol.

Running the length and circumference of the shoe is the main drag, U.S. 278 Business (William Hilton Parkway), which crosses onto Hilton Head right at the "tongue" of the shoe, a relatively undeveloped area. The Cross Island Parkway toll route (U.S. 278), beginning up toward the ankle as you first get on the island, is a quicker route straight to the toe near Sea Pines.

While making your way around the island, always keep in mind that the bulk of it consists of private developments, and local law enforcement frowns on people who aimlessly wander among the condos and villas.

Other than taxi services, there is no public transportation to speak of in Hilton Head, unless you want to count the free shuttle around Sea Pines Plantation. Taxi services include **Yellow Cab** (843/686-6666), **Island Taxi** (843/683-6363), and **Ferguson Transportation** (843/842-8088).

Bluffton and Daufuskie Island

Just outside Hilton Head are two of the Lowcountry's true gems, Bluffton and Daufuskie Island. While Bluffton's outskirts have been taken over by the same gated community and upscale strip mall sprawl spreading throughout the coast, at its core it is a delightfully charming little community on the quiet May River, now called Old Bluffton, where you'd swear you just entered a time warp.

Daufuskie Island still maintains much of its age-old isolated, timeless personality, and the island—still accessible only by boat—is one of the spiritual centers of the Gullah culture and lifestyle.

★ OLD TOWN BLUFFTON

Similar to Beaufort, but even quieter and smaller, historic Bluffton is an idyllic village on the banks of the serene May River. Bluffton was the original hotbed of secession, with Charleston diarist Mary Chesnut famously referring to the town as "the center spot of the fire eaters." During their Civil War occupation, Union troops repaid the favor of those original Bluffton secessionists, which is why only nine homes in Bluffton are of antebellum vintage; the rest were torched in a search for Confederate guerrillas.

The center of tourist activity is "Old Town," the **Old Bluffton Historic District,** several blocks of 1800s-vintage buildings clustered between the parallel Boundary and Calhoun Streets (old-timers sometimes call this "the original square mile"). Many of the buildings are private residences, but most have been converted into art studios and antiques stores.

Heyward House Historic Center

The **Heyward House Historic Center** (70 Boundary St., 843/757-6293, www.heywardhouse.org, Mon.-Fri. 10am-5pm, Sat. 10am-4pm, tours $5 adults, $2 students) is not only open to tours but also serves as Bluffton's

visitors center. Built in 1840 as a summer home for the owner of Moreland Plantation, John Cole, the house was later owned by George Cuthbert Heyward, grandson of Declaration of Independence signer Thomas Heyward. (Remarkably, it stayed in the family until the 1990s.) The Heyward House also sponsors walking tours of the historic district (843/757-6293, $15, by appointment only). Download your own walking tour map at www.heywardhouse.org.

Church of the Cross

Don't fail to go all the way to the end of Calhoun Street, as it dead-ends on a high bluff on the May River at the Bluffton Public Dock. Overlooking this peaceful marsh-front vista is the photogenic **Church of the Cross** (110 Calhoun St., 843/757-2661, www.thechurchofthecross.net, free tours Mon.-Sat. 10am-2pm). The current sanctuary was built in 1854 and is one of only two local churches not burned in the Civil War. The parish itself began in 1767, with the first services on this spot held in the late 1830s. While the church looks as if it were made of cypress, it's actually constructed of heart pine.

Bluffton Oyster Company

You might want to get a gander at the state's last remaining working oyster house, the **Bluffton Oyster Company** (63 Wharf St., 843/757-4010, www.blufftonoyster.com, Mon.-Sat. 9am-5:30pm), and possibly purchase some of their maritime bounty. Larry and Tina Toomer continue to oversee the oyster-harvesting-and-shucking family enterprise, which has its roots in the early 1900s.

SHOPS

Bluffton's eccentric little art studios, most clustered in a two-block stretch on Calhoun Street, are by far its main shopping draw. Named for the Lowcountry phenomenon you find in the marsh at low tide among the fiddler crabs, Bluffton's **Pluff Mudd Art** (27 Calhoun St., 843/757-5551, Mon.-Sat. 10am-5:30pm) is a cooperative of 16 talented young painters and photographers from throughout the area. The **Guild of Bluffton Artists** (20 Calhoun St., 843/757-5590, Mon.-Sat. 10am-4:30pm) features works from many local artists, as does the outstanding **Society of Bluffton Artists** (48 Boundary St., 843/757-6586, Mon.-Sat. 10am-5pm, Sun. 11:30am-3pm). For cool, custom handcrafted pottery, try **Preston Pottery and Gallery** (10 Church St., 843/757-3084, Tues.-Sat. 10am-5pm). Another great Bluffton place is the hard-to-define **Eggs'n'tricities** (71 Calhoun St., 843/757-3446, Mon.-Sat. 10am-5pm). The name pretty much says it all for this fun and eclectic vintage, junk, jewelry, and folk art store.

If you want to score some fresh local seafood for your own culinary adventure, the no-brainer choice is the **Bluffton Oyster Company** (63 Wharf St., 843/757-4010, Mon.-Sat. 9am-5:30pm), the state's only active oyster facility. They also have shrimp, crab, clams, and fish, nearly all of it from the nearly pristine May River on whose banks the facility sits.

For a much more commercially intense experience, head just outside of town on U.S. 278 on the way to Hilton Head to find the dual **Tanger Outlet Centers** (1414 Fording Island Rd., 843/837-4339, Mon.-Sat. 10am-9pm, Sun. 11am-6pm), an outlet-shopper's paradise with virtually every major brand represented.

FOOD
American

Probably the single most popular place in Bluffton is the friendly **Old Town Dispensary** (15 Captains Cove, 843/837-1893, daily 11am-2am, $15-25), just off the Calhoun Street center of activity. This is an outstanding place to go for some cut-above pub/bar food or casual drinks, with plenty of outdoor seating and usually some live music going on.

Another very popular casual spot in Old Town, and frequented by many locals, is **Captain Woody's Bar & Grill** (17 State of Mind St., 843/757-6222, $10-15). Unpretentious and friendly, this is a good place to enjoy a

Bluffton Oyster Company on the May River

burger and a beer in a relaxed, patio-style environment with plenty going on around you.

Breakfast and Brunch

No discussion of Bluffton cuisine is complete without the famous **Squat 'n' Gobble** (1231 May River Rd., 843/757-4242, daily 24 hours). Long a site of gossiping and politicking as well as, um, squatting and gobbling, this humble diner on May River Road is an indelible part of the local consciousness.

Coffee

If you're looking for a coffeehouse in Old Town, go no farther than ★ **Corner Perk** (1297 May River Rd., Fording Island Rd., 843/816-5674, Tues.-Thurs. 7am-4pm., Fri.-Sat. 7am-11pm, Sun. brunch 7am-4pm, $10-20) in The Promenade, just off the main drag. Their coffee is truly wonderful, and the sandwich-heavy lunch menu compares with anything else in town. Upstairs is The Roasting Room, a more upscale, full-service bourbon bar.

French

Most dining in Bluffton is pretty casual, but you'll get the white-tablecloth treatment at **Claude & Uli's Signature Bistro** (1533 Fording Island Rd., 843/837-3336, lunch Mon.-Fri. 11:30am-2:30pm, dinner Mon.-Sat. from 5pm, $18-25) just outside of town in Moss Village. Chef Claude does a great veal cordon bleu as well as a number of fine seafood entrées, such as an almond-crusted tilapia and an excellent seafood pasta.

Mexican

My favorite restaurant in Bluffton is ★ **Mi Tierra** (101 Mellichamp Center, 843/757-7200, lunch daily 11am-4pm, dinner Mon.-Fri. 4pm-9pm, Sat.-Sun. 4pm-10pm, $3-15). They serve very high-quality but unpretentious Tex-Mex-style food in a fun atmosphere at affordable prices.

ACCOMMODATIONS
Under $150

A quality bargain stay right between Bluffton and Hilton Head is the **Holiday Inn Express Bluffton** (35 Bluffton Rd., 843/757-2002, www.ichotelsgroup.com, $120), on U.S. 278 as you make the run onto Hilton Head proper. It's not close to the beach or to Old Town Bluffton, so you'll definitely be using your car, but its central location will appeal to those who want to keep their options open.

Over $300

For an ultra-upscale spa and golf resort environment near Bluffton, the clear pick is the **Inn at Palmetto Bluff** (19 Village Park Square, 843/706-6500, www.palmettobluffresort.com, $650-900) just across the May River. This property was picked recently as the number two U.S. resort by *Condé Nast Traveler* magazine. There are three top-flight dining options on the grounds: the fine-dining **River House Restaurant** (843/706-6542, breakfast daily 7am-11am, lunch or "porch" menu daily 11am-10pm, dinner daily 6pm-10pm, $30-40); the **May River Grill** (Tues.-Sat. 11am-4pm, $9-13) at the golf clubhouse; and the casual **Buffalo's** (843/706-6630, Sun.-Tues. 11:30am-5pm, Wed.-Sat. 11:30am-9pm, $10-15).

DAUFUSKIE ISLAND

Sitting between Savannah and Hilton Head Island and accessible only by water, Daufuskie Island—pronounced "da-FUSK-ee"—has about 500 full-time residents, most of whom ride around on golf carts or bikes (there's only one paved road, Haig Point Road). Once the home of rice and indigo plantations and rich oyster beds—the latter destroyed by pollution and overharvesting—the two upscale residential resort communities on the island, begun in the 1980s, give a clue as to where the future might lie, although the recent global economic downturn, perhaps thankfully, slowed development to a standstill.

The area of prime interest to visitors is the unincorporated western portion, or **Historic District,** the old stomping grounds of Pat Conroy during his stint as a teacher of resident African American children. His old

Who Are the Gullah?

A language, a culture, and a people with a shared history, Gullah is more than that—it's also a state of mind. Simply put, the Gullah are African Americans of the Sea Islands of South Carolina and Georgia. (In Georgia, the term *Geechee*, from the nearby Ogeechee River, is more or less interchangeable.) Protected from outside influence by the isolation of this coastal region after the Civil War, Gullah culture is the closest living cousin to the West African traditions of those brought to this country as slaves.

While you might hear that *Gullah* is a corruption of "Angola," some linguists think it simply means "people" in a West African language. In any case, the Gullah speak what is known as a creole language, meaning one derived from several sources. Gullah combines elements of Elizabethan English, Jamaican patois, and several West African dialects; for example, "goober" (peanut) comes from the Congo *n'guba*. Another creole element is a word with multiple uses; for example, Gullah's *shum* could mean "see them," "see him," "see her," or "see it" in either past or present tense, depending on context. Several white writers in the 1900s published collections of Gullah folk tales, but it wasn't until later linguistic research was done that the Gullah tongue was recognized as something more than just broken English. Lorenzo Dow Turner's groundbreaking *Africanisms in the Gullah Dialect,* published in 1949, traced elements of the language to Sierra Leone in West Africa and more than 300 Gullah words directly to Africa.

Gullah is typically spoken very rapidly, which of course only adds to its impenetrability to the outsider. Gullah also relies on colorful turns of phrase. *"E tru mout"* ("He true mouth") means the speaker is referring to someone who doesn't lie. *"Le een crack muh teet"* ("I didn't even crack my teeth") means "I kept quiet." A forgetful Gullah speaker might say, *"Mah head leab me"* ("My head left me").

Gullah music, as practiced by the world-famous Hallelujah Singers of St. Helena Island, also uses many distinctly African techniques, such as call-and-response (the folk hymn "Michael Row the Boat Ashore" is a good example). The most famous Americans with Gullah roots are late boxer Joe Frazier (Beaufort), hip-hop star Jazzy Jay (Beaufort), NFL great Jim Brown (St. Simons Island, Georgia), and Supreme Court justice Clarence Thomas (Pin Point, Georgia, near Savannah).

Upscale development continues to claim more and more traditional Gullah areas, generally by pricing the Gullah out through rapidly increasing property values. Today, the major pockets of living Gullah culture in South Carolina are in Beaufort, St. Helena Island, Daufuskie Island, Edisto Island, and a northern section of Hilton Head Island.

The old ways are not as prevalent as they were, but several key institutions are keeping alive the spirit of Gullah: the **Penn Center** (16 Martin Luther King Dr., St. Helena, 843/838-2474, www.penncenter.com, Mon.-Sat. 11am-4pm, $4 adults, $2 seniors and children) on St. Helena Island near Beaufort; the **Avery Research Center** (66 George St., Charleston, 843/953-7609, www.cofc.edu/avery, Mon.-Fri. 10am-5pm, Sat. noon-5pm) at the College of Charleston; and **Geechee Kunda** (622 Ways Temple Rd., Riceboro, Georgia, 912/884-4440, www.geecheekunda.com) near Midway off U.S. 17.

one-room schoolhouse of *The Water is Wide* fame, the **Mary Field School,** is still here, as is the adjacent 140-year-old **Union Baptist Church,** but Daufuskie students now have a surprisingly modern new facility (middle school students are still ferried to mainland schools every day). Farther north on Haig Point Road is the new **Billie Burn Museum,** housed in the old Mount Carmel Church and named after the island's resident historian.

On the southern end you'll find the **Bloody Point Lighthouse,** named for the vicious battle fought nearby during the Yamasee War of 1815 (the light was actually moved inland in the early 1900s). Other areas of interest throughout the island include Native American sites, tabby ruins, the old Baptist church, and a couple of cemeteries.

Download a very well-done, free self-guided tour of Daufuskie's historic sites at www.hiltonheadisland.org; look for the "Robert Kennedy Historic Trail Guide" (not a nod to the former attorney general and U.S. senator, but a longtime island resident and historian).

For overnight stays, you can rent a humble but cozy cabin at **Freeport Marina** (843/785-8242, $100-150, golf cart $60 extra per day), near the ferry dock and overlooking the water. There are vacation rental options island-wide as well; go to www.daufuskieislandrentals.com for info on a wide variety of offerings. Sorry, no camping available!

There are no grocery stores as commonly understood on Daufuskie, only a couple of general store-type places. So if you've booked a vacation rental, most grocery items will need to be brought in with you.

For the freshest island seafood, check out the **Old Daufuskie Crab Company** (Freeport Marina, 843/785-6652, daily 11:30am-9pm, $8-22). The deviled crab is the house specialty. The other place to dine out on the island is **Marshside Mama's** (15 Haig Point Rd., 843/785-4755, www.marshsidemamas.com, hours change frequently, $10-15), a laid-back spot to enjoy grouper, gumbo, and Lowcountry boil, and frequent live music. Reservations are strongly encouraged.

For hand-crafted island art, go to **Iron Fish Gallery** (168 Benjies Point Rd., 843/842-9448, call ahead for hours), featuring the work of Chase Allen. His "coastal sculptures" include fanciful depictions of fish, stingrays, and even mermaids.

Transportation and Services

The main public ferry between Daufuskie and Hilton Head is operated by **Calibogue Cruises** (18 Simmons Rd., 843/342-8687, www.daufuskiefreeport.com). Taking off from Broad Creek Marina on Hilton Head, the pleasant short ride—30 minutes each way—brings you in on the landward side of the island. Cost is $33 per person round-trip, or $64 per person round-trip including a meal at the Old Daufuskie Crab Company and a golf cart rental. Ferries run three times a day Monday, Wednesday, and Friday, and twice a day Tuesday, Thursday, Saturday, and Sunday. Ferry reservations are essential!

While the ferry trip and many vacation rentals include the rental of a golf cart, for *a la carte* service—get it?—rent one near Freeport Marina by calling 843/342-8687 (rates vary but hover around $30 per person per day). As the amount of golf carts is limited, I strongly recommend reserving yours in advance. All standard rules of the road apply, including needing a valid driver's license.

Points Inland

It's likely that at some point you'll find yourself traveling inland from Beaufort, given that region's proximity to I-95. While this area is generally more known for offering interstate drivers a bite to eat and a place to rest their heads, there are several spots worth checking out in their own right, especially Walterboro and the Savannah National Wildlife Refuge.

WALTERBORO

Walterboro is chiefly known to the world at large for being one of the best antiquing locales on the East Coast. Indeed, many of the high-dollar antiques shops on Charleston's King Street actually do their picking right here in the local stores, selling their finds at a significant markup in Charleston! (Another advantage Walterboro antiques shopping has over Charleston: plenty of free parking.)

Convenient and walkable, the two-block **Arts and Antiques District** on Washington Street centers on more than a dozen antiques and collectible stores, interspersed with a few gift shops and eateries. The best shop, though by no means the only one you should check out, is **Bachelor Hill Antiques** (255

E. Washington St., 843/549-1300, Mon.-Sat. 9am-6pm, Sun. 9am-4pm), which has several rooms packed with interesting and unique items, from collectibles to furniture to most everything in between.

Sights
★ SOUTH CAROLINA ARTISANS CENTER

Don't miss the **South Carolina Artisans Center** (334 Wichman St., 843/549-0011, www.scartisanscenter.com, Mon.-Sat. 9am-5pm, Sun. 1pm-5pm, free), an expansive and vibrant collection of the best work of local and regional painters, sculptors, jewelers, and other craftspeople, for sale and for enjoyment. The Artisans Center hosts numerous receptions, and every third Saturday of the month they hold live artist demonstrations 11am-3pm.

MUSEUMS

Walterboro boasts three small museums. The relocated and upgraded **Colleton Museum** (506 E. Washington St., 843/549-2303, www. colletonmuseum.org, Tues. noon-6pm, Wed.-Fri. 10am-5pm, Sat. 10am-2pm, free) is one of the best examples of a small-town museum you're likely to find. Adjacent is the farmers market, open Tuesday 2pm-6pm and Saturday 10am-2pm May-end of October.

The **Bedon-Lucas House Museum** (205 Church St., 843/549-9633, Thurs.-Sat. 1pm-4pm, $3 adults, free under age 8) was built by a local planter in 1820. An example of the local style of "high house," built off the ground to escape mosquitoes and catch the breeze, the house today is a nice mix of period furnishings and unadorned simplicity.

The **Slave Relic Museum** (208 Carn St., 843/549-9130, www.slaverelics.org, by appointment, $6 adults, $5 children) houses the Center for Research and Preservation of the African American Culture. It features artifacts, photos, and documents detailing the Atlantic passage, slave life, and the Underground Railroad.

TUSKEGEE AIRMEN MEMORIAL

Yes, the Tuskegee Airmen of World War II fame were from Alabama, not South Carolina. But a contingent trained in Walterboro, at the site of the present-day **Lowcountry Regional Airport** (537 Aviation Way, 843/549-2549), a little north of downtown on U.S. 17. A publicly accessible, low-security area of the airport hosts the **Tuskegee Airmen Memorial,** an outdoor monument

the South Carolina Artisans Center

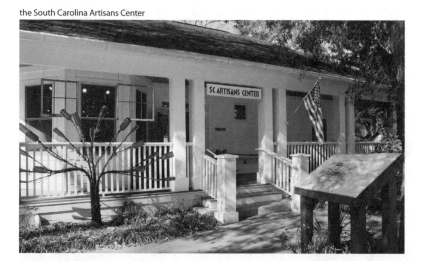

Tuskegee Airmen in Walterboro

In a state where all too often African American history is studied in the context of slavery, a refreshing change is the tale of the Tuskegee Airmen, one of the most lauded American military units of World War II. Though named for their origins at Alabama's Tuskegee Institute, the pilots of the famed 332nd Fighter Group actually completed their final training in South Carolina at Walterboro Army Airfield, where the regional airport now sits.

The U.S. military was segregated during World War II, with African Americans mostly relegated to support roles. An interesting exception was the case of the 332nd, formed in 1941 as the 99th Pursuit Squadron by an act of Congress and the only all-black flying unit in the American military at the time. Mostly flying P-47 Thunderbolts and P-51 Mustangs, the pilots of the 332nd had one of the toughest missions of the war: escorting bombers over the skies of Germany and protecting them from Luftwaffe fighters. Though initially viewed with skepticism, the Tuskegee Airmen wasted no time in proving their mettle.

In fact, it wasn't long before U.S. bomber crews—who were, needless to say, all white—specifically requested that they be escorted by the airmen, who were given the nickname "Red-tail Angels" because of the distinctive markings of their aircraft. While legend has it that the 332nd never lost a bomber, this claim has been debunked. But as Tuskegee Airman Bill Holloman said, "The Tuskegee story is about pilots who rose above adversity and discrimination and opened a door once closed to black America, not about whether their record is perfect." The 332nd's reputation for aggressiveness in air combat was so widely known that the Germans also had a nickname for them—*Schwartze Vogelmenschen*, or "Black Birdmen."

Today Walterboro honors the airmen with a monument on the grounds of the Lowcountry Regional Airport, on U.S. 17 just northeast of town. In an easily accessible part of the airport grounds, the monument features a bronze statue and several interpretive exhibits. Another place to catch up on Tuskegee Airmen history is at the **Colleton Museum** (506 E. Washington St., 843/549-2303, www.colletonmuseum.org, Tues. noon-6pm, Wed.-Fri. 10am-5pm, Sat. 10am-2pm, free), which has a permanent exhibit on the pilots and their history in the Walterboro area.

Walterboro Army Airfield's contribution to the war effort was not limited to the Tuskegee Airmen. Seven of the famed Doolittle Raiders were trained here, there was a compound for holding German prisoners of war, and it was also the site of the U.S. military's largest camouflage school.

to these brave flyers. There's a bronze statue and several interpretive exhibits.

GREAT SWAMP SANCTUARY

Just south of town is the **Great Swamp Sanctuary** (www.thegreatswamp.org, daily dawn-dusk, free), a still-developing ecotourism project focusing on the Lowcountry environment. Located in one of the region's few braided-creek habitats accessible to the public, the 842-acre sanctuary has three miles of walking and biking trails, some along the path of the old Charleston-Savannah stagecoach route. Kayakers and canoeists can paddle more than two miles of winding creeks. There are three entry points to the Great Swamp Sanctuary, all off Jefferies Boulevard. In west-to-east order from I-95: north onto

Beach Road, north onto Detreville Street (this is considered the main entrance), and west onto Washington Street.

Festivals and Events

In keeping with South Carolina's tradition of towns hosting annual events to celebrate signature crops and products, Walterboro's **Colleton County Rice Festival** (http://the-ricefestival.org, free) happens every April. There's a parade, live music, a 5K run, and the crowning of the year's "Rice Queen."

Food

The story of food in Walterboro revolves around ★ **Duke's Barbecue** (949 Robertson Blvd., 843/549-1446, $7), one of the best-regarded barbecue spots in the Lowcountry and one of the top two joints named "Duke's" in the state (the other, by common consensus, is in Orangeburg). The pulled pork is delectable, cooked with the indigenous South Carolina mustard-based sauce.

Accommodations

If you're looking for big-box lodging, the section of Walterboro close to I-95 is chockablock with it. The quality is surprisingly good, perhaps because they tend to cater to Northerners on their way to and from Florida. A good choice is **Holiday Inn Express & Suites** (1834 Sniders Hwy., 843/538-2700, www.hiexpress.com, $85), or try the **Comfort Inn & Suites** (97 Downs Ln., 843/538-5911, www.choicehotels.com, $95).

If you'd like something with a bit more character, there are two B&Bs on Hampton Street downtown. **Old Academy Bed & Breakfast** (904 Hampton St., 843/549-3232, www.oldacademybandb.com, $80-115) has four guest rooms housed in Walterboro's first school building. They offer a full continental breakfast. Note that credit cards are not accepted. Although built recently (by local standards), the 1912 **Hampton House Bed and Breakfast** (500 Hampton St., 843/542-9498, www.hamptonhousebandb.com, $125-145) has three well-appointed guest rooms and offers a full country breakfast. By appointment only, you can see its Forde Doll and Dollhouse Collection, with over 50 dollhouses and oodles of antique dolls.

SAVANNAH NATIONAL WILDLIFE REFUGE

Roughly equally divided between Georgia and South Carolina, the sprawling, 30,000-acre **Savannah National Wildlife Refuge** (912/652-4415, www.fws.gov/savannah, daily dawn-dusk, free) is one of the premier bird-watching and nature-observing locales in the Southeast. The system of dikes and paddy fields once used to grow rice now helps make this an attractive stopover for migrating birds. Bird-watching is best October-April. While you can kayak on your own on miles of creeks, you can also call **Swamp Girls Kayak Tours** (843/784-2249, www.swampgirls.com), who work out of nearby Hardeeville, for a guided tour. The wildlife refuge is about 20 minutes from Savannah, two hours from Charleston, and an hour from Beaufort. To get here, take exit 5 off I-95 onto U.S. 17. Go south to U.S. 170 and look for Laurel Hill Wildlife Drive. Be sure to stop by the **visitors center** (off U.S. 170 at Laurel Hill Wildlife Dr., Mon.-Sat. 9am-4:30pm).

Columbia and the Midlands

The "real" South Carolina, this large area stretching across the wide waist of the Palmetto State, is often neglected in discussions of tourism.

Between the living movie set that is the Lowcountry and the more dramatic landscape of the Upstate, the Midlands—flat and crisscrossed with interstate highways—sometimes seem plain by comparison. But the Midlands have long been something of an honest broker between the Lowcountry and the Upcountry, from Columbia's original role as compromise state capital to the region's default mode as a cultural buffer zone between the insouciant coast and the staunch mountains.

In addition to great fishing, throughout the region there's an abundance of outdoor activity, including some of the best white-water rafting in the South near Columbia and the unique Congaree National Park, home to some of the most ancient old-growth forest on the planet.

PLANNING YOUR TIME

Columbia is an easy city to get around in. Reserve half a day for the Riverbanks Zoo and a minimum of another half day for the other major sights. Two days will allow you to see more of the city, including a night out in the Vista and an evening in Five Points.

Because of the physical breadth of the Midlands, one day is not nearly enough to enjoy the rest of the region outside Columbia. Reserve half a day alone for Congaree National Park. If you only have a day or a day and a half, choose between two areas: the Pee Dee or Santee Cooper.

Previous: Riverbanks Zoo and Garden; South Carolina State House. **Above:** Maurice's Piggie Park BBQ.

Look for ★ to find recommended sights, activities, dining, and lodging.

Highlights

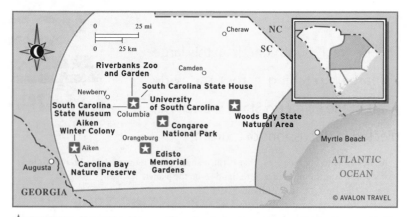

★ **South Carolina State House:** The resilient and grand state capitol features gorgeous grounds and interesting monuments (page 190).

★ **South Carolina State Museum:** Learn all about the Palmetto State in an excellently restored warehouse in the Congaree Vista (page 192).

★ **University of South Carolina:** The elegant Horseshoe area is the oldest, most beautiful part of one of the South's oldest universities (page 192).

★ **Riverbanks Zoo and Garden:** One of the country's best zoos has a dynamic educational and conservation component as well as a beautiful botanical garden (page 193).

★ **Congaree National Park:** This park features an ancient cypress swamp with what may be the tallest old-growth canopy remaining on earth (page 198).

★ **Woods Bay State Natural Area:** This well-preserved Carolina bay features a canoe trail and scenic boardwalk (page 201).

★ **Edisto Memorial Gardens:** The pride of Orangeburg showcases thousands of varieties of roses (page 203).

★ **Aiken Winter Colony:** See the cozy, historic cottages of the wealthy Northerners who put Aiken on the map (page 206).

★ **Carolina Bay Nature Preserve:** This scenic and accessible Carolina bay features a good walking trail around its circumference (page 208).

Columbia and the Midlands

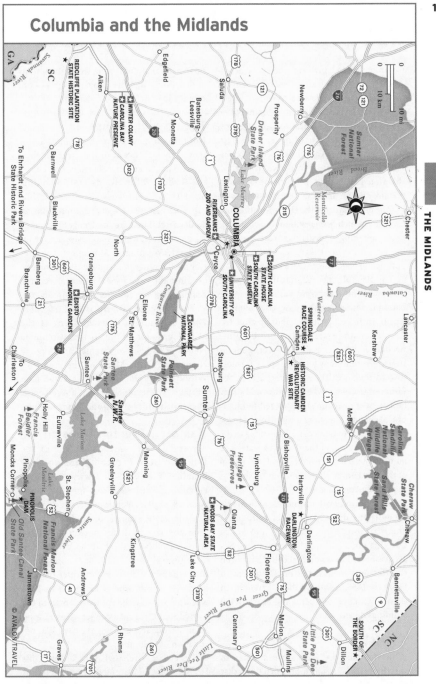

© AVALON TRAVEL

Columbia

Columbia's broad, inviting avenues—a necessity of the rebuilding after General Sherman's torching, now considered a civic signature—are a welcome break from the winding, often cramped streets of Charleston and the predictable Main Streets of dozens of South Carolina hamlets. And while it seems that almost every little burg you drive through in this state has its own little private college—certainly not an unattractive trait—Columbia has the big enchilada, the University of South Carolina, which brings with it that comparatively rare thing in the Palmetto State: a genuine, honest-to-goodness college-town vibe, as opposed to just a town with a college.

The first planned capital in the United States and only the second planned city in the nation (after Savannah, Georgia), Columbia was born in compromise. Shortly after the Revolution and statehood, South Carolina needed a state capital. However, generations of resentment by Upcountry farmers toward their wealthier counterparts in the Lowcountry meant the capital would likely be nowhere near the slave-tended fiefdoms of Charleston. Therefore it was decided to locate the new capital as close as possible to the geographic center of the Palmetto State. The name of the new city would reflect the symbol of the new nation, a feminine figure who was the Uncle Sam of her day.

For reasons still unknown to history, though long debated, General William T. Sherman took a big left turn into South Carolina upon ending his March to the Sea at Savannah. The wrath that could have been Charleston's was visited on Columbia in February 1865. A third of the city went up in flames, with over 300 acres and nearly 1,400 buildings destroyed.

SIGHTS

While the "must-see" picks are limited here to specific attractions, any local will tell you that no trip to Columbia is complete without stops at Five Points and the Congaree Vista (more often "the Vista"), both downtown.

Robert Mills House

Not the oldest but certainly the most architecturally significant of the three antebellum homes to survive Sherman's torching, the **Robert Mills House** (1616 Blanding St., 803/252-7742, www.historiccolumbia.org, Tues.-Sat. 10am-4pm, Sun. 1pm-5pm, $8 adults, $6 children, free under age 5) is named for its designer, whose impressive oeuvre includes the Washington Monument. The interior hosts a range of furniture and decorative arts, including examples of American Federal, English Regency, and French Empire styles.

You can get a **combo ticket** (803/252-7742, $28 adults, $20 children) at the Mills House for all the Historic Columbia Foundation's house museums, including the Hampton-Preston Mansion, the Woodrow Wilson Family Home, and the Mann-Simon Cottage. The last tour at each house begins Tuesday-Saturday at 3pm and Sunday at 4pm.

Hampton-Preston Mansion

Across the street from the Mills House is the 1818 **Hampton-Preston Mansion** (1615 Blanding St., 803/252-7742, www.historiccolumbia.org, Tues.-Sat. 10am-4pm, Sun. 1pm-5pm, $8 adults, $6 children, free under age 6). This classic example of an elite planter's domicile was built for cotton merchant Ainsley Hall (who also had the Mills House built several years later), but soon landed in the hands of an even wealthier planter, Wade Hampton, who at his death in 1835 was widely held to be the richest man in the United States. The mansion served as a Union Army headquarters during the Civil War occupation of Columbia.

Tickets are purchased at the Robert Mills House. You can also buy a **combo ticket**

Columbia

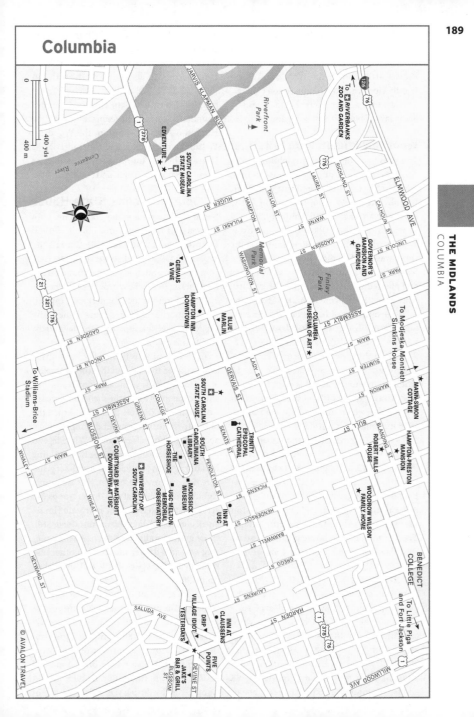

0
400 yds

0
400 m

Congaree River

Riverfront Park

To 126 76

To RIVERBANKS ZOO AND GARDEN

JARVIS KLAPMAN BLVD

1 378

EDVENTURE

SOUTH CAROLINA STATE MUSEUM

HUGER ST.

TAYLOR ST.

PULASKI ST.

HAMPTON ST.

WASHINGTON ST.

Memorial Park

176

RICHLAND ST.

LAUREL ST.

WAYNE ST.

ELMWOOD AVE.

CALHOUN ST.

LINCOLN ST.

GADSDEN ST.

PARK ST.

GOVERNOR'S MANSION AND GARDENS

Finlay Park

To Modjeska Monteith Simkins House

ASSEMBLY ST.

MAIN ST.

SUMTER ST.

MARION ST.

BULL ST.

COLUMBIA MUSEUM OF ART

MANN-SIMON COTTAGE

BLANDING ST.

HAMPTON-PRESTON MANSION

ROBERT MILLS HOUSE

WOODROW WILSON FAMILY HOME

21 321 176

To Williams-Brice Stadium

GADSDEN ST.

LINCOLN ST.

PARK ST.

ASSEMBLY ST.

BLOSSOM ST.

DEVINE ST.

COLLEGE ST.

GREENE ST.

WHALEY ST.

MAIN ST.

WHEAT ST.

HEYWARD ST.

SALUDA AVE.

GERVAIS & VINE

HAMPTON INN DOWNTOWN

BLUE MARLIN

GERVAIS ST.

LADY ST.

SOUTH CAROLINA STATE HOUSE

SOUTH CAROLINIANA LIBRARY

THE HORSESHOE

USC MELTON MEMORIAL OBSERVATORY

UNIVERSITY OF SOUTH CAROLINA

COURTYARD BY MARRIOTT DOWNTOWN AT USC

MCKISSICK MUSEUM

SENATE ST.

PENDLETON ST.

TRINITY EPISCOPAL CATHEDRAL

PICKENS ST.

HENDERSON ST.

BARNWELL ST.

GREGG ST.

LAURENS ST.

HARDEN ST.

INN AT USC

DRIP

VILLAGE IDIOT

YESTERDAYS

INN AT CLAUSSENS

FIVE POINTS

JAKE'S BAR & GRILL

DEVINE ST.

SALUDA AVE.

BLOSSOM ST.

MILLWOOD AVE.

BENEDICT COLLEGE

To Little Pigs and Fort Jackson

1 378 76

1

© AVALON TRAVEL

(803/252-7742, $28 adults, $20 children) at the Mills House for all the Historic Columbia Foundation's house museums, including the Robert Mills House, the Woodrow Wilson Family Home, and the Mann-Simon Cottage. The last tour at each house begins Tuesday-Saturday at 3pm and Sunday at 4pm.

Woodrow Wilson Family Home

The Wilson family arrived in Columbia from Augusta, Georgia, during Reconstruction, when the future president's father, Joseph Ruggles Wilson, took a job at the Presbyterian Theological Seminary, housed in what's now the Mills House. Woodrow Wilson, who went by the name Tommy at the time, was 14 years old. Woodrow's mother, Jessie, held sway over the extensive gardens and planted the magnolias in the front yard, which can be seen from Hampton Street. The Wilsons only stayed in the house for a couple of years. Today, the **Woodrow Wilson Family Home** (1705 Hampton St., 803/252-7742, www.historiccolumbia.org, Tues.-Sat. 10am-4pm, Sun. 1pm-5pm, $8 adults, $6 children, free under age 6) is open for tours. Historically, the key object in the collection is the bed in which the president was born in 1856 in Staunton, Virginia.

Tickets are purchased at the Robert Mills House. You can also buy a **combo ticket** (803/252-7742, $28 adults, $20 children) at the Mills House for all the Historic Columbia Foundation's house museums, including the Robert Mills House, the Hampton-Preston Mansion, and the Mann-Simon Cottage. The last tour at each house begins Tuesday-Saturday at 3pm and Sunday at 4pm.

Mann-Simon Cottage

Born into slavery near Charleston in 1799, Celia Mann somehow escaped servitude and made her way to Columbia to work as a midwife. By 1844 she was living in the **Mann-Simon Cottage** (1403 Richland St., 803/252-7742, www.historiccolumbia.org, Tues.-Sat. 10am-4pm, Sun. 1pm-5pm, $8 adults, $6 children, free under age 6), one of

a precious handful of antebellum homes in South Carolina owned by free blacks.

Tickets are purchased at the Robert Mills House. You can also buy a **combo ticket** (803/252-7742, $28 adults, $20 children) at the Mills House for all the Historic Columbia Foundation's house museums, including the Hampton-Preston Mansion, the Woodrow Wilson Family Home, and the Robert Mills House. The last tour at each house begins Tuesday-Saturday at 3pm and Sunday at 4pm.

★ South Carolina State House

South Carolina is a pretty small state, both in area and in population. But the **South Carolina State House** (1101 Gervais St., 803/734-2430, www.discoversouthcarolina.com, www.scstatehouse.gov, grounds daily dawn-dusk, free), whose grounds cover nearly 20 acres, is one of the grandest state capitols in the nation. Free guided tours of the entire capitol are available Monday-Saturday and the first Sunday of the month.

In 1865 General William Sherman and his army assailed the city, and the still incomplete State House took several cannonballs (you can still see the spots where the shells hit). Once in Columbia, the Yankees promptly burned the old State House to the ground along with just about everything else in town. While legend has it that Sherman spared the new building because it wasn't actually where the legislature had approved secession, this isn't quite right. The truth is that the Union troops did set fire to the interior of the new State House, and a good bit of damage was sustained. Still, those granite walls stood firm. A temporary roof was added after the war, but otherwise the State House was to sit idle and unfinished until 1907.

A controversial highlight is at the entrance on Gervais Street, at the **Confederate Monument.** At one time, the rebel Stars and Bars flew over the State House. However, in the wake of the murders of nine worshippers at the historically black Emanuel AME Church in Charleston in 2015, the old Confederate battle flag was furled by order of

the South Carolina State House

the governor and the state legislature. It is no longer present on the State House grounds.

The **African American History Monument** is a comparatively late addition to the property and the first of its kind on any American capitol grounds. The dozen vignettes on the monument depict various chapters in the struggle for civil rights from slavery through today. At the base of the monument are four rubbing stones, each representing a different region of Africa from which slaves were imported.

The imposing and impressive **George Washington Statue** at the capitol's front steps is sculpted of bronze on a granite base and is supposedly Washington's exact height: six feet, two inches tall. If you're here after hours, you may notice joggers running up and down the front steps, *Rocky*-style.

Trinity Episcopal Cathedral

The beautiful buffed-brick **Trinity Episcopal Cathedral** (1100 Sumter St., 803/771-7300, www.trinitysc.org), near the State House, is a fine example of Gothic Revival church architecture, and a recent renovation has made it even more attractive. Its congregation has roots back to the very first backcountry Episcopalian church in the state, around 1812.

The current sanctuary hosts deceased luminaries in the attached cemetery, including five governors of South Carolina and three Confederate generals (and one who was both: Wade Hampton III). Good construction and

Trinity Episcopal Cathedral

benevolent wind patterns (and divine intervention?) saved the church from Yankee fires in 1865.

★ South Carolina State Museum

The mother lode of all history of the Palmetto State, the **South Carolina State Museum** (301 Gervais St., 803/898-4921, www.scmuseum.org, Mon. and Wed.-Fri. 10am-5pm, Tues. 10am-8pm, Sat. 10am-6pm, Sun. noon-5pm, $13.95 adults, $11.95 children, free under age 3) occupies the 1893 Columbia Mill textile building. Open since 1988, there are over 70,000 artifacts in its growing collection. There's a constant menu of rotating exhibits as well as a standing collection of art, archaeology, and natural history. Kids love the giant shark display, a 43-foot-long replica of a prehistoric shark skeleton typical of the species that once roamed this area back when water levels were significantly higher than today. But the real highlights are the detailed and vibrant exhibits on particular segments of the human history of South Carolina.

Housed within the State Museum complex is the small but well-tended **South Carolina Relic Room & Military Museum** (301 Gervais St., 803/737-8095, www.crr.sc.gov, Tues.-Sat. 10am-5pm, 1st Sun. of the month 1pm-5pm, $6 adults, $3 youth, free under age 12, $1 1st Sun. of the month), which maintains an interesting collection of artifacts and memorabilia highlighting the state's significant contributions to American military history, with a strong focus on the Civil War era. A combo ticket ($9) provides admission to both the State Museum and the Relic Room.

EdVenture

The new-fangled children's museum **EdVenture** (211 Gervais St., 803/779-3100, www.edventure.org, Tues.-Sat. 9am-5pm, Sun. noon-5pm, $11.50), within the State Museum complex but in a separate building, was built specifically for those ages 12 and under. In it are over 350 hands-on exhibits, mostly concentrating on science and nature. A highlight

is "Eddie," a 40-foot-tall schoolboy within whose simulated innards kids can climb and slide.

Columbia Museum of Art

The small but well-done **Columbia Museum of Art** (Main St. and Hampton St., 803/799-2810, www.columbiamuseum.org, Tues.-Fri. 11am-5pm, Sat. 10am-5pm, Sun. noon-5pm, $12 adults, $5 children, free under age 5) is in a suitably modern-looking building, erected in 1998. The highlight of its permanent collection is the Samuel H. Kress Collection on the upper floor, including some wonderful Renaissance and baroque pieces. The most notable single works here are Botticelli's matchless *Nativity* and Claude Monet's *The Seine at Giverny*. Occasionally hours and admission cost are different during special exhibits; check the website for details.

★ University of South Carolina

Columbia isn't just the state capital; it's a college town as well. The **University of South Carolina** (USC, 803/777-0169, www.sc.edu) hosts nearly 30,000 students at its main campus in Columbia, although apparently only a few attend during summer, which is dead compared to the busy fall and spring.

On Sumter Street at College Street you'll find the wrought-iron gates opening onto **The Horseshoe**, the oldest and most beautiful part of campus. The grand **McKissick Museum** (816 Bull St., 803/777-7251, www.artsandsciences.sc.edu, Mon.-Fri. 8:30am-5pm, Sat. 11am-3pm, free), a New Deal-era public works project, houses USC's many collections and has diverse exhibits on public life and history in the state. There are two galleries on the 2nd floor, a natural history component on the 3rd floor, and a visitors center on the 1st floor.

The key building to note during your walking tour of The Horseshoe is one near the Sumter Street entrance, the **South Caroliniana Library** (910 Sumter St., 803/777-3131, www.sc.edu, Mon.-Fri.

Walter Edgar's Journal

He's originally from Alabama, but you could call University of South Carolina professor Walter Edgar the modern voice of the Palmetto State. From the rich diversity of barbecue to the inner workings of the poultry business and the charms of beach music, Edgar covers the gamut of South Carolina culture and experience on his popular weekly radio show *Walter Edgar's Journal*, airing on South Carolina public radio stations throughout the state.

Currently director of the USC Institute of Southern Studies, the Vietnam vet and certified barbecue contest judge explains the show like this: "On the *Journal* we look at current events in a broader perspective, trying to provide context that is often missing in the mainstream media." More specifically, Edgar devotes each one-hour show to a single guest, usually a South Carolinian—by birth or by choice—with a unique perspective on some aspect of state culture, business, arts, or folkways. By the time the interview ends, you not only have a much deeper understanding of the topic of the show but of the interviewee as well. And because of Edgar's unique way of tying strands of his own vast knowledge and experience into every interview, he'll also leave you with a deeper understanding of South Carolina itself.

In these days of media saturation, a public radio show might sound like a rather insignificant perch from which to influence an entire state. But remember that South Carolina is a small, close-knit place, a state of Main Street towns rather than impersonal metro areas. During any given show, many listeners in Edgar's audience will know his guests on a personal basis. And by the end of the show, the rest of the listeners will feel as if they did.

Listen to *Walter Edgar's Journal* Friday at noon on South Carolina public radio, with a repeat Sunday at 8pm. Hear podcasts of previous editions at www.scetv.org.

8:30am-5pm, Sat. 9am-1pm, free). Designed by renowned American architect Robert Mills, who also designed Columbia's premier house museum, the Caroliniana is the first freestanding college library in the country (two fireproof wings were added in 1927). The library has one of the most significant collections on Southern history anywhere, with a particularly distinguished reading room full of stately busts and Harry Potter-esque alcoves. It's open to the public; all you need is a photo ID. Keep in mind that it's open only when classes are in session.

Governor's Mansion and Gardens

The executive branch of the Palmetto State is headquartered at the **Governor's Mansion and Gardens** (800 Richland St., 803/737-1710, www.scgovernorsmansion.org, gardens Mon.-Fri. 9am-5pm, free). Built in 1855 as the Arsenal Military Academy, the building, which now houses the governor and family, survived the burning of the city in 1865

and hosted its first chief executive in 1869. The six rooms of the mansion open to the public contain an impressive collection of furnishings and artwork from various eras. Call or visit the website to make an appointment for a free tour.

★ Riverbanks Zoo and Garden

One of the nation's best, if underrated, zoos and South Carolina's most popular single attraction, **Riverbanks Zoo and Garden** (500 Wildlife Pkwy., 803/779-8717, www. riverbanks.org, fall-winter daily 9am-5pm, spring-summer Mon.-Fri. 9am-5pm, Sat.-Sun. 9am-6pm, $15.95 adults, $13.50 children, free under age 2) is a unique combo site. Not only do you get a crackerjack zoo, with nearly 400 species represented and an extensive environmental and educational component, but there's a beautiful botanical garden as well. A $36 million expansion includes a new seal/sea lion exhibit, an upgraded grizzly bear environment, and more kids' activities.

Some tips on enjoying Riverbanks: It gets

hot in Columbia. Go early or late in the day to see the animals at their best. Regardless of the heat, Riverbanks begins attracting heavy crowds just before lunchtime. If crowds bother you, get there right as it opens. When you enter, take stock of the rotating schedule of exhibits, programs, showtimes, and feeding times *before* you set off on your trek through the zoo.

Riverbanks couldn't be easier to get to. It's just off I-26 at the Greystone Boulevard exit.

ENTERTAINMENT

Columbia is a fun town with plenty of nightlife, especially when USC is in session. In addition to the campus's cultural offerings, there are two main areas to remember for entertainment, dining, and shopping: Five Points, the intersection of Harden and Greene Streets and Saluda Avenue; and the Vista (sometimes called the Congaree Vista), a more recently restored area closer to downtown amid former mill buildings.

Riverbanks Zoo and Garden

Festivals and Events

The main public event on the calendar for downtown Columbia is March's annual **St. Patrick's Day Festival** (www.stpats5points. com, $15) in Five Points. The conglomeration of bars and the cozy streets make for a vivacious Celtic celebration. There are five stages of live music, various kids' activities, and, of course, a big parade.

Each October, Five Points hosts the **Columbia Blues Festival** (803/733-8452, www.wordofmouthproductions.org), a celebration of that indigenous American art form, mostly relying on regional talent. Also in October comes the biggest single local event, the **South Carolina State Fair** (1200 Rosewood Dr., 803/799-3387, www.scstatefair.org, $8 adults, $2 children) at the sprawling state fairgrounds near Williams-Brice Stadium.

Nightlife

As you'd expect, nightlife here is plentiful, boisterous, and centers on the college scene,

especially in Five Points. The Vista appeals to visitors as well as trendy and well-heeled locals. There's no smoking in all bars, restaurants, and public places in Columbia.

Any discussion of nightlife in Columbia, and specifically in Five Points, should begin with **Jake's Bar & Grill** (2112 Devine St., 803/708-4788, Tues.-Fri. 4pm-4am, Sat. 2pm-2am, Sun. 5pm-2am). Formerly called Rockafella's, it often hosted Hootie and the Blowfish when they were getting their start, and it remains the quintessential Five Points neighborhood joint.

In the Vista, for great live bar bands go to the spacious and bustling **Tin Roof** (1022 Senate St., 803/771-1558, www.tinroofbars. com). This is a South Carolina outpost of a Nashville chain of revival juke joints and "shotgun shacks" catering to college crowds. The closest thing to a Five Points-style dive in the Vista is **The Whig** (1200 Main St., 803/931-8852, daily 4pm-2am, kitchen until 10pm), a bohemian-slacker joint with what's generally considered the best jukebox in town.

Performing Arts

The nearly half-century-old **South Carolina Philharmonic** (721 Lady St., 803/771-7937, www.scphilmarmonic.com) plays most of its classical music concerts at the **Koger Center for the Arts** (1051 Greene St., 803/777-7500, www.koger.sc.edu) under the baton of Morihiko Nakahara.

Columbia City Ballet (www.columbiacityballet.com), a professional troupe, generally dances at the Koger Center for the Arts. They offer one of the more eclectic seasons you'll find outside New York City, with a ballet about Dracula every Halloween, and even a ballet chronicling the history of Hootie and the Blowfish. Of course, there's an annual holiday *Nutcracker* as well.

SHOPPING

Other than malls, the main shopping area in Columbia is at Five Points. The Vista also has a growing range of good stores.

As with much of South Carolina, the capital has some good antiques action, mostly in the West Columbia area. **Old Mill Antique Mall** (310 State St., 803/796-4229, www.oldantiquemill.com, Mon.-Sat. 10am-5:30pm, Sun. 1:30pm-5:30pm), represents vendors on a consignment basis. **763 Antique Mall** (763 Meeting St., 803/796-1516, www.763antiquemall.com, Mon.-Sat. 10am-6pm, Sun. 1:30pm-6pm) is in an 11,000 square foot space and has a wide range of collectibles.

The acclaimed **Blue Sky Gallery** (733 Saluda Ave., 803/779-4242, www.blueskyart.com, by appointment) in Five Points is where you'll find original work from none other than Blue Sky himself, aka Warren Edward Johnson, a nationally renowned local artist who specializes in murals and folk art. Call for an appointment.

Sid Nancy (733 Saluda Ave., 803/779-6454, www.shopsidnancy.com, Mon.-Fri. noon-8pm, Sat. 11am-7pm, Sun. 1pm-3pm) in Five Points, as the name might indicate, is an awesome vintage and thrift store with a definite cutting-edge post-punk appeal. Adjacent is the excellent consignment shop **Revente**

(737 Saluda Ave., 803/256-3076, www.shoprevente.com, Mon.-Sat. 10am-6pm, Sun. noon-6pm), which tends to cater to the upper end of the scale, though with some great bargains if your timing is right.

Serious vinyl junkies should head straight to Five Points to check out **Papa Jazz** (2014 Greene St., 803/256-0096, www.papajazz.com, Mon.-Sat. 10am-7pm, Sun. 1pm-6pm). Besides the eponymous genre, they deal in used vinyl of all types, including rare funk records and the occasional punk gem. It's a tiny store packed to the gills with music, but it has been a Columbia tradition for over 25 years.

RECREATION

Because of its position at the confluence of the Saluda, Broad, and Congaree Rivers and the presence of Lake Murray nearby, Columbia is a haven for water-based pastimes. Generally speaking, most put-in spots are in West Columbia, using the large Gervais Street Bridge from downtown as a major landmark. The **Three Rivers Greenway** (803/765-2200, www.riveralliance.org, daily dawn-dusk, free) joins several different hiking and biking paths and provides numerous river access points.

A great place to put in on the Saluda River is **Saluda Shoals Park** (5605 Bush River Rd., 803/731-5208, www.icrc.net, daily dawn-dusk, $4 per vehicle), a 350-acre park on the Saluda River outside of town with a good launch ramp. The park offers periodic guided kayak trips; call for details.

There are several good outfitters in town for rental, purchase, or guided tours. **Adventure Carolina** (1107 State St., 803/796-4505, www.adventurecarolina.com) runs several trips on all area rivers, including a quick and easy selection of three-hour, three-mile paddles (about $50 pp). They also rent anything you might need. **River Runner Outdoor Center** (905 Gervais St., 803/771-0353, www.riverrunner.us, Mon.-Sat. 10am-6pm) is the designated outfitter for Saluda Shoals Park but will rent for any trip at about $40 per day.

On the other side of the rivers in West

Columbia and the suburb of Cayce are the **West Columbia Riverwalk** (from town, cross over the Gervais St. Bridge, take a left on Alexander Rd., and you'll see the amphitheater and parking lot on the left) and the **Cayce Riverwalk** (take Blossom St. over the river, then a left onto Axtell Dr./Jessamine St., and the entrance is on the left).

Spectator Sports

As part of the Southeastern Conference, the **University of South Carolina's Gamecocks** (www.gamecocksonline.cstv.com) play football in front of a passionate fan base at **Williams-Brice Stadium** (1127 George Rogers Blvd., 803/254-2950). They play basketball downtown at the **Colonial Center** (801 Lincoln St., 803/576-9200).

The brand-new **Columbia Fireflies** (www.columbiafireflies.com) play baseball in the also brand-new **Spirit Communications Park** (1640 Freed St., 803/726-4487, single game tickets $10), built especially for them. The Single-A level farm team of the New York Mets made a big impact their inaugural year in 2017 by signing former University of Florida and NFL player Tim Tebow to play for them.

FOOD

Columbia may not be challenging Charleston on the food front anytime soon, but a growing number of very tasty establishments have sprung up in the Five Points and Vista districts to go along with other longtime favorites in town. And if you're a barbecue fan, you're definitely in luck.

American

Columbians swear by the pimento cheeseburgers and the pimento cheese fries at **Rockaway's** (2719 Rosewood Dr., 803/256-1075, daily 11am-11pm, $8), an under-the-radar, locals-only type place in a nondescript building on the south side of the USC campus. For a brewpub, **Hunter Gatherer Brewery** (900 Main St., 803/748-0540, Tues.-Sat. 4pm-midnight, $10) has an excellent kitchen, and

many locals insist the best burger in town is actually here.

Barbecue and Ribs

Maurice's Piggie Park BBQ (1600 Charleston Hwy., 803/796-0220, www.mauricesbbq.com, Sun.-Thurs. 10am-10pm, Fri.-Sat. 10am-11pm, $7-12) in West Columbia is the real thing: mustard-based Carolina pulled pork, and lots of it. This barbecue is the traditional Midlands variety, in a yellow mustard sauce.

Many locals insist however that ★ **Little Pigs** (4927 Alpine Rd., 803/788-8238, www.littlepigs.biz, Wed. 11am-2pm, Thurs.-Sat. 11am-9pm, $8) outside downtown near Fort Jackson has much better 'cue, despite not cooking with wood (a sticky issue with connoisseurs). This is all-you-can-eat buffet-style dining in a simple setting, with the focus purely on the pig itself—literally, since you can see it all right there in the buffet line.

Classic Southern

Not Columbia's best restaurant, but certainly its best-known, ★ **Yesterday's** (2030 Devine St., 803/799-0196, www.yesterdaysssc.com, Sun.-Thurs. 11:30am-midnight, Fri.-Sat. 11:30am-1am, $6-12), in the heart of Five Points, is as close to a Southern institution as the city offers. This simple, always-crowded diner has a menu perfect for a Southern gameday meal for the whole family: "Confederate fried" steak, special-recipe fried chicken, fried catfish, and, of course, the signature meat loaf. Yes, meat loaf. They also have all kinds of sandwiches, including wraps, burgers, clubs, and southwestern chicken.

Coffee, Tea, and Sweets

Probably the best cuppa joe in Columbia is at **Drip** (729 Saluda Ave., 803/661-9545, www.dripcolumbia.com, Mon.-Sat. 7am-6pm, Sun. 8am-6pm) in the heart of Five Points, which, as the name implies, specializes in the hot trend of pour-over drip coffee. There is also wine and beer.

A favorite, if quirky, spot in the Vista is

Nonnah's (930 Gervais St., 803/779-9599, Mon.-Fri. 11:30am-2pm and 5pm-10pm, Sat. 6pm-midnight), an eatery better known for its bar scene and for its great desserts.

Mediterranean and Middle Eastern

Generally considered one of the best restaurants in Columbia and certainly the most romantic, ★ **Gervais & Vine** (620A Gervais St., 803/799-8463, www.gervine.com, Mon.-Sat. 4:30pm-close, $8-10) specializes in Spanish-style tapas. An extensive vibrant menu of both hot and cold tapas awaits, including seared pork tenderloin with cucumber-melon salsa and lavender honey, and marinated manchego cheese with thyme and garlic.

New Southern

A longtime favorite with locals, visitors, and the college crowd alike, the **Blue Marlin** (1200 Lincoln St., 803/799-3838, www.bluemarlincolumbia.com, lunch Mon.-Fri. 11:30am-2:30pm, dinner Mon.-Thurs. 5pm-10pm, Fri. 5pm-11pm, Sat. 4pm-11pm, Sun. 11:30am-9pm, $16-25) in the Vista is known for its mix of Lowcountry and New Orleans-style entrées, like the oyster and shrimp Bienville, seafood gumbo, and shrimp and grits. Each table gets a community-style bowl of collard greens.

Vegetarian

The premier vegan and vegetarian spot in Columbia is **Blue Cactus Café** (2002 Greene St., 803/929-0782, Tues.-Fri. 11am-3pm and 5pm-9pm, Sat. noon-9pm, $7-10). While the veggie burrito is to die for, carnivores will be pleased at the various spicy meat dishes offered, especially in southwestern and Korean cuisine.

ACCOMMODATIONS

Columbia has plenty of lodging but is somewhat underserved in terms of quality accommodations for travelers and businesspeople. This is slowly changing, however. These are the best picks close to major attractions.

Under $150

Perhaps the most beloved stay in Columbia is the ★ **Inn at USC** (1619 Pendleton St., 866/455-4753, www.innatusc.com, $145), a real hidden gem right on campus. A particular emphasis is placed on a certain clubby collegiality. A plus is the complimentary cooked-to-order breakfast in the Palmetto Room.

The **Courtyard by Marriott Downtown at USC** (630 Assembly St., 803/799-7800, www.marriott.com, $120-125) puts you a short walk from several performing arts facilities, the State House, and the Vista. There's a small and somewhat windy rooftop pool.

There aren't many bed-and-breakfasts in Columbia—thanks to General Sherman, the stock of nostalgic old homes is small—but one well-regarded B&B is the **1425 Inn** (1425 Richland St., 803/252-7225, $130-150). Formerly the Richland Inn, this property has had a slight but tasteful makeover since a management change.

$150-300

It's hard to beat the ★ **Hampton Inn Downtown** (822 Gervais St., 803/231-2000, www.hamptoninncolumbia.com, $159) for its combination of location and service. Right in the Vista and close by the State House, this property has the usual high standards associated with the Hampton brand, along with the usual price premium. The only problematic thing about this property is its continuing tight parking issue.

Housed in a former bakery building, the **Inn at Claussen's** (2003 Greene St., 803/765-0440, www.theinnatclaussens.com, $150-200) is the premier lodging in Five Points proper.

INFORMATION AND SERVICES

Visitors Centers

The main visitors center in the area is the **Columbia Regional Visitors Center** (1101 Lincoln St., 803/545-0000, Mon.-Fri. 8am-6pm, Sat. 10am-4pm, Sun. 1pm-5pm, www.columbiacvb.com), on the upper floor of the Columbia Metropolitan Convention Center in the Vista. The Lake Murray area has its own, the **Capital City/Lake Murray Country Visitors Center** (2184 North Lake Dr., Irmo, 800/725-3935, www.scjewel.com, Mon.-Fri. 9am-5pm, Sat. 10am-4pm, Sun. 1pm-5pm), northwest of town near the lake. The university runs an excellent visitors center as well, the **University of South Carolina Visitors Center** (816 Bull St., 803/777-0169, www. sc.edu/visitorcenter, Mon.-Fri. 8:30am-5pm, Sat. 11am-3pm) in the McKissick Museum. Visitor parking is available at the corner of Pendleton and Bull Streets.

TRANSPORTATION
Getting There
Columbia is served by **Columbia Metropolitan Airport** (CAE, 3000 Aviation Way, 803/822-5000, www.columbiaairport.com), southwest of town, which hosts American, Delta, and United.

If you're driving, three interstate highways—I-20, I-26, and I-77—intersect near the city. Signage is plentiful and accurate from all three.

Amtrak (850 Pulaski St., 803/252-8246 or 800/872-7245, www.amtrak.com) has a station downtown with daily New York-Miami *Silver Star* trains. There's a **Greyhound bus station** (2015 Gervais St., 803/256-6465, www.greyhound.com, daily 24 hours) downtown as well.

Getting Around
The airport has numerous **car rental** kiosks, including Alamo, Avis, Budget, Hertz, and Thrifty. In town you'll find an abundance of Enterprise (www.enterprise.com) locations; several Hertz locations, including one downtown (508 Gervais St., 803/252-2561, www. hertz.com); and a Budget location downtown (408 Blossom St., 803/779-3707, www.budget. com).

The **Central Midlands Regional Transit Authority** (803/255-7100, www.gocmrta. com) is the city's public transportation system. Buses run throughout the area, including a full schedule of downtown routes. Single trips are $1.50, or you can purchase a 10-ride pass for $10.

Outside Columbia

★ CONGAREE NATIONAL PARK
There's literally nothing like it on the planet. Set on a pristine tract of land close to Columbia's sprawl but seemingly a galaxy away, **Congaree National Park** (100 National Park Rd., 803/776-4396, www.nps. gov/cong, daily dawn-dusk, free) contains the most ancient stands of old-growth cypress left in the world. It is, quite simply, one of my favorite places. And like many truly great experiences, it's free.

Adjacent to the **Harry Hampton Visitor Center** (daily 8:30am-5pm), which has a great gift shop in addition to good educational exhibits, you'll embark on a system of elevated boardwalks and trails, 20 miles in total, that takes you into and through a good portion

of Congaree's 22,000 acres. A well-done self-guided tour brochure explains the fascinating aspects of this unique environment, almost unknown today.

You'll see cypresses towering over 130 feet into the air (Congaree is said to have the tallest forest canopy on earth, taller than the boreal forests of Canada and the Himalayas). At ground level you'll see hundreds of cypress "knees," parts of the trees' root systems that jut aboveground. You'll see unbelievably massive loblolly pines—a larger, immeasurably grander species than the sad slash pine tree farms that took over much of the South's available acreage with the arrival of the big paper plants in the 1930s.

You'll have the rare experience of seeing what an old-growth forest actually looks like

Congaree National Park

and why it's so peaceful: Because the canopy shuts off so much light, there is almost no understory. You can walk among the great trees as if you were in a scene from *Lord of the Rings*. You'll view gorgeous Weston Lake, actually an oxbow lake that was once part of the Congaree River, isolated as the river changed course over time. You'll see—and much more often, hear—a wide range of wildlife, including owls, waterfowl, and several species of woodpecker, including the rare red-cockaded woodpecker.

You can kayak Cedar Creek, or take one of the free guided canoe tours every Saturday and Sunday, with canoes provided. And serious hikers will enjoy the expansive series of trails that go even deeper into the wilderness than the standard boardwalk loop (sorry pedal-pushers—no bikes are allowed on the trails or boardwalks).

CAMDEN

Camden's attractive and practical geographic location on the Wateree River was recognized by Native Americans. The town's main drag, Broad Street, is actually on the route of the old Catawba trading path. Archaeologists now think the great and influential Creek town of Cofitachequi, which gained fame for its contact with Spanish explorer Hernando De Soto, was headquartered nearby. Most notably, it was the home of Mary Boykin Chesnut, famed Civil War diarist. Camden's resurgence came in the late 1800s, when it became home to a series of affluent Northerners who brought their wealth and their love of horses to town. To this day Camden is a major equestrian center, nicknamed the "Steeplechase Capital of the World."

Historic Camden Revolutionary War Site

Unlike most historic battlefields in the state, the **Historic Camden Revolutionary War Site** (803/432-9841, www.historiccamden.net, Tues.-Sat. 10am-5pm, Sun. 2pm-5pm, free) commemorates a British victory. In this "Empire Strikes Back" scenario, American general Horatio Gates, hero of the Battle of Saratoga, and his combined force of Continental troops and untrained militia were defeated by a large British force from Charleston under the command of Lord Cornwallis, better known to history for surrendering to George Washington at Yorktown several years later. The 107-acre "outdoor museum" includes the townsite of Camden, the oldest inland city in South Carolina. One caveat: This is not the actual battle site, which is several miles away and largely uninterpreted. To get to the actual battlefield, go north from Historic Camden about seven miles on U.S. 521, then take a left onto Flat Rock Road. The marker commemorating the battle is about two miles on the right.

Springdale Race Course

Northwest of town is the nearly 100-year-old **Springdale Race Course** (200 Knights Hill Rd., 803/432-6513), which also hosts the town's two biggest steeplechase events. At the entrance to the track, you'll find the **National Steeplechase Museum** (803/432-6513, www.nationalsteeplechase-museum.org, Sept.-May Wed.-Sat. 10am-4pm, other times by appointment, free), containing a well-managed and exhaustive collection of vintage photos, artifacts, trophies, racing colors, and archival records. Get to Springdale Race Course by taking U.S. 521 (Broad St.) north through Camden, and then turn left onto Knights Hill Road. The track is a little way up on the right.

Food and Accommodations

The best-regarded eating spot in the Camden area is actually a short drive outside Camden in Boykin, a historic little hamlet just south

of town on U.S. 521, past I-20. **The Mill Pond Steakhouse** (84 Boykin Mill Rd., 803/424-0261, www.themillpondsteakhouse.com, Tues.-Sat. 5pm-10pm, $20-40) serves awesome high-end, connoisseur-style steaks and Southern classics like crab cakes and shrimp and grits.

There are several great B&Bs in town, chief among them the outstanding **Bloomsbury Inn** (1707 Lyttleton St., 803/432-5858, www.bloomsburyinn.com, $150-180), widely rated one of the best in the United States. The 1849 property itself is of great historical importance as the onetime home of James and Mary Chesnut, he a Confederate general and she a famous wartime diarist.

The Pee Dee

Named for the Pee Dee River running through it, this region in the extreme northeast of the state—always called "the Pee Dee," not just "Pee Dee"—is largely off the tourism radar. That's a shame, because it offers a particularly relaxing, rolling landscape and a plethora of charming small towns. Though Florence is by far the major city in the region—largely due to its location straddling the region's interstate highways—it has very little to offer. Where possible, stay off the beaten path to explore the region further.

Cheraw Historic District

The beguiling little town of Cheraw on the Pee Dee River is my favorite place in the Pee Dee and one of the Palmetto State's great, but underrated, gems. How gemlike? To tour some of its historic buildings, you simply sign out the keys at the little visitors center. Only in South Carolina, folks. Primarily known today as the birthplace of jazz great Dizzy Gillespie, Cheraw—pronounced "chuh-RAW"—was actually one of the first settlements in the state, dating from the 1730s.

The **Cheraw Visitors Bureau** (221 Market St., 843/537-8425, www.cheraw.com,

Mon.-Fri. 9am-5pm) inside the chamber of commerce building puts out an excellent walking-tour map; call or stop by to get one. You can even make appointments to tour sites on the weekend, but make sure to call ahead.

A natural first stop is the place where Cheraw's favorite son grew up, the **Dizzy Gillespie Home Site Park** (300 block of Huger St., daily dawn-dusk, free). Get here by taking Huger Street a couple of blocks north of Market Street as you come into town. A particularly cool aspect of the park is the chrome fence along Huger Street, illustrating several bars from Gillespie's biggest hit, "Salt Peanuts." (No statue of Dizzy? No worries. There's a nice one a few blocks farther into town.) The premier event in Cheraw, as you'd expect, given its favorite son, is the **South Carolina Jazz Festival** (various venues, 843/537-8420, www.scjazzfestival.com, $20 per day), held each autumn.

Carolina Sandhills National Wildlife Refuge

Established in 1939, **Carolina Sandhills NWR** (23734 U.S. 1, 843/335-8401, www.fws.gov/carolinasandhills, daily dawn-dusk, free)

is one of the last, best places to find the once-ubiquitous longleaf pine and wiregrass habitat, home of the endangered red-cockaded woodpecker. Several well-maintained hiking trails allow you to fully explore and observe this rare ecosystem, and a handful of lakes are available for fishing; a state fishing license (www.dnr.sc.gov) is required.

Darlington Raceway

Darlington Raceway (1301 Harry Byrd Hwy./U.S. 52, 843/395-8499, www.darlingtonraceway.com, dates vary, $35-150) is the granddad of all NASCAR tracks, the first ever to host a major race. While it's not as plush as the ritzier raceways built to accommodate the sport's push to gentrify its ranks, this is still an impressive sight right on U.S. 52. Racing fans can celebrate the return of the NASCAR Cup Series Southern 500 to its customary slot on Labor Day weekend. If you're not in town that weekend, you can call ahead for tours (Mon.-Fri., $5 pp). Sharing a parking area is the **Darlington Raceway Stock Car Museum** (1301 Harry Byrd Hwy./U.S. 52, 843/395-8862, www.darlingtonraceway.com, Mon.-Fri. 10am-5pm, Sat. 10am-4pm, Sun. 11am-4pm, $5 adults, free under age 13).

★ Woods Bay State Natural Area

The best site associated with Florence is actually south of town in the country, near tiny Olanta but still conveniently close to I-95. **Woods Bay State Natural Area** (11020 Woods Bay Rd., 843/659-4445, www.south-carolinaparks.com, daily 9am-6pm, free) is one of the largest remaining Carolina bays, a unique and somewhat mysterious geological phenomenon. These elliptical depressions, scattered throughout the Carolinas and all oriented in a northwest-southeast direction, are typified by a cypress-tupelo bog environment. There's also a rich variety of flora and fauna, including the Cooper's hawk and southern twayblade orchid.

Although the signage is good, it can still be a little tricky getting here. The quickest route is I-95 exit 146, but if you're coming from Florence, take U.S. 52 (Irby St.) through the city and turn right onto U.S. 301 south of town. When you get to Olanta, start looking for the brown signs for Woods Bay. To get back on I-95, take a left onto Woods Bay Road and continue on to little Shiloh. I-95 is a short distance away.

Cheraw is the birthplace of the great jazz artist Dizzy Gillespie.

SOUTH OF THE BORDER

As you're traveling along I-95, you'll inevitably notice billboards with a stereotyped Mexican named Pedro with a penchant for puns exhorting people to visit **South of the Border** (I-95 and U.S. 301/501, 843/774-2411, www.thesouthoftheborder.com, daily 24 hours, free). Begun in 1950 by Al Schafer as a beer stand servicing a dry North Carolina county just across the state line—"south of the border"—the entertainment empire near Dillon gradually grew to encompass motels, restaurants (Mexican and otherwise), gas stations, RV campgrounds, fireworks stands, sprawling gift shops, and even an adult entertainment store, the Dirty Old Man's Shop. At one point, South of the Border, which covers nearly 150 acres, had its own police and fire departments.

In 1997, the racist content of the billboards was watered down, and employees stopped wearing "Pedro" name tags. Today, a more evolved world and vastly increased entertainment options mean that South of the Border is a ghost town. The main landmark is the 75-foot sombrero-clad Pedro himself, between whose massive legs you can drive your car.

TRANSPORTATION

Air

The airport serving the Pee Dee is **Florence Regional Airport** (FLO, 2100 Terminal Dr., 843/669-5001, www.florencescairport.com), which hosts American Airlines. However, most travelers drive to the Pee Dee or arrive at larger airports in the region such as Greenville, Charleston, or Charlotte.

Car

Interstate highways I-95 and I-20 intersect in the Pee Dee, and they are by far the dominant arteries. Other major highways include U.S. 1 from Camden to Cheraw; U.S. 301, which largely parallels I-95 to the east; and U.S. 52 from Cheraw through Darlington to Florence.

Florence Regional Airport has several **car rental** kiosks, including Hertz, Budget, and Avis. There's an Enterprise location (213 S. Coit St., 843/317-6857) downtown. Hartsville has a couple of locations, including Hertz (1 N. 2nd St., 843/662-7930) and Enterprise (826 N. 5th St., 843/857-9088).

Train

Two cities in the Pee Dee have **Amtrak** (www.amtrak.com) passenger train stations with daily New York City-Miami *Silver Meteor* trains: Florence (807 E. Day St.) and Dillon (100 N. Railroad Ave.), near the North Carolina border.

Bus

Greyhound (www.greyhound.com) has bus stations in Florence (611 S. Irby St., 843/662-8407) and in Sumter (129 S. Harvin St., 803/775-3849).

The Santee Cooper Region

As primordial as Lakes Marion and Moultrie seem to be, they're actually artificial. Both are by-products of a New Deal-era hydroelectric project under the auspices of the Santee Cooper Authority, named after the two rivers impounded to form the lakes. One of the largest public works projects in history, the Santee Cooper project was so expansive that eventually the entire region would be known by the same name; the area's chief utility company also goes by that moniker. World War II interrupted the clearing of Lake Marion—hence all those gnarled cypress trees still poking above the waves to this day. Somewhere under its waters, in fact, is Pond Bluff, the old homestead of "the Swamp Fox," Francis Marion himself.

★ Edisto Memorial Gardens

By far the main attraction in Orangeburg is **Edisto Memorial Gardens** (200 Riverside Dr., 800/545-6153, www.orangeburg.sc.us/gardens, daily dawn-dusk, free). The "memorial" aspect is because they're dedicated to the memory of local veterans who died in both world wars. But other than the nice sculpture at the entrance, there is little else remotely military about this wonderful free venue right next to Orangeburg's downtown.

As a nod to the city's popular annual Festival of Roses, the keynotes are the vast fields of heirloom roses in a dazzling variety of colors, which you'll be able to see approximately April-November, with May being the best month. You can't pick the roses, but you can just about get lost wandering among the rows. A scenic duck pond provides a relaxing backdrop. The site takes on added brilliance—literally—in November and December, as Christmas-themed light displays occupy seemingly every corner of the gardens.

The biggest event of the year is the **Festival of Roses** (803/534-6821, www.festivalofroses.com, free), held, fittingly, the weekend before Mother's Day. About 30,000 people attend this weekend-long event, which culminates in a Parade of Roses downtown, with a special float carrying the Queen of Roses.

Food in Orangeburg largely begins and ends with ★ **Duke's Barbecue**, the legacy of the legendary Earl Duke. There are two locations, one uptown (789 Chestnut St., 803/534-9418, call for hours, $8) and one downtown (1298 Whitman St., 803/534-2916, call for hours, $8). Connoisseurs of 'cue clearly prefer the original, more Spartan spot on Whitman Street downtown, commonly referred to around town as "the one by the Pepsi plant." In both cases, you get freshly cooked pulled pork served all-you-can-eat buffet-style with a local version of the indigenous mustard-based sauce, plenty of sweet tea, and loaves of Sunbeam white bread on the tables. Both locations serve what could be the finest examples of the traditional South Carolina side called hash, a pork-based stew. Duke's hours vary; call ahead to make sure they're open.

LAKES MARION AND MOULTRIE

Wild-looking Lake Marion on the Santee River, known for its plethora of striped bass, is the larger of the two lakes, covering over 100,000 acres. To the south, more manicured Lake Moultrie on the Cooper River covers about 60,000 acres and is known for its massive catfish; blue cats over 40 pounds are not uncommon, and some over 50 pounds have been caught. There are numerous marinas, public landings, and fish camps around the circumference of both lakes.

Santee National Wildlife Refuge

Located an easy jaunt off I-95, **Santee NWR** (2125 Fort Watson Rd., 803/478-2217, www.fws.gov/santee, daily dawn-dusk, free)

Lake Marion in the Santee National Wildlife Refuge

actually comprises several federally run locations on the eastern shore of Lake Marion. The well-done **visitors center** (Tues.-Fri. 8am-4pm, 1st, 2nd, and 3rd Sat. of the month 8am-4pm) is at the main Bluff Unit of the refuge, with a nice overlook of the lake and an easy walk down to the sandy shore. A very short drive away is the site of Fort Watson, built by the British on a 3,000-year-old Indian mound. Francis Marion caused the British surrender of Fort Watson in 1781. Each October sees a Revolutionary War encampment at the site in honor of the victory.

Bird-watchers will enjoy the rich variety of migratory ducks, geese, and swans that make their way to Santee NWR November-February.

Pinopolis Dam

The tallest single-step lock in North America and the second tallest in the world, the Pinopolis Dam at the south end of Lake Moultrie separates the impounded lake from the Cooper River. If you're in a boat or kayak, it's a whopping 75-foot, half-hour drop from the lake to the 1940s-era Tailrace Canal, a short trip on which takes you to the river. For a guided kayak tour that includes a jaunt through the lock, contact **Blackwater**

Adventures (843/761-1850, www.blackwateradventure.com, about $50).

Francis Beidler Forest

The **Francis Beidler Forest** (336 Sanctuary Rd., Harleyville, 843/462-2150, www.sc.audubon.org, Tues.-Sun. 9am-5pm, $8 adults, $4 ages 6-18, free under age 6) is jointly owned by The Nature Conservancy and the Audubon Society. It conserves a rare and special 15,000-acre habitat in the blackwater Four Holes Swamp. An 1,800-acre section of the forest contains some of the largest and most ancient old-growth stands of bald cypress and tupelo trees in the world.

To get here from Charleston, take I-26 west out of town to exit 187. Make a left onto Highway 27 south to U.S. 78, where you turn right. Veer right on U.S. 178, and then take a right on Francis Beidler Forest Road. To get to the visitors center, veer right onto Mims Road after a few miles.

Recreation

A good way for the casual traveler to enjoy the lakes is at **Santee State Park** (251 State Park Rd., 803/854-2408, www.southcarolinaparks.com, daily 6am-10pm, $2 adults, free under age 16) on Lake Marion near the town of Santee. A nature-based boat tour of the lake (Wed. and Fri.-Sun., call for times) run by **Fish Eagle Tours** (803/854-4005) departs from the Tackle Shop. The park also has two boat ramps.

All fishing on the lakes for those over age 16 requires a valid South Carolina fishing license, available at any tackle shop, online (www.dnr.sc.gov), or by phone (888/434-7472). A seven-day nonresident license is $11. A total of 40 game fish can be kept any one day, with no more than 10 black bass, 5 striped bass, and only 1 catfish over 36 inches long.

There are three golf courses of note on Lake Marion around the town of Santee: **Santee Cooper Country Club** (630 Santee Dr., 803/854-2467, www.santeecoopergolf.com, $30-60), the area's first; **Lake Marion Golf Course** (9069 Old Hwy. 6, 803/854-2554, www.santeecoopergolf.com, $27-51), built in 1979; and **Santee National Golf Club** (8638 Old Hwy. 6, 803/854-3531, www.santeenational.com, $40-60). **Wyboo Golf Club** (1 Warrens Way, 803/478-7899, www.wyboogolfclub.com, $40-50), a Tom Jackson design near Manning (take I-95 exit 119), is consistently rated one of the top 10 public courses in South Carolina. There are tons of golf packages available in the area; call the Santee Cooper Country Commission (800/227-8510) for more info.

Food

Any discussion of great food in South Carolina must include ★ **Sweatman's Bar-b-que** (1313 Gemini Dr., 803/492-7543, Fri.-Sat. 11:30am-9:30pm, $8-15), outside the town of Holly Hill on the western side of the lakes. People drive two or three hours, literally from the other side of the state, just to eat here on a weekend. While a certain amount of this popularity is driven by the media's trendy fondness for "authentic" Americana—Sweatman's proudly displays signed items by TV gourmand Anthony Bourdain—there's no doubt that this is a special kind of place, if a humble one.

They cook their pork the old-fashioned way: the proverbial whole hog, slow-cooked over wood in a blockhouse out back. The

result is served buffet-style, in two types: the dry white portion, the "inside meat," and the glazed outer portion, "the outside meat." Don't miss the "cracklin's," crunchy fried pigskin.

Sweatman's closes for most of August. To get here, take I-95 exit 90 and then head east on U.S. 176, which becomes Main Street in Holly Hill. Turn left onto Highway 453 and head north for a few miles, and Sweatman's is on the right. When in Holly Hill looking for the turn, keep in mind that Highway 453 is not contiguous through town. You're looking for the spur of Highway 453 that begins on the west side of the railroad tracks.

Sweatman's has only one serious competitor in the area, and that's ★ **McCabe's Bar-B-Que** (480 N. Brooks St., 803/435-2833, Thurs.-Sat. 5:30pm-9pm, $10) on the eastern side of Lake Marion in the town of Manning. The pork is finely pulled, and the sauce is the tangy, kicky Pee Dee-style pepper-and-vinegar variety. Served with that distinctive hash side dish and sliced tomatoes, this plate is often considered the equal of Sweatman's.

MONCKS CORNER

The town of Moncks Corner, seat of Berkeley County, is at the southern tip of Lake Moultrie at the headwaters of the Cooper River; it is a gateway of sorts to the greater Charleston area.

Mepkin Abbey

The burg of Moncks Corner is actually named for a person, not a vocation, but nonetheless that's where you'll find a fully active, practicing Trappist monastery, **Mepkin Abbey** (1098 Mepkin Abbey Rd., 843/761-8509, www.mepkinabbey.org, Tues.-Fri. 9am-4:30pm, Sat. 9am-4pm, Sun. 1pm-4pm, free), notable for the fact that it's not only open to visitors but welcomes them.

The beautiful abbey and grounds on the Cooper River are on what was once the plantation of great Carolina statesman Henry Laurens, whose ashes are buried here, and later the home of the famous publisher Henry Luce and his wife, Clare Boothe Luce. The focal point of natural beauty is the Luce-commissioned **Mepkin Abbey Botanical Garden** (Tues.-Sun.), a 3,200-acre tract with a camellia garden designed by noted landscape architect Loutrel Briggs, a native New Yorker who made Charleston his adopted home.

When they're not in prayer, the monks generally observe silence. In accordance with the emphasis the order puts on the spiritual value of manual labor, farming is the main physical occupation, with the monks' efforts producing eggs, honey, preserves, soap, and even compost from the gardens, all of which you can purchase in the abbey gift shop in the reception center, which will always be your first stop. Tours of the abbey itself are usually given Tuesday-Sunday 11:30am and 3pm.

INFORMATION AND SERVICES

The centrally located visitors center for Santee Cooper is the **Santee Cooper Country Visitor Information Center** (9302 Old Hwy. 6, Santee, 803/854-2131, www.santeecoopercountry.org) in the town of Santee, right off I-95.

TRANSPORTATION

I-95 goes directly through Santee Cooper, making it one of the more accessible parts of South Carolina. U.S. 301 is another key route, cutting through the region and serving Orangeburg before briefly joining I-95 and crossing Lake Marion to Manning. U.S. 17 is the main road to Moncks Corner.

A car is a must in Santee Cooper, unless you're planning on simply boating to the lakes from the Intracoastal Waterway, which is theoretically possible. Rental cars are available in Orangeburg from **Enterprise** (1624 Saint Matthews Rd., 803/534-0143, www.enterprise.com) and **Hertz** (907 Chestnut St., 803/534-0447, www.hertz.com).

Aiken

There are towns with horses, and then there are horse towns. Aiken is the latter. How can you tell the difference? Let's put it this way: Horses have the right of way over cars within Aiken city limits. Indeed, roads in Aiken's Horse District are intentionally kept unpaved so as not to cause stress to tender equine hooves. Several Kentucky Derby winners have Aiken roots, including Pleasant Colony (1981), Swale (1984), and Sea Hero (1993). Visitors can enjoy the clean retro-tinged downtown area, with its wide attractive streets and its very good selection of cafés, restaurants, and stores, a clear cut above most South Carolina towns its size.

SIGHTS

Aiken manages a good mix of horse-related attractions and those having nothing to do with our fast four-legged friends. The majority of attractions in town, whether horsey or not, make the most of Aiken's easygoing natural beauty and optimistic all-American atmosphere.

★ Winter Colony

The old homes of the wealthy Northerners who really put Aiken on the map are almost all privately owned. But a drive or a walk through the **Winter Colony Historic Districts** (www.nationalregister.sc.gov), which are three nationally recognized areas, will give you a good idea not only of their wealth but of their taste as well. Major sectors include the area just west of the intersection of Richland Avenue and Laurens Street; Highland Park Drive near the railroad tracks; the Hitchcock Woods-Hopelands-Rye Patch area off Whiskey Road, south of downtown; and the matchless oak-lined canopy along Boundary Street. Key estates—all private—in the Winter Colony include **Let's Pretend,**

Aiken

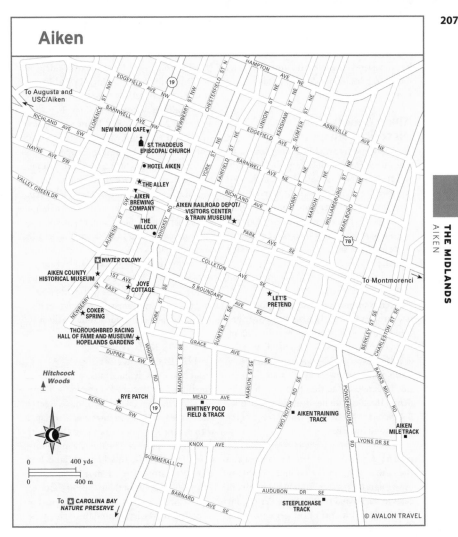

Joye Cottage, and **Sandhurst.** The best way to tour the historic areas of Aiken, including the Winter Colony, is to join the city's tour (803/642-7631, www.cityofaikensc.gov, Sat. 10am, $15) leaving from the Visitors Center and Train Museum (406 Park Ave.) downtown.

You'll often hear the phrase **Horse District** in Aiken. This is actually an informal name for the residential area within the Winter Colony near two vintage racetracks,

the Aiken Mile Track (Banks Mill Rd.) and the Aiken Training Track (538 Two Notch Rd.). Keep in mind that during the warmer months there are precious few horses to see—most will be racing or training up north (this is, after all, a *winter* colony).

Aiken Railroad Depot

The Aiken Railroad Depot, also called the **Visitors Center and Train Museum** (406 Park Ave., 803/293-7846, www.

aikenrailroaddepot.com, Wed.-Fri. 10am-5pm, Sat. 10am-2pm, free) is a beautifully restored facility based in the old 1899 Southern Railway Depot. It centers on nine HO-gauge model train dioramas depicting stops on the historic railroad.

Aiken County Historical Museum

For a good look at area history, housed within a beautiful historic building, check out the **Aiken County Historical Museum** (433 Newberry St., 803/642-2015, http://aiken-county.net, Tues.-Sat. 10am-5pm, Sun. 2pm-5pm, free). While the exhibits are okay, you might honestly be more impressed by the 32-room great house itself, called Banksia (after a variety of rose).

Hopelands Gardens

The gently meandering, exquisitely done outdoor arboretum called **Hopelands Gardens** (1700 Whiskey Rd., 803/642-7631, daily 10am-dusk, free) is, like many sights in Aiken, a legacy of transplanted Northern wealth. Hope Iselin, widow of a wealthy industrialist, gave this 14-acre estate to the city as a public garden in the 1960s on her death at age 102. It's believed that she herself planted some of the cedars and live oaks.

Walking the grounds is a peaceful, lush experience for both the dedicated botanist and the casual visitor alike. Monday nights in May-August bring free outdoor evening concerts to the Roland H. Windham Performing Arts Stage at the rear of the gardens. Bring a blanket and a picnic and enjoy the music.

Also on the grounds is the Dollhouse, once a playhouse and erstwhile schoolroom of the Iselin kids. Actually an old Sears Roebuck catalog house, today the Dollhouse hosts the Aiken Garden Club Council. It's open to the public every Sunday 2pm-5pm, and during the Christmas season it is decorated in fine holiday fashion.

To get here from downtown, just head south on Chesterfield Street, which shortly turns into Whiskey Road.

Thoroughbred Racing Hall of Fame and Museum

Set in the restored old Iselin carriage house (natch) in a corner of Hopelands Gardens is the **Thoroughbred Racing Hall of Fame and Museum** (803/642-7631, http://aiken-racinghalloffame.com, Sept.-May Tues.-Fri. and Sun. 2pm-5pm, Sat. 10am-5pm, June-Aug. Sat. 10am-5pm, Sun. 2pm-5pm, free). Hope Iselin, who bequeathed Hopelands to the city, was quite a horse maven in addition to an amateur horticulturalist, and this is another component of her legacy to Aiken. Staffed by volunteers, this is the kind of humble, underfunded, but achingly sincere museum that makes up in spirit what it lacks in the wow factor.

Downstairs is the actual Hall of Fame, a suitably clubby-looking collection of actual racing silks from famous horses that have trod local tracks, along with all kinds of historical and pedigree information on them.

★ Carolina Bay Nature Preserve

Easily Aiken's most underrated attraction, the **Carolina Bay Nature Preserve** (Whiskey Rd. and Price Ave., daily dawn-dusk, free) is one of the few sights in town not associated with rich people, horses, or both. Owned by the city and protected by the Aiken County Open Land Trust, this lush wetland just across the street from a municipal recreation facility is one of thousands of Carolina bays—elliptical depressions whose origins are shrouded in mystery—found throughout the mid-Atlantic and southeastern United States.

Like most Carolina bays, Aiken's is far from pristine, having been farmed for many years. But this particular specimen is a great example of a restored Carolina bay, with some indigenous flora reintroduced, including a wildflower meadow. A discreet system of pumps keeps it full of water and conversely keeps it from overflowing and flooding the surrounding development. More and more birds are visiting the bay as the years go by. A trail takes you around the circumference of

Carolina Bay Nature Preserve

the bay, and the scenery is beautiful at each point; you can even fish.

To get here, take Whiskey Road well south of Hopelands Gardens until you get to Price Avenue, where you turn east; the preserve parking area is shortly ahead on the left.

Hitchcock Woods

Once the fox-hunting grounds of Thomas Hitchcock, New Yorker and avid sportsman, **Hitchcock Woods** (South Boundary Rd. and Whiskey Rd., 803/642-0528, www.hitchcockwoods.org, daily dawn-dusk, free) is now considered the largest urban forest preserve in the country at a whopping 2,000 acres. It's a great place to hike and stroll, though oddly—given that any number of horse-related activities is allowed—no bicycling is allowed. There are seven main entrances, each with a kiosk that has maps to the woods; or go to the website for a printable, delightfully *Lord of the Rings*-like map. The closest entrance to downtown is on South Boundary Road west of Laurens Street. Another is on Coker Spring Road just west of the spring.

Tours

The key tour in Aiken is provided by the city (803/642-7631, www.visitaikensc.com, Sat. 10am, $15), leaving from the Visitors Center and Train Museum (406 Park Ave.) downtown. Lasting about two hours, it takes you by trolley to all significant areas of town, including through the Winter Colony, with a stop for a walk through Hopelands Gardens. Call for reservations or information.

SHOPPING

There are at least half a dozen antiques shops downtown, many with Sunday hours—a nice change from a lot of sleepy South Carolina towns. The most notable examples are **Aiken Antique Mall** (112 Laurens St., 803/648-6700, Mon.-Sat. 10am-6pm, Sun. 1:30pm-6pm), **Aiken Antiques and Auction** (1060A Park Ave., 803/642-0107, Mon.-Sat. 9am-6pm, Sun. 1:30pm-6pm), and **Swan Antique Mall**

High Cotton and Hot Steam

The big cotton boom of the early 1800s in South Carolina created a demand for a quick way to get the cash crop to market in Charleston, then hotly competing with Savannah, Georgia, for the title of nation's leading cotton export center. That's how South Carolina became home to the first steam rail system in the world, an incredibly little-known fact today.

In 1827, the South Carolina Canal and Rail Road Company was chartered to build a line that would expedite trade from the Upcountry. The resulting 137-mile Charleston-Hamburg line, begun in 1833, was at the time the longest railroad in the world. By 1858 the line was joined with tracks going all the way to Memphis, Tennessee.

However, competing railroads—such as subsequent tracks to Greenville and Augusta—kept profit margins on the Charleston-Hamburg line so low that further expansion was not feasible. With the rise of Augusta and then Atlanta as major rail centers, the line gradually became a backwater run. While the original line stayed in some form of service until the 1980s, its glory days were far in the past.

Today, U.S. 78 roughly follows the old railbed through towns like Aiken, Blackville, Williston, and, of course, tiny Branchville, which became the world's first rail junction when a spur to Columbia was built off the Charleston-Hamburg line.

(321 Richland Ave., 803/643-9922, Mon.-Sat. 10am-5:30pm, Sun. 1pm-5pm). **The Iron Pony** (210 York St., 803/642-5004, Wed.-Sat. 11am-5pm) is set in an antebellum home.

If you like paintings of horses, boy, are you in luck. **Equine Divine** (135 Laurens St., 803/642-9772, www.equinedivineonline. com, Mon.-Sat. 10am-5pm) deals in plenty of equestrian-related artwork and doodads, and it even stays open an hour later during polo season. **Jackson Gallery** (300 Park Ave., 803/648-7397, by appointment) features high-end horse sculpture.

FOOD

Good dining options are scattered throughout the central downtown area, with several in "The Alley," a short lane off Laurens Street.

American

The **Aiken Brewing Company** (140 Laurens St., 803/502-0707, www.aikenbrewingcompany.com, Mon.-Sat. 11am-2am, $10) is a popular restaurant and microbrewery at the entrance to The Alley. While it is best known for its surprisingly wide selection of handcrafted brews, it also offers above-average bar food, such as quesadillas and beer-battered (of course) chicken tenders and wings.

Coffee and Treats

For a cup of joe, some hipster attitude, and a light wrap, sandwich, or sweet treat, go to ★ **New Moon Cafe** (116 Laurens St., 803/643-7088, http://newmoondowntown. com, Mon.-Fri. 8am-5pm, Sat.-Sun. 9am-2pm, $5), certainly the closest thing to an alternative place in this preppy town, although note the weird hours.

ACCOMMODATIONS

The most important thing to remember about staying in Aiken is that all lodging is at a premium during the week of the Masters golf tournament, held each year in early April in nearby Augusta, Georgia.

Under $150

For an interesting and remarkably inexpensive stay right downtown, try the **Hotel Aiken** (235 Richland Ave., 803/648-4265, www.hotelaiken.com, $65-100), a historic property built in 1898 at the height of the Winter Colony's glory. Renovated in 2001, it still retains a certain well-worn patina. However, this isn't where to go for peace and quiet: The hotel's two attached bars, the clubby **Polo Tavern** and the ritzy **One Hundred Laurens,** are centers of downtown nightlife. In fact, things

the Aiken Brewing Company

get so noisy that the guest rooms directly over the bar area are discounted.

$150-300

For a truly grand historic hotel experience downtown, try ★ **The Willcox** (100 Colleton Ave., 877/648-2200, www.thewillcox.com, $185-425), which once hosted Franklin D. Roosevelt as well as a throng of well-heeled visitors during Aiken's Winter Colony glory days.

INFORMATION
AND SERVICES

The main **Aiken Visitors Center** (113 Laurens St., 803/642-7557, www.aikenis.com) is inside the historic Holley Building. The **Visitors Center and Train Museum** (406 Park Ave., 803/293-7846, www.aikenrailroaddepot.com) also features good visitor info.

TRANSPORTATION

Aiken is very accessible either from I-20 just to the north or directly from Augusta, Georgia, via U.S. 78, which is called Jefferson Davis Highway in Augusta and becomes Richland Avenue in downtown Aiken.

The closest airport to Aiken is the small **Augusta Regional Airport** (AGS, 1501 Aviation Way, 706/798-3236, www.flyags.com) in Georgia, hosting carriers Delta Connection and American Eagle. Indeed, when in Aiken it's important to remember that much larger Augusta is a short drive away and is for all intents and purposes considered a part of the local economy.

In Aiken, there's a **Greyhound bus station** (153 Pendleton St., 803/648-6894, www.greyhound.com).

Greenville and the Upstate

C onservative in culture and world-view, the Upstate—you'll also hear it called the Upcountry—is the fastest-growing region of South Carolina.

As such, it's becoming much more diverse each passing year, but the area's hospitality and small-town values remain largely intact. You don't read about it much in the history books, but the Upstate was the most pivotal theater of the American Revolution, in which groups of Upcountry militia and Loyalist Tories savagely battled back and forth while the uniformed regular armies in New England were at a stalemate.

By far the region's main metro area, Greenville is rapidly outpacing its reputation for conservatism. It does so through a devotion to smart urban redevelopment and a forward-looking business sense that has allowed it to move beyond the old mill-based economy that long ago moved offshore.

In the northernmost part of the state, along the fringes of the Blue Ridge Mountains, you'll find stunning natural beauty and plenty of outdoor recreation, all at prices much lower than in the heavily visited havens across the border in trendier North Carolina.

PLANNING YOUR TIME

You can spend as much or as little time in the Upstate as you want. For the full flavor, you'll need at least three days and two nights. Remember to budget time to explore Greenville's Main Street. For a more focused stay—say, one devoted to hiking or fishing along the Cherokee Foothills Scenic Highway (Hwy. 11)—a couple of nights, or perhaps even one, will do.

Previous: riding horses in the Upstate; Falls Park on the Reedy. **Above:** Trinity Church in downtown Greenville.

Look for ★ to find recommended
sights, activities, dining, and lodging.

Highlights

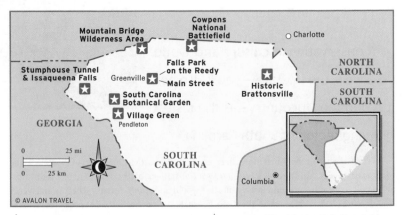

★ **Falls Park on the Reedy:** This rolling green oasis is in excellently restored downtown Greenville (page 215).

★ **Greenville's Main Street:** A nationally renowned example of walkable urban redesign (page 215).

★ **Cowpens National Battlefield:** This interpretive site commemorates a key Patriot victory in the American Revolution (page 226).

★ **Stumphouse Tunnel and Issaqueena Falls:** This fun twofer features a tunnel with a unique history and a scenic waterfall (page 230).

★ **Mountain Bridge Wilderness Area:** The wildest area of the Upstate combines Jones Gap State Park with Caesars Head State Park (page 232).

★ **South Carolina Botanical Garden:** The state's official gardens are on the scenic campus of Clemson University (page 234).

★ **Pendleton Village Green:** This historic hamlet has a delightful central square (page 236).

★ **Historic Brattonsville:** Living history and educational fun for the whole family can be found at this restored Upcountry village (page 238).

Greenville

Greenville, South Carolina, might be the coolest city you've never heard of. It's a source of frustration to Greenville residents that so few of their fellow Americans—heck, even their fellow South Carolinians—are aware of the city's modern renaissance. Greenville has its fair share of well-scrubbed block-long megachurches, but the only crusade most residents of Greenville seem to be on is spreading the word that their city—inevitably pronounced in the local foothills twang as "GRUHN-vul"—is actually a rapidly growing and increasingly wealthy city nestled in the scenic foothills of the Appalachians.

Like much of the Upstate, modern-day Greenville is located on what used to be the heart of the Cherokee Nation. The first white settler of note was Richard Pearis, who began a plantation around 1770 in what's now downtown Greenville at East Court and South Main Streets.

By the turn of the 20th century, Greenville began promoting itself as the "Textile Center of the South." After World War II, that slogan was expanded to "Textile Center of the World." In the 1960s, however, as farsighted community and business leaders foresaw the coming decline of the U.S. textile industry, Greenville began pursuing a more diversified economy, concentrating on increasing foreign investment.

SIGHTS
★ Falls Park on the Reedy

In a fun quirk of fate, Greenville's most historic spot, the place it began, is also its coolest visitor attraction. **Falls Park on the Reedy** (864/232-2273, www.greatergreenville.com, daily dawn-dusk, free), a rambling, manicured, eclectic outdoor experience along the Reedy River, is where Richard Pearis, the area's first nonnative settler, set up his trading post and gristmill in 1768 on what was then Cherokee land. The scenic **Reedy River Falls**

powered Pearis's mill and helped spawn the city you see today. While the Pearis mill is long gone, you can still see some ruins of the later Vardry and McBee mills from the early 1800s on the riverbank.

You can keep up with the historical events that happened here through a series of markers, but Falls Park is more of an all-around pedestrian experience. Walk the 355-foot **Liberty Bridge**—the only curved pedestrian suspension bridge in the country—over the Reedy River Falls, and see the nearby **Falls Cottage**, built by George Dryer in 1840.

★ Greenville's Main Street

To get the true feel of Greenville's revitalization, take a leisurely walk down historic **Main Street**, which in a nice reversal of the usual situation was actually narrowed from four lanes to the current cozy two. The renovated area—one of the most well-done I've seen in the country—runs roughly from the Hyatt Regency Hotel slightly downhill to the newest restored area, the West End. In between are quality stores, cafés, and restaurants of all descriptions, all under a particularly well-crafted and shady tree canopy.

Shoeless Joe Jackson Museum

With memorabilia from the life and career of Greenville's favorite native son, the **Shoeless Joe Jackson Museum** (356 Field St., 864/235-6280, www.shoelessjoejackson.org, Sat. 10am-4pm and Greenville Drive home game nights, free) suitably sits adjacent to the Fluor Field minor-league ballpark in the historic West End. The house, formerly the home of Joe and his family, was moved to this site from 119 East Wilborn Street, and it houses a variety of photos and artifacts, all in a cozy, loving setting. Parking next to the museum is free except on Greenville Drive game days.

Greenville and the Upstate

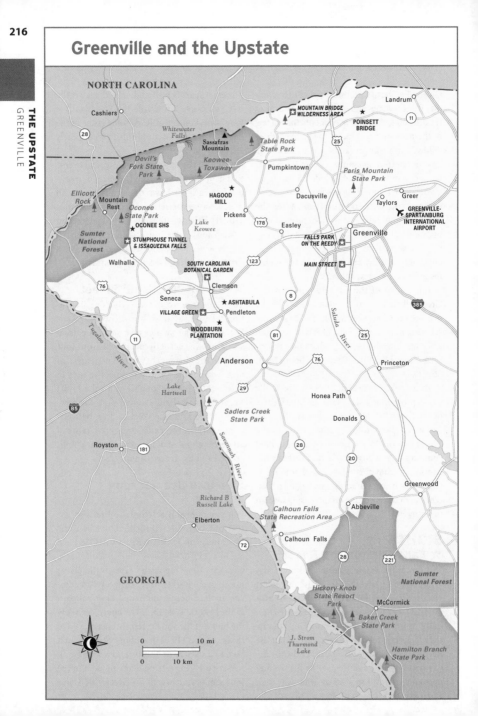

NORTH CAROLINA

Landrum

Cashiers

Whitewater
Falls

MOUNTAIN BRIDGE
WILDERNESS AREA

POINSETT
BRIDGE

Sassafras
Mountain

Table Rock
State Park

Devil's
Fork State
Park

Keowee-
Toxaway

Pumpkintown

Paris Mountain
State Park

Ellicott
Rock

Mountain
Rest

Oconee
State Park

HAGOOD
MILL

Dacusville

Greer

Taylors

GREENVILLE-
SPARTANBURG
INTERNATIONAL
AIRPORT

OCONEE SHS

Lake
Keowee

Pickens

178

Sumter
National
Forest

STUMPHOUSE TUNNEL
& ISSAQUEENA FALLS

Easley

Greenville

FALLS PARK
ON THE REEDY

Walhalla

SOUTH CAROLINA
BOTANICAL GARDEN

123

MAIN STREET

76

Clemson

Saluda
River

Seneca

ASHTABULA

8

VILLAGE GREEN

Pendleton

385

11

WOODBURN
PLANTATION

81

25

Tugaloo
River

Anderson

76

Princeton

Lake
Hartwell

29

Honea Path

85

Sadlers Creek
State Park

Donalds

Royston

181

28

20

Savannah
River

Greenwood

Richard B
Russell Lake

Calhoun Falls
State Recreation Area

Abbeville

Elberton

72

Calhoun Falls

28

221

Sumter
National
Forest

Hickory Knob
State Resort
Park

McCormick

GEORGIA

Baker Creek
State Park

J. Strom
Thurmond
Lake

Hamilton Branch
State Park

0   10 mi

0   10 km

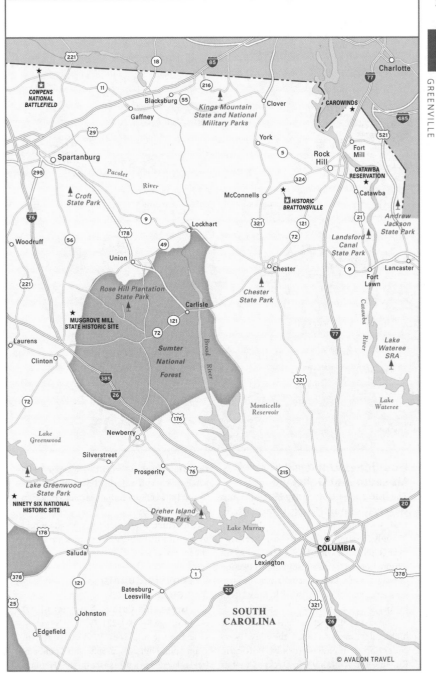

Greenville

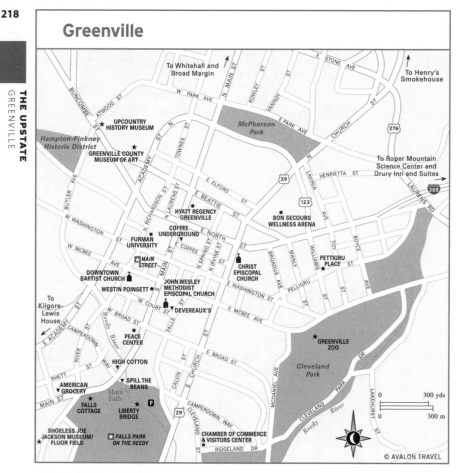

Bob Jones University Museum and Gallery

The **Bob Jones University Museum and Gallery** (1700 Wade Hampton Blvd., 864/770-1331, www.bjumg.org, Tues.-Sun. 2pm-5pm, $5 adults, $3 students, free ages 6-12), referred to as "Greenville's best-kept secret," deserves national praise for its outstanding collection of religious art. The museum hosts the largest single array of such artwork in the western hemisphere.

The main gallery at the museum, and the highlight for most visitors, is the Old Masters collection. It includes work by Botticelli, Rubens, and Anthony van Dyck, as well as

the often stunning works by lesser-known artists such as the starkly beautiful *Crucifix* by the 14th-century Italian painter Francesco di Vannuccio.

Unfortunately, the gallery is closed for renovation until 2019. Check the museum's website for updates.

Greenville County Museum of Art

The **Greenville County Museum of Art** (420 College St., 864/271-7570, www.greenvillemuseum.org, Tues.-Wed. and Fri.-Sat. 11am-5pm, Thurs. 11am-8pm, Sun. 1pm-5pm, free) is located in a nice space on the "Heritage

downtown Greenville

Paris Mountain State Park

My favorite park in the Greenville area, and one of South Carolina's coolest state parks (and that's saying a lot), is **Paris Mountain State Park** (2401 State Park Rd., 864/244-5565, www.southcarolinaparks.com, daily 8am-sunset, $2 adults, free under age 16). This is yet another of the state parks built by the Civilian Conservation Corps in the mid-1930s, with many of the sturdily built, evocative structures typical of that effort. To get to Paris Mountain State Park, take the North Pleasantburg Drive/Highway 291 exit from I-385. Go north on Piney Mountain Road, take a right onto State Park Road, and continue to the park entrance.

TOURS

Carriage rides downtown are available from **Whispering Winds Carriage Co.** (864/220-3650, www.downtowncarriage.com, Fri.-Sat. 6pm-11pm, adults $15, under five $5). They last about half an hour and depart from the Westin Poinsett and Courtyard Marriott.

For more detailed guided tours, check out **Greenville History Tours** (864/567-3940, www.greenvillehistorytours.com, $12, culinary tour $39), which offers several options.

ENTERTAINMENT AND EVENTS

Since the closure of longtime local favorite The Handlebar, the local live music scene has been hurting. Trying to pick up the slack is **The Radio Room** (2845 N. Pleasantburg Dr., 864/263-7868, www.wpbrradioroom.com), an excellent hipster dive bar a bit north of downtown that books the best indie touring bands.

In the restored West End across from Falls Park is **Chicora Alley** (608 S. Main St., 864/232-4100, www.chicoraalley.com, Tues.-Sat. 5pm-2am, Sun.-Mon. 5pm-midnight), a great place to grab a bite, have a brew, and listen to reggae or jazz.

One might not rank the **Greenville Symphony Orchestra** (GSO, 200 S. Main St., 864/232-0344, www.greenvillesymphony.org) among the world's greatest ensembles,

Green" downtown at the corner of Academy and College Streets. The feather in its cap is the resident collection, always on display, of 32 of what Andrew Wyeth himself called his best watercolors. The museum also has an eclectic collection of American contemporary artists such as Josef Albers, Jasper Johns, Andy Warhol, Edward Hopper, and Romare Bearden.

Upcountry History Museum

Also at Heritage Green is the **Upcountry History Museum** (540 Buncombe St., 864/467-3100, www.upcountryhistory.org, Tues.-Sat. 10am-5pm, Sun. 1pm-5pm, $6 adults, $4 ages 4-12, free under age 4).

Greenville Zoo

The smallish **Greenville Zoo** (150 Cleveland Park Dr., 864/467-4300, www.greenvillezoo.com, daily 10am-4:30pm, $8.75 adults, $5.50 children, free under age 4) is good for an hour or so of fun if you're in the downtown area. It comprises 10 acres tucked into verdant Cleveland Park.

The Story of Shoeless Joe

With the possible exception of another controversial man with the same surname—civil rights leader Jesse Jackson—Greenville's most famous native son is Joseph Jefferson "Shoeless Joe" Jackson, one of a handful of baseball players whose name is mentioned in the same breath as Babe Ruth (who eagerly took hitting tips from the South Carolinian, in fact). Baseball purists remember him for his powerful natural swing and his claim on the third-highest career batting average at .356. But to much of the general public, he's best known for his role in the Black Sox gambling scandal, which he seems to have actually had little to do with.

Born in next-door Pickens County in 1888 (or 1889, some scholars believe), Jackson began working in a textile mill while still a young child, and had no formal education. In those days each mill fielded its own team, and "textile ball" was a popular local pastime for mill workers and area spectators alike. Jackson soon became a standout on the Brandon Mill nine, gaining his nickname when, during a game in nearby Anderson, he took the batter's box in his socks because his new cleats were aggravating a bad blister. After he then swatted a triple, a frustrated fan of the opposing team called Jackson a "shoeless son of a gun," and the name stuck—along with an unfortunate image of a clueless Southern bumpkin.

In 1908 Jackson went on to play minor-league ball for the Greenville Spinners. He was then signed for a short stint with the Philadelphia Athletics, an unproductive relationship that soon had him moonlighting around the South Atlantic League with the Savannah minor-league team. Settling into life in the big leagues, he went on to a five-year run with the Cleveland Indians, chalking up a .408 batting average his rookie season. The gangly left fielder signed with the Chicago White Sox in 1915, and he still holds the career triples and batting average records for that team.

Jackson's aw-shucks persona would come back to haunt him during the 1919 Black Sox scandal, when the White Sox were accused of throwing that year's World Series. Although he had by far the best performance of both teams during the series, his output dipped notably in the games the White Sox lost. The Chicago papers had a field day savaging the Southerner when under oath he admitted he'd participated. Modern scholarship has shown, however, that an unscrupulous lawyer manipulated him into making the admission. Years later, his teammates admitted he was at none of the meetings where the fix was discussed.

While the jury acquitted Jackson, baseball commissioner Kennesaw Mountain Landis banned him from the sport anyway. A hangdog Jackson returned to the familiar South, opening up a successful dry-cleaning business back in Savannah. He also quietly managed and played on several Georgia semipro and "outlaw" teams. He moved back to Greenville with his wife in 1933, continuing to play and manage. For the rest of his life Jackson proclaimed his innocence, though he fatalistically accepted his tarnished place in history. While working at a Greenville liquor store he owned late in life, none other than the great Ty Cobb and sportswriter Grantland Rice came in. According to Rice, after Cobb paid for his bottle, he asked Jackson, "Don't you know me, Joe?" Jackson said, "Sure, I know you, Ty, but I wasn't sure you wanted to speak to me. A lot of them don't."

Jackson died of a heart attack in 1951 and is buried in Woodlawn Memorial Park in Greenville, section 5, plot 333. You can find a striking bronze statue of Shoeless Joe in downtown Greenville in the West End on Main Street. The **Shoeless Joe Jackson Museum** (356 Field St., 864/235-6280, www.shoelessjoejackson.org, Sat. 10am-4pm and Greenville Drive home game nights, free) is adjacent to the ballpark in the West End. Once the Jackson family home, the structure was moved from 119 East Wilborn Street to this location. Another effort to honor him is the dedication of **Shoeless Joe Jackson Memorial Park** (406 West Ave., 864/288-6470, daily dawn-dusk, free), farther out on the West End on the site of an old ball field where the man himself once played.

Today, Jackson's legacy is in a bit of a renaissance, and you can find out more about the advocacy effort to get him into the Baseball Hall of Fame at www.blackbetsy.com, a website bearing the nickname of his favorite bat.

but it is an impressive group nonetheless and is the city's performing arts crown jewel. The GSO now plays most of its concerts at the Peace Center Concert Hall on the banks of the Reedy River.

My favorite Greenville event—and perhaps the most surprising one to outsiders who assume the city is populated by clueless hayseeds—is the summer-long **Upstate Shakespeare Festival** (Falls Park, S. Main St., 864/787-4016, performances May-Aug. Thurs.-Sun. 7pm, free). The festival brings two complete productions by the Bard downtown, separated by a period classic by another well-known playwright. The setting is the rolling Falls Park, where the audience lolls around on the grass, enjoys a bottle of wine and a picnic dinner, and takes in the show in the gradually cooling air of a fine Upstate evening.

SHOPPING

Shopping in Greenville comes in two forms: on Main Street and off. Don't neglect Main Street's restored West End.

The most unique shopping experience on Main Street is at the **Mast General Store** (111 N. Main St., 864/235-1883, Mon.-Thurs. 10am-6pm, Fri.-Sat. 10am-9pm, Sun. noon-5pm), a branch of a North Carolina-based regional chain. This hard-to-define and sprawling store, restored to a 1920s vibe, has camping gear, outdoor clothing, preppy clothes, local books, maps, gifts, and an entire candy section in the back.

Paying homage to one of the area's largest employers is **Michelin on Main** (550 S. Main St., 864/241-4450), which contains every kind of Michelin-branded thing you can imagine. The funky **Christopher Park Gallery** (608-A S. Main St., 864/232-6744, www.chickenmanart.com) in the West End has a variety of outsider paintings and sculptures and locally crafted jewelry. On the other end of Main is the **Mary Praytor Gallery** (26 S. Main St., 864/235-1800, www.themarypraytorgallery.com, Tues.-Sat. 10am-5pm), which features eclectic folk art and contemporary paintings from regional artists.

Despite its bland name, the **Clothing Warehouse** (123 N. Main St., 864/467-1238, www.theclothingwarehouse.com, Mon.-Wed. 11am-8pm, Thurs.-Sat. 11am-9pm, Sun. 11am-7pm), a branch of a popular Southern chain, is the hippest vintage clothing and shoe store in town, with a great selection from various eras.

Into beading? Try **The Beaded Frog** (233 N. Main St., 864/235-2323, www.beadedfrog.com, Tues.-Wed. and Fri.-Sat. 11am-5:30pm, Thurs. 11am-8pm, Sun. 1pm-5pm), a locally owned store with every type of bead you could imagine. Take the kids to **O. P. Taylor's** (117 N. Main St., 864/467-1984, www.optaylors.com, Mon.-Sat. 10am-6pm, Sun. 1pm-5pm), a fine toy store with a variety of European toys, Thomas the Tank Engine gear, and games. As military surplus stores go, **Greenville Army Store** (660 S. Main St., 864/232-3168, www.greenvillearmystore.com, Mon.-Sat. 9:30am-5:30pm) is outstanding—which makes sense when one considers it's been in business for half a century and has served many generations of martial Upstaters.

There aren't many indie record stores left in the United States, but a great one is still thriving at **Horizon Records** (2-A W. Stone Ave., 864/235-7922, http://blog.horizonrecords.net), catering to true music enthusiasts since 1975 with a variety of new and used product on CD, DVD, and vinyl. Owner Gene Berger and his helpful staff often host some fairly high-profile musicians for workshops and in-house concerts; check the website for details.

SPECTATOR SPORTS

If you ask the typical Greenville resident what is the most important sports event in the area, they'll say Clemson football. But technically speaking, a more pertinent spectator pastime in Greenville comes courtesy of the **Greenville Drive** (945 S. Main St., 864/240-4528, www.greenvilledrive.com, box seats $8), an affiliate of the Boston Red Sox playing in the South Atlantic League. They play in the retro-style Fluor Field in the historic West

End, built in 2005 as a nearly exact facsimile of Boston's Fenway Park.

FOOD
Barbecue

Don't be put off by the nondescript exterior and small dining room at ★ **Henry's Smokehouse** (240 Wade Hampton Blvd., 864/232-7774, www.henryssmokehouse. com, call for hours, $4-10). This is one of the best, if not *the* best, Upstate barbecue joints and a true Greenville tradition, even though they have taken on some trappings of Midlands 'cue cooking, offering a mustard-based sauce. If the mustard sauce is too much of an acquired taste for you, they also offer the indigenous Upcountry tomato-based sauce. There are two other locations, one on Woodruff Road and the other in nearby suburban Simpsonville.

Classic Southern

Like its older sister location in Charleston, ★ **High Cotton** (550 S. Main St., 864/335-4200, www.mavericksouthernkitchens.com, daily 5:30pm-10pm, Sun. jazz brunch 10am-2pm, $20-40) deals in robust, no-nonsense takes on Southern and American classics. Meats and game are a particular specialty. Reservations are recommended.

The word *quaint* seems to be applied quite often to dining at **Mary's Restaurant at Falls Cottage** (615 S. Main St., 864/298-0005, www.fallscottage.com, Tues.-Sat. 11am-2pm, Sun. 10am-2pm, $10-15), and rightly so for an experience in this daintily restored little cottage scenically overlooking Falls Park. Breakfast buffet, lunches, and brunches are popular. Reservations are strongly recommended.

Coffee, Tea, and Sweets

The java trend has hit Greenville big time, and while there is indeed a Starbucks on Main Street, there are some excellent indie coffeehouses in the restored downtown area as well. If you're walking near Falls Park on the Reedy, take a coffee and snack break at **Spill**

the Beans (531 S. Main St., 864/242-6355, http://stbdowntown.com, Mon.-Sat. 6:30am-11pm, Sun. 1:30pm-9:30pm), right at the entrance to the park. Besides a great selection of coffees, they have the best fresh, hot (and huge!) waffles in town and good yogurt and smoothie offerings.

For truth in advertising, you can't beat **Coffee Underground** (1 E. Coffee St., 864/298-0494, www.coffeeunderground.info, Mon.-Thurs. 7am-11pm, Fri. 7am-midnight, Sat. 8am-midnight, Sun. 8am-10pm), literally located underground and on Coffee Street. Walk down the stairs below ground level at the intersection of Main and Coffee Streets to enter this spacious bistro with an art gallery atmosphere, which also hosts frequent theatre performances. There is a nice brunch menu in addition to breakfast and snack goodies.

New Southern

Trendy **American Grocery Restaurant** (732 S. Main St., 864/232-7665, www.americangr. com, Tues.-Sat. 6pm-10pm, $15-25) is not a grocery store at all but an upscale advocate for *very* locally sourced organic and all-natural meats and produce.

ACCOMMODATIONS

Visitors to Greenville will be pleasantly surprised at the low rates for lodging compared to other American metropolitan areas, a surprise made even more pleasant by the generally high standards.

Under $150

The best accommodations value in Greenville, the **Drury Inn and Suites** (10 Carolina Point Pkwy., 800/378-7946, www.druryhotels.com, $96-175) has excellent facilities, classy decor, prompt, attentive service, and most rooms under $150.

The best and most popular B&B in town is ★ **Pettigru Place** (302 Pettigru St., 864/242-4529, www.pettigruplace.com, $115-195), and not only because of its proximity to scenic Cleveland Park and being a 20-minute walk from Main Street's activity. Pettigru's five guest rooms are decorated tastefully along particular themes.

$150-300

The only four-diamond hotel in Greenville and easily its most pedigreed, the ★ **Westin Poinsett** (120 S. Main St., 864/421-9700, www.westinpoinsettgreenville.com, $185-245) isn't for those who insist on a brand-new building. This is a historic inn built in 1925, and the elegantly simple guest rooms and decor reflect this. The staff is professional and friendly, and you can't beat the location—right on top of the old town center on bustling Main Street.

Anchoring the east end of Main Street's revitalization is the **Hyatt Regency Greenville** (220 N. Main St., 864/235-1234, www.greenville.hyatt.com, $159-259), which is somewhat dated in its monolithic style, typical of the chain. When people downtown talk about going "up near the Hyatt," this is what they're referencing.

INFORMATION AND SERVICES

The main visitors center in Greenville is the **Greenville Downtown Visitor Center** (206 S. Main St., 864/233-0461, www.greenvilecvb.com, Mon.-Fri. 8:30am-5pm). Another one close by is the **Greenville Convention and Visitors Bureau** (631 S. Main St., 864/421-0000, www.greenvillecvb.com, Mon.-Fri. 8:30am-5pm), which has brochures and maps only.

TRANSPORTATION
Air

This rapidly growing metro area is served by the **Greenville-Spartanburg International Airport** (GSP, 864/877-7426, www.gspairport.com), the busiest in the state, at I-85 exit 57. Airlines here include Allegiant (www.allegiant-air.com), American Airlines (www.aa.com), Delta (www.delta.com), Southwest (www.southwest.com), and United (www.ual.com).

Train

Trains stop at the **Greenville Amtrak Station** (1120 W. Washington St., 864/255-4221, www.amtrak.com), with daily service in each direction on the New Orleans-New York City *Crescent*.

Car

The main routes into Greenville are I-85 and I-185, which enters the city from the west side and becomes Mills Avenue, then shortly becomes Church Street. From there, most attractions of interest are to the west (on your left) as you drive into town. Signage is generally excellent in Greenville.

A spur off I-85 called I-385 enters Greenville from the east and runs by the airport. Keep in mind, however, that this is a toll road. There really is no need to use it unless you are coming in and out of the airport. Laurens Road (U.S. 276) on the other side of the airport leads into town in virtually the same place.

Bus

Greenlink (864/467-5000, www.ridegreen-link.com) is an all-biodiesel fleet with various routes throughout Greenville County. Each ride is $1.25, and transfers are $0.50. Children under age six ride free.

Spartanburg

Not as enveloped in new construction as Greenville or as thick with newer residents, Spartanburg retains its small-town attitude while hosting a growing contingent of progressive thinkers. The late legendary gospel great Ira Tucker was from here, as is the Southern rock group the Marshall Tucker Band (no relation to Ira, and no, there's not actually anyone in the band named Marshall Tucker).

One of the Revolutionary War's key engagements took place at nearby Cowpens, where a combined force of colonial militia and Continental Army soldiers soundly defeated a British contingent of redcoats and Loyalists. Spartanburg resident Kate Barry entered legend as South Carolina's own version of Paul Revere, warning local commanders of the approach of the British in time for them to prepare for the battle.

The town got its modern name in 1785, when it was named for the local Spartan Rifles militia regiment. In the nineteenth century, Spartanburg, along with Greenville, grew in importance as major textile centers. It was during this time that Spartanburg got its nickname, "Hub City."

SIGHTS
Morgan Square

The best place to start your explorations in Spartanburg is downtown at **Morgan Square** (daily 24 hours), the center of the city's efforts to transform into a model of pedestrian-friendly downtown redevelopment. Nearby is a throwback to Spartanburg's rail heyday, the restored **Magnolia Street Train Depot** (Magnolia St. and Morgan Ave.), which now hosts the local Amtrak station, the visitors bureau, and the **Hub City Farmer's Market** (Sat. 8am-noon).

Seay House

Vernacular architecture buffs will enjoy viewing the oldest extant building in Spartanburg, the **Seay House** (106 Darby Rd., 864/596-3501, Apr.-Oct. Sat. 11am-5pm, $5), built by farmer Kinsman Seay around 1800. Take Crescent Drive off John B. White Boulevard, and then a left onto Darby Road.

Morgan Square in downtown Spartanburg

Hatcher Garden and Woodland Preserve

Hatcher Garden and Woodland Preserve

The delightful **Hatcher Garden and Woodland Preserve** (832 John B. White Sr. Blvd., 864/574-7724, www.hatchergarden.org, daily dawn-dusk, free) was the labor of love of Harold and Josephine Hatcher, who in 1969 began planting over 10,000 trees and flowering bushes to realize their vision of a community garden. Now an expertly and lovingly tended 10-acre public garden, the site boasts gorgeous flower displays, little ponds, and tastefully arranged viewing platforms.

Walnut Grove Plantation

The most notable historic structure in the Spartanburg area is the **Walnut Grove Plantation** (1200 Otts Shoals Rd., Roebuck, 864/576-6546, Apr.-Oct. Tues.-Sat. 11am-5pm, Sun. 2pm-5pm, Nov.-Mar. Sat. 11am-5pm, $6 adults, $3 children, free under age 6), outside of town in little Roebuck. It was built in 1765 on land granted by King George III to the family of planter Charles Moore.

BMW Zentrum

Although it's technically located in Greer, right next door, Spartanburg tends to claim the **BMW Zentrum** (1400 Hwy. 101 S., Greer, 888/868-7269, www.bmwusfactory.com/zentrum) as its own. Currently the only place outside Germany where BMWs are manufactured, the Zentrum is an interesting hybrid exhibit combining a factory and a museum. You can't miss the Zentrum—it's between Greenville and Spartanburg right on I-85. Take exit 60 and follow the signs.

While tours of the factory itself have been suspended until 2018 so that a billion-dollar renovation can take place, you can visit on-site static displays for free, featuring numerous vintage and noteworthy BMWs.

Spartanburg Museum of Art

The aggressively local **Spartanburg Museum of Art** (200 E. St. John St., 864/948-5364, www.spartanburgartmuseum.org, Tues.-Sat. 10am-5pm, Sun. 1pm-5pm, $5 adults, $3 students and ages 4-17, free under age 4, first Thurs. of the month free) began with the acquisition of *The Girl with Red Hair* by Robert Henri in 1907. Since then, the museum has acquired over 400 pieces of art and sculpture for its permanent collection, which focuses on regional artists. It's housed in the big Chapman Cultural Center downtown.

Spartanburg Regional Museum of History

In the same building as the Museum of Art is the **Spartanburg Regional Museum of History** (200 E. St. John St., 864/596-3501, Tues.-Wed. and Fri.-Sat. 10am-5pm, Thurs. 10am-8pm, Sun. 1pm-5pm, $5 adults, $3 students and ages 4-17, free under age 4, first Thurs. of the month free), run by the Spartanburg County Historical Association. Perhaps the single most historically important item in the collection is the Pardo Stone, a boulder supposedly bearing graffiti from the first Spanish explorer to come through the Upstate, Juan Pardo.

★ Cowpens National Battlefield

The most significant historic site in the Spartanburg area is **Cowpens National Battlefield** (4001 Chesnee Hwy., 864/461-2828, www.nps.gov/cowp, daily 9am-5pm, free), which commemorates one of the key victories over the British in the Revolutionary War. Fought literally in an old cattle pasture, hence the name, the dreaded British cavalry colonel Banastre Tarleton was driven from the field by a combined force of General Daniel Morgan's continentals and local militia (Morgan is memorialized with a park bearing his name in nearby downtown Spartanburg). The British would remain on the defensive for the rest of the war.

In addition to seeing the battlefield and learning about the history of the period in the interpretive center, the other big attraction at Cowpens is the trails, some of which have historical significance. The 1.3-mile **Battlefield Trail** includes exhibits, the 1856 Washington Light Infantry Monument, and the Green River Road, along which the battle was fought. If you want to stay in your car, take the 3.8-mile **Auto Loop Road,** which includes exhibits and parking areas with short trails to the Green River Road, an 1818 log cabin, and a picnic area.

April-October you can take advantage of free one-hour guided walks of the battlefield (Sat. 9:30am, Sun. 1:30pm). Each year on the weekend closest to January 17, the anniversary of the battle, the park celebrates with various demonstrations of period weaponry and a cool living-history encampment.

Poinsett Bridge

The oldest bridge in the state is the beautiful little 14-foot **Poinsett Bridge** (Callahan Mountain Rd., Lyman), built around 1820 by Joel T. Poinsett, city father of Greenville and the man for whom the poinsettia is named. Get there by taking U.S. 25 north past its intersection with Highway 11 and turn right onto Old Highway 25. Take a right onto Callahan Road.

ENTERTAINMENT AND EVENTS

Nightlife

On Morgan Square you can't miss the popular, cavernous **Delaney's Irish Pub** (117 W. Main St., 864/583-3100, Mon.-Sat. 11am-2am, Sun. 3pm-2am). They have a great selection of beer on tap and in the bottle as well as a very good menu of pub food. Dating from 1938, the **Nu-Way Restaurant and Lounge** (373 E. Kennedy St., 864/582-9685) is Spartanburg's version of every town's lovable old dive. This is the place to go for that ironically hip night out on the town, not to mention some truly satisfying burgers.

Performing Arts

Some vibrant stuff goes on downtown at the **Hub-Bub** (149 S. Daniel Morgan Ave., Ste. 2, 864/582-0056, www.hub-bub.com, admission varies). Housed in a former Nash Rambler dealership, Hub-Bub hosts over 100 evenings a year of concerts, film, art exhibits, plays, and workshops, almost all of it with a countercultural edge for this conservative area.

The very definition of a "multiuse" venue, the beautiful **Chapman Cultural Center** (200 E. St. John St., 864/542-2787, www.chapmanculturalcenter.org, admission varies) next to Barnet Park has a 500-seat theater that hosts performances by several local theater groups as well as Ballet Spartanburg. It also houses the city's two main museums, the Spartanburg Museum of Art and the Spartanburg Regional Museum of History.

SHOPPING

My favorite shop in Spartanburg is the non-profit **Hub City Bookshop** (186 W. Main St., 864/577-9349, www.hubcity.org, Mon.-Thurs. 10am-7pm, Fri.-Sat. 10am-9pm), which has a great selection of new and used tomes and also serves as the central meeting point for the Hub City Writers Project and houses the Hub City Press. There's also an attached coffee shop.

How South Carolina Saved America

Cowpens National Battlefield

To read most history books, you'd think the Revolutionary War took place almost entirely in Boston. But South Carolina was the location of the conflict's fiercest fighting, suffering the most men killed of all 13 colonies. Savage and personal, the fighting here usually involved not uniformed regulars but Patriot and Tory militia.

In a span of 90 days, Upstate South Carolina hosted two of the most important Patriot victories of the war, Kings Mountain and Cowpens. Sent to pacify the backcountry's independent-minded Scots-Irish colonists, British major Patrick Ferguson led 1,000 Tory militiamen to a stronghold at the base of Kings Mountain on the border of the Carolinas. On October 7, 1780, an equal number of Appalachian militiamen assaulted the position using tactics they'd learned fighting Native Americans. Rather than marching as a unit and shooting en masse as a European army would, each militiaman fired at will as he attacked, hiding behind rocks to reload.

The battle seesawed for an hour. The end came when Ferguson, attempting to rally his men, was riddled with eight bullets. As the Tory line collapsed, colonists initially sounded the cry "Tarleton's Quarter!," an ironic reference to the brutal British colonel Banastre Tarleton, infamous for murdering prisoners. But cooler heads prevailed, and 700 Loyalists were taken prisoner.

By January 1781 many Kings Mountain veterans had joined General Daniel Morgan, who chose a large cattle-grazing area—literally, the "cow pens"—outside modern-day Spartanburg to make a stand. Learning from the debacle at Camden, Morgan picked a wide-open battlefield with no place for potentially panicking militiamen to run and hide. To further bolster the colonists, he posted regular Continental Army troops behind them.

Thinking the retreating militiamen were panicking, Tarleton's men advanced into a firestorm of bullets. Sending militiamen out on both wings, Morgan surrounded the British in a classic double envelopment, studied by military leaders to this day.

In a very real way, Cowpens led directly to American victory in the war. With the exception of his stronghold at Charleston, General Cornwallis wrote off South Carolina and moved his troops into North Carolina instead. A series of engagements led to his retreat up the Virginia coast to Yorktown, where, bottled up by Washington's army and the French fleet, he was forced to surrender.

You can visit both battle sites today, at **Kings Mountain National Military Park** (2625 Park Rd., 803/222-3209, www.nps.gov/kimo, Labor Day-Memorial Day daily 9am-5pm, Memorial Day-Labor Day daily 9am-6pm, free) near Blacksburg and **Cowpens National Battlefield** (4001 Chesnee Hwy., 864/461-2828, www.nps.gov/cowp, daily 9am-5pm, free) near Gaffney.

SPORTS AND RECREATION
Hiking and Biking

Spartanburg is becoming a mecca of sorts for bicyclists. The city is the launching point for the **Assault on Mt. Mitchell** (www.freewheelers.info) each May, an amateur race over 100 miles long taking participants from Spartanburg to Mount Mitchell, North Carolina, the highest point east of the Mississippi River.

The main recreation area close to Spartanburg is **Croft State Natural Area** (450 Croft State Park Rd., 864/585-1283, www.southcarolinaparks.com, daily 7am-9pm, $2 adults, free under age 16), which offers 12 miles of biking and hiking trails within its massive acreage, once a U.S. Army training ground. As the Palmetto Trail nears completion, a section is expected to join Croft with the rest of the trail.

FOOD
Asian

A great Thai place, right downtown on Morgan Square, is **Lime Leaf** (101 E. Main St., 864/542-2171, Mon.-Fri. 11:30am-3pm and 5pm-10pm, Sat. 5pm-11pm, $9-15). For a sushi fix, check out **Wasabi** (1529 John B. White Sr. Blvd., 864/576-8998, www.wasabispartanburg.com, Tues.-Sat. 11:30am-2:30pm and 5pm-10pm, $5-10).

Classic Southern

No visit to Spartanburg is complete without a visit to the **Beacon Drive-In** (255 John B. White Blvd., 864/585-9387, www.beacondrivein.com, Mon.-Sat. 6:30am-10pm, $5-7). As is the case with many surviving greasy spoon-type places with retro allure, the media hype now surrounding the Beacon doesn't quite match the food, which is really very simple when you get down to it. The signature offering is the Chili Cheese A-Plenty, which sounds like a chili dog but is actually a burger topped with chili and cheese ("A-Plenty" means you get a huge mound of fries and onion rings tossed on top).

Once considered the best barbecue place in Spartanburg, **Wade's Restaurant** (1000 N. Pine St., 864/582-3800, www.eatatwades.com, Mon.-Sat. 10:45am-8:30pm, Sun. 10:45am-3pm, $6-9) has branched out and now deals out all kinds of Southern comfort food, meat-and-two style, including collard greens, fried chicken, and dinner rolls. Wednesday nights are big here, so if you don't like waiting in line, be forewarned.

Coffee, Tea, and Sweets

The most happening coffee and sweet-treat shop in town is ★ **The Coffee Bar** (188-A W. Main St., 864/582-1227, www.littlerivercoffeebar.com, Mon.-Thurs. 7am-7pm, Fri.-Sat. 7am-9pm), located in the historic Masonic Temple downtown and adjacent to the Hub City Bookshop and the nonprofit goings-on there.

Pizza

There's a continuing rivalry over who has the best pizza in Spartanburg: **Venus Pie Pizza** (400 E. Main St., 864/582-4200, Mon.-Tues. 11:30am-9pm, Wed. 11:30am-9:30pm, Thurs.-Fri. 11:30am-10:30pm, Sat. 11:30am-10pm, $6-12) or **The Mellow Mushroom** (464 E. Main St., 864/582-5495, Mon.-Thurs. 11am-10pm, Fri.-Sat. 11am-midnight, Sun. noon-9pm, $7-14) down the block. The former is a totally local venture, while the latter is a regional chain.

ACCOMMODATIONS
Under $150

The first and still best-regarded B&B in Spartanburg is the award-winning ★ **Inn on Main** (319 E. Main St., 864/585-5001, www.innonmainofspartanburg.com, $95-155). Located in a historic 1904 building right on the main drag, Inn on Main offers six distinctive, exquisitely furnished suites that wouldn't be out of place in one of the classic B&Bs in Charleston or Beaufort (and at about half the price). The beds alone, some of which are genuine antiques, will wow you. Of course, you get the requisite full Southern breakfast served in a clubby setting typical of the inn's common areas. Keep in mind they discourage kids under age 12.

The spacious **Spartanburg Marriott at Renaissance Park** (299 N. Church St., 864/596-1211, $109-179) has 240 smoke-free rooms within walking distance of the downtown area.

TRANSPORTATION

While Spartanburg does have its own small municipal airport, **Spartanburg Downtown Memorial Airport** (SPA, 500 Ammons Rd., 864/574-8552, www.cityof-spartanburg.org), it has no commercial flights, and most visitors fly into the area at the much larger **Greenville-Spartanburg International Airport** (GSP, 2000 GSP Dr., 864/877-7426, www.gspairport.com), a short

distance west of town along I-85. Another option is **Charlotte-Douglas International Airport** (CLT, 5501 Josh Birmingham Pkwy., 704/359-4000, www.clt.com), 70 miles east of Spartanburg in North Carolina.

Amtrak (290 Magnolia St., 800/872-7245, www.amtrak.com) has a station downtown, with daily service in each direction on the New Orleans-New York City *Crescent*. There's also a **Greyhound bus station** (100 N. Liberty St., www.greyhound.com).

Public transportation by bus in Spartanburg is offered by **Spartanburg Area Regional Transit Agency (SPARTA)** (100 N. Liberty St., 864/562-4287, www.spartabus. com). Fares run $1.25 per trip, and eight interlocking routes take you all over town, including the mall area.

Along the Blue Ridge

While the landscape is not as stark as north of the border, the Blue Ridge in South Carolina has the dual advantages of being both more easily accessible and much less expensive than the increasingly upscale area of the North Carolina mountains.

ELLICOTT ROCK WILDERNESS AREA

One of the oldest trails in the Southeast can be found in the **Ellicott Rock Wilderness Area** (803/561-4000, www.fs.fed.us, year-round daily, free), which has acreage in three states. It takes you through the Chattooga River gorge in the Sumter National Forest, with about half the trail in North Carolina and a small portion in Georgia. Ellicott Rock itself, once inaccurately considered the meeting point of the three states, is actually in North Carolina. You can reach it on one of the trails in the wilderness area.

Get here by taking Forest Road 708 (Burrells Ford Rd.) west of Highway 107.

There's a parking area near the Burrells Ford Campground, and it's a short hike to the Chattooga River. Since the Chattooga River became designated a Wild and Scenic River, you can no longer drive your car all the way into **Burrells Ford Campground** in the Sumter National Forest. But if you don't mind hiking a short distance, you'll be happy to be away from the RV crowd. As you'd expect, this is a no-frills campground, with a hand-pumped well and minimal toilet facilities.

OCONEE STATE PARK

One of the gems of the Civilian Conservation Corps era in South Carolina, **Oconee State Park** (624 State Park Rd., Mountain Rest, 864/638-5353, www.southcarolinaparks.com, during daylight saving time daily 7am-9pm, other seasons Sun.-Thurs. 7am-7pm, Fri.-Sat. 7am-9pm, $2 adults, free under age 16), a few miles north of Walhalla, is also one of the Upstate's most popular campgrounds. Its two lakes are picturesque, with paddleboat

camping at Oconee State Park

and johnboat rentals available ($10 per day). There's a good network of trails on-site, including the beginning of the Foothills Trail.

★ STUMPHOUSE TUNNEL AND ISSAQUEENA FALLS

This combo free attraction, a neat place to bring the family, is overseen by the nearby town of Walhalla as part of a conservation agreement among the town, local landowners, and a few nonprofit groups. You'll find it clearly marked on the east side of Highway 28 several miles north of Walhalla. If you're up this way checking out the Chattooga River, there's no reason not to stop by.

The **Stumphouse Tunnel** (864/638-4343, daily 8am-5pm, free) is a cool (literally) and possibly slightly frightening experience that kids will either really enjoy or be really petrified of. You won't know until you get them here. In the early 1800s somebody hatched a plan to run a railroad from Charleston to the Midwest, to be known as the Blue Ridge Rail Line. The line was built from Charleston to nearby Pendleton, but one big problem remained: Stumphouse Mountain was in the

way. Residing in a hastily formed rough-and-rowdy burg called, suitably enough, Tunneltown, 1,500 workers managed to dig about 1,600 feet of the planned mile-long tunnel through the mountain before funds ran out. Then the Civil War started, and thus ended the Blue Ridge Line.

The 25-foot-high tunnel stayed empty until the 1940s, when Clemson University professor Paul Miller discovered that the tunnel's interior stayed a consistent 56°F with 85 percent humidity year-round, making it a perfect natural cooler to store and age the signature Clemson blue cheese.

Today, a walk in the tunnel—about 500 feet of it is still open—is like a scary, albeit very low-budget, thrill ride. Take your flashlight if you go inside because once you're a few feet in, there is no light at all. If you're brave enough, you'll eventually come to a brick doorway, behind which is another couple of hundred feet of even darker tunnel before it's finally closed off.

A short walking distance from Stumphouse Tunnel is another charming attraction, **Issaqueena Falls** (864/638-4343, daily 8am-5pm, free). It's a popular place to visit and

The Legend of Issaqueena Falls

Oconee County lore says that sometime in the late 1700s, Cherokee maiden Issaqueena fell in love with an English trader named Allan Francis. When the local Cherokee planned an attack on an English outpost, Issaqueena got on her pony and took a 96-mile ride to warn the settlers, which fittingly ended at the English fort at Ninety Six. She began a family with Francis back at Stumphouse Mountain where she had grown up.

But one day a group of Cherokee attempted to kidnap Issaqueena. She ran from them, but they eventually caught up to her at the 200-foot waterfall at the base of the mountain. Legend has it that Issaqueena pretended to fling herself to her death over the falls but actually hid under a ledge until her pursuers left. Another version has it that she hid under the falls because the Cherokee supposedly thought evil spirits dwelled in waterfalls.

So is the story true? In the frontier memoirs of Ann Matthews, we read about an Indian woman who "disliked very much to think that the white women who had been so good to her in giving her clothes and bread and butter in trading parties would be killed, [so] she became determined to let them know their danger […] and walked 96 miles in twenty-four hours spreading news as she went." Other accounts confirm this story. Some recent scholars, however, doubt her existence at all, citing an abundance of elaborately embellished tales from the Victorian era about comely Indian maidens falling in love with white settlers.

If she did exist, however, perhaps the best clue to Issaqueena's psychology has as much to do with lineage as with love. Legend says that Issaqueena was actually one of the Choctaw people kidnapped by the Cherokee, and her given name at birth was Cateechee.

admire the water's forceful path down over the rocks, many of which you can climb out on if you're feeling adventurous.

OCONEE STATION STATE HISTORIC SITE

Not to be confused with nearby Oconee State Park, **Oconee Station State Historic Site** (500 Oconee Station Rd., 864/638-0079, www.southcarolinaparks.com, daily 9am-6pm, free) is a much smaller park with no camping facilities, geared toward the enjoyment of two historic sites within it as well as a popular and easily accessible waterfall.

The main structure is **Oconee Station** (Sat.-Sun. 1pm-5pm, free), a reconstructed late-1700s blockhouse (fort), used to defend what was then the frontier against Cherokee and other Native American attacks. The other structure is the **William Richards House** (Sat.-Sun. 1pm-5pm, free), built in 1805 by the Irish settler of that name and used as a trading post.

Get here by taking Highway 11 (Cherokee Foothills Scenic Byway) north of West Union

and Walhalla a few miles and following the signs.

DEVIL'S FORK STATE PARK

Don't be put off by the name—**Devil's Fork State Park** (161 Holcombe Circle, 864/944-2639, www.southcarolinaparks.com, spring-summer daily 7am-9pm, fall-winter Sat.-Thurs. 7am-6pm, Fri. 7am-8pm, $2 adults, free under age 16) is one of the easier and more picturesque modern, non-Civilian Conservation Corps South Carolina state parks. Its claim to fame is being the only public access to Lake Jocassee, which despite its artificial nature is pretty picturesque. As you might expect, this park, with four boat ramps, is popular with boaters and anglers (Jocassee is the only lake in South Carolina offering both trophy trout and smallmouth bass).

KEOWEE-TOXAWAY STATE NATURAL AREA

At the halfway point between the two ends of the Cherokee Foothills Scenic Byway (Hwy.

11) lies **Keowee-Toxaway State Natural Area** (108 Residence Dr., Sunset, 864/868-2605, www.southcarolinaparks.com, during daylight saving time daily 7am-9pm, other seasons Sat.-Thurs. 9am-6pm, Fri. 9am-8pm, free). This is one of the state's newer and smaller campgrounds, built in the 1970s on 1,000 acres of land donated by Duke Power, which is also responsible for the existence of Lake Keowee, on which the site resides and under which are the remains of an ancient Cherokee town.

While you're here, or even if you're just driving by, don't miss the **Cherokee Heritage Interpretive Center** (daily 11am-noon and 4pm-5pm, free) on-site. There's a modest museum explaining the natural and human history of the area, including the inundation of the ancient village of Keowee.

TABLE ROCK STATE PARK

A very popular state park with the casual RV crowd as well as with serious hikers is **Table Rock State Park** (158 E. Ellison Ln., 864/878-9813, www.southcarolinaparks.com, during daylight saving time Sun.-Thurs. 7am-9pm, Fri.-Sat. 7am-10pm, other seasons Sun.-Thurs. 7am-7pm, Fri.-Sat. 7am-9pm, $2 adults, free under age 16), just off Highway 11, the Cherokee Foothills Scenic Byway. With two lakes, well-appointed cabins, tent and RV sites, and some exceptional examples of Civilian Conservation Corps handiwork, there is plenty to do and see. But perhaps the key element is Table Rock itself, dominating the northern sky-scape and compelling hikers like a large magnet. Serving as the eastern trailhead for the 76-mile-long Foothills Trail, the park provides access to several strenuous but ultimately rewarding journeys.

Just off the Cherokee Foothills Scenic Highway is **The Inn at Table Rock** (117 Hiawatha Tr., 864/878-0078, www.theinnattablerock.com, $129-179). This six-room historic Victorian offers a bucolic, sumptuous setting on four acres, with views of Table Rock and the Blue Ridge. They discourage guests under age 18.

★ MOUNTAIN BRIDGE WILDERNESS AREA

By far the most wild and woolly nature experience in the Upstate is at **Mountain Bridge Wilderness Area** (8155 Geer Hwy./U.S. 276, Cleveland, 864/836-6115, www.southcarolinaparks.com, spring-summer daily 9am-9pm, fall-winter daily 9am-6pm, $2 adults, free under age 16), just shy of the border with North Carolina. Technically speaking, this site actually comprises two well-known parks, **Caesars Head State Park** and **Jones Gap State Park,** but these are very atypical South Carolina state parks, so don't be fooled by the designation.

The focal point of the area is the hike to Caesars Head, a fancifully shaped 3,622-foot-tall rock outcropping along the Blue Ridge Escarpment. The other major landmark is the 420-foot **Raven Cliff Falls,** one of the most stunning cataracts in the state. It waits at the end of a moderately strenuous 2.2-mile hike, with a suspension bridge available for your scenic vertigo-inducing pleasure.

Campers will find 24 primitive trail-side sites ($8-20), 18 of which have fire rings and 6 of which allow no fires. You must have a permit in advance to camp in the Mountain Bridge Wilderness; call 866/345-7275 or go to the website.

GETTING AROUND

Getting around is quite easy. The main route is Highway 11, the Cherokee Foothills Scenic Byway, running roughly east-west along the base of the Blue Ridge. Other key routes are U.S. 76 in the northwest corner, which takes you from Westminster up to the Chattooga River and into Georgia; Highway 28, which links Highway 11 and U.S. 76 through the cute town of Walhalla; and U.S. 276, a spur from Highway 11 to the Caesars Head area.

Waterfalls of the Upstate

Because of South Carolina's location on the Blue Ridge Escarpment—the so-called "Blue Wall" marking the sudden end of the Appalachians—it contains dozens of waterfalls, from grand to humble. While there are plenty of brochures and websites out there guiding you to the locations of South Carolina's waterfalls, keep in mind that some falls are significantly more difficult to get to than others, especially if there has been a recent rain to turn the old logging roads into muck. Also remember that some of the more remote falls require strenuous, if enjoyable, hikes.

Issaqueena Falls

Here is a sampling of some of the more accessible falls in the Upstate. For more info, go to www.alleneasler.com/waterfalls.html or www.sctrails.net.

- At 420 feet, **Raven Cliff Falls** are the highest in South Carolina, and by some measures, the highest in the eastern United States. Get here by way of a moderately strenuous 4.4-mile round-trip hike out of Caesars Head State Park in the Mountain Bridge Wilderness Area. There's a parking area off U.S. 276.

- Table Rock State Park has several smaller falls on its network of trails, with most on the two-mile **Carrick Creek** loop.

- **Issaqueena Falls** just north of Walhalla on Highway 28 comes with its own legend of a love-struck Cherokee princess. The parking area is near the head of the falls, and there's a nice trail down the falls with a scenic overlook.

- **Spoon Auger Falls** up near the Chattooga River in the northwest corner of the state has a 40-foot drop. It's a short hike out of the Burrells Ford Campground parking area. To get here from Walhalla, take Highway 107 north 17 miles to Forest Road 708 (Burrells Ford Rd.). The parking lot is three miles ahead.

- The comically misnamed **Hidden Falls** are easily found within Oconee State Park. Get to this 40-foot cascade by taking the two-mile yellow-blazed Hidden Falls Trail.

- Just up the road on Highway 11 are the 60-foot **Station Cove Falls,** easily found on a short trail within the Oconee Station State Historic Site.

- The picturesque 30-foot **Reedy Branch Falls** are very easy to get to. From Westminster, take U.S. 76 about 15 miles north and look for a pull-off on the left after you pass Chattooga Ridge Road on the right. The falls are about a 300-yard walk from the road.

- Perhaps the easiest cascade to find—and one of the more enjoyable—is 30-foot **Chau-Ram Falls** in Oconee County's Chau-Ram County Park. (The name derives from the Chauga River and Ramsey Creek.) Drive west of Westminster on U.S. 76 for about three miles; the park entrance is on the left. Unlike most local waterfalls, this one has a nice campground nearby.

Clemson and Vicinity

Like any great American college town, the home of the Clemson University Tigers is vocally proud of its local sports teams. This is especially true in the wake of their dramatic NCAA Football National Championship win in 2017, Clemson University's second. If you're the type to scoff at the Southern passion for college football—or if you're a fan of the Tigers' archrival, the University of South Carolina—OR if you don't like the color orange—you might not enjoy Clemson very much.

Sights

The following attractions are all on the Clemson University campus, which welcomes visitors. Catch a campus tour at the **Clemson University Visitors Center** (109 Daniel Dr., 864/656-4789, www.clemson.edu) most days at 9:45am and 1:45pm.

JOHN C. CALHOUN HOME

The ancestral home of the great South Carolina statesman and subsequently that of his daughter and Thomas Clemson, the **John C. Calhoun Home** (101 Fort Hill St., 864/656-2475, www.clemson.edu, Mon.-Sat. 10am-noon and 1pm-4:30pm, Sun. 2pm-4:30pm, $5 adults, $2 ages 6-12, free under age 6) is the spiritual center of Clemson. Also known as Fort Hill, the Greek Revival mansion, a National Historic Landmark, is essentially all that remains of the original plantation.

★ SOUTH CAROLINA BOTANICAL GARDEN

The official botanical garden of the Palmetto State since 1992, the **South Carolina Botanical Garden** (150 Discovery Ln., 864/656-3405, www.clemson.edu, daily dawn-dusk, free) takes up the entire southeastern tip of the Clemson campus and is a delightful place to stroll, relax, and take in the aromas of the tens of thousands of types of plants, flowers, and herbs planted on the site's 300 acres. There are 70 acres of display gardens, including the impressive camellia garden, a dwarf conifer garden, a hosta garden, and a butterfly garden. A 40-acre arboretum and nearly 100 acres of woodlands with walking trails complete the outdoor package. The best times to visit are spring and fall; in the summer there are significantly fewer flowering plants, and the heat can be stifling.

Within the grounds of the South Carolina Botanical Garden is the **Bob Campbell Geology Museum** (140 Discovery Ln., 864/656-4600, www.clemson.edu/public/geomuseum, Wed.-Sat. 10am-5pm, Sun. 1pm-5pm, closed home football Sat., free), which has its roots in a small rock collection in the Clemson geology department.

the South Carolina Botanical Garden

Entertainment and Events

Like everything else in Clemson, local entertainment here moves with the ebb and flow of student life—especially during football season.

NIGHTLIFE

The most famous college bar in Clemson is **The Esso Club** (129 Old Greenville Hwy., 864/654-5120, www.theessoclub.com), on the edge of campus. As the name indicates, it's in an old gas station, built in 1933 on what was then the main road to Atlanta. You could actually fill up your car until the mid-1980s, when it became a full-time bar and tavern.

The other key watering hole in town is the **Tiger Town Tavern** (368 College Ave., 864/654-5901, www.tigertowntavern.com), aka Triple T's. Upstairs is Top of Tiger Town Tavern, a "private club"—meaning that for a few bucks a year its members can drink there on Sundays. You can too if you come as a current member's guest and pony up.

Sports and Recreation

SPECTATOR SPORTS

Clemson University plays about seven Saturday home football games during the regular season, August-November. During this time, everything in town focuses on the game, to the exclusion of all else except basic bodily functions. Many attractions in town are closed on home football Saturdays. The games are played in **Clemson Memorial Stadium** (Centennial Blvd., 864/656-2118, www.clemsontigers.com), aka "Death Valley," at the western edge of campus. You can buy advance tickets to a Clemson University home game at the school's official ticket site (www.clemsontigers.com) or by calling the school directly at 800/253-6766.

Food

Whatever you do in Clemson, don't miss a stop by the Hendrix Student Center on campus, where you'll find ★ **'55 Exchange** (864/656-2155, www.clemson.edu/icecream, Aug.-May Mon.-Fri. 11:30am-6pm, Sat.-Sun.

1pm-6pm, June-July Mon.-Thurs. 11:30am-8pm, Fri. 11:30am-6pm, Sat.-Sun. 1pm-6pm, $4-10). They have what I believe to be the best ice cream and milk shakes on the planet, courtesy of the Clemson University Dairy Sciences Department. Open to the public, this little corner shop—named for the Clemson graduating class that funded its opening—features rich, robust ice cream in the old style, served in a multitude of equally fresh and tasty cones and edible cups.

Considered the finest of fine dining in Clemson, **Pixie & Bill's** (1058 Tiger Blvd., 864/654-1210, www.tigergourmet.com, lunch Mon.-Fri. 11:30am-1:30pm, dinner Mon.-Sat. 5:30pm-9:30pm, $18-26) is a favorite of students and visiting alumni alike.

Accommodations

There are several nice places to stay in Clemson, but don't stay near Tiger Boulevard unless you enjoy the sound of trains—there are busy railroad tracks that cut through town in that area. Also keep in mind that rates here skyrocket on home-game weekends.

Not near the train tracks and right next to the campus's Walker Golf Course—and like that facility, completely open to the public—is the **James F. Martin Inn** (100 Madren Center Dr., 864/654-9020, www.clemson.edu, $100). Many of its 89 guest rooms overlook Lake Hartwell. There's an outdoor pool, tennis courts, Wi-Fi, and included continental breakfast.

The circa-1837 **Sleepy Hollow Bed and Breakfast** (220 Issaqueena Tr., 864/207-1540, www.sleepyhollow.ws, $100-175) is reportedly the site of the introduction of Percheron horses and Jersey cows to South Carolina, in addition to what's purported to be the state's largest white oak tree out back. A full breakfast is offered on weekends and a continental breakfast is served during the week.

PENDLETON

Right next door to Clemson and basically contiguous with it, the significantly older Pendleton is one of the most impossibly

Carolina Kitsch

the Jockey Lot and Farmers Market

Need a T-shirt that says "Jesus was nailed for my sins"? How about a NASCAR handbag? Some used gospel CDs? Karate movies on VHS? Fresh grapefruit by the basket? Over-the-counter medicines for a buck? You'll find it all and then some in the dollar-store-run-wild atmosphere of the sprawling **Jockey Lot and Farmers Market** (4530 U.S. 29, Belton, 864/224-2027, www.jockeylot. com, Sat. 7am-5pm, Sun. 8am-5pm, free), which claims to be South Carolina's single most-visited attraction and the South's biggest flea market. *Attraction* really isn't the word, however, because this is hardly intended for tourists; it's mostly for the benefit of budget shoppers from around the Upstate, who jam the sheds and roam the display tables of this huge complex, just over twenty miles southwest of Greenville and Anderson on U.S. 29. Table after table of merchandise, ranging from personal junk to odd lots of cheap Chinese-made stuff, spread before you like a vast discount smorgasbord. Honestly, the sheer bulk of the offerings can be overwhelming.

Walk slowly through the place, soaking in the rustic vibe. Smile and talk with people as you pass. If you're really meant to buy something here, it will jump out at you. Most of this stuff… you can live without.

cute small towns you'll ever see. Founded in 1790, Pendleton's origin came over a century after Charleston's founding, but you'll find this Upstate town oddly familiar if you've been to that great Lowcountry city: Most of the finer buildings in Pendleton were built by Lowcountry planters who kept summer homes here.

Sights
★ VILLAGE GREEN
Pendleton's main claim to fame is its central **Village Green** (125 E. Queen St.,

864/646-3782, www.pendleton-district.org). Now surrounded by cute shops and cafés, it's the center of the area of Pendleton that's in the National Register of Historic Places—over 50 buildings in town date from before 1850. The focal point is the circa-1828 **Farmers Society Hall** (255 Old Depot Rd., 864/646-8161) in the center of the green.

ASHTABULA
Stately **Ashtabula** (444 Hwy. 88, 864/646-7249, www.pendletonhistoricfoundation.org, Thurs.-Sun. 1pm-4pm, $6 adults, $2 children),

pronounced "ash-ta-BYEW-la," was built in the 1820s by Charleston's well-connected Lewis Ladson Gibbes. He was a descendant of the first English settler in South Carolina, Dr. Henry Woodward, and married Maria Henrietta Drayton, daughter of Dr. Charles Drayton of Drayton Hall fame and Esther Middleton, of the magnificent Middleton Place and sister of Arthur Middleton, who signed the Declaration of Independence.

WOODBURN PLANTATION

Another magnificent home with historical roots is **Woodburn Plantation** (328 U.S. 76, 864/646-7249, www.pendletonhistoric-foundation.org, Fri. 2:30pm-5pm, $6 adults, $2 children). Like Ashtabula, it is a very short drive from Pendleton, although on the other side of town. And like Ashtabula, this four-story house with high ceilings, spacious verandas, and great cross-ventilation was owned as a summer home by a Lowcountry planter and statesman, in this case Charles Cotesworth Pinckney.

HISTORIC TOURS

Try **Historic Pendleton District Tours** (125 E. Queen St., 864/646-3782), inside the historic Hunter's Store building, which also houses the **Pendleton District Historical, Recreational, and Tourism Commission** (864/646-3782, Mon.-Fri. 9am-4:30pm, Sat. 10am-3pm); they can hook you up with materials to take your own self-guided tour.

Shopping

Antiques buffs will find themselves in heaven in Pendleton, with several good stores ringing the Village Green. Keep in mind that store hours are not always religiously observed. The best is **Past Times** (165 S. Mechanic St., 864/654-5985, Tues.-Sat. 11am-5pm), which boasts the largest collection of vintage Edgefield pottery in the nation. Colonial and Shaker furniture is the specialty of **The Renaissance Man** (130 S. Mechanic St., 864/646-8862).

Old English District

In the early days of the Revolution, this area was considered safe ground for British soldiers and settlers due to the Loyalist sentiments of the local population. All that changed due to the heavy-handed occupation by the redcoats. With Loyalists in shorter supply than promised, the British soon found themselves on the run, especially after key defeats at Cowpens and Kings Mountain.

KINGS MOUNTAIN NATIONAL MILITARY PARK

Nestled against the North Carolina border (the actual town of Kings Mountain is in the Tar Heel State) is **Kings Mountain National Military Park** (2625 Park Rd., 803/222-3209, www.nps.gov/kimo, Labor Day-Memorial Day daily 9am-5pm, Memorial Day-Labor

Day daily 9am-6pm, free). The site marks the battle of October 7, 1780, when American militia defeated a band of Loyalists under British major Patrick Ferguson. While the Patriots clearly carried the day, only later did it become clear that the Battle of Kings Mountain was the turning point in the Revolutionary War, after which the British never again gained the offensive.

Kings Mountain is the end point of the **Overmountain Victory National Historic Trail** (864/936-3477, www.nps.gov/ovvi), marking the route of the victorious militia forces through the Carolinas. It's important to note that this is a federal site, therefore no battle reenactments are allowed.

Not to be confused with the nearby Kings Mountain State Park, campers can spend the night within the National Military Park only

Historic Brattonsville

at the Garner Creek campsite, intended for a single large party. No reservations are taken, but you must get a permit (free) at the park's visitors center. Oh, and another catch: It's a three-mile hike to the campsite.

KINGS MOUNTAIN STATE PARK

Not to be confused with the adjacent National Military Park of the same name, **Kings Mountain State Park** (1277 Park Rd., Blacksburg, 803/222-3209, www.southcaro-linaparks.com, during daylight saving time daily 7am-8pm, other seasons daily 8am-6pm, $2 adults, free under age 16) offers plenty to do amid the picturesque setting of one of the classic South Carolina state parks built in the 1930s by the Civilian Conservation Corps. There are miles of good trails, two fishing lakes with boat rentals ($20 per day), and a living-history farm replicating the look, feel, and livestock of a typical piedmont farm in the early 1800s.

For the horse lover, there are 20 miles of equestrian trails that connect to the National Military Park. The state park has 15

equestrian campsites ($12)—but bring your own horse. For regular campers, the park has a whopping 115 RV and gravel tent sites with electricity and water ($16-18) and 10 primitive campsites with no water or electricity ($12-13).

★ HISTORIC BRATTONSVILLE

Near the town of McConnells, **Historic Brattonsville** (1444 Brattonsville Rd., 803/684-2327, www.chmuseums.org, Tues.-Sat. 10am-5pm, Sun. 1pm-5pm, $6 adults, $3 ages 4-17, free under age 4) includes the site of the Revolutionary War battle of Huck's Defeat, a pivotal victory of Patriot militia over the Tories. But the chief allure of this 775-acre site is the impressive grouping of more than 30 well-restored historic structures (although not all are open to the public), including the circa-1840 visitors center, a reconstruction of a backwoods log cabin, and a mid-1800s milk barn and hog pen. The crown jewel is the 1766 **William Bratton House,** probably the oldest building in this part of the state and where some scenes in Mel Gibson's *The Patriot* were filmed.

Background

The Landscape

GEOGRAPHY

The story of South Carolina's geography begins with the Appalachian mountain chain. It's in Appalachia where so much of the coast's freshwater—in the form of rain—comes together and flows southeast—in the form of rivers—to the Atlantic Ocean. A feature called the **Blue Ridge Escarpment,** or Blue Wall, demarcates the mountains, and its steep face is responsible for most of the many waterfalls in the state.

Moving east, the next level down from the Appalachians is the **piedmont** region (in South Carolina often called simply the Upstate). The piedmont is a rolling, hilly area, the eroded remains of an ancient mountain chain now long gone.

At the piedmont's eastern edge is the **fall line,** so named because it's there where rivers make a drop toward the sea, generally becoming navigable. This slight but noticeable change in elevation—which actually marked the shoreline about 60 million years ago—not only encouraged trade but has provided water power for mills for hundreds of years. Many inland cities of the region, like Columbia, trace their origin and commercial success to their strategic location on the fall line.

Around the fall line zone in the **upper coastal plain** you can sometimes spot **sand hills,** usually only a few feet in elevation, generally thought to be the vestigial remains of primordial sand dunes and offshore sandbars. Well beyond the fall line and the sometimes nearly invisible sand hills lies the **lower coastal plain,** gradually built up over a 150-million-year span by sedimentary runoff from the Appalachian Mountains, which were then as high or even higher than the modern-day Himalayas.

The coastal plain was sea bottom for much of the earth's history, and in some eroded areas you can see dramatic proof of this in prehistoric shells, shark teeth, fossilized whale bones, and oyster beds, often many miles inland. In some places, calcium from these ancient shells has provided a lush home for distinct groups of unique plants, called **disjuncts.**

At various times over the last 50 million years, the coastal plain has submerged, surfaced, and submerged again. At the height of the last major ice age, when global sea levels were very low, the east coast of North America extended out nearly 100 miles farther than the present shoreline. (We now call this former coastal region the **continental shelf.**) The coastal plain has been in roughly its current form for about the last 15,000 years.

Rivers

Visitors from drier climates are sometimes shocked to see how huge the rivers can get in the South, wide and voluminous as they saunter to the sea, their seemingly slow speed belying the massive power they contain. South Carolina's big **alluvial,** or sediment-bearing, rivers originate in the region of the Appalachian mountain chain.

The **blackwater river** is a particularly interesting Southern phenomenon, duplicated elsewhere only in South America and one example each in New York and Michigan. While alluvial rivers generally originate in highlands and carry with them a large amount of sediment, blackwater rivers—the Edisto River being the chief example—tend to originate in low-lying areas and move slowly toward the sea, carrying with them very little sediment. Their dark tea color comes from the

---

Previous: Revolutionary War reenactors at Brattonsville; Charleston's Pineapple Fountain.

tannic acid of decaying vegetation all along the banks, washed out by the slow, inexorable movement of the river toward the sea. While I don't necessarily recommend drinking it, despite its dirty color, blackwater is for the most part remarkably clean and hygienic.

Carolina Bays

An interesting regional feature of the state is the **Carolina bay,** an elliptical depression rich with biodiversity, thousands of which are found all along the coast from Delaware to Florida. While at least 500,000 have been identified, new laser-based imaging technology is enabling the discovery of thousands more, previously unnoticed.

Though not all Carolina bays are in the Carolinas, many are, and that's where they were first documented. They're called "bays" not for the water within them—indeed, many hold little or no water at all—but for the proliferation of bay trees often found inside. Carolina bays can be substantially older than the surrounding terrain, with many well over 25,000 years old. Native Americans referred to the distinctive wetland habitat within a Carolina bay as a pocosin.

Theories abound as to their origin. One claims that they're the result of wave action from when the entire area was underwater in primordial times. The most popular, if unproven, theory is that they are the result of a massive meteor shower in prehistoric times. Certainly their similar orientation, roughly northwest-southeast, makes this intuitively possible as an impact pattern. Further bolstering this theory is the fact that most Carolina bays are surrounded by sand rims, which tend to be thicker on the southeast edge.

An old theory, once discredited but now gaining new credence, is that Carolina bays are the result of a disintegrating comet that exploded on entry into the earth's atmosphere somewhere over the Great Lakes. Apparently, if you extend the axes of all the Carolina bays, that's where they converge. This theory takes on an ominous edge when one realizes that the same comet is also blamed for a mass extinction of prehistoric animals such as the mammoth.

The Intracoastal Waterway

You'll often see its acronym, ICW, on signs—and you'll probably hear many mispronounce it "intercoastal"—but the casual visitor might actually find the Intracoastal Waterway difficult to spot. Relying on a natural network of interconnected estuaries and channels, combined with artificial cuts, the ICW often blends in rather subtly with the already extensive network of creeks and rivers in the area.

Mandated by Congress in 1919 and maintained by the U.S. Army Corps of Engineers, the Atlantic portion of the ICW runs from Key West to Boston and carries recreational and barge traffic away from the perils of offshore currents and weather. Even if they don't use it specifically, kayakers and boaters often find themselves on it at some point during their nautical adventures.

Estuaries

Most biologists will tell you that the coastal plain is where things get interesting. The place where a river interfaces with the ocean is called an estuary, and it's perhaps the most interesting place of all. Estuaries are heavily tidal in nature (indeed, the word derives from *aestus,* Latin for tide), and feature brackish water and heavy silt content.

South Carolina typically has about a 6-8-foot tidal range, and the coastal ecosystem depends on this steady ebb and flow for life itself. At high tide, shellfish open and feed. At low tide, they literally clam up, keeping saltwater inside their shells until the next tide comes.

Waterbirds and small mammals feed on shellfish and other animals at low tide, when their prey is exposed. High tide brings an influx of fish and nutrients from the sea, in turn drawing predators like dolphins, who often come into tidal creeks to feed.

It's the estuaries that form the most compelling and beautiful sanctuaries for the area's incredibly rich diversity of animal species. Many estuaries are contiguous with those of other rivers; Charleston Harbor, formed by the confluence of the Ashley and Cooper Rivers, is an excellent example of that phenomenon.

Salt Marsh

All this water action in both directions—freshwater coming from inland, saltwater encroaching from the Atlantic—results in the phenomenon of the salt marsh, the single most recognizable and iconic geographic feature of the South Carolina coast, also known simply as "wetlands." (Freshwater marshes are rarer, Florida's Everglades being perhaps the premier example.)

Far more than just a transitional zone between land and water, marshes are also nature's nursery. Plant and animal life in marshes tends not only to be diverse but to encompass multitudes. You may not see its denizens easily, but on close inspection you'll find the marsh absolutely teeming with creatures. Visually, the main identifying feature of a salt marsh is its distinctive reedlike marsh grasses, adapted to survive in brackish water. Like estuaries, marshes and all life in them are heavily influenced by the tides, which bring in nutrients.

The marsh has also played a key role in human history as well, for it was here where the massive rice and indigo plantations grew their signature crops, aided by the natural ebb and flow of the tides. While most wetlands you see look quite undisturbed, very little of it could be called pristine.

In the heyday of the rice plantations, much of the entire coastal salt marsh was crisscrossed by the canal-and-dike system of the paddy fields. You can still see evidence almost everywhere in the area if you look hard enough (the best time to look is right after takeoff or before landing in an airplane, since many approaches to regional airports take you over wetlands). Any time you see a low, straight ridge running through a marsh, that's likely the eroded overgrown remnant of an old rice field dike. Kayakers occasionally

find old wooden water gates, or "trunks," on their paddles.

In the Lowcountry, you'll often hear the term **pluff mud.** This refers to the area's distinctive variety of soft, dark mud in the salt marsh, which often has an equally distinctive odor that locals love but some visitors have a hard time getting used to. Extraordinarily rich in nutrients, pluff mud helped make rice a successful crop in the marshes of the Lowcountry.

In addition to their huge role as wildlife incubators and sanctuaries, wetlands are also one of the most important natural protectors of the health of the coastal region. They serve as natural filters, cleansing runoff from the land of toxins and pollutants before it hits the ocean. They also help humans by serving as natural hurricane barriers, their porous nature helping to ease the brunt of the damaging storm surge.

Beaches and Barrier Islands

The beaches of South Carolina are almost all situated on barrier islands, long islands parallel to the shoreline and separated from the mainland by a sheltered body of water. Because they're formed by the deposit of sediment by offshore currents, they change shape over the years, with the general pattern of deposit going from north to south (meaning the northern end will begin eroding first). Most of the barrier islands are geologically quite young, only having formed within the last 25,000 years or so. Natural erosion by currents and by storms, combined with the accelerating effects of dredging for local port activity, has quickened the decline of many barrier islands. Many beaches in the area are subject to a mitigation of erosion called **beach renourishment,** which generally involves redistributing dredged material closely offshore so that it will wash up on and around the beach.

As the name indicates, barrier islands are another of nature's safeguards against hurricane damage. Historically, the barrier islands have borne the vast bulk of the damage done by hurricanes in the region. Sullivan's Island near Charleston was submerged by 1989's Hurricane Hugo. Like the marshes, barrier islands also help protect the mainland by absorbing the brunt of the storm's wind and surging water.

Wiregrass and Longleaf Ecosystems

In prehistoric times, most of South Carolina's upper coastal plain was covered by what's known as a wiregrass or longleaf pine ecosystem. Wiregrass (*Aristida stricta*) is a foot-tall species of hardy grass that often coexists with forests of longleaf pine (*Pinus palustris*), a relative of the slash pine now used as a cash crop throughout the South. The longleaf pine is fire-dependent, meaning it only reproduces after wildfire—usually started by lightning—releases its seed cones.

Wiregrass savanna and old-growth forests of longleaf pine once covered about 100 million acres, most of the Southeast. Within about 200 years, however, settlers had deforested the region. Currently only a few good examples remain in South Carolina, especially the Carolina Sandhills National Wildlife Refuge, Lynchburg Savanna Heritage Preserve, and Longleaf Pine Heritage Preserve.

Contrary to Hollywood portrayals, no one ever needed a machete to tear their way through an old-growth forest. Because the high, thick tree canopy allows little but wiregrass to grow on the forest floor, Native Americans and early settlers could walk through these primordial forests with ease.

CLIMATE

One word comes to mind when one thinks about Southern climate: *hot.* That's the first word that occurs to Southerners as well, but virtually every survey of why residents are attracted to the area puts the climate at the top of the list. Go figure. How hot is hot? The average high for July, the region's hottest month, in Charleston is about 89°F. While that's nothing compared to Tucson or Death Valley, coupled with the region's notoriously

high humidity it can have an altogether miserable effect.

Technically South Carolina has a **humid subtropical** climate. During summer, the famous high-pressure system called the **Bermuda High** settles over the entire southeastern United States, its rotating winds pushing aside most weather coming from the west. This can bring drought as well as a certain sameness that afflicts the area. Heat aside, there's no doubt that one of the most difficult things for a nonnative to adjust to in the South is the humidity. The average annual humidity in Charleston is about 55 percent in the afternoons and a whopping 85 percent in the mornings. The most humid months are August and September. There is no real antidote to humidity—other than air conditioning, that is—though many film crews and other outside workers swear by the use of Sea Breeze astringent. If you and your traveling partner can deal with the strong minty odor, dampen a hand towel with the astringent, drape it across the back of your neck, and go about your business. Don't assume that because it's humid you shouldn't drink fluids. Just as in any hot climate, you should drink lots of water if you're going to be out in the Southern heat.

If you're on the South Carolina coast, you'll no doubt grow to love the steady ocean breeze during the day. But at night you may notice the wind changing direction and coming from inland. That's caused by the land cooling at night and the wind rushing toward the warmer water offshore. This shift in wind current is mostly responsible for that sometimes awe-inspiring, sometimes just plain scary phenomenon of a typical Southern **thunderstorm.** Seemingly within the space of a few minutes on a particularly hot and still summer day, the afternoon is taken over by a rapidly moving stacked storm cloud called a **thunderhead,** which soon bursts open and pours an unbelievable amount of rain on whatever is unlucky enough to be beneath it, along with frequent huge lightning strikes. Then, almost as quickly as it came on, the storm subsides, and the sun comes back out again as if nothing had happened. August-September is by far the rainiest time, with averages well over six inches for each of these months. July is also quite wet, with over five inches on average.

Winters are pretty mild but can seem much colder than they actually are because of the dampness in the air. The coldest month is January, with a high of about 58°F for the month and an average low of 42°F. You're highly unlikely to encounter snow in the area, and if you do, it will likely only be skimpy flurries that a resident of the Great Lakes region wouldn't even notice as snow. But don't let this lull you into a false sense of security. If such a tiny flurry were to hit, be aware that most people down here have no clue how to drive in rough weather and will not be prepared for even such a small amount of snowfall. Visitors from snow country are often surprised by how completely a Southern city will shut down when that rare few inches of snow hits.

Hurricanes

The major weather phenomenon for residents and visitors alike is the mighty hurricane. These massive storms, with counterclockwise-rotating bands of clouds and winds pushing 200 mph, are an ever-present danger to the southeast coast June-November, with the most serious danger period around Labor Day.

Tornadoes—especially those that come in the "back door" through the Gulf of Mexico and overland—are a very present danger with hurricanes. As hurricanes die out over the land, they can spawn literally dozens of tornadoes, which in many cases prove more destructive than the hurricanes that spawned them.

Local TV, websites, and print media can be counted on to give more than ample warning in the event a hurricane is approaching the area during your visit. Whatever you do, do not discount the warnings; it's not worth it. If the locals are preparing to leave, you should too.

Typically, when a storm is likely to hit the area, there will first be a suggested evacuation. But if authorities determine there's an overwhelming likelihood of imminent hurricane damage, they will issue a **mandatory evacuation order.** What this means in practice is that if you do choose to stay behind, you cannot count on any type of emergency services or help.

Generally speaking, the most lethal element of a hurricane is not the wind but the **storm surge,** the wall of ocean water that the winds drive in front of them onto the coast. During 1989's Hurricane Hugo, Charleston's Battery was inundated with a storm surge of over 12 feet, with an amazing 20 feet reported farther north at Cape Romain.

ENVIRONMENTAL ISSUES

The coast of South Carolina in particular is currently experiencing a double whammy, environmentally speaking: Not only are its distinctive wetlands extraordinarily sensitive to human interference, but this is also one of the most rapidly developing parts of the country. New and often poorly planned subdivisions and resort communities are popping up all over the place. Vastly increased port activity is also taking a devastating toll on the salt marsh and surrounding barrier islands. Combine all that with the South's often skeptical attitude toward environmental activism and you have a recipe for potential ecological disaster.

Thankfully, there are some bright spots. More and more communities are seeing the value of responsible planning and not greenlighting every new development sight unseen. Land trusts and other conservation organizations are growing in size, number, funding, and influence. The large number of marine biologists in these areas at various research and educational institutions means there's a wealth of education and talent available to advise local governments and citizens on how best to conserve the area's natural beauty.

Hilton Head Island is a longtime trendsetter for sustainable development, dating back to the insistence of its original residential developer, Charles Fraser, that the Sea Pines development interfere as little as possible with the island's ecosystem. But in South Carolina, the city of Charleston and Charleston County are leading the pack on environmental issues right now—perhaps because its wealth and comparatively large size mean it has so much more to lose if things go badly. Planners estimate that the Charleston area will have to accommodate about 250,000 new residents over the next 25 years, and there's a clear consensus locally that the time to act is now. One concrete step Charleston County has taken is devoting part of a new transportation sales tax to its new comprehensive greenbelt plan to help responsibly guide the next 25 years of development here. It calls for at least $12 million to go to preserving rural green space and nearly $2 million to conserve remaining urban green space.

Marsh Dieback

The dominant species of marsh grass, *Spartina alterniflora* (pronounced "spar-TINE-uh") and *Juncus roemerianus,* thrive in the typically brackish water of the coastal marsh estuaries, their structural presence helping to stem erosion of banks and dunes. While drought and blight have taken their toll on the grass, increased coastal development and continued channel deepening have also led to a steady creep of ocean saltwater farther and farther into remaining marsh stands.

The Paper Industry

Early in the 20th century, the Southeast's abundance of cheap undeveloped land and plentiful free water led to the establishment of massive pine tree farms to feed coastal pulp and paper mills. Chances are that if you used a paper grocery bag recently, it was made in a paper mill in the South. But in addition to making a whole lot of paper bags and providing lots of employment for residents through the decades, the paper industry also gave the area lots of air and water pollution, stressed local water supplies (it takes a lot of water to make paper from trees), and took away natural species diversity from the area by devoting so much acreage to a single crop, pine trees.

Currently the domestic paper industry is reeling from competition from cheaper Asian lumber stocks and paper mills. As a result, an interesting—and not altogether welcome—phenomenon has been the wholesale entry of Southeast paper companies into the real estate business. Discovering they can make a whole lot more money selling or developing tree farms for residential lots than making paper bags, pulp and paper companies are helping to drive overdevelopment in the region by encouraging development on their land rather than infill development closer to urban areas. So, in the long run, the demise of the paper industry in the South may not prove to be the net advantage to the environment that was anticipated.

Aquifers

Unlike parts of the western United States, where individuals can enforce private property rights to water, the South has generally held that the region's water is a publicly held resource. The upside of this is that everybody has equal claim to drinking water without regard to status or income or how long they've lived here. The downside is that industry also has the same free claim to the water that citizens do—and they use a heck of a lot more of it.

Currently most of South Carolina gets its water from aquifers, which are basically huge underground caverns made of limestone. Receiving **groundwater** drip by drip, century after century, from rainfall farther inland, the aquifers essentially act as massive sterile warehouses for freshwater, accessible through wells. The aquifers have human benefit only if their water remains fresh. Once saltwater from the ocean begins intruding into an aquifer, it doesn't take much to render all of it unfit for human consumption—forever. What keeps that freshwater fresh is natural water pressure, keeping the ocean at bay. But nearly a century ago, paper mills began pumping millions and millions of gallons of water out of coastal aquifers. Combined with the dramatic rise in coastal residential development and a continuing push to deepen existing shipping channels, the natural water pressure of the aquifers has decreased, leading to measurable saltwater intrusion at several points under the coast.

Currently, state and local governments are increasing their reliance on **surface water** (treated water from rivers and creeks) to relieve the strain on the underground aquifer system. But it's too soon to tell if that has contained the threat from saltwater intrusion.

Nuclear Energy

South Carolina has four nuclear power plants, in the Greenville, Hartsville, and Jenkinsville areas, and in York County. They are major job providers and are likely to remain a major driver of the state's economy well into the future.

Looming upstream of the entire area is the massive Cold War-era nuclear bomb plant called Savannah River Site, near Aiken. Groundwater in the area has already shown measurable amounts of radioactivity from the site, and activists have long warned of potential catastrophe from its aging infrastructure. Most activity there is now limited to environmental cleanup.

Air Pollution

Despite growing awareness of the issue, air pollution is still a big problem in the coastal region. Paper mills still operate, putting out their distinctive rotten-eggs odor, and auto emissions standards are notoriously lax in South Carolina. The biggest culprit, though, are coal-powered electric plants, which are the norm throughout the region and which continue to pour large amounts of toxins into the atmosphere.

Plants and Animals

PLANTS

The most iconic plant life of the coastal region is the **Southern live oak** (*Quercus virginiana*). Named because of its evergreen nature, a live oak is technically any one of a number of evergreens in the *Quercus* genus, many of which grow in South Carolina, but in local practice the name almost always refers to the Southern live oak. Capable of living over 1,000 years and possessing wood of legendary resilience, the Southern live oak is one of nature's most magnificent creations. The timber value of live oaks has been well known since the earliest days of the American shipbuilding industry—when the oak dominated the entire coast inland of the marsh—but their value as a canopy tree has finally been widely recognized by local and state governments.

Fittingly, the other iconic plant life of the coastal region grows on the branches of the live oak. Contrary to popular opinion, **Spanish moss** (*Tillandsia usneoides*) is neither Spanish nor moss. It's an air plant, a wholly indigenous cousin to the pineapple. Also contrary to folklore, Spanish moss is not a parasite nor does it harbor parasites while living on an oak tree—although it can after it has already fallen to the ground. Also growing on the bark of a live oak, especially right after a rain shower, is the **resurrection fern** (*Polypodium polypodioides*), which can stay dormant for amazingly long periods of time, only to spring back to life with the introduction of a little water. You can find live oak, Spanish moss, and resurrection fern anywhere in the **maritime forest** ecosystem of coastal South Carolina, a zone generally behind the **interdune meadows,** which is itself right behind the beach zone.

Far and away South Carolina's most important commercial tree is the pine, used for paper, lumber, and turpentine. Rarely seen in the wild today due to tree farming, the dominant species is now the **slash pine** (*Pinus*

BACKGROUND
PLANTS AND ANIMALS

elliottii), often seen in long rows on either side of rural highways. Before the introduction of large-scale monoculture tree farming, however, a rich variety of native pines flourished in the **upland forest** inland from the maritime forest, including **longleaf** (*Pinus palustris*) and **loblolly** (*Pinus taeda*) pines. Longleaf forest covered nearly 100 million acres of the southeastern coastal plain when the Europeans arrived; within 300 years most of it would be cut down or harvested.

Right up there with live oaks and Spanish moss in terms of instant recognition would have to be the colorful, ubiquitous **azalea**, a flowering shrub of the *Rhododendron* genus. Over 10,000 varieties have been cultivated through the centuries, with quite a wide range of them on display during blooming season, March-April, on the South Carolina coast (slightly earlier farther south, slightly later farther north). The area's other great floral display comes from the **camellia** (*Camellia japonica*), a large, cold-hardy evergreen shrub that generally blooms in late winter (Jan.-Mar.). An import from Asia, the southeastern coast's camellias are close cousins to *Camellia sinensis,* also an import and the plant from which tea is made. Other colorful ornamentals of the area include the ancient and beautiful **Southern magnolia** (*Magnolia grandiflora*), a native plant with distinctive large white flowers that evolved before the advent of bees; and the **flowering dogwood** (*Cornus florida*), which, despite its very hard wood—great for daggers, hence its original name "dagwood"—is actually quite fragile. An ornamental imported from Asia that has now become quite obnoxious in its aggressive invasiveness is the **mimosa** (*Albizia julibrissin*), which blooms March-August.

Moving into watery areas, you'll find the remarkable **bald cypress** (*Taxodium distichum*), a flood-resistant conifer recognizable by its tufted top, its great height (up to 130 feet), and its distinctive "knees," parts of the root that project above the waterline and which are believed to help stabilize the tree in lowland areas. Much prized for its beautiful pest-resistant wood, great stands of ancient cypress once dominated the marsh along the coast; sadly, overharvesting and destruction of wetlands has made the magnificent sight of this ancient, dignified species much less common. The acres of **smooth cordgrass** for which the Golden Isles are named are plants of the *Spartina alterniflora* species. (A cultivated cousin, *Spartina anglica,* is considered invasive.) Besides its simple natural beauty, *Spartina* is also a key food source for marsh denizens. Playing a key environmental role on the coast are **sea oats** (*Uniola paniculata*). This wispy, fast-growing perennial grass anchors sand dunes and hence is a protected species (it's a misdemeanor to pick them).

South Carolina isn't called the "Palmetto State" for nothing. Palm varieties are not as common up here as in Florida, but you'll definitely encounter several types along the coast. The **cabbage palm** (*Sabal palmetto*), for which South Carolina is named, is the largest variety, up to 50-60 feet tall. Its "heart of palm" is an edible delicacy, which coastal Native Americans boiled in bear fat as porridge. In dunes and sand hills you'll find clumps of the low-lying **saw palmetto** (*Serenoa repens*). The **bush palmetto** (*Sabal minor*) has distinctive fan-shaped branches. The common **Spanish bayonet** (*Yucca aloifolia*) looks like a palm, but it's actually a member of the agave family.

ANIMALS
On Land

Perhaps the most iconic land animal—or semi-land animal, anyway—of South Carolina is the legendary **American alligator** (*Alligator mississippiensis*), the only species of crocodilian native to the area. Contrary to their fierce reputation, locals know these massive reptiles, 6-12 feet long as adults, to be quite shy. If you come in the colder months, you won't see them at all, since alligators require an outdoor temperature over 70°F to become active and feed (indeed, the appearance of alligators was once a well-known symbol of spring in the area). Often all you'll see is a couple of eyebrow ridges sticking out of the water, and a gator lying still in a shallow creek can easily be mistaken for a floating log. But should you see one or more gators basking in the sun—a favorite activity on warm days for these cold-blooded creatures—it's best to admire them from afar. A mother alligator, in particular, will destroy anything that comes near her nest. Despite the alligator's short, stubby legs, they run amazingly fast on land—faster than you, in fact.

If you're driving on a country road at night, be on the lookout for **white-tailed deer** (*Odocoileus virginianus*), which, besides being quite beautiful, also pose a serious road hazard. Because coastal development has dramatically reduced the habitat—and therefore the numbers—of their natural predators, deer are very plentiful throughout the area, and as you read this they are hard at work devouring vast tracts of valuable vegetation. No one wants to hurt poor little Bambi, but the truth is that area hunters perform a valuable service by culling the local deer population, which is in no danger of extinction anytime soon.

South Carolina hosts large populations of playful **river otter** (*Lontra canadensis*). Not to be confused with the larger sea otters off the West Coast, these fast-swimming members of the weasel family inhabit inland waterways and marshy areas, with dominant males sometimes ranging as much as 50 miles within a single waterway. As strict carnivores, usually of fish, otters are a key indicator of the health of their ecosystem. If they're thriving, water and habitat quality are likely to be pretty high. If they're not, something's going badly wrong.

While you're unlikely to encounter an otter, if you're camping, you might easily run into the **raccoon** (*Procyon lotor*), an exceedingly intelligent and crafty relative of the bear, sharing that larger animal's resourcefulness in stealing your food. Though nocturnal, raccoons will feed whenever food is available. Raccoons can grow so accustomed to human presence as to almost consider themselves part of the family, but resist the temptation to get close to them. Rabies is prevalent in the raccoon population, and you should always, always keep your distance.

Another common campsite nuisance, the **opossum** (*Didelphis virginiana*) is a shy, primitive creature that is much more easily discouraged. North America's only marsupial, an opossum's usual "defense" against predators is to play dead. That said, however, they have an immunity to snake venom and often feed on the reptiles, even the most poisonous ones.

Opossums are native to the area, but another similarly slow-witted, slow-moving creature is not: the **nine-banded armadillo** (*Dasypus novemcinctus*). In centuries past, these armor-plated insect-eaters were mostly confined to Mexico, but they are gradually working their way northward. Obsessive diggers, armadillos cause quite a bit of damage to crops and gardens. Sometimes jokingly called "possum on the half shell," armadillos, like opossums, are frequent roadkill on South Carolina highways.

While you're highly unlikely to actually see a **red fox** (*Vulpes vulpes*), you might very well see their distinctive footprints in the mud of a marsh at low tide. These nocturnal hunters, a nonnative species introduced by European settlers, range the coast seeking mice, squirrels, and rabbits.

Once fairly common in South Carolina, the **black bear** (*Ursus americanus*) has suffered from hunting and habitat destruction and is extremely rare in the state.

In the Water

Humankind's aquatic cousin, the **Atlantic bottle-nosed dolphin** (*Tursiops truncatus*) is a well-known and frequent visitor to the coast, coming far upstream into creeks and rivers to feed. Children, adults, and experienced sailors alike all delight in encounters with the mammals, sociable creatures who travel in family units. When not occupied with feeding or mating activities—both of which can get surprisingly rowdy—dolphins show great curiosity about human visitors to their habitat. They will gather near boats, surfacing often with the distinctive chuffing sound of air coming from their blowholes. Occasionally they'll even lift their heads out of the water to have a look at you; consider yourself lucky indeed to have such a close encounter. Don't be fooled by their cuteness, however. Dolphins live life with gusto and aren't scared of much. They're voracious eaters of fish, amorous and energetic lovers, and will take on an encroaching shark in a heartbeat.

Another beloved part-time marine creature of the barrier islands of the coast is the **loggerhead turtle** (*Caretta caretta*). Though the species prefers to stay well offshore the rest of the year, females weighing up to 300 pounds come out of the sea each May-July to dig a shallow hole in the dunes and lay over 100 leathery eggs, returning to the ocean and leaving the eggs to hatch on their own after two months. Interestingly, the mothers prefer to nest at the same spot on the same island year after year. After hatching, the baby turtles then make a dramatic, extremely dangerous (and extremely slow) trek to the safety of the waves, at the mercy of various predators. A series of dedicated research and conservation efforts are working hard to protect the loggerheads' traditional nursery grounds to ensure the survival of this fascinating, lovable, and threatened species. Cape Island within the Cape Romain National Wildlife Refuge accounts for about a quarter of all loggerhead nests in South Carolina and is the leading nesting site north of Florida. Other key sites include Kiawah, Edisto, and Hilton Head Islands.

Of course, the coastal waters and rivers are chockablock with fish. The most abundant and sought-after recreational species in the area is the **spotted sea trout** (*Cynoscion nebulosus*), followed by the **red drum** (*Sciaenops ocellatus*). Local anglers also pursue many varieties of **bass, bream, sheepshead,** and **crappie.** It may sound strange to some accustomed to considering it a "trash" fish, but many types of **catfish** are not only plentiful here but are a common and well-regarded food source. Many species of **flounder** inhabit the silty bottoms of estuaries all along the coast. Farther offshore are game and sport fish like **marlin, swordfish, shark, grouper,** and **tuna.**

Each March, anglers jockey for position on coastal rivers for the yearly running of the **American shad** (*Alosa sapidissima*) upstream to spawn. This large (up to eight pounds) catfish-like species is a regional delicacy as a seasonal entrée as well as for its tasty roe. There's a catch limit of eight shad per person per season. One of the more interesting fish species in the area is the endangered **shortnose sturgeon** (*Acipenser brevirostrum*). A fantastically ancient species that has evolved little in hundreds of millions of years, this small freshwater fish is known to exist in the estuaries of the ACE Basin. Traveling upriver to spawn in the winter, the sturgeons remain around the mouths of waterways the rest of the year, venturing near the ocean only sparingly.

Crustaceans and shellfish have been a key food staple in the area for thousands of years, with the massive shell middens of the coast being testament to Native Americans' healthy appetite for them. The beds of the local variant, the **eastern oyster** (*Crassostrea virginica*), aren't what they used to be due to overharvesting, water pollution, and disruption of habitat. In truth, these days most local restaurants import the little filter-feeders from the Gulf of Mexico. Oysters spawn May-August, hence the old folk wisdom about eating oysters only in months with the letter "r" so as not to disrupt the breeding cycle.

Each year April-January, shrimp boats up and down the southeastern coast trawl for **shrimp,** most commercially viable in two local species, the white shrimp (*Litopenaeus setiferus*) and the brown shrimp (*Farfantepenaeus aztecus*). Shrimp are the most popular seafood item in the United States and account for bringing hundreds of millions of dollars in revenue into the coastal economy. While consumption won't slow down anytime soon, the South Carolina shrimping industry is facing serious threats, both from species decline due to pollution and overfishing and from competition from shrimp farms and the Asian shrimp industry.

Another important commercial crop is the **blue crab** (*Callinectes sapidus*), the species used in such Lowcountry delicacies as crab cakes. You'll often see floating markers bobbing up and down in rivers throughout the region. These signal the presence directly below of a crab trap, often of an amateur crabber. A true living link to primordial times, the alien-looking **horseshoe crab** (*Limulus polyphemus*) is frequently found on beaches of the coast during the spring mating season (it lives in deeper water the rest of the year). More closely related to scorpions and spiders than crabs, the horseshoe has evolved hardly a lick in hundreds of millions of years. Any trip to a local salt marsh at low tide will likely uncover hundreds of **fiddler crabs** (*Uca pugilator* and *Uca pugnax*), so-named for the way the males wave their single enlarged claws in the air to attract mates. (Their other, smaller claw is the one they actually eat with.) The fiddlers make distinctive burrows in the pluff mud for sanctuary during high tide, recognizable by the little balls of sediment at the entrances (the crabs spit out the balls after sifting through the sand for food).

One charming beach inhabitant, the **sand dollar** (*Mellita quinquiesperforata*), has seen its numbers decline drastically due to being entirely too charming for its own good. Beachcombers are now asked to enjoy these flat little cousins to the sea urchin in their natural habitat and to refrain from taking them home. Besides, they start to smell bad when they dry out. The **sea nettle** (*Chrysaora quinquecirrha*), a less-than-charming beach inhabitant, is a jellyfish that stings thousands of people on the coast each year (although only for those with severe allergies are the stings potentially life-threatening). Stinging their prey before transporting it into their waiting mouths, the jellyfish also sting when disturbed or frightened. Most often, people are stung by stepping on the bodies of jellyfish washed up on the sand. If you're stung by a jellyfish, don't panic. You'll probably experience a stinging rash for about half an hour. Locals say applying a little baking soda or vinegar helps cut the sting. (Some also swear fresh urine will do the trick, and I pass that tip along to you purely in the interest of thoroughness.)

In the Air

When enjoying the marshlands of the coast, consider yourself fortunate to see an endangered **wood stork** (*Mycteria americana*), although their numbers are on the increase. The only storks to breed in North America, these graceful long-lived birds (routinely living over 10 years) are usually seen on a low flight path across the marsh, although at some birding spots beginning in late summer you can find them at a **roost,** sometimes numbering over 100 birds. Resting at high tide, they fan out over the marsh to feed at low tide on foot. Old-timers sometimes call them "Spanish buzzards" or simply "the preacher." Often confused with the wood stork is the gorgeous **white ibis** (*Eudocimus albus*), distinguishable by its orange bill and black wingtips. Like the wood stork, the ibis is a communal bird that roosts in colonies. Other similar-looking coastal denizens are the white-feathered **great egret** (*Ardea alba*) and **snowy egret** (*Egretta thula*), the former distinguishable by its yellow bill and the latter by its black bill and the tuft of plumes on the back of its head. Egrets are in the same family as herons. The most magnificent is the **great blue heron** (*Ardea herodias*). Despite their imposing height—up to four feet tall—these waders are shy. Often you hear them rather than see them, a loud shriek of alarm that echoes over the marsh. So how to tell the difference between all these wading birds at a glance? It's actually easiest when they're in flight. Egrets and herons fly with their necks tucked in, while storks and ibis fly with their necks extended.

Dozens of species of shorebirds comb the beaches, including **sandpipers, plovers,** and the wonderful and rare **American oystercatcher** (*Haematopus palliatus*), instantly recognizable for its prancing walk, dark brown back, stark white underside, and long bright-orange bill. **Gulls** and **terns** also hang out wherever there's water. They can frequently be seen swarming around incoming shrimp boats, attracted by the catch of little crustaceans.

The chief raptor of the salt marsh is the fish-eating **osprey** (*Pandion haliaetus*). These large grayish birds of prey are similar to eagles but are adapted to a maritime environment, with a reversible outer toe on each talon (the better for catching wriggly fish) and closable nostrils so they can dive into the water after prey. Very common all along the coast, they like to build big nests on top of buoys and channel markers in addition to trees. The **bald eagle** (*Haliaeetus leucocephalus*) is making a comeback in the area thanks to increased federal regulation and better education of trigger-happy locals. Of course, as we all should have learned in school, the bald eagle is not actually bald but has a head adorned with white feathers. Like the osprey, they prefer fish, but unlike the osprey will settle for rodents and rabbits.

Inland among the pines you'll find the most common area woodpecker, the huge **pileated woodpecker** (*Dryocopus pileatus*) with its huge crest. Less common is the smaller, more subtly marked **red-cockaded woodpecker** (*Picoides borealis*). Once common in the vast primordial pine forests of the Southeast, the species is now endangered, its last real refuge being the big tracts of relatively undisturbed land on military bases and national wildlife refuges.

Insects

Down here they say that God invented bugs to keep the Yankees from completely taking over the South. And insects are probably the most unpleasant fact of life in the southeastern coastal region. The list of annoying indigenous insects must begin with the infamous **sand gnat** (*Culicoides furens*), scourge of the lowlands. This tiny and persistent nuisance, a member of the midge family, lacks the precision of the mosquito with its long proboscis. No, the sand gnat is more torture master than surgeon, brutally gouging and digging away its victim's skin until it hits a source of blood. Most prevalent in the spring and fall, the sand gnat is drawn to its prey by the carbon dioxide trail of its breath. While long sleeves and long pants are one way to keep gnats at bay, that causes its own discomfort because of the region's heat and humidity. The only real antidote to the sand gnat's assault—other than never breathing—is the Avon skin-care product Skin So Soft, which has taken on a new and wholly unplanned life as the South's favorite anti-gnat lotion. Grow to like the scent, because the more of this stuff you lather on, the better. In calmer moments grow to appreciate the great contribution sand gnats make to the salt marsh ecosystem—as food for many species of birds and bats.

Running a close second to the sand gnat are the over three dozen species of highly aggressive **mosquito,** which breeds anywhere a few drops of water lie stagnant. Not surprisingly, massive populations blossom in the rainiest months, in late spring and late summer. Like the gnat, the mosquito—the biters are always female—homes in on its victim by trailing the plume of carbon dioxide exhaled in the breath. More than just a biting nuisance, mosquitoes are now carrying West Nile disease, signaling a possibly dire threat to public health. Local governments in the region pour millions of dollars of taxpayer money into massive pesticide spraying programs from helicopters, planes, and trucks. While that certainly helps stem the tide, it by no means eliminates the mosquito population. This is just as well, because like the sand gnat, the mosquito is an important food source for many species, including bats and dragonflies. Alas, Skin So Soft has little effect on the mosquito. Try over-the-counter sprays, anything smelling of citronella, and wearing long sleeves and long pants when weather permits.

But undoubtedly the most viscerally

loathed of all pests on the Lowcountry and Georgia coasts is the so-called "palmetto bug," or **American cockroach** (*Periplaneta americana*). These black, shiny, and sometimes grotesquely massive insects—up to two inches long—are living fossils, virtually unchanged over hundreds of millions of years. And perfectly adapted as they are to life in and among wet, decaying vegetation, they're unlikely to change a bit in 100 million more years. While they spend most of their time crawling around, usually under rotting leaves and tree bark, the American cockroach can indeed fly—sort of. There are few more hilarious sights than a room full of people frantically trying to dodge a palmetto bug that has just clumsily launched itself off a high point on the wall. Because the cockroach doesn't know any better than you do where it's going, it can be a particularly bracing event—though the insect does not bite and poses few real health hazards. Popular regional use of the term *palmetto bug* undoubtedly has its roots in a desire for polite Southern society to avoid using the ugly word *roach* and its connotations of filth and unclean environments. But the colloquialism actually has a basis in reality. Contrary to what anyone tells you, the natural habitat of the American cockroach—unlike its kitchen-dwelling, much-smaller cousin the German cockroach—is outdoors, often up in trees. They only come inside human dwellings when it's especially hot, especially cold, or especially dry outside. Like you, the palmetto bug is easily driven indoors by extreme temperatures and by thirst. Other than visiting the Southeast during the winter, when the roaches go dormant, there's no convenient antidote for their presence. The best way to keep them out of your life is to stay away from decaying vegetation and keep doors and windows closed on especially hot nights.

History

BEFORE THE EUROPEANS

Based on studies of artifacts found throughout the state, anthropologists know that the first humans arrived in South Carolina at least 13,000 years ago, at the tail end of the last ice age. However, a still-controversial archaeological dig in the state, the Topper Site on the Savannah River near Allendale, has found artifacts that some scientists say are about 50,000 years old.

In any case, during this **Paleo-Indian Period,** sea levels were over 200 feet lower than present levels, and large mammals such as woolly mammoths, horses, and camels were hunted for food and skins. However, rapidly increasing temperatures, rising sea levels, and efficient hunting techniques combined to quickly kill off these large mammals, relics of the Pleistocene era, ushering in the **Archaic Period** in what's now the southeastern United States. Still hunter-gatherers, Archaic Period Indians began turning to small game such as deer, bears, and turkeys, supplemented with fruit and nuts. The latter part of the Archaic era saw more habitation on the coasts, with an increasing reliance on fish and shellfish. It's to this time that the great **shell middens** of the Georgia and South Carolina coasts trace their origins. Basically serving as trash heaps for discarded oyster shells, as the middens grew in size they also took on a ceremonial status, often being used as sites for important rituals and meetings. Such sites are often called **shell rings,** and the largest yet found was over nine feet high and 300 feet in diameter. Hilton Head Island, for example, has two remaining shell rings. Using ground-penetrating radar, archaeologists are finding more and more Archaic Period shell middens and rings all the time.

The introduction of agriculture and improved pottery techniques about 3,000 years ago led to the **Woodland Period** of Native

American settlement. Extended clan groups were much less migratory, establishing year-round communities of up to 50 people, who began the practice of clearing land to grow crops. The ancient shell middens of their ancestors were not abandoned, however, and were continually added onto. Native Americans had been cremating or burying their dead for years, a practice which eventually gave rise to the construction of the first **mounds** during the Woodland Period. Essentially built-up earthworks sometimes marked with spiritual symbols, often in the form of animal shapes, mounds not only contained the remains of the deceased but items like pottery to accompany the deceased into the afterlife.

Increased agriculture led to increased population, and with that population growth came competition over resources and a more formal notion of warfare. This period, about AD 800-1600, is termed the **Mississippian Period.** It was the Mississippians who would be the first Native Americans in what's now the continental United States to encounter European explorers and settlers after Columbus. The Native Americans who would later be called **Creek Indians** were the direct descendants of the Mississippians in lineage, language, and lifestyle. Described by later European accounts as a tall, proud people, the Mississippians often wore elaborate body art and, like the indigenous inhabitants of Central and South America, used the practice of **head shaping,** whereby an infant's skull was deliberately deformed into an elongated shape by tying the baby's head to a board for about a year. By about AD 1400, change came to the Mississippian culture for reasons that are still not completely understood. In some areas, large chiefdoms began splintering into smaller subgroups in an intriguing echo of the medieval feudal system going on concurrently in Europe. In other areas, however, the rise of a handful of more powerful chiefs subsumed smaller communities under their influence. In either case, the result was the same: The landscape of the Southeast became less peopled as

many of the old villages, built around huge central mounds, were abandoned, some suddenly. As tensions increased, the contested land became more and more dangerous for the poorly armed or poorly connected. Indeed, at the time of the Europeans' arrival, much of the coastal area was more thinly inhabited than it had been for many decades.

THE SPANISH ARRIVE

The first known contact by Europeans on the southeastern coast came in 1521, roughly concurrent with Cortés's conquest of Mexico. A party of Spanish slavers ventured into what's now Port Royal Sound from Santo Domingo in the Caribbean. Naming the area Santa Elena, they kidnapped a few Indian slaves and left, ranging as far north as the Cape Fear River in present-day North Carolina, and by some accounts even farther up the coast.

The first serious exploration of the coast came in 1526, when Lucas Vázquez de Ayllón and about 600 colonists made landfall at Winyah Bay near present-day Georgetown. They didn't stay long, however, immediately moving down the coast and trying to set down roots in the St. Catherine's Sound area of modern-day Liberty County, Georgia. That colony—called San Miguel de Gualdape—was the first European colony in North America (the continent's oldest continuously occupied settlement, St. Augustine, Florida, wasn't founded until 1565). The colony also brought with it the seed of a future nation's dissolution: slaves from Africa. San Miguel lasted only six weeks due to political tension and a slave uprising.

Hernando De Soto's infamous expedition of 1539-1543 began in Florida and went through southwest Georgia before crossing the Savannah River somewhere near modern-day North Augusta, South Carolina. He immediately came in contact with emissaries from the Cofitachequi empire of Mississippian Indians. The powerful Cofitachequi empire was the culmination of years of consolidation among regional nations. They had attained a high level of sophistication and military and economic prowess, with the rule of their eponymous queen, Cofitachequi, recognized for about 250 miles in every direction—in other words, over almost all of what is now South Carolina. When De Soto and his men arrived near the Cofitachequi capital, near modern-day Camden, he was met on the shores of the Wateree River by Queen Cofitachequi herself. She had heard the tales of De Soto's previous atrocities against Native American villages who refused to aid him in his quest for gold, and she was savvy enough to receive him diplomatically. According to a Spanish account, the queen "was a young girl of fine bearing, and she spoke to the governor quite gracefully and at her ease," carried on a platform covered with pillows.

While De Soto found no fabled cities of gold, he was impressed by the quality and quantity of the Cofitachequi's great homes and the copper and pearls they had amassed. In true conquistador fashion, De Soto decided to take the queen hostage to guarantee his safe passage through the rest of her empire. The queen proved smarter than her captor, however. During their journey across South Carolina, at one point she excused herself into the woods to attend to bodily functions. She immediately vanished, heading back to her people.

Long after his departure and eventual death from fever in Alabama, De Soto's legacy was felt throughout the Southeast in the form of various diseases for which the indigenous Mississippian people had no immunity whatsoever: smallpox, typhus, influenza, measles, yellow fever, whooping cough, diphtheria, tuberculosis, and bubonic plague. While the barbaric cruelties of the Spanish certainly took their toll, far more damaging were these deadly diseases to a population totally unprepared for them. As the viruses they introduced ran rampant, the Europeans themselves stayed away from this area for several decades after the ignominious end of De Soto's quest. During that quarter century, the once-proud Mississippian culture, ravaged by disease, disintegrated into a shadow of its former greatness.

The French Misadventure

The Spanish presence in South Carolina was briefly threatened by the ill-fated establishment of Charlesfort in 1562 by French Huguenots under Jean Ribault. Part of a covert effort by the Protestant French admiral Coligny to send Huguenot colonizing missions around the globe, Ribault's crew of 150 first explored the mouth of the St. Johns River near present-day Jacksonville, Florida, before heading north to Port Royal Sound and present-day Parris Island, South Carolina.

After establishing Charlesfort, Ribault returned to France for supplies. In his absence, religious war had broken out in his home country. Ribault sought sanctuary in England but was clapped in irons anyway. Meanwhile, most of Charlesfort's colonists grew so demoralized they joined another French expedition led by René Laudonnière at Fort Caroline on the St. Johns River. The remaining 27 built a ship to sail from Charlesfort back to France; 20 of them survived the journey, which was cut short in the English Channel when they had to be rescued.

Ribault himself was dispatched to reinforce Fort Caroline, but was headed off by a contingent from the new fortified Spanish settlement at St. Augustine. The fate of the French presence on the southeast coast was sealed when not only did the Spanish take Fort Caroline but a storm destroyed Ribault's reinforcing fleet. Ribault and all survivors were killed as soon as they struggled ashore. To keep the French away for good and cement Spain's hold on this northernmost part of their province of La Florida, the Spanish built the fort of Santa Elena directly on top of Charlesfort. Both layers are currently being excavated and studied today on Parris Island, near a golf course on the U.S. Marine camp.

Juan Pardo's Expedition

The next serious Spanish expedition into South Carolina began on the coast in 1566, when Juan Pardo set out from Santa Elena on Parris Island. Pardo and his party of 125 soldiers were on a mission to explore the hinterland and scout a location for a road to the main Spanish silver mines in Mexico. Inland, he encountered the Cofitachequi nation, much diminished since De Soto's time. Because they had set out without pack animals and serious supplies of their own, the Spanish obtained most of their food from local Indians, whether by request or by force. At all Indian villages he encountered, Pardo delivered the traditional *requerimiento,* a formal notification of the jurisdiction of the Spanish crown and the primacy of Christianity.

Before heading into present-day North Carolina and into Appalachia, Pardo stopped for a time near modern Spartanburg, South Carolina. A rock supposedly bearing an inscription of Pardo's name was overturned by a local farmer and is currently in the Spartanburg County Museum.

The Mission Era

With Spanish dominance of the region ensured for the near future, the lengthy mission era began. It's rarely mentioned as a key part of U.S. history, but the Spanish missionary presence in Florida and on the Georgia coast was longer and more comprehensive than its much more widely known counterpart in California. While the purpose of the missions was to convert as many Indians as possible to Christianity, they also served to further consolidate Spanish political control. It was a dicey proposition, as technically the mission friars served at the pleasure of the local chiefs. But the more savvy of the chiefs soon learned that cooperating with the militarily powerful Spanish—with the friars came soldiers—led to more influence and more supplies. Frequently it was the chiefs themselves who urged for more expansion of the Franciscan missions.

The looming invasion threat to St. Augustine from English adventurer and privateer Sir Francis Drake was a harbinger of trouble to come, as was a Guale uprising in 1597. The Spanish consolidated their positions near St. Augustine, and Santa Elena was abandoned. As Spanish power waned, in 1629 Charles I of England laid formal claim to what is now the Carolinas, Georgia, and much of Florida, but made no effort to colonize the area. By 1706 the Spanish mission effort in the Southeast had fully retreated to Florida. In an interesting postscript, 89 Native Americans—the sole surviving descendants of Spain's southeastern missions—evacuated to Cuba with the final Spanish exodus from Florida in 1763.

ENTER THE ENGLISH

South Carolina is a product of the **English Restoration,** when the monarchy returned to power after the grim 11-year tenure of Oliver Cromwell, who had defeated Royalist forces in the English Civil War. The attitudes of the Restoration era—expansionist, confident, mercantile—is key to understanding the character of South Carolina even today. Historians dispute exactly how close-minded Cromwell was, but there's no debating the puritanical tone of his reign as British head of state. Theater was banned, as was most music, except for hymns. Hair was close-cropped, and dress was extremely conservative. Most disturbing of all for the holiday-loving English, the observation of Christmas and Easter was strongly discouraged because of their supposedly pagan origins.

Enter Charles II, son of the beheaded Charles I. His ascent to the throne in 1660 signaled a release of all the pent-up creativity and energy of the British people, stagnant under Cromwell's repression. The arts returned to their previous importance. Foreign policy became aggressive and expansionist. Capitalists again sought profit. Fashion made a comeback, and dandy dress and long hair for both men and women were all the rage. This, then, is the backdrop for the first English settlement of what is now South Carolina. The first expedition was by a Barbadian colonist, William Hilton, in 1663. While he didn't establish a new colony, he did leave behind his name on the most notable geographic feature he saw—Hilton Head Island.

In 1665 King Charles II gave a charter to eight **Lords Proprietors** to establish a colony, generously to be named Carolina after the monarch himself. (One of the Proprietors, Lord Ashley Cooper, would see not one but both rivers in the Charleston area named after him.) Remarkably, none of the Proprietors ever set foot in the colony they established for their own profit. Before their colony was even established, the Proprietors themselves set the stage for the vast human disaster that would eventually befall it. They encouraged slavery by promising that each colonist would receive 20 acres of land for every black male slave and 10 acres for every black female slave brought to the colony within the first year.

In 1666 explorer Robert Sandford officially claimed Carolina for the king, in a ceremony on modern-day Seabrook or Wadmalaw Island. The Proprietors then sent out a fleet of three ships from England, only one of which, the *Carolina,* would make it the whole way. After stops in the thriving English colonies of Barbados and Bermuda, the ship landed in Port Royal. They were greeted without violence, but the fact that the local indigenous people spoke Spanish led the colonists to conclude that perhaps the site was too close for comfort to Spain's sphere of influence. A Kiawah chief, eager for allies against the fierce, slave-trading Westo people, invited the colonists north to settle instead. So the colonists—148 of them, including three African slaves—moved 80 miles up the coast and in 1670 pitched camp on the Ashley River at a place they dubbed Albemarle Point after one of their lost ships. Living within the palisades of the camp, the colonists farmed 10-acre plots outside the walls for sustenance. The Native Americans of the area were of the large and influential Cusabo people of the Creek Nation, and are sometimes even today known as the Settlement Indians. Subgroups of the Cusabo whose names live on today in South Carolina geography were the Kiawah, Edisto, Wando, Stono, and Ashepoo.

A few years later some colonists from Barbados, which was beginning to suffer the effects of overpopulation, joined the Carolinians. The Barbadian influence, with an emphasis on large-scale slave labor and a caste system, would have an indelible imprint on the colony. Indeed, within a generation a majority of settlers in the new colony would be African slaves. By 1680, however, Albemarle Point was feeling growing pains as well, and the Proprietors ordered the site moved to Oyster Point at the confluence of the Ashley and Cooper Rivers (the present-day Battery). Within a year Albemarle Point was abandoned, and the walls of Charles Towne were built a few hundred yards up from Oyster Point on the banks of the Cooper River.

The original Anglican settlers were quickly joined by various **Dissenters,** among them French Huguenots, Quakers, Congregationalists, and Jews. A group of Scottish Presbyterians established the short-lived Stuart Town near Port Royal in 1684. Recognizing this diversity, the colony in 1697 granted religious liberty to all "except Papists," meaning Roman Catholics. The Anglicans attempted a crackdown on Dissenters in 1704, but two years later Queen Anne stepped in and ensured religious freedom for all Carolinians (again with the exception of Roman Catholics, who wouldn't be a factor in the colony until after the American Revolution).

The English settlements quickly gained root as the burgeoning deerskin trade increased exponentially. Traders upriver, using an ancient network of trails, worked with local Native Americans, mostly Cherokees, to exploit the massive numbers of deer in the American interior. The deerskin trade had a deleterious effect on the indigenous population, as men were gone from their villages much longer than in previous times, when hunting trips had been for sustenance only. By the mid-1700s, the deer population had been so overharvested that the Cherokees had trouble feeding themselves. This led to the need to purchase or barter for food from the English, a dependency that would lead inexorably to violence in years to come.

But before that conflict would come, other scores had to be settled.

Henry Woodward: Colonial Indiana Jones

He's virtually unsung in the history books, and there are no movies made about him, but Dr. Henry Woodward, the first English settler in South Carolina, lived a life that is the stuff of novels and screenplays. Educated in medicine in London, Woodward first tried his hand in the colony of Barbados. But Barbados, crowded and run by an elite, was no place for a young man with a sense of adventure but no contacts in the sugar industry. Still in his teens, Woodward left Barbados in Captain Robert Sandford's 1664 expedition to Carolina. Landing in the Cape Fear region, Sandford's cohort made its way down to Port Royal Sound to contact the Cusabo Indians. In 1666, in what is perhaps the New World's first "cultural-exchange program," Woodward volunteered to stay behind while the rest of the expedition returned to England with a Native American named Shadoo.

Woodward learned the local language and established political relations with surrounding Native American groups, actions for which the Lords Proprietors granted him temporary "formall possession of the whole Country to hold as Tennant att Will." The Spanish had different plans, however. They came and kidnapped the young Englishman, taking him to what turned out to be a very permissive state of house arrest at the Spanish stronghold of St. Augustine in Florida. Surprising the Spanish with his request—in Latin, no less—to convert to Catholicism, Woodward was popular and well-treated. An excellent student of the Catechism, Woodward became a favorite of the Spanish governor and was even promoted to official surgeon. During that time, he studied Spanish government, commerce, and culture, with the same diligence with which he had studied the Indians a year earlier. In 1668, Woodward was "rescued" by English privateers—pirates, really—under the command of Robert Searle, who'd come to sack St. Augustine. Woodward's sojourn with the pirates would last two years, during which he was kept on board as ship's surgeon. Was the pirate raid a coincidence? Or, as some scholars suggest, was Woodward really one of history's greatest spies? We will probably never know.

Incredibly, the plot thickens. In another coincidence, in 1670 Woodward was rescued when the pirates shipwrecked on the Caribbean island of Nevis. His rescuers were none other than the settlers on their way to found Charles Towne. On landfall, Woodward asserted his previous experience in the area to direct the colonists away from Port Royal to an area of less Spanish influence. That same year he began a series of expeditions to contact indigenous people in the Carolina interior—the first non-Spanish European to set foot in the area. Using economic espionage gained from the Spanish, Woodward's goal was to jump-start the trade in deerskins that would be the bulwark of the Charles Towne colony. Woodward's unlikely 1674 alliance with the aggressive Westo people was instrumental in this burgeoning trade. As if all this weren't enough, in 1680 Woodward, now with property of his own on Johns Island, would introduce local farmers to a certain strange crop recently imported from Madagascar: rice.

Woodward made enemies, however, of settlers who were envious of his growing affluence and suspicious of his friendship with the Westo. His outspoken disgust with the spread of Indian slavery brought a charge against him of undermining the interests of the crown. But Woodward, by now a celebrity of sorts, returned to England to plead his case directly to the Lords Proprietors. They not only pardoned him but made him their official Indian agent—with a 20 percent share of the profits. Woodward would never again see the land of his birth. He returned to the American colonies to trek inland, making alliances with groups of Creek Indians in Spanish-held territory. Hounded by Spanish troops, Woodward fell ill of a fever somewhere in the Savannah River valley. He made it to Charleston and safety but never fully recovered and died around 1690—after living the kind of life you usually only see in the movies.

The Yamasee War

Within 20 years the English presence had expanded throughout the Lowcountry to include Port Royal and Beaufort. Charles Towne became a thriving commercial center, dealing in deerskins with traders in the interior and with foreign concerns from England to South America. Its success was not without a backlash, as the local Yamasee people became increasingly disgruntled at the settlers' growing monopolies on deerskin and the slave trade. Slavery was a sad and common fact of life from the earliest days of European settlement in the region. Indians were the most frequent early victims, with not only white settlers taking slaves from among them but the Indians themselves conducting slaving raids on each other, often selling hostages to eager colonists.

As rumors of war spread, on Good Friday, 1715, a delegation of six white Carolinians went to the Yamasee village of Pocataligo to address some of the Yamasee's grievances in the hopes of forestalling violence. Their effort was in vain, however, as Yamasee warriors murdered four of them in their sleep, the remaining two escaping to sound the alarm. The treacherous attack signaled the beginning of the two-year Yamasee War, which would claim the lives of nearly 10 percent of the colony's population and an unknown number of Native Americans—making it one of the bloodiest conflicts in American history. Energized and ready for war, the Yamasee attacked Charles Town itself and killed about 90 of the 100 or so white traders in the interior, effectively ending commerce in the area. As Charles Towne began to swell with refugees from the hinterland, water and supplies ran low, and the colony was in peril.

After an initially poor performance by the Carolina militia, a professional army—including armed African slaves—was raised. Well trained and well led, the new army more than held its own despite being outnumbered. A key alliance with local Cherokees was all the advantage the colonists needed to turn the tide for good. While the Cherokees never received the overt military backing from the settlers

that they sought, they did garner enough supplies and influence to convince their Creek rivals, the Yamasee, to begin the peace process. The war-weary settlers, eager to get back to life and to business, were eager to negotiate with them, offering goods as a sign of their earnest intent. By 1717 the Yamasee threat had subsided, and trade in the region began flourishing anew.

No sooner had the Yamasee War ended, however, when a new threat emerged: the dread pirate Edward Teach, a.k.a. Blackbeard. Entering Charleston harbor in May 1718 with his flagship *Queen Anne's Revenge* and three other vessels, he promptly plundered five ships and began a full-scale blockade of the entire settlement. He took a number of prominent citizens hostage before finally departing northward.

Slavery Expands

While it was the Spanish who introduced slavery to the New World—of Indians as well as of Africans—it was the English-speaking settlers who dramatically expanded the institution.

For the English colonists, the Blackbeard episode was the final straw. Already disgusted by the lack of support from the Lords Proprietors during the Yamasee War, the humiliation of the pirate blockade was too much to take. So to almost universal agreement in the colony, the settlers threw off the rule of the Proprietors and strenuously lobbied in 1719 to become a crown colony, an effort that came to final fruition in 1729.

While this outward-looking and energetic place—whose name would morph into Charlestown, and then simply Charleston—was originally built on the backs of merchants, with the introduction of the rice and indigo crops in the early 1700s it would increasingly be built on the backs of slaves. For all the wealth gained through the planting of indigo, rice, and cotton seeds, another seed was sown by the Lowcountry plantation culture. The area's total dependence on slave labor would soon lead to a disastrous war, a conflict signaled for decades to those smart enough to read the signs. By this time Charleston was firmly established as the key American port for the importation of African slaves, accounting for about 40 percent of the trade. As a result, the black population of the coast outnumbered the white population by more than three to one. The very real fear of violent slave uprisings had great influence over not only politics but day-to-day affairs.

These fears were eventually realized in the great **Stono Rebellion** on September 9, 1739. Twenty African American slaves led by an Angolan known only as Jemmy met near the Stono River near Charleston. Marching with a banner that read "Liberty," they seized guns with the plan of marching all the way to Spanish Florida and sanctuary in the wilderness. On the way they burned seven plantations and killed 20 whites. A militia eventually caught up with them, killing 44 escaped slaves and losing 20 of their own. The prisoners were decapitated and had their heads spiked on every milepost between the spot of that final battle and Charleston. The result was not only a 10-year moratorium on slave importation into Charleston, but a severe crackdown on the education of slaves—a move that would have damaging implications for generations to come.

Spain Vanquished

In 1729, Carolina was divided into north and south. In 1731, a colony to be known as Georgia, after the new English king, was carved out of the southern part of the Carolina land grant specifically to provide a military buffer to protect Carolina. A young English general, aristocrat, and humanitarian named James Edward Oglethorpe gathered together a group of Trustees—similar to Carolina's Lords Proprietors—to take advantage of that grant. Like Carolina, the Georgia colony also emphasized religious freedom. While to modern ears Charleston's antipathy toward "papists" and Oglethorpe's original ban of Roman Catholics from Georgia might seem incompatible with this goal, the reason was a coldly pragmatic one for the time: England's two

main global rivals, France and Spain, were both staunchly Catholic countries.

In 1742 Oglethorpe defeated a Spanish force on St. Simons Island, Georgia, in the **Battle of Bloody Marsh.** That clash marked the end of Spanish overtures on England's colonies in America. With first the French and then the Spanish effectively shut off from the American East Coast, the stage was set for an internal battle between England and its burgeoning colonies across the Atlantic.

The Coming of the "Crackers"

In the mid-1700s, Scots-Irish settlers from Pennsylvania and Virginia came down the **Great Wagon Road** along the Appalachians to enter upstate South Carolina in great numbers. Although many of these independent farmers owned slaves, generally they were far less sympathetic to slavery than coastal residents, and certainly much less dependent on it. Calvinist in religion and self-reliant in outlook, these "crackers"—called that either because of the sound of their whips as they drove their wagons or from the Gaelic word *craic,* meaning to boast—grew to become a formidable political force in South Carolina.

The interior began filling up with Scottish, Irish, German, and Swiss settlers. Their subsequent demands for political representation led to tension with the coastal inhabitants, typically depicted through the years as an Upcountry versus Lowcountry competition.

In later years the Scots-Irish of the Upstate would go on to contribute two of South Carolina's most prominent figures, Andrew Jackson and John C. Calhoun. Ironically, the men would find themselves on opposing sides of the nation-shattering question of secession.

The Cherokee War

By 1750 the Cherokees of the Upstate were the most numerous and important Native American allies of English settlers in South Carolina. However, tired of being ripped off by white traders against whom they had little recourse, the Cherokees grew increasingly embittered, their morale further shattered by a particularly devastating outbreak of the plague. They began to play the English against the French to the west, who were generally more ethical in their relations with indigenous populations. Isolated violence by the Cherokees against English settlers—much of which was subsumed within what's now known as the French and Indian War—was also on the upswing.

An attack on some white settlers in 1759 convinced South Carolina's Governor James Lyttleton to put his foot down. He demanded that the Cherokees surrender those responsible, knowing full well that they had no centralized governmental authority capable of doing so. When the Cherokees cobbled together a delegation to Charleston to negotiate, Lyttleton promptly had the Indian emissaries taken hostage and held at Fort Prince George on the Keowee River (the site is now submerged under the reservoir of Lake Keowee). However, the Cherokee answered subterfuge with subterfuge. They invited the fort's commander, Lieutenant William Coytmore, outside the walls under a flag of truce to bargain for the hostages' release. They then ambushed Coytmore and his unarmed men, killing the lieutenant. The English furiously responded by immediately murdering all 22 hostages within the fort.

Thus all-out war came to the Upstate, between the Cherokees and the English, their former allies. Violence flared throughout the colony. A war party massacred 50 settlers near present-day Abbeville. An Indian assault on the outpost at Ninety Six was barely repulsed. An entire surrendered garrison, marching from Tennessee to Fort Prince George, was murdered. While the first phase of the Cherokee War favored the Cherokees—accustomed as they were to guerrilla tactics—the tide would soon turn. Ever-larger deployments of regular British Army troops were dispatched to Cherokee land, both to protect settlers as well as to sack and burn Cherokee towns wholesale.

In a foreshadowing of the total war that General William Sherman would later unleash on the South, in 1761 a massive British force under General James Grant burned fields and crops throughout the Midlands and Upcountry, depriving the Cherokees of sustenance for the winter ahead. In September 1761, the Cherokees signed a peace treaty with the colony, ceding most of its eastern lands. The Cherokees would later embark on a disastrous alliance with the crown during the American Revolution, but for the time being they were neutralized, and South Carolina settlers could focus on a larger, much more powerful enemy: the crown. The brutal lessons learned fighting the Cherokees would come in handy.

REVOLUTION AND A NEW NATION

It's a persistent but inaccurate myth that the affluent elite on the southeastern coast were reluctant to break ties with England. While the Lowcountry's cultural and economic ties to England were certainly strong, the **Stamp Act** and the **Townshend Acts** combined to turn public sentiment against the mother country there as elsewhere in the colonies. South Carolinian planters like Christopher Gadsden, Henry Laurens, John Rutledge, and Arthur Middleton were early leaders in the movement for independence.

At war's outbreak, the British failed to take Charleston—fourth-largest city in the colonies—in June 1776. The episode gave South Carolina its "Palmetto State" moniker when redcoat cannonballs bounced off the palm tree-lined walls of Fort Moultrie on Sullivan's Island. The British under General Sir Henry Clinton successfully took the city, however, in 1780, holding it until 1782. The area's two major cities were captured—Savannah fell to the British in 1778—but the war raged on in the surrounding area. Indeed, throughout the Carolinas the fighting was as vicious as anything yet seen on the North American continent. With over 130 known military engagements occurring in South Carolina, that colony sacrificed more combatants during the war than any other.

The struggle became a guerrilla war of colonists versus the British as well as a civil war between Patriots and Loyalists, or **Tories.** Committing what would today undoubtedly be called war crimes, the British routinely burned homes, churches, and fields, and killed recalcitrant civilians. In response, Patriots of the Lowcountry formed a group of deadly guerrilla soldiers under legendary leaders such as Francis Marion, "the Swamp Fox," and Thomas Sumter, "the Gamecock." Using unorthodox tactics perfected in years of backcountry Indian fighting, the Patriots of the Carolinas attacked the British in daring hit-and-run raids staged from the swamps and marshes and from the hills and forests.

Although the British originally assumed they would be supportive of the crown, Upstate Carolinians were swayed by the resurgence of violence by the Cherokees, newly allied with the British. The savagery of the repeated frontier massacres—some of which, it must be said, were encouraged by the British—hardened the Upcountry settlers against redcoat and Indian alike. Some of them, such as Andrew Jackson, would take their anti-Indian prejudice to extremes.

In all, the Scots-Irish of the Upstate would play a key role—some historians say *the* key role—in turning the tide of the American Revolution. South Carolina militiamen would defeat Loyalist forces in two pivotal battles of the war, at Cowpens and Kings Mountain. The unexpected show of patriotism from Upcountry settlers put a dagger in Lord Cornwallis's ill-fated Southern Strategy and led inevitably to the British retreat through North Carolina to Yorktown, Virginia, and ignominy.

In all, four South Carolinians signed the Declaration of Independence: Thomas Heyward Jr., Thomas Lynch Jr., Arthur Middleton, and Edward Rutledge.

The Cotton Boom

True to form, the new nation wasted no time in asserting its economic strength. Rice planters from Georgetown north of Charleston on down to the Altamaha River in Georgia built on their already impressive wealth, becoming the new nation's richest men by far—with fortunes built on the backs of the slaves working in their fields.

Charleston was still by far the largest, most powerful, and most influential city in the Southeast. While most Lowcountry planters spent the warmer months away from the mosquito- and malaria-infested coast, Charleston's elite grew so fond of their little peninsula that they took to living in their "summer homes" year-round, becoming absentee landlords of their various plantations. As a result of this affluent, somewhat hedonistic atmosphere, Charleston became an early arts and cultural center for the whole country.

In 1786, a new crop was introduced that would only enhance the financial clout of the coastal region: cotton. A former Loyalist colonel, Roger Kelsal, sent some seed from Anguilla in the West Indies to his friend James Spaulding, owner of a plantation on St. Simons Island, Georgia. This crop, soon to be known as **Sea Island cotton** and considered the best in the world, would supplant rice as the crop of choice for coastal plantations. Plantations on Hilton Head, Edisto, Daufuskie, and Kiawah Islands would make the shift to this more profitable product and amass even greater fortunes for their owners. With the boom in cotton, there needed to be a better way to get that cash crop to market quickly. In 1827, the South Carolina Canal and Rail Road Company was chartered to build a line that would expedite cotton trade from the Upcountry down to the port of Charleston. The resulting 137-mile Charleston-Hamburg line, begun in 1833, was at the time the longest railroad in the world.

Secession

Much of the lead-in to the Civil War focused on whether slavery would be allowed in the newest U.S. territories in the West, but there's no doubt that all figurative roads eventually led to South Carolina. During Andrew Jackson's presidency in the 1820s, his vice president, South Carolina's John C. Calhoun, became a thorn in Jackson's side with his aggressive advocacy for the concept of **nullification,** which Jackson strenuously rejected. In a nutshell, Calhoun said that if a state decided that the federal government wasn't treating it fairly—in this case with regard to tariffs that were hurting the cotton trade in the Palmetto State—it could simply nullify the federal law, superseding it with law of its own.

As the abolition movement gained steam and tensions over slavery rose, South Carolina congressman Preston Brooks took things to the next level. On May 22, 1856, he beat fellow senator Charles Sumner of Massachusetts nearly to death with his walking cane on the Senate floor. Sumner had just given a speech criticizing pro-slavery forces—including a relative of Brooks's—and called slavery "a harlot." (In a show of support, South Carolinians sent Brooks dozens of new canes to replace the one he broke over Sumner's head.)

In 1860, the national convention of the Democratic Party, then the dominant force in U.S. politics, was held in—where else?—Charleston. Rancor over slavery and state's rights was so high that they couldn't agree on a single candidate to run to replace President James Buchanan. Reconvening in Maryland, the party split along sectional lines, with the Northern wing backing Stephen A. Douglas. The Southern wing, fervently desiring secession, deliberately chose its own candidate, John Breckenridge, in order to split the Democratic vote and throw the election to Republican Abraham Lincoln, an outspoken opponent of the expansion of slavery. During that so-called **Secession Winter** before Lincoln took office, seven states seceded from the union, first among them the Palmetto State, followed by Mississippi, Florida, Alabama, Georgia, Louisiana, and Texas.

A UNION DISSOLVED

Five days after South Carolina's secession on December 21, 1860, U.S. Army Major Robert Anderson moved his garrison from Fort Moultrie in Charleston harbor to nearby Fort Sumter. Over the next few months and into the spring, Anderson would ignore many calls to surrender, and Confederate forces would prevent any Union resupply or reinforcement. Shortly before dawn on April 12, 1861, Confederate batteries around Charleston—ironically none of which were at the Battery itself—opened fire on Fort Sumter for 34 straight hours, until Anderson surrendered on April 13.

In a classic example of why you should always be careful what you wish for, the secessionists had been too clever in pushing for Lincoln. Far from prodding the North to sue for peace, the fall of Fort Sumter instead caused the remaining states in the union to rally around the previously unpopular tall man from Illinois. Lincoln's skillful—some would say cunning—management of the Fort Sumter standoff meant that from then on out, the South would bear history's blame for initiating the conflict that would claim over half a million American lives.

After Fort Sumter, the remaining four states of the Confederacy—Arkansas, Tennessee, North Carolina, and Virginia—seceded. The Old Dominion was the real prize for the secessionists, as Virginia had the South's only ironworks and by far the largest manufacturing base.

War on the Coast

In November 1861, a massive Union invasion armada landed in Port Royal Sound in South Carolina, effectively taking the entire Lowcountry and Sea Islands out of the war. Charleston, however, did host two battles in the conflict. The **Battle of Secessionville** came in June 1862, when a Union force attempting to take Charleston was repulsed on James Island with heavy casualties. The next battle, an unsuccessful Union landing on Morris Island in July 1863, was immortalized by the movie *Glory*.

The 54th Massachusetts Regiment, an African American unit with white

Old Hickory's Legacy

Although many histories of Andrew Jackson, seventh president of the United States, say he was born in North Carolina, don't tell that to South Carolinians. They're sure Old Hickory is one of their own. If you don't believe them, get into your time machine and ask Andrew Jackson himself. He always insisted he was born in a log house in South Carolina a couple of miles from the border with the Tar Heel State.

In any case, we know that Old Hickory was born in what's called the Waxhaws region, straddling the border of the Carolinas roughly in the area of modern-day Charlotte and its suburbs to the south. Like much of the Upstate, the area was generally immune to the charms of the Lowcountry planters, whom they thought of as a pampered elite. While owning slaves was certainly a part of the entire state's economy, it was noticeably less important in the Upstate.

This sensitivity to the needs and basic dignity of the common man would go on to inform Jackson's time in the White House. Prior to Jackson's presidency, only white male landowners could vote in the United States. Setting the stage for gradually increasing suffrage gains—such as for African American men, and later for all women—Jackson changed the system so that owning land was not a requirement to vote.

Jackson had noticeably less populist sympathy for Native Americans, however. As a product of the rough Carolina frontier, the site of generations of savage wars between settlers and local indigenous people, he grew up with a strong bias against the region's original inhabitants. This enmity would see its awful height in the Trail of Tears, a direct result of Jackson's Indian Removal Act of 1830. The most famous—and possibly apocryphal—example of Jackson's literal "my way or the highway" approach came in 1831, when the Supreme Court, under Chief Justice John Marshall, ruled against the state of Georgia's action to take Cherokee land. In response, Jackson supposedly said, "John Marshall has made his decision—now let him enforce it."

Another development that didn't necessarily have such sanguine results was his introduction of the patronage system, in other words, "to the victor go the spoils." Before Jackson, civil servants kept their jobs regardless of which team was in the White House. Afterward, bureaucrats became political appointees. While today patronage is generally thought of as leading to corruption and cronyism, at the time Jackson intended it as an antidote to what he saw as a creeping aristocracy in the government and another example of the venal self-centered nature of the Lowcountry planter elite.

One of Jackson's key philosophies, a sharp distrust of banks, did not survive his time in office. Although he fought strenuously against the undue influence of the banking industry on the American body politic, no one could say he was successful in light of their power today.

Learn more about Old Hickory when you're in the state of his birth (according to the man himself, anyway) by visiting **Andrew Jackson State Park** (196 Andrew Jackson Park Rd., 803/285-3344, www.southcarolinaparks.com, during daylight saving time daily 9am-9pm, other seasons daily 8am-6pm, $2 adults, free under age 15).

commanders, performed so gallantly in its failed assault on the Confederate Battery Wagner that it inspired the North and was cited by abolitionists as further proof that African Americans should be given freedom and full citizenship rights. Another invasion attempt on Charleston would not come, but it was besieged and bombarded for nearly two years (devastation made even worse by a massive fire, unrelated to the shelling, that destroyed much of the city in 1861).

White Southerners evacuated the coastal cities and plantations for the hinterland, leaving behind only slaves to fend for themselves. In many coastal areas, African Americans and Union garrison troops settled into an awkward but peaceful coexistence.

In Savannah, to the south, General William Sherman concluded his **March to the Sea** in 1864, famously giving the city to Lincoln as a Christmas present. While staunch Confederates, city fathers were wise enough to know what would happen to their accumulated wealth and fine homes should they be foolhardy enough to resist Sherman's army of war-hardened veterans, most of them farm boys from the Midwest with a pronounced distaste for the "peculiar institution" of slavery.

Aftermath

The only military uncertainty left was in how badly Charleston, the "cradle of secession," would suffer for its sins. Historians and local wags have long debated why Sherman spared Charleston, the hated epicenter of the Civil War. Did he fall in love with the city during his brief posting there as a young lieutenant? Did he literally fall in love there, with one of its legendarily beautiful and delicate local belles? We may never know for sure, but it's likely that the Lowcountry's marshy, mucky terrain simply made it too difficult to move large numbers of men and supplies from Savannah to Charleston proper. So Sherman turned his terrifying battle-hardened army inland toward the state capital, Columbia, which would not be so lucky. Most of Charleston's once-great plantation homes were also put to the torch.

For the African American population of South Carolina, however, it was not a time of sadness but the great Day of Jubilee. Soon after the Confederate surrender, black Charlestonians held one of the largest parades the city has ever seen, with one of the floats being a coffin bearing the sign "Slavery is dead."

As for the place where it all began, a plucky Confederate garrison remained underground at Fort Sumter throughout the war, as the walls above them were literally pounded into dust by the long Union siege. The garrison quietly left the fort under cover of night on February 17, 1865. Major Robert Anderson, who surrendered the fort at the war's beginning, returned to Sumter in April 1865 to raise the same flag he'd lowered exactly four years earlier. Three thousand African Americans attended the ceremonies, including the son of Denmark Vesey. Later that same night, Abraham Lincoln was assassinated in Washington DC.

Reconstruction

A case could be made that slavery need not have led the United States into Civil War. The U.S. government had banned the importation of slaves long before, in 1808. The great powers of Europe would soon ban slavery altogether (Spain in 1811, France in 1826, and Britain in 1833). Visiting foreign dignitaries in the mid-1800s were often shocked to find the practice in full swing in the American South. Even Brazil, the world center of slavery, where 4 out of every 10 slaves taken from Africa were brought (less than 5 percent came to the United States), would ban slavery in 1888. Still, the die was cast, the war was fought, and everyone had to deal with the aftermath.

For a brief time, Sherman's benevolent dictatorship on the coast held promise for an orderly postwar future. In 1865 he issued his sweeping "40 acres and a mule" order seeking dramatic economic restitution for coastal Georgia's free blacks. Politics reared its ugly head in the wake of Lincoln's assassination, however, and the order was rescinded, ushering in the chaotic Reconstruction era, echoes of which linger to this day. Nonetheless, that period of time in the South Carolina and Georgia Sea Islands served as an important incubator of sorts for the indigenous African American culture of the coast—called Gullah in South Carolina and Geechee in Georgia. Largely left to their own devices, these insulated farming and oystering communities held to their old folkways, many of which exist today.

Even as the trade in cotton and naval stores resumed to even greater heights than before, urban life and racial tensions became more and more problematic. Urban populations swelled as freed blacks from all over the depressed countryside rushed into the cities. As one of them, his name lost to history, famously said: "Freedom was freer in Charleston." It was during this time that some gains were made by African Americans, albeit with little support from the white population. Largely under duress, the University of South Carolina became the first Southern university to grant degrees to black students. The historically black, Methodist-affiliated Claflin College in Orangeburg was founded in 1869. While the coast and urban areas saw more opportunities for African Americans, tensions remained high in the countryside. The Edgefield District along the Savannah River, in particular, saw long periods of standoff between heavily armed black and white militias.

Largely with the support of those white militia groups, in 1876 the old guard of the Democratic Party returned to power in South Carolina with the election of former Confederate General Wade Hampton III to the governor's office. Supported by a violent paramilitary group called the Red Shirts, Hampton used his charisma and considerable personal reputation to attempt to restore South Carolina to its antebellum glory—and undo Reconstruction in the process.

"Pitchfork" Ben

The natural antipathy between the Lowcountry and the Upstate came to a head with the Populist movement of the 1890s. While the movement itself was short-lived, the empowerment it gave to South Carolina's long-ignored poor white farmers marked a permanent shift. A direct impact was the establishment of the agriculturally oriented Clemson College (later Clemson University) in 1889 specifically to counter the influence of the University of South Carolina in Columbia, which was perceived by some as an elite institution. The white farmers' standing became immeasurably enhanced by the new state constitution of 1895. With new poll taxes and literacy tests designed to dramatically hinder black voting, the constitution effectively ushered in the Jim Crow era in South Carolina.

The man behind the new charter was Benjamin Ryan Tillman of Trenton, South Carolina, who posed as the friend of the rural white South Carolinian but was essentially a career politician. He was also an extreme and unrepentant racist, as evidenced by this inflammatory quote, one of many like it:

> We of the South have never recognized the right of the negro to govern white men, and we never will. We have never believed him to be the equal of the white man, and we will not submit to his gratifying his lust on our wives and daughters without lynching him.

Tillman quickly rose in the newly nascent state Democratic Party and went on to become a U.S. senator from 1895 to 1918. Not only the main spokesman for the state's white backlash after the Civil War, he also ensured the supremacy of the Upstate in most internecine political battles, a legacy that lives on, more or less, to this day.

RENAISSANCE AND DEPRESSION

While the aftermath of the Civil War was painful, it was by no means bereft of activity or profit. The reunification of the states marked the coming of the Industrial Revolution, and in many quarters of the South, the cotton, lumber, and naval stores industries not only recovered but exceeded antebellum levels. A classic South Carolina example was in Horry County, where the town of Conway exploded as a commercial center for the area logging industry. By 1901 the first modest resort had been built on nearby Myrtle Beach, and the area rapidly became an important vacation area—a role it serves to this day.

The textile industry ramped up as well, and the Upstate became the new world center of the trade—gaining a certain amount of regional revenge by taking business from the once-dominant New England textile industry. For some parts of South Carolina, it was specifically an influx of Northern money after Reconstruction that heralded a mini boom. The classic example of this is in Aiken, where the heralded Winter Colony was responsible for much of the affluent, equestrian culture that reigns there even now.

The **Spanish-American War** of 1898

was a major turning point for the South. For most Southerners, it was the first time since the Civil War that they were enthusiastically patriotic about being Americans. The southeastern coast felt this in particular, as it was a staging area for the invasion of Cuba. Charlestonians cheered the exploits of their namesake heavy cruiser the USS *Charleston,* which played a key role in forcing the Spanish surrender of Guam.

Bernard Baruch, a South Carolinian, Wall Street financial wizard, and presidential adviser, would make many Americans more familiar with the state's natural beauty. After his acquisition of the old Hobcaw Barony near Georgetown in 1905, he hosted many a world leader there, including President Franklin D. Roosevelt and British Prime Minister Winston Churchill.

Charleston would elect its first Irish American mayor, John Grace, in 1911. Though it wouldn't open until 1929, the first Cooper River Bridge joining Charleston with Mount Pleasant was the child of the Grace administration, which is credited today for modernizing the Holy City's infrastructure (as well as tolerating high levels of vice during Prohibition) and making possible much of the civic gains to follow.

A major change that came during this time is rarely remarked on in history books: This was when South Carolina became a majority white state for the first time since the early colonial days. With thousands of African Americans leaving for more tolerant pastures and more economic opportunity in the North and the West—a move known as the **Great Migration**—the demographics of the state changed accordingly.

The arrival of the tiny but devastating boll weevil all but wiped out the cotton trade on the coast after the turn of the 20th century, forcing the economy to diversify. Naval stores and lumbering were the order of the day at the advent of **World War I**, the patriotic effort of which did wonders in repairing the wounds of the Civil War, still vivid in many local memories.

A major legacy of World War I that still greatly influences life in the Lowcountry is the Marine Corps Recruit Depot Parris Island, which began life as a small Marine camp in 1919.

The Roaring '20s

In the boom period following World War I, Charleston entered the world stage and made some of its most significant cultural contributions to American life. The dance called the Charleston, originated on the streets of the Holy City and popularized in New York, would sweep the world. The Jenkins Orphanage Band, often credited with the dance, traveled the world, even playing at President Taft's inauguration.

In the visual arts, the Charleston Renaissance took off, specifically intended to introduce the Holy City to a wider audience. Key work included the Asian-influenced work of self-taught painter Alice Ravenel Huger Smith and the etchings of Elizabeth O'Neill Verner. Edward Hopper was a visitor to Charleston during that time and produced several noted watercolors. The Gibbes Art Gallery, now the Gibbes Museum of Art, opened in 1905.

Recognizing the cultural importance of the city and its history, in 1920 socialite Susan Pringle Frost and other concerned Charlestonians formed the Preservation Society of Charleston, the oldest community-based historic preservation organization in the country.

In 1924, lauded Charleston author DuBose Heyward wrote the locally set novel *Porgy.* With Heyward's cooperation, the book would soon be turned into the first American opera, *Porgy and Bess,* by George Gershwin, who labored over the composition in a cottage on Folly Beach. Ironically, *Porgy and Bess,* which premiered with an African American cast in New York in 1935, wouldn't be performed in its actual setting until 1970 because of segregation laws.

And in a foreshadowing of a future tourist boom, the Pine Lakes golf course opened in

Myrtle Beach in 1927, the first on the Grand Strand.

A NEW DEAL

Alas, the good times didn't last. The Great Depression hit the South hard, but since wages and industry were already behind the national average, the economic damage wasn't as bad as elsewhere in the country. As elsewhere in the South and indeed across the country, public works programs in President Franklin D. Roosevelt's New Deal helped not only to keep locals employed but contributed greatly to the cultural and archaeological record of the area. The Public Works of Art Project stimulated the visual arts. The Works Progress Administration renovated the old Dock Street Theatre in Charleston, and theatrical productions once again graced that historic stage. You can still enjoy the network of state parks built in South Carolina by the Civilian Conservation Corps.

The New Deal also left its mark on South Carolina in the form of numerous hydroelectric projects, which involved the damming of rivers and the flooding of thousands of acres of land, much of it inhabited. Lakes Marion, Moultrie, Hartwell, Russell, and Thurmond are all artificial byproducts of these massive engineering projects. Used for recreation today, they played a vital role in the electrification of rural South Carolina and in the huge war effort that was soon to come.

WORLD WAR II AND THE MODERN ERA

With the attack on Pearl Harbor and the coming of World War II, life in the United States and in South Carolina would never be the same. Military funding and facilities swarmed the area, and populations and long-depressed living standards rose as a result. Here are some key developments:

- The Charleston Navy Yard became the city's largest employer, and the population soared as workers crowded in.

- Fort Jackson near Columbia became one of the U.S. Army's largest infantry training grounds, and Colonel Jimmy Doolittle's famed Tokyo Raiders trained for their daring missions over Lake Murray.

- Camp Croft near Spartanburg opened, training 250,000 infantrymen during the war.

- Down in Walterboro, the Tuskegee Airmen, a highly decorated group of African American fighter pilots, trained for their missions escorting bombing raids over Germany. Walterboro also hosted a large German POW camp.

- The Marine Corp Recruit Depot Parris Island expanded massively, training nearly 250,000 recruits 1941-1945.

- The entire 1944 graduating class of the Citadel in Charleston was inducted into the armed forces—possibly the only time an entire class was drafted at once.

The Postwar Boom

Up in Aiken, the construction of the sprawling Savannah River Site hydrogen-bomb plant in the early 1950s forced the relocation of thousands of citizens, mostly low-income African Americans. Although environmentally problematic, the site has continued to provide many jobs to the area.

Myrtle Beach and the Grand Strand were already the breeding ground of that unique South Carolina dance called the shag. The postwar era marked the shag's heyday, as carefree young South Carolinians flocked to beachfront pavilions to enjoy this indigenous form of music, sort of a white variation on the regional black rhythm and blues of the time.

The postwar U.S. infatuation with the automobile—and its troublesome child, the suburb—brought exponential growth to the great cities of the coast. The first bridge to Hilton Head Island was built in 1956, leading to the first of many resort developments, Sea Pines, in 1961. On many outlying islands, electricity came for the first time. With rising coastal populations came pressure to demolish more and more fine old buildings to put parking lots and high-rises in their place. A backlash grew among the cities' elites, aghast at the destruction of so much history. The immediate postwar era brought about the formation of both the Historic Charleston Foundation, which began the financially and politically difficult work of protecting historic districts from the wrecking ball of "progress." They weren't always successful, but the work of these organizations—mostly older women from the upper crust—laid the foundation for the successful coastal tourist industry to come, as well as preserving important American history for the ages.

Civil Rights

Contrary to popular opinion, the civil rights era wasn't just a blip in the 1960s. The gains of that decade were the fruits of efforts begun decades earlier. Many of the efforts involved efforts to expand black suffrage. Though African Americans had secured the nominal right to vote years before, primary contests were not under the jurisdiction of federal law. As a result, Democratic Party primary elections—the de facto general elections because of that party's total dominance in the South at the time—were effectively closed to African American voters. In Charleston, the Democratic primary was opened to African Americans for the first time in 1947.

In 1960 the Charleston Municipal Golf Course voluntarily integrated to avoid a court battle. Lunch counter sit-ins happened all over South Carolina, including the episode of the "Friendship Nine" in Rock Hill. Martin Luther King Jr. visited South Carolina in the late 1960s, speaking in Charleston in 1967 and helping reestablish the Penn Center on St. Helena Island as not only a cultural center but a center of political activism as well. The hundred-day strike of hospital workers at the Medical University of South Carolina in 1969—right after King's assassination—got national attention and was the culmination of Charleston's struggle for civil rights. By the end of the 1960s, the city council of

Charleston had elected its first black alderman, and the next phase in local history began.

The South Carolinian most closely associated with the civil rights era is the Reverend Jesse Jackson. Although the Greenville native has operated out of Chicago for most of his career, his early work with Martin Luther King in the South put an indelible stamp on the struggle for civil rights.

While South Carolina avoided much of the large-scale violence that plagued many other parts of the country during the civil rights era, there was one exception. A drive to peacefully integrate a whites-only bowling alley in Orangeburg turned violent one February night in 1968 when a crowd of African Americans confronted local police. When police opened fire with buckshot, 3 men were killed and nearly 30 wounded in what would be known as the "Orangeburg Massacre."

Both major universities in the state integrated without major incident in 1963: first Clemson University (then Clemson College) followed rapidly by the University of South Carolina. Only eight years after the University of South Carolina integrated, an African American was elected student body president.

A Coast Reborn

While the story of the South Carolina coastal boom actually begins in the 1950s with Charles Fraser's development of Sea Pines Plantation on Hilton Head—forever changing that barrier island—the decade of the 1970s was pivotal to the future success of the South Carolina coast.

In Charleston, the historic tenure of Mayor Joe Riley began in 1975, and as of this writing he is still in that office. The Irish American has broken precedents and forged key alliances, reviving not only the local economy but tamping down age-old racial tensions. Beginning with downtown's Charleston Place, Riley embarked on a series of high-profile public works projects to reinvigorate the then-moribund Charleston historic area. King

Street would soon follow. Tourism in the Holy City increased 60 percent 1970-1976.

The coast's combination of beautiful scenery and cheap labor proved irresistible to the movie and TV industry, which began filming many series and movies in the area in the 1970s, which continues to this day. Beaufort in particular would emerge from its stately slumber as the star of several popular films, including *The Great Santini* and *The Big Chill*. Of course, Myrtle Beach had been a leisure getaway for generations, but with the 1980s and the building of the Barefoot Landing retail and lodging development—followed by many others like it—the Grand Strand entered the first tier of American tourist destinations, where it remains.

Charleston received its first major challenge since the Civil War in 1989 when Hurricane Hugo slammed into the South Carolina coast just north of town. The Holy City, including many of its most historic locations, was massively damaged, with hardly a tree left standing. In a testament to the toughness beneath Charleston's genteel veneer, the city not only rebounded but came back stronger. In perhaps typically mercantile fashion, Charlestonians used the devastation of Hugo as a reason to introduce a new round of residential construction to the entire area, particularly the surrounding islands.

The most recent phenomenon on the coast has been the exponential increase in golf and retirement communities in the Beaufort-Bluffton area. The largest development, Sun City, has brought thousands of retirees to a habitat that is not naturally able to support this level of human density. Despite a recent emphasis on more environmentally friendly development, it remains to be seen whether local and state planners and elected officials will have the wisdom to regulate the more land- and water-intensive projects.

Change Comes to the Upstate

Greenville was still calling itself the "Textile Capital of the World" as late as 1980, but the mill culture of the Upstate had largely disintegrated by the 1950s, victim of the car culture and increased opportunity elsewhere. By the 1970s the industry was further threatened by international competition.

By the dawn of the 1990s, however, the Upstate was well positioned to attract foreign capital to fill the void left by the almost complete annihilation of the textile industry. In 1988, European tire maker Michelin ushered in this new era by locating a manufacturing facility near Greenville. In 1992, German auto manufacturer BMW announced its North American factory would be based in Spartanburg County. Today, the Upstate hosts literally hundreds of foreign firms, and the resulting influx of both money and transplants from other regions and countries has brought rapid socioeconomic change to the region, the most visible being Greenville's Main Street, once an unsightly four-lane affair, now shrunk to a pedestrian-friendly two lanes and augmented with cozy shops, restaurants, and hotels.

Conservatism and Controversy

South Carolina's movement into the future, while inexorable, has been slow and fraught with missteps, most of them related to the state's long embrace of political and social conservatism. The most notable example was the controversy in the late 1990s over the display of the Confederate battle flag over the State House in Columbia, the last Southern capitol to continue a practice begun as a protest of integration in the 1960s. Facing a vast boycott of the entire state by the National Collegiate Athletic Association, including a threat to remove the lucrative Final Four basketball tournament, the state relented—sort of. While moving the flag might seem like a no-brainer—indeed, the business community was strongly supportive of the move—no state politician wanted to be the one to risk the ire of conservative white "heritage"-minded voters, not an insignificant voting bloc in South Carolina. After a dramatic debate in the legislature that was quite emotional on both sides, a compromise solution was found in 2000 that left neither side satisfied: The rebel banner was moved to a different location on the State House grounds. After the Charleston church shooting in 2015, the flag was finally moved to the nearby Confederate Relic Room and Museum.

A more ironically humorous episode involving the State House came in 2003, when the inscription on the statue of archconservative U.S. Senator Strom Thurmond was changed to acknowledge the former segregationist's illegitimate children by an African American mistress. A truly unfortunate controversy ensued during the presidential election campaign of 2000, when an appearance by then-candidate George W. Bush at Bob Jones University in Greenville brought out the news that the school's longtime ban on interracial dating was still in effect. President Bob Jones III immediately rescinded the ban.

A lesser echo took place in Greenville during the 2008 election campaign, when a Catholic bishop in Greenville stated that any parishioner who voted for Barack Obama was not eligible for Communion, supposedly because of the Democrat's pro-choice position on the abortion issue. Although the Vatican quickly invalidated the bishop's ill-timed policy, it was another embarrassment for the state.

Not all the controversies have had to do with race, however. The once all-male Citadel in Charleston is still struggling with the issue of gender following a 1990s court decision requiring them to open their doors to female applicants. In 1994 Shannon Faulkner became the first female to enter Citadel day classes. Her physical unreadiness and relentless hazing by fellow students combined to force her departure shortly thereafter. In 1996 another four women enrolled, and two left because they were harassed in a similar fashion. The first female graduate—who was also the daughter of the college commandant—got her degree in 1999. Today, female day-students at the Citadel are more common (night graduate courses have been coed for quite a while). But episodes of sexual harassment are still alleged to be more common than on typical campuses.

Government and Economy

GOVERNMENT

For many decades, the South was completely dominated by the Democratic Party. Originally the party of slavery, segregation, and Jim Crow, the Democratic Party began attracting Southern African American voters in the 1930s with the election of Franklin D. Roosevelt. The allegiance of black voters was further cemented in the Truman, Kennedy, and Johnson administrations. The region would remain solidly Democratic until a backlash against the civil rights movement of the 1960s drove many white Southerners, ironically enough, into the party of Lincoln, the Republicans. This added racial element, so confounding to Americans from other parts of the country, remains just as potent today.

The default mode in the South is that white voters are massively Republican and black voters massively Democratic. Since South Carolina is 69 percent white, there is an overwhelming Republican dominance. The GOP currently controls the governor's mansion and both houses of the state legislature. However, the coastal areas and parts of the Midlands, with their large, predominantly Democratic African American populations, function somewhat separately from this realignment.

But don't make the mistake of assuming that local African Americans are particularly liberal because of their voting habits. Deeply religious and traditional in background and upbringing, African Americans in South Carolina are among the most socially conservative people in the region, even if their choice of political party does not always reflect that.

South Carolina's presidential primary is the first in the South, and as such carries more than its share of influence.

ECONOMY

South Carolina has experienced over a century's worth of profound changes in economy and business. The rice-growing industry moved offshore in the late 1800s, and the center of the cotton trade moved to the Gulf states in the early 1900s. That left timber as the main cash crop all up and down the coast, specifically huge pine tree farms to feed the pulp and paper business. For most of the 20th century, the largest employers along the coast were massive sulfur-spewing paper mills that had as big an effect on the local environment as on its economy. But even that is changing as Asian competition is driving paper companies

to sell off their tracts for real estate development—from an environmental perspective, not necessarily a more welcome scenario.

Despite the decline of major industries in the area—textile, furniture, and fishing—many towns and cities have made a deft transition into the global economy. Of course, tourism is also an important factor in the local economies of the area, particularly in seasonal resort-oriented areas like Hilton Head, Myrtle Beach, and Kiawah and Seabrook Islands. Charleston also has a well-honed tourism infrastructure, bringing at least $5 billion per year into the local economy; it is routinely voted one of the top three American cities to visit.

Another huge economic development on the coast has been the exponential growth of the Charleston seaport. From the 1990s on, the quickened pace of globalization has brought enormous investment, volume, and expansion to area port facilities.

People and Culture

Contrary to how the state is portrayed in the media, South Carolina is hardly exclusive to natives with thick flowery accents who still obsess over the Civil War and eat grits three meals a day. As you will quickly discover, the entire coastal area and much of the Upstate is becoming heavily populated with transplants from other parts of the country. In some of these places, you can actually go quite a long time without hearing even one of those Scarlett O'Hara accents.

Some of this is due to the region's increasing attractiveness to professionals and artists, drawn by the temperate climate, natural beauty, and business-friendly environment. Part of it is due to its increasing attractiveness to retirees, most of them from the frigid Northeast. Indeed, in some places, chief among them Hilton Head, the most common accent is a New York or New Jersey one, and a Southern accent is rare.

In any case, don't make the common mistake of assuming you're coming to a place where footwear is optional and electricity is a recent development (although it's true that many of the islands didn't get electricity until the 1950s and 1960s). Because so much new construction has gone on in the South in the last 25 years or so, you might find some aspects of the infrastructure—specifically the roads and the electrical utilities—actually superior to where you came from.

POPULATION

The 2010 U.S. Census put South Carolina's population at 4,679,230. Population statistics for individual cities are quite misleading because of South Carolina's notoriously strict annexation laws, which make it nearly impossible for a city to annex growing suburbs. For example, while the cities of Greenville and Spartanburg are listed as having populations of approximately 58,000 and 37,000, respectively, in practice this is grossly inaccurate; the combined Greenville-Spartanburg area actually has well over one million residents. The city of Anderson technically has only about 27,000 residents, but Anderson County has over 200,000.

In rough order of rank, the largest official metropolitan areas in South Carolina are Columbia (767,000), Charleston, North Charleston, and Summerville (664,000), Greenville, Mauldin, and Easley (636,000), Myrtle Beach, North Myrtle Beach, and Conway (329,000), Florence (200,000), and Hilton Head and Beaufort (170,000).

Racial Makeup

Its legacy as the center of the U.S. slave trade and plantation culture means that South Carolina continues to have a large African American population, about 28 percent of the total. The coast has a higher percentage, with Charleston at about 31 percent African American and Georgetown about 40 percent. Portions of the Midlands are heavily African American as well; Orangeburg, for example, is 60 percent black. The Upstate has the lowest proportion of African Americans. Seneca, for example, is only 8 percent black; Spartanburg and nearby Gaffney have the highest proportions in the Upstate, at about 20 percent.

One unfortunate legacy of South Carolina's history is the residual existence of a certain amount of de facto segregation. Visitors are often shocked to see how some residential areas even today still break sharply on racial lines—as do schools, with most public schools mostly black and most private schools overwhelmingly white. However, despite persistent media portrayals, overt racism is extremely rare in the areas covered in this book. In remote areas an interracial couple might get some disapproving looks, but in any urban area, hardly anyone will bat an eye.

The Hispanic population, as elsewhere in the United States, is growing rapidly, but statistics can be misleading. Although Hispanic populations are growing at a triple-digit clip in the region, they still remain only about 5 percent of South Carolina's total population. Bilingual signage is becoming more common but is still quite rare.

RELIGION
The Coast

The Lowcountry, and Charleston in particular, is unusual in the Deep South for its wide variety of religious faiths. While South Carolina remains overwhelmingly Protestant—over 80 percent of all Christians in the state are members of some Protestant denomination, chief among them Southern Baptist and Methodist—the coast's cosmopolitan polyglot history has made it a real melting pot of faiths.

The Lowcountry was originally dominated by the Episcopal Church (known as the Anglican Church in other countries), but from early on it was also a haven for those of other faiths. Various types of Protestant groups soon arrived, including French Huguenots and Congregationalists. Owing to vestigial prejudice from the European realpolitik of the founding era, the Roman Catholic presence in South Carolina was late in arriving, but once it came, it was there to stay, especially on the coast.

Most unusually of all for the Deep South, Charleston had a large Jewish population that was a key participant in the city from the very first days of settlement. Sephardic Jews, primarily of Portuguese descent, were among the first settlers. One of them, Judah Benjamin, spent a lot of time in the Carolinas and became the Confederacy's secretary of state. Indeed, up to about 1830, South Carolina had the largest Jewish population of any state in the union.

The Midlands

Because of the large numbers of German and Swiss settlers that came to the Midlands, the region has more of a Lutheran quality today. There is even a notable Mennonite presence, particularly in Blackville and Abbeville.

Local Food

- **Blenheim Ginger Ale:** Generally pronounced "BLEN-um," this heady and addictive retro-style brew is still obtainable at country roadside stores throughout the state. Even if they don't have a beat-up Blenheim sign out front, feel free to inquire inside.

- **Boiled peanuts:** Usually pronounced "ball peanuts" and sold from roadside stands, this soft, salty, mouthwatering treat—usually served in plastic grocery bags—is just the ticket on a hot South Carolina day.

- **Chick-fil-A:** This Atlanta-based chain, which you'll often find inside South Carolina malls, boasts a signature pressure-cooked chicken sandwich. Enjoy them only Monday-Saturday, though—the owners are devout Christians and give all their employees Sunday off to observe the Sabbath.

- **Coca-Cola:** In local patois it's "Coke-Cola." In any case, never call it "pop"—in South Carolina that's not a soft drink, it's the sound a firecracker makes.

- **Duke's:** It seems almost every little town in the state has a barbecue place called Duke's. At one time most of them had a pedigree descending from the Earl Duke dynasty of Orangeburg, but these days many are independently owned.

- **Iced tea:** Down here it's just "ice tea," or even just "tea," and the default mode is sweet to extremely sweet. If you want it unsweetened, or "unsweet," you'll have to ask. You'll usually get a lemon wedge in any case.

- **Piggly Wiggly:** Based in Memphis, Tennessee, "the Pig" is the supermarket of choice for much of South Carolina, especially in semirural areas.

The Upstate

The Upstate was first settled by Presbyterians, hard-shell Baptists, and various Christian fundamentalists. Their collective attitude was much more sternly moralistic, and this conservatism has colored the region's sensibilities to this day. The Greenville area in particular is a hotbed of fundamentalism, with the archconservative Bob Jones University the premier example. Sprawling, well-attended **megachurches** dot the region and are increasingly the focal point of religious activity—to the dismay of the pastors of smaller, older churches.

And, of course, who could forget the tragicomic reign of televangelists Jim and Tammy Faye Bakker? Though both Midwesterners, their now-defunct religious empire, Heritage USA in Fort Mill, South Carolina, became a byword for kitsch and corruption.

MANNERS

The prevalence and importance of good manners is the main thing to keep in mind about the South. While it's tempting for folks from more outwardly assertive parts of the world to take this as a sign of weakness, that would be a major mistake. Bottom line: Good manners will take you a long way here. Southerners use manners, courtesy, and chivalry as a system of social interaction with one goal above all: to maintain the established order during times of stress. A relic from a time of extreme class stratification, etiquette and chivalry are ways to make sure that the elites are never threatened—and, on the other hand, that even those on the lowest rungs of society are afforded at least a basic amount of dignity. But as a practical matter, it's also true that Southerners of all classes, races, and backgrounds rely on the observation of manners as a way to sum up people quickly. To any Southerner, regardless of class or race, your use or neglect of basic manners and proper respect indicates how seriously they should take you—not in a socioeconomic sense, but in the big picture.

The typical Southern sense of humor—equal parts irony, self-deprecation, and good-natured teasing—is part of the code. Southerners are loath to criticize another individual directly, so often they'll instead take the opportunity to make an ironic joke. Self-deprecating humor is also much more common in the South than in other areas of the country. Because of this, you're also expected to be able to take a joke yourself without being too sensitive.

Etiquette

It's rude here to inquire about personal finances, along with the usual no-go areas of religion and politics. Here are some other specific etiquette tips:

- **Basics:** Be liberal with "please" and "thank you," or conversely, "no, thank you" if you want to decline a request or offering.

- **Eye contact:** With the exception of very elderly African Americans, eye contact is not only accepted in the South, it's encouraged. In fact, to avoid eye contact in the South means you're likely a shady character with something to hide.

- **Handshake:** Men should always shake hands with a *very* firm, confident grip and appropriate eye contact. It's OK for women to offer a handshake in professional circles, but is otherwise not required.

- **Chivalry:** When men open doors for women here—and they will—it is not thought of as a patronizing gesture but as a sign of respect. Also, if a female of any age or appearance drops an object on the floor, don't be surprised if several nearby males jump to pick it up. This is considered appropriate behavior and not at all unusual.

- **The elderly:** Senior citizens—or really anyone obviously older than you—should

be called "sir" or "ma'am." Again, this is not a patronizing gesture in the South but is considered a sign of respect. Also, in any situation where you're dealing with someone in the service industry, addressing them as "sir" or "ma'am" regardless of their age will get you far.

- **Bodily contact:** Interestingly, though public displays of affection by romantic couples are generally frowned upon here, Southerners are otherwise pretty touchy-feely once they get to know you. Full-on body hugs are rare, but Southerners who are well acquainted often say hello or good-bye with a small hug.

- **Driving:** With the exception of the interstate perimeter highways around the larger cities, drivers in the South are generally less aggressive than in other regions. Cutting sharply in front of someone in traffic is taken as a personal offense. If you need to cut in front of someone, poke the nose of your car a little bit in that direction and wait for a car to slow down and wave you in front. Don't forget to wave back as a thank-you. Similarly, using a car horn can also be taken as a personal affront, so use your horn sparingly, if at all. In rural areas, don't be surprised to see the driver of an oncoming car offer a little wave. This is an old custom, sadly dying out. Just give a little wave back; they're trying to be friendly.

THE GUN CULTURE

One of the most misunderstood aspects of the South is the value the region places on the personal possession of firearms. No doubt, the 2nd Amendment to the U.S. Constitution ("A well regulated Militia, being necessary to the security of a free State, the right of the people to keep and bear Arms, shall not be infringed") is well known here and fiercely protected, at the governmental and at the grassroots levels. But while guns are indeed more casually accepted in everyday life in the South, the reason for this has less to do with personal safety than with the rural background of the region and its long history of hunting. If you're traveling on a back road and you see a pickup truck with a gun rack in the back containing one or more rifles or shotguns, this is not intended to be menacing or intimidating. Chances are the driver is a hunter, nothing more.

State laws do tend to be significantly more accommodating of gun owners here than in much of the rest of the country. It is legal to carry a concealed handgun in South Carolina with the proper permit, and you need no permit at all to possess a weapon for self-defense. However, there are regulations regarding how a handgun must be conveyed in automobiles.

South Carolina now has a so-called "stand your ground" law, whereby if you're in imminent lethal danger, you do not first have to try to run away before resorting to deadly force to defend yourself.

Essentials

Transportation

AIR

There are six key airports serving South Carolina. **Charleston International Airport** (CHS, 5500 International Blvd., 843/767-1100, www.iflychs.com) is served by the major national airlines and is a primary gateway to the entire coast. **Columbia Metropolitan Airport** (CAE, 3000 Aviation Way, 803/822-5000, www.columbiaairport. com) is a good access point for the center of the state, and **Greenville-Spartanburg International Airport** (GSP, 2000 GSP Dr., Greer, 864/877-7426, www.gspairport.com) is a good point of entry for the upper half of the state.

Because of the lack of interstate highway coverage in this area, **Myrtle Beach International Airport** (MYR, 1100 Jetport Rd., 843/448-1589, www.flymyrtlebeach.com) is best used only if Myrtle Beach is your primary destination. **Savannah/Hilton Head International Airport** (SAV, 400 Airways Ave., 912/964-0514, www.savannahairport. com), off I-95 in Savannah, Georgia, is perhaps the best access point to enjoy the lower portion of the South Carolina coast, and definitely Hilton Head.

CAR

South Carolina is extremely well served by the U.S. interstate highway system. The main interstate arteries into the region are the north-south I-95, I-77, and I-85, and the east-west I-20 and I-26. Charleston has a perimeter interstate, I-526 (the Mark Clark Expressway). Columbia's perimeter is I-126. Greenville has two, I-185 and I-386; Spartanburg's is I-585.

Keep in mind that despite being heavily traveled, the Myrtle Beach area is not served by any interstate highway. A common landmark road through the coastal region is U.S. 17, which used to be known as the Coastal Highway and currently goes by a number of local incarnations as it winds its way along the coast.

Unfortunately, the stories you've heard about speed traps in small South Carolina towns are correct. Always strictly obey the speed limit, and if you're pulled over, always deal with the police respectfully and truthfully, whether or not you agree with their judgment.

Winter driving in South Carolina is generally easy, since it rarely snows. During periods of heavy rainfall, however, unpaved roads can become quite muddy. Should you be unlucky enough to be on the coast during a mandatory hurricane evacuation, be aware that some roads, especially interstate highways, will become one-way westbound for all lanes to streamline the evacuation. In any case, always follow all law enforcement directions. For updates on planned slowdowns due to construction projects, go to www.dot.state.sc.us.

South Carolina's copious network of interstate highways offers numerous **rest stops.** They are often a very welcome sight, since the state's heavily rural nature means services can be hard to come by on the road. The following is a list of rest areas.

- **I-95:** Mile markers 5 (northbound near the Georgia border), 17 (Ridgeland, no facilities), 47 (south of Walterboro), 99 (Santee), 139 (south of Florence), 171 (north of Florence), and 195 (southbound at the North Carolina border).

- **I-26:** Mile markers 63 (north of Newberry), 123 (south of Columbia), 150 (eastbound at Orangeburg), 152 (westbound at Orangeburg), 202 (westbound at Summerville), and 204 (eastbound at Summerville).

- **I-85:** Mile markers 17 (northbound at Anderson), 24 (southbound at Anderson), and 89 (Gaffney).
- **I-20:** Mile marker 93 (Camden).
- **I-77:** Mile marker 66 (south of Rock Hill).

While all rest stops are clean, safe, and well equipped, remember there is no gasoline sold at any of them.

Car Rentals

Unless you're going to hunker down in one city, you will need auto transportation to enjoy South Carolina. Renting a car is easy and fairly inexpensive as long as you play by the rules, which are simple. You need either a valid driver's license from any U.S. state or a valid International Driving Permit from your home country, and you must be at least 25 years old.

If you do not either purchase insurance coverage from the rental company or already have insurance coverage through the credit card you rent the car with, you will be 100 percent responsible for any damage caused to the car during your rental period. While purchasing insurance at the time of rental is by no means mandatory, it might be worth the extra expense just to have that peace of mind.

Key rental car companies include **Hertz** (www.hertz.com), **Avis** (www.avis.com), **Thrifty** (www.thrifty.com), **Enterprise** (www.enterprise.com), and **Budget** (www.budget.com). Some rental car locations are in the cities, but the vast majority of outlets are at airports, so plan accordingly. The airport locations have the bonus of generally being open for longer hours than their in-town counterparts.

TRAIN

Passenger rail service in the car-dominated United States is far behind that in other developed nations, both in quantity and quality. Many towns and cities in South Carolina are served by the national rail system, **Amtrak** (www.amtrak.com), which is pretty good, if erratic at times.

With the notable exception of the Grand Strand, South Carolina is well-served by Amtrak. You'll find stations in Camden, Charleston, Clemson, Columbia, Florence, Greenville, and Spartanburg. The closest Amtrak station to the Beaufort/Hilton Head area is in Yemassee.

BUS

South Carolina is well-served by the privately owned bus company **Greyhound** (www.greyhound.com), which has stops throughout the state, including Aiken, Anderson, Beaufort, Camden, Charleston, Columbia, Florence, Georgetown, Greenville, Myrtle Beach, Orangeburg, Spartanburg, Sumter, and Walterboro. While rates are reasonable and the vehicles are high-quality, this is by far the slowest possible way to travel around the state, as buses stop frequently and sometimes for lengthy periods of time.

BOAT

One of the coolest things about the South Carolina coast is the prevalence of the Intracoastal Waterway, a combined artificial and natural sheltered seaway from Miami to Maine. Many boaters enjoy touring the coast by simply meandering up or down the Intracoastal, putting in at marinas along the way.

Recreation

STATE PARKS AND NATURAL AREAS

South Carolina has one of the best state park systems in the United States, with a total of 46 parks and natural areas. Seventeen of the parks were built by the Civilian Conservation Corps during FDR's New Deal and boast distinctive, rustic, and well-made architecture. While primitive camping is available in South Carolina, the general preference here is for plusher surroundings more conducive to a family vacation. Many state parks offer fully equipped rental cabins with modern amenities that rival a hotel's. Generally speaking, such facilities tend to sell out early, so make reservations as soon as you can. Keep in mind that during the high season (Mar.-Nov.) there are minimum rental requirements. Be aware that the closer you are to the Appalachian Mountains, the higher the rainfall. Be prepared to camp wet if you're camping in the Upstate near the Blue Ridge. Dogs are allowed in state parks, but they must be leashed at all times.

While admission and lodging expenses are very reasonable at South Carolina state parks, long-term visitors can save money on frequent visits by purchasing a **State Park Passport** ($75), which covers a full year of admission from the date of purchase. You currently can't get them online but must charge by phone (803/734-0156). Get one online at www.southcarolinaparks.com.

NATIONAL WILDLIFE REFUGES

There are seven federally administered National Wildlife Refuges (NWR) in South Carolina:

- **ACE Basin NWR** (www.fws.gov/acebasin)
- **Cape Romain NWR** (www.fws.gov/caperomain)
- **Carolina Sandhills NWR** (www.fws.gov/carolinasandhills)
- **Pinckney Island NWR** (www.fws.gov/pinckneyisland)
- **Santee NWR** (www.fws.gov/santee)
- **Savannah NWR** (www.fws.gov/savannah)
- **Waccamaw NWR** (www.fws.gov/waccamaw)

Admission is generally free. Access is limited to daytime hours (sunrise-sunset). Keep in mind that some hunting is allowed on some refuges.

BEACHES

Some of the best beaches in the country are in South Carolina. While upscale amenities aren't always there and they aren't very surfer-friendly, the area's beaches are outstanding for anyone looking for a relaxing scenic getaway.

By law, beaches in the United States are fully accessible to the public up to the high-tide mark during daylight hours, even if the beachfronts are private property and even if the only means of public access is by boat.

It is a misdemeanor to disturb sea oats, those wispy, waving, wheat-like plants among the dunes. Their root system is vital to keeping the beach intact. Also never disturb a turtle nesting area, whether it is marked or not.

The barrier islands of the Palmetto State have seen more private development than their Georgia counterparts. Some Carolina islands, like Kiawah, Fripp, and Seabrook, are not even accessible unless you are a guest at their affiliated resorts. This means that if you're not a guest, the only way to visit the beaches there is by boat, which I really don't advise.

The Grand Strand, of course, has many miles of beach, from North Myrtle Beach on down to Huntington Beach State Park. Charleston-area beaches include **Folly Beach, Sullivan's Island,** and **Isle of Palms.** Moving down the coast, some delightful beaches are at **Edisto Island** and **Hunting Island,** which both feature state parks with lodging.

Hilton Head Island has about 12 miles of beautiful family-friendly beaches, and while most of the island is devoted to private golf resorts, the beaches remain accessible to the general public with parking at four points: Driessen Beach Park, Coligny Beach Park, Alder Lane Beach Access, and Burkes Beach Road.

KAYAKING AND CANOEING

In the Grand Strand, you can enjoy kayaking on the Waccamaw River and Winyah Bay. Some key kayaking and canoeing areas in the Charleston area are Cape Romain National Wildlife Refuge, Shem Creek, Isle of Palms, Charleston Harbor, and the Stono River.

Farther south in the Lowcountry are the Ashepoo, Combahee, and Edisto blackwater rivers, which combine to form the ACE Basin. Next is Port Royal Sound near Beaufort. The Hilton Head-Bluffton area has good kayaking opportunities at Hilton Head's Calibogue Creek and Bluffton's May River.

Inland, some great kayaking opportunities can be found at many state parks and natural areas, including Congaree National Park and Woods Bay State Natural Area. You can also kayak or canoe on any of the great artificial reservoirs that dot inland South Carolina, including Lake Jocassee, Lake Hartwell, and Lake Marion.

FISHING AND BOATING

In coastal South Carolina, because of the large number of islands and wide area of salt marsh, life on the water is largely inseparable from life on the land. Fishing and boating are very common pursuits, and fish species include spotted sea trout, channel bass, flounder, grouper, mackerel, sailfish, whiting, shark, amberjack, and tarpon.

Freshwater fishing on the many artificial lakes in South Carolina is a huge business and a major driver of the state's economy. You'll find largemouth bass, bream, catfish, and crappie, among many more. Key freshwater fishing locations are Lakes Jocassee and Keowee in the Upstate; the "freshwater coast" along the Savannah River and Lakes Hartwell, Russell, and Thurmond; and the twin lakes of the Santee Cooper region, Marion and Moultrie.

It's easy to fish on piers, lakes, and streams, but if you're over age 16, you need to get a nonresident fishing license from the state. A nonresident fourteen-day license is $11. Go to www.dnr.sc.gov for more information or to purchase a license online.

The most popular places for **casual anglers** are the various public piers throughout the area. There are public fishing piers at North Myrtle Beach, Folly Beach, Edisto Beach State Park, and Hunting Island State Park. Two nice little public docks are at the North Charleston Riverfront Park on the grounds of the old Charleston Navy Yard and the Bluffton public landing on the May River. Many anglers cast off from abandoned bridges unless signage dictates otherwise, and fishing charters and marinas are common throughout the region.

GOLF

The first golf club in the United States was formed in Charleston, and South Carolina as a whole is one of the world's golf meccas. There is a great variety of facilities, from tony courses like the Pete Dye-designed Ocean Course at the **Kiawah Island Golf Resort** or **Harbour Town** on Sea Pines Plantation in Hilton Head, to the more **budget-conscious** courses in the Santee Cooper region, Myrtle Beach, and North Myrtle Beach.

Don't be shy about pursuing golf packages that combine lodging with links access.

South Carolina, especially the coastal area, is currently suffering from something of a glut of golf courses, and you can find some great deals online.

Travel Tips

WOMEN TRAVELING ALONE

Women should take the same precautions they would take anywhere else in the United States. Many women traveling to this region have to adjust to the prevalence of traditional chivalry. In the South, if a man opens a door for you, it's considered a sign of respect, not condescension.

Another adjustment is the possible assumption that two or three women who go to a bar or tavern together might be there to invite male companionship. This misunderstanding can happen anywhere, but in some parts of the South it might be more prevalent.

While small towns are generally very friendly and law-abiding, some are more economically depressed than others and hence prone to more crime. Always take common-sense precautions no matter how bucolic the setting may be.

TRAVELERS WITH DISABILITIES

While the vast majority of attractions and accommodations make every effort to comply with federal law regarding those with disabilities, as they're obligated to do, the historic nature of much of this region means that some structures simply cannot be retrofitted for maximum accessibility. This is something you'll need to find out on a case-by-case basis, so call ahead.

GAY AND LESBIAN TRAVELERS

Despite the region's essential conservatism, many areas in this state can be considered quite gay friendly, especially in bigger cities like Charleston. Visit **QNotes** (www.q-notes.com) for more information on LBGTQ resources in the state.

SENIOR TRAVELERS

Both because of the large proportion of retirees in South Carolina and because of the South's traditional respect for the elderly, the state is quite friendly to senior citizens. Many accommodations and attractions offer a seniors discount, which can add up over the course of a trip. Always inquire before making a reservation, however, as check-in time is sometimes too late.

TRAVELING WITH PETS

While the United States is very pet friendly, that friendliness rarely extends to restaurants and other indoor locations. More and more accommodations are allowing pet owners to bring pets, often for an added fee, but inquire before you arrive. In any case, keep your dog on a leash at all times. Some beaches in the area permit dog-walking at certain times of the year, but as a general rule, keep dogs off beaches unless you see signs saying otherwise.

Health and Safety

CRIME

While crime rates are generally above national averages in much of the state, especially in inner-city areas, incidents of crime in the more heavily touristed areas are no more common than elsewhere. In fact, these areas might be safer because of the amount of foot traffic and police attention.

By far the most common crime against visitors is simple theft, primarily from cars. (Pickpocketing, thankfully, is quite rare in the United States). Always lock your car doors. Conversely, only leave them unlocked if you're absolutely comfortable living without whatever's inside at the time. As a general rule, I try to lock valuables—such as CDs, a recent purchase, or my wife's purse—in the trunk. (Just make sure the "valet" button, allowing the trunk to be opened from the driver's area, is disabled.)

Should someone corner you and demand your wallet or purse, just give it to them. Unfortunately, the old advice to scream as loud as you can is no longer the deterrent it once was, and in fact may hasten aggressive action by the robber.

A very important general rule to remember is not to pull over for cars you do not recognize as law enforcement, no matter how urgently you might be asked to do so. This is not a common occurrence, but a possibility you should be aware of. A real police officer will know the correct steps to take to identify him or herself. If you find yourself having to guess, then do the safe thing and refuse to stop.

If you are the victim of a crime, *always call the police.* Law enforcement wants more information, not less, and at the very least you'll have an incident report in case you need to make an insurance claim for lost or stolen property.

Remember that in the United States as elsewhere, no good can come from a heated argument with a police officer. The place to prove a police officer wrong is in a court of law, perhaps with an attorney by your side, not at the scene.

For emergencies, always call 911.

AUTO ACCIDENTS

If you're in an auto accident, you're bound by law to wait for police to respond. Failure to do so can result in a "leaving the scene of an accident" charge or worse. In the old days, cars in accidents had to be left exactly where they came to rest until police gave permission to move or tow them. However, the states in this guide have recently loosened regulations so that if a car is blocking traffic as a result of an accident, the driver is allowed to move it enough to allow traffic to flow again. That is, if the car can be moved safely; if not, you're not required to move it out of the way.

Since it's illegal to drive without auto insurance, I'll assume you have some. And because you're insured, the best course of action in a minor accident, where injuries are unlikely, is to patiently wait for the police and give them your side of the story. In my experience, police react negatively to people who are too quick to start making accusations against other people. After that, let the insurance companies deal with it; that's what they're paid for.

If you suspect any injuries, call 911 immediately.

ILLEGAL DRUGS

Marijuana, heroin, methamphetamine, and cocaine and all its derivatives are illegal in the United States with only a few exceptions, none of which apply to South Carolina. The use of ecstasy and similar mood-elevators is also illegal.

ALCOHOL

The drinking age in all of the United States is 21. Most restaurants that serve alcoholic beverages allow those under 21 inside. Generally speaking, if only those over 21 are allowed inside, you will be greeted at the door by someone asking to see identification. These people are often poorly trained, and anything other than a state driver's license may confuse them, so be forewarned.

Drunk driving is a problem on U.S. roads. Always drive defensively, especially late at night, and obey all posted speed limits and road signs—and never assume the other driver will do the same. You may never drive with an open alcoholic beverage in the car, even if it belongs to a passenger.

GETTING SICK

Unlike most developed nations, the United States has no comprehensive national health care system. Visitors from other countries who need nonemergency medical attention are best served by going to freestanding medical clinics. The level of care is typically very good, but unfortunately you'll be paying out of pocket for the service.

For emergencies, however, do not hesitate to go to the closest hospital emergency room, where the level of care is generally also quite good, especially for trauma. Worry about payment later; emergency rooms in the United States are required to take true emergency cases whether or not the patient can pay for services.

Pharmaceuticals

Unlike in many other countries, antibiotics are available in the United States only on a prescription basis and are not available over the counter. Most cold, flu, and allergy remedies are available over the counter. While homeopathic remedies are gaining popularity in the United States, they are nowhere near as prevalent as in Europe.

Medications with the active ingredient ephedrine are available in the United States without a prescription, but their purchase is now tightly regulated to cut down on the use of these products to make the illegal drug methamphetamine.

NOT GETTING SICK
Vaccinations

As of this writing, there are no vaccination requirements to enter the United States. Contact your embassy before coming to confirm this before arrival, however.

In the autumn, at the beginning of flu season, preventive influenza vaccinations, simply called "flu shots," often become available at easily accessible locations like clinics, health departments, and even supermarkets.

Humidity, Heat, and Sun

There is only one way to fight the South's high heat and humidity, and that's to drink lots of fluids. A surprising number of people each year refuse to take this advice and find themselves in various states of dehydration, some of which can land you in a hospital. Remember: If you're thirsty, you're already suffering from dehydration. The thing to do is keep drinking fluids before you're thirsty, as a preventative action rather than a reaction.

Always use sunscreen, even on a cloudy day. If you do get a sunburn, get a pain relief product with aloe vera as an active ingredient. On extraordinarily sunny and hot summer days, don't even go outside between the hours of 10am and 2pm.

HAZARDS
Insects

Because of the recent increase in the mosquito-borne West Nile virus, the most important step to take in staying healthy in the Lowcountry and Southeast coast—especially if you have small children—is to keep mosquito bites to a minimum. Do this with a combination of mosquito repellent and long sleeves and long pants, if possible. Not every mosquito bite will give you the virus; in fact, chances are quite slim that one will. But don't take the chance if you don't have to.

The second major step in avoiding insect nastiness is to steer clear of **fire ants,** whose large gray or brown dirt nests are quite common in this area. They attack instantly and in great numbers, with little or no provocation.

They don't just bite; they inject you with poison from their stingers. In short, fire ants are not to be trifled with. While the only real remedy is the preventative one of never coming in contact with them, should you find yourself being bitten by fire ants, the first thing to do is to stay calm. Take off your shoes and socks and get as many of the ants off you as you can. Unless you've had a truly large number of bites—in which case you should seek medical help immediately—the best thing to do next is wash the area to get any venom off, and then disinfect it with alcohol if you have any handy. Then a topical treatment such as calamine lotion or hydrocortisone is advised. A fire ant bite will leave a red pustule that lasts about a week. Try your best not to scratch it so that it won't get infected.

Outdoor activity, especially in woodsy, undeveloped areas, may bring you in contact with another unpleasant indigenous creature, the tiny but obnoxious **chigger,** sometimes called the redbug. The bite of a chigger can't be felt, but the enzymes it leaves behind can lead to a very itchy little red spot. Contrary to folklore, putting fingernail polish on the itchy bite will not "suffocate" the chigger, because by this point the chigger itself is long gone. All you can do is get some topical itch or pain relief and go on with your life. The itching will eventually subside.

For **bee stings,** the best approach for those who aren't allergic to them is to immediately pull the stinger out, perhaps by scraping a credit card over the bite, and apply ice if possible. A topical treatment such as hydrocortisone or calamine lotion is advised. In my experience, the old folk remedy of tearing apart a cigarette and putting the tobacco leaves directly on the sting does indeed cut the pain. But that's not a medical opinion, so do with it what you will. A minor allergic reaction can be quelled by using an over-the-counter antihistamine. If the victim is severely allergic to bee stings, go to a hospital or call 911 for an ambulance.

Threats in the Water

While enjoying area beaches, a lot of visitors become inordinately worried about **shark attacks.** Every couple of summers there's a lot of hysteria about this, but the truth is that you're much more likely to slip and fall in a bathroom than you are even to come close to being bitten by a shark in these shallow Atlantic waters.

A far more common fate for area swimmers is to get stung by a **jellyfish,** or sea nettle. They can sting you in the water, but most often beachcombers are stung by stepping on beached jellyfish stranded on the sand by the tide. If you get stung, don't panic; wash the area with saltwater, not freshwater, and apply vinegar or baking soda.

Lightning

The southeastern United States is home to vicious, fast-moving thunderstorms, often with an amazing amount of electrical activity. Death by lightning strike occurs often in this region and is something that should be taken quite seriously. The general rule of thumb is that if you're in the water, whether at the beach or in a swimming pool, and hear thunder, get out of the water immediately until the storm passes. If you're on dry land and see lightning flash a distance away, that's your cue to seek safety indoors. Whatever you do, do not play sports outside when lightning threatens.

Information and Services

MONEY

Automated teller machines (ATMs) are available in all the urban areas covered in this guide. Be aware that if the ATM is not owned by your bank, not only will that ATM likely charge you a service fee, but your bank may charge you one as well. While ATMs have made traveler's checks less essential, traveler's checks do have the important advantage of accessibility, as some rural and less-developed areas have few or no ATMs. You can purchase traveler's checks at just about any bank.

Establishments in the United States only accept the national currency, the U.S. dollar. To exchange foreign money, go to any bank.

Generally, establishments that accept credit cards will feature stickers on the front entrance with the logo of the particular cards they accept, although this is not a legal requirement. The use of debit cards has dramatically increased in the United States. Most retail establishments and many fast-food chains are now accepting them. Make sure you get a receipt whenever you use a credit card or a debit card.

Tipping

Unlike many other countries, service workers in the United States depend on tips for the bulk of their income. In restaurants and bars, the usual tip is 15 percent of the pretax portion of the bill for acceptable service, 20 percent (or more) for excellent service. For large parties, usually six or more, a 15-18 percent gratuity is sometimes automatically added to the bill.

It's also customary to tip hotel bell staff about $2 per bag when they assist you at check-in and checkout of your hotel; some sources recommend a minimum of $5.

For taxi drivers, 15 percent is customary as long as the cab is clean, smoke-free, and you were treated with respect and taken to your destination with a minimum of fuss.

INTERNET ACCESS

Visitors from Europe and Asia are likely to be disappointed at the quality of Internet access in the United States, particularly the area covered in this guide. Fiber-optic lines are still a rarity, and while many hotels and B&Bs now offer in-room Internet access—some charge, some don't, so make sure to ask ahead—the quality and speed of the connection might prove poor.

Wireless (Wi-Fi) networks also are less than impressive, although that situation continues to improve on a daily basis in coffeehouses, hotels, and airports. Unfortunately, many Wi-Fi access points in private establishments are for rental only.

PHONES

Generally speaking, the United States is behind Europe and much of Asia in terms of cell phone technology. Unlike Europe, where "pay-as-you-go" refills are easy to find, most American cell phone users pay for monthly plans through a handful of providers. Still, you should have no problem with cell phone coverage in urban areas. Where it gets much less dependable is in rural areas and on beaches. Bottom line: Don't depend on having cell service everywhere you go. As with a regular landline, any time you face an emergency, call 911 on your cell phone.

All phone numbers in the United States are seven digits preceded by a three-digit area code. You may have to dial a 1 before a phone number if it's a long-distance call, even within the same area code.

Resources

Suggested Reading

NONFICTION

Ferling, John E. *Almost a Miracle: The American Victory in the War of Independence.* New York: Oxford University Press, 2007. Not only perhaps the best single volume detailing the military aspects of the Revolutionary War, but absolutely indispensable for learning about the key role of the Carolinas and Georgia in it.

Klein, Maury. *Days of Defiance: Sumter, Secession, and the Coming of the Civil War.* New York: Vintage, 1999. A gripping and vivid account of the lead-up to war, with Charleston as the focal point.

Robinson, Sally Ann. *Gullah Home Cooking the Daufuskie Island Way.* Chapel Hill: UNC Press, 2007. Subtitled *Smokin' Joe Butter Beans, Ol' 'Fuskie Fried Crab Rice, Sticky-Bush Blackberry Dumpling, and Other Sea Island Favorites,* this cookbook by a native Daufuskie Islander features a foreword by Pat Conroy.

Todd, Leonard. *Carolina Clay: The Life and Legend of the Slave Potter Dave.* New York: W. W. Norton, 2008. A fascinating exploration of the world of the largely anonymous African American artisans who created the now-hot genre known as Edgefield pottery. We know the story of one of them, the man simply known as Dave, because he was literate enough to sign his name to his amazing works—an extremely unusual (and dangerous) act for the time.

Woodward, C. Vann, ed. *Mary Chesnut's Civil War.* New Haven, CT: Yale University Press, 1981. The Pulitzer Prize-winning compilation of the sardonically funny and quietly heartbreaking letters of Charleston's Mary Chesnut during the Civil War.

FICTION

Caldwell, Erskine. *God's Little Acre.* Athens: University of Georgia Press, 1995. Scandalous in its time for its graphic sexuality, Caldwell's best-selling 1933 novel chronicles socioeconomic decay in the mill towns of South Carolina and Georgia during the Great Depression.

Conroy, Pat. *The Lords of Discipline.* New York: Bantam, 1985. For all practical purposes set at the Citadel, this novel takes you behind the scenes of the notoriously insular Charleston military college.

Conroy, Pat. *The Water Is Wide.* New York: Bantam, 1987. Immortal account of Conroy's time teaching African American children in a two-room schoolhouse on "Yamacraw" (actually Daufuskie) Island.

Kinsella, W. P. *Shoeless Joe.* New York: Houghton Mifflin, 1982. Magical realist novel about a man who hears a voice telling him to "build it and they will come" and constructs a baseball diamond in an Iowa cornfield. Later adapted into the hit film *Field of Dreams* starring Kevin Costner and—with a totally out-of-place New York accent—Ray Liotta as Greenville, South Carolina, native "Shoeless" Joe Jackson.

Poe, Edgar Allan. *The Gold Bug*. London: Hesperus Press, 2007. Inspired by his stint there with the U.S. Army, the great American author set this classic short story on Sullivan's Island, South Carolina, near Charleston.

Internet Resources

TOURISM AND RECREATION

Discover South Carolina
http://discoversouthcarolina.com
The state's official tourism website.

South Carolina State Parks
www.southcarolinaparks.com
This site offers historical and visitor information for South Carolina's excellent network of state park sites, including camping reservations.

NATURE

South Carolina Department of Natural Resources
www.dnr.sc.gov
Advice on how best to enjoy South Carolina's great outdoors, whether you're an angler, a kayaker, a bird-watcher, a hiker, or a biker.

HISTORY AND CULTURE

South Carolina Information Highway
www.sciway.net
An eclectic cornucopia of interesting South Carolina history and assorted background facts makes for an interesting Internet portal into all things Palmetto State.

Index

QR

S

List of Maps

Photo Credits

Title page photo: blooming magnolia © Jaimie Tuchman | Dreamstime; page 4 © Wollwerth | Dreamstime. com; page 5 (top) Meunierd | Dreamstime.com, (bottom) © Jim Morekis; page 6 (top left) © Bandu | Dreamstime.com, (top right) © Marieclaire66 | Dreamstime.com, (bottom) © Sepavo | Dreamstime.com; page 7 (top) © Andykazie | Dreamstime.com, (bottom left) © Crlocklear | Dreamstime.com, (bottom right) © Jilllang | Dreamstime.com; page 8 © Dccastelhano | Dreamstime.com; page 9 (top) © Meunierd | Dreamstime.com, (bottom left) © Gnagel | Dreamstime.com, (bottom right) © Cvandyke | Dreamstime. com; pages 10-11 © Chinklephotographer | Dreamstime.com; page 12 (top) © Sepavo | Dreamstime. com, (bottom) Courtesy of Pinehurst Resort; page 13 (top) © Jim Morekis, (bottom) © Kirkikisphoto | Dreamstime.com; page 15 © Pipehorse | Dreamstime.com; page 16 © Jim Morekis; page 19 © Dcslim | Dreamstime.com; page 20 © Jim Morekis; page 21 © Wilsilver77 | Dreamstime.com; page 24 (both) © Jim Morekis; page 25 © Jim Morekis; page 31 © Jim Morekis; page 33 © Jim Morekis; page 37 © Jim Morekis; page 38 © Wickedgood | Dreamstime.com; page 40 © Jim Morekis; page 41 © Jim Morekis; page 44 © Jim Morekis; page 45 © Jim Morekis; page 46 © Jim Morekis; page 48 © Jim Morekis; page 50 © Jim Morekis; page 54 © Tinamou | Dreamstime.com; page 59 © Jim Morekis; page 67 © Wickedgood | Dreamstime. com; page 84 © Jim Morekis; page 88 © Jim Morekis; page 94 (top) © Jim Morekis, (bottom) © Jim Morekis; page 95 © Kirkikisphoto | Dreamstime.com; page 100 © Jim Morekis; page 103 © Jim Morekis; page 105 © Jim Morekis; page 106 © Jim Morekis; page 108 (both) © Jim Morekis; page 116 © Jim Morekis; page 126 © Marynag | Dreamstime.com; page 131 © Jim Morekis; page 133 © Jim Morekis; page 138 (both) © Jim Morekis; page 139 © Jim Morekis; page 143 © Jim Morekis; page 145 © Kzlobastov | Dreamstime.com; page 151 © Jim Morekis; page 152 © Jim Morekis; page 154 © Jim Morekis; page 155 © Jim Morekis; page 157 © Jim Morekis; page 159 © Jim Morekis; page 161 © Appalachianviews | Dreamstime.com; page 164 © Jim Morekis; page 165 © Jim Morekis; page 171 © Cfarmer | Dreamstime.com; page 177 © Jim Morekis; page 181 © Jim Morekis; page 184 (top) © Jim Morekis, (bottom) © Americanspirit | Dreamstime. com; page 185 © Jim Morekis; page 191 (both) © Jim Morekis; page 194 © Jim Morekis; page 199 © Jim Morekis; page 201 © Jim Morekis; page 204 © Pxlman | Dreamstime.com; page 209 © Jim Morekis; page 211 © Jim Morekis; page 212 (both) © Jim Morekis; page 213 © Jim Morekis; page 219 © Jim Morekis; page 224 © Jim Morekis; page 225 © Jim Morekis; page 227 © Jim Morekis; page 230 © Jim Morekis; page 233 © Jim Morekis; page 234 © Jim Morekis; page 236 © Jim Morekis; page 238 © Jim Morekis; page 239 (top) © Kmm7553 | Dreamstime.com, (bottom) 123rf.com; page 276 (top) Wellesenterprises | Dreamstime.com, (bottom) Ltishankov | Dreamstime.com

Also Available

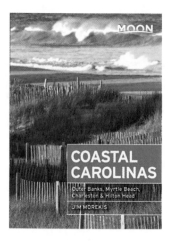

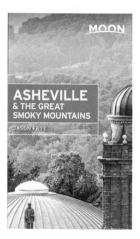

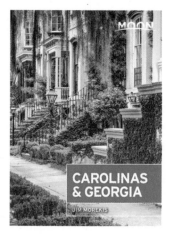

MAP SYMBOLS

Expressway	○ City/Town	✈ Airport	⚓ Golf Course
Primary Road	◉ State Capital	✈ Airfield	◻ Parking Area
Secondary Road	⊛ National Capital	▲ Mountain	⊜ Archaeological Site
Unpaved Road	★ Point of Interest	✛ Unique Natural Feature	⚑ Church
Feature Trail	• Accommodation		⚑ Gas Station
Other Trail		🁢 Waterfall	
Ferry	▼ Restaurant/Bar		⬡ Glacier
Pedestrian Walkway	■ Other Location	▲ Park	⬡ Mangrove
Stairs	∧ Campground	☗ Trailhead	⬡ Reef
		⛷ Skiing Area	⬡ Swamp

CONVERSION TABLES

°C = (°F - 32) / 1.8
°F = (°C x 1.8) + 32
1 inch = 2.54 centimeters (cm)
1 foot = 0.304 meters (m)
1 yard = 0.914 meters
1 mile = 1.6093 kilometers (km)
1 km = 0.6214 miles
1 fathom = 1.8288 m
1 chain = 20.1168 m
1 furlong = 201.168 m
1 acre = 0.4047 hectares
1 sq km = 100 hectares
1 sq mile = 2.59 square km
1 ounce = 28.35 grams
1 pound = 0.4536 kilograms
1 short ton = 0.90718 metric ton
1 short ton = 2,000 pounds
1 long ton = 1.016 metric tons
1 long ton = 2,240 pounds
1 metric ton = 1,000 kilograms
1 quart = 0.94635 liters
1 US gallon = 3.7854 liters
1 Imperial gallon = 4.5459 liters
1 nautical mile = 1.852 km

MOON SOUTH CAROLINA
Avalon Travel
Hachette Book Group
1700 Fourth Street
Berkeley, CA 94710, USA
www.moon.com

Editor: Rachel Feldman
Series Manager: Kathryn Ettinger
Copy Editor: Brett Keener
Graphics and Production Coordinator: Elizabeth Jang
Cover Design: Faceout Studios, Charles Brock
Interior Design: Domini Dragoone
Moon Logo: Tim McGrath
Map Editor: Kat Bennett
Cartographers: Stephanie Poulain, Karin Dahl
Proofreader: Ann Seifert
Indexer: Greg Jewett

ISBN-13: 978-1-64049-246-2

Printing History
1st Edition — 1999
7th Edition — February 2018
5 4 3 2 1

Front cover photo: Charleston's historic French Quarter at twilight © Sean Pavone / Alamy Stock Photo

Back cover photo: Myrtle Beach © Meunierd | Dreamstime

Printed in Canada by Friesens